# U.S. Latino
# Literatu
# Today

# U.S. Latino Literature Today

**Gabriela Baeza Ventura**

University of Houston

PEARSON

Longman

New York   San Francisco   Boston
London   Toronto   Sydney   Tokyo   Singapore   Madrid
Mexico City   Munich   Paris   Cape Town   Hong Kong   Montreal

Vice President and Editor in Chief: Joseph Terry
Managing Editor: Erika Berg
Executive Marketing Manager: Ann Stypuloski
Production Manager: Denise Phillip
Project Coordination, Text Design, and Electronic Page Makeup: Electronic Publishing Services Inc., NYC
Cover Design Manager: Wendy Ann Fredericks
Cover Designer: Nancy Sacks
Cover Art: *Comunidad*, 2001. José Ramirez/RamirezArt.com
Senior Manufacturing Buyer: Dennis J. Para

For permission to use copyrighted material, grateful acknowledgment is made to the copyright holders on pp. 317–321, which are hereby made part of this copyright page.

**Library of Congress Cataloging-in-Publication Data**

U.S. Latino literature today / [edited by] Gabriela Baeza Ventura.
    p. cm.
Includes bibliographical references and index.
ISBN 0-321-19843-3 (pbk.)
    1. American literature—Hispanic American authors. 2. Hispanic Americans—Literary collections. 3. Hispanic American literature (Spanish) 4. Hispanic Americans. I. Ventura, Gabriela Baeza.
PS508.H57U8 2005
B10.9'868—dc22                                                    2004008654

Please visit our website at http://www.ablongman.com

ISBN 0-321-19843-3

# Dedication

*To Bogar, as always*

# Contents

### Prose

### Essay

### Drama

# Exile and Immigration

### Poetry

# Transcultural

## *Prose*

## *Drama*

## *Essay*

# Preface

This anthology offers a wide spectrum of Latino creative expression. In doing so, it affords the reader the opportunity to navigate the works of authors who are at times negotiating with issues of being Latino in a country different from theirs, and at others reaffirming their stake in America and the American dream. The works included here open windows to worlds that are perhaps new or unexplored, and in this way encourage the reader to see this literature as one that is not foreign but very much a part of the United States.

Recognizing that the ethnicities of U.S. Latino writers are as wide-ranging as the themes and characters they write about, this anthology features works by writers of Cuban, Mexican, Puerto Rican, and Central and South American descent. It contains a variety of genres that will allow professors to provide students with a strong vision of Latino literature in the United States. The author biographies and current Web sites are included to facilitate professors' research and to allow students their own investigations into the major Latino voices in America today. In addition to works by well-established Hispanic authors, this anthology also includes works published in the new millennium to present a broad and dynamic representation of the Latino literary landscape.

## *Organization*

In my travels to trade and educational shows and conferences, I have had the opportunity to meet instructors and discuss with them the literature they teach. There seems to be great demand for anthologies and textbooks that have a clear theoretical and historical framework, that are written in plain, practical language, and that can assist students in identifying the salient themes, trends, styles, and authors of U.S. Latino literature.

With these characteristics in mind, I found that one of the clearest and soundest approaches to this literature is based on an understanding of the cultural trends that have characterized Latinos in the United States throughout history: the development of a native culture on U.S. soil; the intellectual and artistic culture that has always accompanied exiles from Latin America; the constant immigration to the United States, particularly from Mexico and the Caribbean; and the rise of a transcultural environment in which people can enjoy their homeland's culture while living in the United States. This dynamic scheme—native, exile and immigrant, and transcultural—has characterized Latino life since the beginning of the nineteenth century and has made for a literary evolution that reflects these preoccupations and orientations down to the present. To reflect this tendency, this book follows this organization.

The "Native" component contains works that discuss the need to demand justice and equality for U.S. Latinos who are discriminated against and abused. Some of the works also reflect themes that pertain to identity issues, such as split personalities that are a result of living in two cultures. The selections included in the "Exile and Immigration" section speak to the problems of living in the United States as guests. These authors are concerned with returning to their homelands, and they focus on aspects of life in the United States that are cruel and inhospitable. The "Transcultural" component presents the work of authors whose writing priority is no longer preoccupied with returning to their homeland or claiming rights denied to U.S. Latinos. They are focused on presenting approaches to life in the United States in all its aspects and do not revolve around a specific theme.

Each part begins with an introduction that contextualizes and provides background on authors and works so students can gain a deeper understanding of U.S. Latino literature. The selections in each part are divided into the four literary genres to provide flexibility to instructors who may not want to teach the material following the overarching themes. Each genre section includes a variety of well-known authors as well as contemporary authors who have recently begun to publish. The makeup is two-thirds old and one-third new, which facilitates the presentation of contemporary authors who conform to new trends in Latino literature.

## *Features*

The following features help provide a deeper and more informed understanding of Latino literature in the United States.

- **Thematic organization**—Part One: Native; Part Two: Exile and Immigration; Part Three: Transcultural—helps contextualize works and enables students to gain greater insight and understanding into each selection.
- **Introductions**—a general one at the beginning of the book as well as an introduction at the beginning of each of the three parts—provide background and context to help students engage with the selections.
- **Brief author biographies** accompany each selection.
- **Breadth of selections** featuring the works of a diversity of well-established authors alongside more contemporary writers to demonstrate new trends in Latino literature.
- Represents authors from a **range of nationalities and cultures** within the Latino/Hispanic community, including beyond the usual three: Mexican, Puerto Rican, and Cuban.

- **Thought-provoking questions**—designed to stimulate classroom discussion and trigger ideas for essays—are included on each of the three sections of the book in an appendix.
- **English translations of Spanish terms** are provided in footnotes within each selection.
- **Key interpretive devices**—a list of Latino films, a historical timeline, and a list of author Web pages—are also included.

## *Acknowledgments*

I would like to acknowledge Nicolás Kanellos for his guidance and dedication to Latino Studies in its entirety. I would also like to thank Erika Berg, Rebecca Gilpin, and Barbara Santoro for their patience and dedication to this project. This work would not be complete without the astute and thoughtful suggestions of professors who reviewed this anthology in its various stages: Meredith Abarca, University of Texas at El Paso; Carol Adams, Western Washington University; Robert D. Aguirre, Wayne State University; José Amaya, Iowa state University; Laura Barbas-Rhoden, Wofford College; Cordelia C. Candelaria, Arizona State University; Norma E. Cantú, University of Texas at San Antonio; Balance Chow, San Jose University; Elizabeth J. Clark, LaGuardia Community College; Ignacio Corona, Ohio State University; Maria E. Cotera, Michigan State University; Michael Hames-Garcia, Binghamton University; Jose Jara, Mira Costa Community College; Jaime Mejia, Southwest Texas State University; Yeganeh Modirzadeh, DeAnza College; Alejandro Guillermo Murguia, San Francisco State University; Adela Navarro, Western Michigan University; William A. Nericcio, San Diego State University; Barbara H. Paul-Emil, Bentley College; Marco Portales, Texas A&M University; Gerald Resendez, Califorina State University of Northridge; Travis Silcox, Sacramento City College; Perce Smith, Sonoma State University; and Virgil Suárez, Florida State University.

Finally, I would like to recognize the invaluable support of my family, especially my lifetime companion, Bogar, and my little sister, Georgina Baeza; my sister-friend Carolina Villarroel; my coworkers Linda M. Garza and Lalis Mendoza; and my students at the University of Houston.

*Gabriela Baeza Ventura*

# Introduction

atino literature has existed in the United States from the colonial period—well before the United States was settled, before it was a united country—as has been proven by many Latino literature scholars' research.[1] But it is only now, at the beginning of the twenty-first century, that these works are being recognized for their literary quality and are quickly becoming a significant component of literature curriculums throughout the United States. This acknowledgment of Latino literature is also a result of the latest census, which tells us that the population of Latinos in the United States is steadily increasing to represent a place in the majority.

The rise of Latino population and culture has been anticipated in many ways over the years and through a variety of media. José Martí, in his famous essay "Our America," predicted that Latinos throughout the world would unite to create the majority and thus become empowered to take political action in the United States.[2] In the 1990s, when Ricky Martin sang for soccer's World Cup, everyone in the United States turned to acknowledge the Latin pop singer who opened the door for other Latino and Latin American singers, such as Christina Aguilera and Shakira. In the film industry, we witnessed the rebirth of Mexican cinema with films such as *Amores Perros, Y tu mamá también, El crimen del Padre Amaro,* and *Frida,* many of which were nominated for Oscars. One of the most important responses to the census results is the increase in the number of Hispanic/Latino works from major publishing houses—a clear sign that the desire to read Latino literature is growing strongly in the United States.

*U.S. Latino Literature Today* is intended to raise awareness of Latino and Latina literary production and promote the work of established and contemporary writers such as Alicia Gaspar de Alba, Pat Mora, Julia Alvarez, Sandra María Esteves, Martín Espada, José Martí, Virgil Suárez, and Dolores Prida and by spoken word artists such as Olga Angelina García Echeverría, Leticia Hernández-Linares, and Nancy Mercado, to name a few. The works of these authors, and many others, reveal that Latino literature is not only that produced by the

---

[1]Please refer to Nicolás Kanellos's research and the introductions to *En otra voz: Antología de la literatura hispana de los Estados Unidos* (Houston: Arte Público Press, 2002); *Herencia: The Anthology of Hispanic Literature of the United States* (New York: Oxford, 2002); and *Hispanic Periodicals in the US: Origins to 1960* (Houston: Arte Público Press, 2000).

[2]"Nuestra América." *Obras Completas.* (Editorial de Ciencias Sociales. La Habana, 1975): 15–23.

three major components of the Latino population in the United States—Mexicans, Puerto Ricans, and Cubans—but is enriched and influenced by writers from *all* Latin American countries living in the United States.

## METHODOLOGY FOR THIS BOOK

All anthologists must make selections. The selections in this text were chosen because they allow readers to understand and analyze the production of authors studied in a typical Latino literature curriculum. The selections represent some of the most anthologized authors as well as writers who have not been previously published or anthologized. This balance allows new writers to have their work read and analyzed in literature courses. Readers are encouraged to experiment with the work of contemporary writers as well as learn of newer trends in Latino literature. Instead of selections being listed by literary genre or country, the works are divided into the following categories: Native, Exile and Immigrant, and Transcultural. These categories demonstrate that the Latino experience in the United States often begins with a desire to remain in touch with one's native homeland. This thematic approach also helps in uniting Latinos and Latinas; it facilitates comparisons and differentiation of people who share similar experiences as they strive to make a living in the United States. This approach offers professors and teachers an opportunity to break boundaries between ethnic groups and to incorporate voices often left out of anthologies.

The categories serve as guides to evaluate the works within. They are not to be thought of as closed or rigid; in fact, a dynamic is created by their interaction. Authors are constantly moving between them, many times unknowingly. The purpose is to raise questions that lead students to research other authors they enjoy reading and place them within these categories, as the divisions are applicable not only to Latino literature but to all U.S. literature.

The selections encompass most literary genres: poetry (including spoken word), prose, drama, and the essay. Also included are works by many Latin American authors who are now living and writing in the United States, including Victor Montejo, exiled from Guatemala; Mario Bencastro, exiled from El Salvador; and Alicia Partnoy, exiled from Argentina. The selections present a variety of experiences that Latinos confront while living and adjusting to life in the United States, away from their native homes.

Here is a brief description of each category; a more detailed explanation precedes each section.

## NATIVE LITERATURE

(like the U.S.)

In the Native classification, we discover that there is no longer a desire to return to *allá* ("over there"), the homeland. The author or characters believe that the United States is their land, and that they belong here. Among their most significant goals is to protest discrimination and influence U.S. politics in order to obtain civil, cultural, and indigenous rights. The characters and authors promote Hispanism, a sense of community that stems from the fact that the Spanish language can establish liaisons between Spanish-speaking groups across the United States; they believe that they are a unique group, and they create their own communities such as the Chicano Aztlán[3] and the Nuyorican Loisaida (Lower East Side of New York City), among others. Many writers in this group encounter cultural conflicts in deciding whether they most identify with U.S. culture or that of their homeland. Their patriotism and nationalism may be tested and redefined. The language in which they express their creativity moves between English, Spanish, bilingualism, and Spanglish (the mixture of Spanish and English). The characters are hybrid and new in that they identify with their country of origin as well as with the United States; some identify with the indigenous tribes of the Americas and are therefore not easily categorized. Writers in this category masterfully combine their native culture with U.S. culture, creating new expressions such as poems that mix English and Spanish as well as speech and literature prose styles. Themes presented in these works include identity search, psychological confusion, and discrimination in coming of age, forging a confident hybrid identity within the United States, recovering roots and family and national histories, etc. For example, Luis Valdez's play *The Shrunken Head of Pancho Villa* demonstrates some of the issues associated with being part of U.S. society. Valdez discusses issues of discrimination for Mexican families who are part of U.S. communities but are abused as a result of their ethnicity. The hybrid character in this case must choose between his Chicano identity and that of a U.S. citizen.

## EXILE AND IMMIGRANT LITERATURE    *(don't like the U.S.)*

Literature that is considered Exile is preoccupied with the country left behind; therefore, the focus is on the *allá* ("over there"), with a constant mention of a return to the homeland. The Exile author's primary interest in living in the United States is to protest what is happening in his or her native land—making a case against colonization by and despotism in powerful countries, as in *El laúd del desterrado,* by Cuban poets who protested Spain's colonial administration of their island in the nineteenth century. Some recurring literary expressions in these works are references to Babylonian captivity, where people cannot communicate because everyone speaks his or her own language, and Paradise lost, referring to people who feel completely lost in the United States, a foreign land that is inhospitable and not welcoming. Authors and characters present a political and revolutionary nationalism that also depicts nostalgia and disillusionment about the way their land has changed as a result of colonial repression. In other words, writers speak of being true and committed to their countries of origin by not Americanizing or forgetting their origin, and many harshly criticize the involvement of the United States or any other powerful country in their countries to advance U.S. territory or economic gains, as is the case of Central American literature. Most of the authors represent an elite group of

---

[3]In Chicano folklore, *Aztlán* is often appropriated as the name for that portion of Mexico that was taken over by the United States after the Mexican-American War of 1846, on the belief that this area represents the point of parting of the Aztec migrations.

individuals with the means to travel and the connections to voice their opinions in U.S. media, as José Martí did by writing in many important journals and newspapers in the United States. These writers demand that other exiles express themselves with linguistic purity. That is, using the most elegant Spanish and the most traditional verse forms, such as the sonnet— a traditional poem written in fourteen lines and divided into four stanzas, the first two stanzas having four lines and the last two three each. This, on one hand, allowed exiles to demonstrate to the United States and any other place of exile that they were educated and worthy of that country's help. On the other hand, they created role models for the exiles who read their work. For that reason, the characters depicted in Exile literature are heroes—classic, epic, and tragic figures who must live and travel through the United States in an effort to obtain help solving problems in the homeland. Exile takes a toll on the patriotic figure who sacrifices all for the love of his or her native country.

Immigrant literature raises questions such as: where do I belong? am I Latin American or American? how can I be one or the other when both reject me? should I hyphenate my identity: Mexican-American, Cuban-American, Costa Rican-American, Puerto Rican-American? This category is extremely significant, as this literature represents the process that most immigrants experience as they adjust to life in the United States. In this literature, we are privy to characters and authors who question whether they should stay *aquí* (here in the United States) or return to *allá* (homeland). Many find that they are not welcomed in either and, with a foot on each side of the border, discover they are as much a part of their native country as they are American. Thus, it is not uncommon to find texts, like *Lucas Guevara*,[4] in which we witness this type of questioning process. In this novel, as in much of Immigrant literature, the message sent to Latin Americans who may be thinking about migrating to the United States is to stay home; it is better to suffer at home than in a foreign land.[5] This message, however, does not always reach the destined reader—those who are about to migrate, therefore, are constantly reminded that they must preserve their native culture. This can only be accomplished if the language, traditions, and customs, as well as their Catholicism, are kept. Anyone who does not uphold these values is reprimanded in all possible ways because there is fear of Americanization. One of the ways in which they are reprimanded is through the use of terms such as *agringados* ("anglicized"), *pochos* ("half-breeds"), *renegados* ("sellouts"), *pelonas* ("short-haired women"), and *americanos* ("Americans"). These are common names for those who do not abide by these values. All or some of the derogatory terms are used on those who are easily enamored of American ways. Communities such as

---

[4]This novel was written by Alirio Díaz Guerra and is considered the first novel of immigration. It was discovered and reprinted in English and Spanish by Nicolás Kanellos. (Houston: Arte Público Press, 2002).

[5]*The Adventures of Don Chipote or, When Parrots Breastfeed,* by Daniel Venegas, presents this clearly when he states that "Mexicans will make it big in the United States . . . when parrots breast-feed." (Houston: Arte Público Press, 2000): 160.

*México de afuera*[6] ("Mexico outside" in San Antonio and El Paso, Texas; Los Angeles, California; Chicago, Illinois), *Trópico en Manhattan* ("Tropics in Manhattan" in New York), *Pequeña Habana* ("Little Havana" in Florida), and *Harlem español* ("Spanish Harlem" in New York) are established throughout the United States in an effort to maintain each Latin American community intact. Each reinforces respect for and upholds the values listed above.

But writers in this category realize it is not enough to reinforce the traditional customs of their native land; they must also fight for labor and human rights and against exploitation and racism here in the United States. Laborers and a small community of elite impresarios—who often were exiled for political rather than economic reasons and who had to learn to survive on their own in the United States—compose Immigrant literature. The language in which they write is filled with neologisms (*jamenegs*—ham and eggs), and regional and popular dialects. The characters they depict are typical men and women who represent the new and innocent immigrant mesmerized by the wonders of U.S. culture. Some of the themes in this literature reflect conflicts between generations, domestic dramas in which families must confront changes in children who grow up as U.S. citizens and no longer identify with their parents' culture. An example is *The Super,* a play by the Cuban writer Iván Acosta, which masterfully describes the difficulty of living in the United States. Acosta touches on issues that affect families with children who learn to enjoy the benefits of living in the United States and no longer want to be Cuban.

## TRANSCULTURAL LITERATURE

This section is dedicated to authors who try to bridge the gap between their native culture and the United States through their writing. Authors within this category demonstrate that they are no longer worried about returning to their countries because with the advances in technology, this can easily be accomplished by computer or telephone. As a matter of fact, being in two places at once is not a thing of the future or something out of the ordinary but a state of mind.

This section features authors whose texts evidence the participation of several worlds in one space and offers examples of how it is that these worlds complement each other. The selections present views that diverge from the search for identity; writers are no longer only focused on presenting works that try to identify who they are or why they belong in the United States. Often, writers no longer experiment with this concern because many realize that they do not need to identify one identity because they can and should have many. Authors in this category share the perspective that Latinos in the United States must create identities that facilitate their accommodation to a new country; at the same time, these identities must also enable them to keep strong ties with their original countries although they live in an Anglo-American environment. The writers reflect on their experiences in North America, often as

---

[6]This community was established in the early part of the twentieth century when Mexican citizens living the United States began to worry about losing Mexican women to the Anglo race. It was termed by Ignacio G. Lozano, a newspaper impresario and community leader in San Antonio, Texas.

minorities but also as survivors on many levels of racism, discrimination, and abuse, looking to overcome the circumstances that inform who Latinos are based on the language they speak and the customs or traditions they uphold. Authors and characters represent immigrants in search of better opportunities who discover that life in the United States, in many cases, *does* provide economically for them and for their families back home, although this involves working at low-paying jobs such as cleaning houses or harvesting, jobs that take a toll on their bodies and lives. Many authors enrich this connection with the countries left behind through the material objects that are purchased and sent back: a radio, a television, a VCR, a computer—all items that are symbolically charged as examples of life away from the native land. They are symbols of transculturation in that through them images and ideas on U.S. life and culture are transmitted.

## CONCLUSION

The primary role of this book is to provide readers essential data to learn of Latinos in the United States through the literature they produce—literature that reflects their visions and experiences. Readers will find that these texts chronicle life for many Latinos in the United States. Latinos who traveled to *El Norte* ("The North") seeking a better life, in search perhaps of the American Dream so popular in Latin countries, may discover that living in the United States can be difficult, even more so than living in the place they left behind. Little by little, those who migrated last night or ten years ago are faced with significant moments that force them to reconfigure their identities, helping them realize that, in these times, life in the United States does not necessarily break all ties with one's country. Those ties are reinforced with the coming and going between one's country and the United States, whether via conventional methods of transportation or through computer and telephone lines in addition to television signals that serve to reinforce cultural values and traditions. Besides learning about Latinos who live in the United States, readers will also gain an appreciation of these works as literature—literature that has a significant place in the American canon for its particular merits.

## A NOTE ON TERMINOLOGY

I use the terms *Latino* and *Latina* rather loosely to refer to people of Latin American descent living in the United States. These terms complicate the condition of the people to whom they apply. I have also used *Hispanic* in an effort to redefine and reappropriate a name that was given by U.S. government agencies to people of Spanish-speaking origins. The terms are interchangeable, and I use them all in this book.

# U.S. Latino Literature Today

# Native

Throughout the years, researchers and scholars have discovered books and spaces in which Spanish-speakers participated to create what we now consider Latino literature. Spanish-speaking people in the United States have been expressing their creativity through writing before what we presently know as the United States was founded. *they were even here first* One example of this creative endeavor is *The Account* by the Spanish explorer Álvar Núñez Cabeza de Vaca in 1542. The literature of exploration of the new colonies also produced epic poems such as *La Florida,* written by a Franciscan friar, Alonso Gregorio de Escobedo, at the end of the sixteenth century, and *La Historia de la Nueva México,* published in 1610 and written by Gaspar Pérez de Villagrá, a Mexican who was appointed to the Juan de Oñate expedition to New Mexico. All four historical pieces *history literature* demonstrate that literature was produced and published by peoples of Hispanic descent in the New World.

The newspaper industry in the nineteenth century also evidences some of the first literary expressions by Spanish-speaking peoples who found in this medium the forum through which they could voice their opinions and creativity. *everyone = informed* *El Misisipí* and *El Mensajero Luisianés,* published in New Orleans in 1808 and 1809 respectively, are two of the first Spanish newspapers to be published in the United States, and they provided citizens with news and other information in Spanish. Their founders understood the need to provide Spanish speakers information on current events as well as important data from their homelands.

María Amparo Ruiz de Burton published her two novels, *The Squatter and the Don* *really great novel* (1885) and *Who Would Have Thought It* (1872) in the latter part of the nineteenth century. She wrote her novels under the pseudonym of C. Loyal and was one of the first Mexican writers to publish in English. There are many authors who in the fashion of Ruiz de Burton wrote in English and were conscious of the need to publish their works, such as Leonor Villegas de Magnón, who wrote *The Rebel/La Rebelde,* a novel based on her experiences in the Mexican Revolution.

*began to write in English so their work would get recognized.*

These works are examples of literary expression that precede the literature included in the Native category of this anthology.

Native literature, for the purpose of this anthology, parts from the assumption that both authors and characters believe and understand that they are part of the United States, that this land is *their* land. Writers in this category, unlike exiles and immigrants, do not question their pertinence to the United States. Among their most significant *goals* is to protest discrimination and influence US politics in order to obtain civic, cultural, and indigenous rights, as was done by many writers in the nineteenth century, when the United States claimed territories that belonged to Mexico through the 1848 Treaty of Guadalupe Hidalgo. Californios (Mexican natives of California) immediately sought *outlet* newspapers as the medium through which they could voice their concerns, as in the case of Platón Vallejo, who tried to tell his side of the story—a story of colonialism—and Pablo de la Guerra, who sent articles to newspapers protesting the occupation of land by squatters.

Latino writers throughout the years have continued to protest the treatment they *treated* have received as members of a minority at the hands of authority figures who are given *unfairly* complete authority to mistreat and abuse. Benjamin Alire Sáenz, in his essay "Exile," underlines this concern when he discusses his situation within a border/*frontera* culture, where he is constantly confused with illegal immigrants because he does not look "American." Sáenz cites several episodes in which immigration agents and police officers approach him to demand that he prove his US citizenship. Sáenz highlights that many of these officials are authorized to judge whether a person is an illegal alien based on his *or her* appearance—that is, they have the right to enforce a subjective evaluation that *racist* is often biased and erroneous. An evaluation not uncommon of authority figures who have not yet learned to see others, people who may be different from them culturally and ethnically, as human beings.

Miguel Algarín's "Taos Pueblo Indians: 700 According to Bobby's Last Census" and Tomás Rivera's "Zoo Island" masterfully employ the image of the zoo to describe how Anglo and non-Anglo communities interact in the United States. Rivera portrays a migrant Mexican community observed by Anglos as they drive by their campsites every Sunday in the same way in which Algarín presents the Taos Pueblo Indians, who open the doors to their pueblo to have foreigners come and participate in their economy. Both texts attest to the fact that the image of the other, the foreigner, that which is not like me, marks not only Latinos but also other minorities in the United States. Rivera and Algarín complicate Anglos' perception of minorities while at the same time they invite Latinos to question their own views on Anglos and minorities. Aren't Native Americans oppressed and mistreated? Are Latinos, then, to question how they see the Anglo? Who casts the evaluating glance? How does this affect one or the other? *questions of perception of each other*

The cultural conflict of deciding whether one most identifies with US culture or that of the homeland is evidenced by some authors in this category. Patriotism and nationalism is tested and redefined. Some authors confront this issue by speaking of their country's history, while others focus on the language, as do Rafael Campo and Lorna Dee Cervantes. Campos, in "Belonging," takes readers back to Cuba only to discover that life there is no different than that in the United States. He concludes that the history of Cubans is no longer found in Cuba. It is elsewhere; those who were expelled from the country when Fidel Castro took over probably write it.

Lorna Dee Cervantes, in a similar process, faces her identity as Mexican, American, and Chicana.[1] She claims that she did not learn to speak Spanish and alludes to her grandmother, with whom she cannot communicate because the two lack a language in common. For that reason, she feels trapped on a refugee ship, one that will never dock because it oscillates between several language worlds—English, Spanish, and Spanglish.

In Native literature, we find that characters and authors promote Hispanism across the United States, they believe that they are a unique group, and although they create their own communities such as the Chicano "Aztlán" and the Nuyorican[2] "Loisaida" (Lower East Side) among others they are still part of a bigger entity: Hispanics/Latinos. Alurista, in his poem "El sarape de mi personalidad" (The Sarape of My Personality) shares this vision when he explains, in plain terms, that he is made of many shades and peoples, that he is unique in that he is not monolithic, this his life and identity are chromatic because he lives in the United States, a place where cultures are in constant contact with each other, creating a sense of camaraderie where each shares with the next the best that it can offer. Tato Laviera, in "AmeRícan," also speaks of the solidarity established between all peoples: "We gave birth to a new generation,/AmeRícan salutes all folklores, / european, indian, black, spanish, / and anything else compatible."

Identity search, psychological confusion, discrimination in coming-of-age experiences that forge a confident hybrid identity within the United States, and the recovery of roots and family and national histories are some of the themes that Native literature explores. Luis Valdez's play *Los Vendidos* (The Sellouts) analyzes the theme of a hybrid identity through the symbolism of the sellout. In the play, Valdez presents a variety of characters that are to be sold when an American woman comes to Honest Sancho's store to purchase the Mexican needed to fill out a minority quota at a political rally. Valdez toys with the idea that any person can be a sellout if the price is right. Valdez criticizes those who sell themselves and casts a critical glance at the stereotypes that US culture creates for Latinos.

---

[1]Mexican American, female.
[2]Person of Puerto Rican descent who lives in New York.

In sum, native literature presents authors and characters who claim rights and privileges as US citizens. This literature is written in English, Spanish, or both languages, depending on what the author deems appropriate to transmit his or her message. The themes vary from the search of identity to discrimination to assessment of life in the United States among others. The authors represent some of the best literary work produced by Latinos in the past century.

# POETRY

# Miguel Algarín

Miguel Algarín was born in Santurce, Puerto Rico, in 1941, and moved with his family in the early 1950s to New York City. One of the founders and leaders of the Nuyorican literary movement, both as a writer and as owner-administrator of the Nuyorican Poet's Café, he is dedicated to the oral performance of literature. Algarín received degrees in literature from the University of Wisconsin and Pennsylvania State University, after which he worked as a professor at Rutgers University. He has written plays and prose, but he is most known for the creation of bilingual poetry that employs jazz-salsa to mystical, avant-garde verse. He translated the work of Pablo Neruda and, with Miguel Piñero, edited *Nuyorican Poetry: An Anthology of Puerto Rican Words and Feelings* (1976), introducing the world of the Nuyorican to a broad audience.

## Taos Pueblo Indians: 700 strong according to Bobby's last census

It costs $1.50 for my van to enter
Taos Pueblo Indian land,
adobe huts, brown tanned Indian red skin
reminding me of brown Nuyorican people,
young Taos Pueblo Indians

Primary works by Miguel Algarín: *On Call* (Houston: Arte Público Press, 1980); *Time's Now/Ya es tiempo* (Houston: Arte Público Press, 1985); Miguel Algarín and Miguel Piñero, *Nuyorican Poetry: An Anthology of Puerto Rican Words and Feelings* (New York: William Morrow, 1976).

ride the back of a pick up truck
with no memories of mustangs
controlled by their naked calves and thighs,
rocky, unpaved roads, red brown dirt,
a stream bridged by wide trunk planks,
young warriors unloading thick trunks
for the village drum makers to work,
tourists bringing the greens,
Indian women fry flour and bake bread,
older men attend curio shops,
the center of the village is a parking lot
into which America's mobile homes
pour in with their air conditioned cabins, color
T.V., fully equipped kitchens, bathrooms
with flushing toilets and showers,
A.M. & F.M. quadrophonic stereo sound,
cameras, geiger counters, tents,
hiking boots, fishing gear and mobile telephones,
"restricted" signs are posted round the parking lot
making the final stage for the zoo
where the natives approach selling
American Jewelry made in Phoenix
by a foster American Indian from Brooklyn
who runs a missionary profit making turquoise jewelry shop
"Ma, is this clean water?
do the Indians drink out of this water?
is it all right for me to drink it?"
the young white substitute teacher's daughter
wants to drink some Indian water,
young village school children recognize her,
and in her presence the children snap
quick attentive looks that melt into
"boy am I glad I'm not in school"
gestures as we pass,
but past, past this living room zoo,
out there on that ridge
over there, over that ridge,
on the other side of that mountain,

is that Indian land too?
are there leaders and governments over that ridge?
does Indian law exist there?
who would the Pueblo Indian send
to a formal state meeting
with the heads of street government,
who would we plan war with?
can we transport arms earmarked for ghetto
warriors, can we construct our street
government constitutions on your land?
when orthodox Jews from Crown Heights
receive arms from Israel in their territorial struggle
with local Brooklyn Blacks,
can we raise your flag
in the Lower East Side
as a sign of our mutual treaty of protection?
"hey you you're not supposed to walk in our water,"
"stay back we're busy making bread,"
these were besides your "restricted zones"
the most authoritative words
spoken by your native tongue,
the girl's worry about her drinking water
made Raúl remove his Brazilian made shoes
from the Pueblo Indian drinking cup,
the old woman's bread warning
froze me dead on the spot
"go buy something in the shop,
you understand me, go buy something,"
I didn't buy I just strolled on by the curio shops
till I came across Bobby the police officer,
taught at Santa Fe, though he could've gone on to Albuquerque,
Taos Pueblo Indians
sending their officers of the law to be trained
in neighboring but foreign cities like in New Mexico
proves that Taos Pueblo Indians
ignore that a soldier belongs to his trainer
that his discipline, his habitual muscle response
belongs to his drill sergeant master:
"our laws are the same as up in town"

too bad Bobby! they could be your laws,
it's your land!
then flashing past as I leave Taos Bobby speeds
towards the reservation in a 1978 GMC van with two red flashers
on top bringing Red Cross survival rations to the Taos Pueblo Indians
respectfully frying bread for tourists
behind their sovereign borders.

∴ Chicano ∴ person of Mex. orgin or descent.

# Alurista

Alurista is the pen name for Alberto Baltazar Urista Heredia, who was born in Mexico City in 1947 and migrated to California as an adolescent. He earned a Ph.D. in Spanish literature from the University of California, San Diego, in 1982. Alurista has had a profound impact on the emerging concept of Chicanismo in the late 1960s, particularly regarding the indigenous aspects of Chicano cultural heritage. At San Diego State University in 1967, he helped establish the Chicano Student Movement of Aztlán (MECHA) and the Chicano Studies Program, and in 1969 he promulgated the concept and symbol of Aztlán—the mythological home of the Aztec peoples in the Southwest United States. His use of bilingualism and Chicano Spanish, along with the cultural and intellectual diversity of his themes—pre-Columbian beliefs, pop culture, American rock, barrio experiences, and so on—present an original and provocative mix. His poetry combines social protest with the quest for self-determination reaffirming Chicano culture and dignity of Chicano people that include the latter collections *Floricanto, Nationchild Plumaroja* (1972), *Timespace Huracán* (1976), and *Spik in Glyph?* (1981).

## el sarape de mi personalidad

el sarape de mi personalidad[1]
　　comes in fantastic colors
basic
　　essentially fundamentales[2]

---

Primary works by Alurista: *Floricanto en Aztlán* (Los Angeles: UCLA Chicano Cultural Center, 1971); *Return: Poems Collected and New* (Ypsilanti: Bilingual Review/Press, 1982).

[1]My personality's serape
[2]Fundamental

you know that i would be up hung
to say
    it didn't really pang
y mi clamor no era rojo
    sangre[3]
the nectar with which death feeds
pero crema
amarillento y pasivo[4]
insensitive and lame
    lazy you say!
how blind
    the spectrum of my wool is life itself
enacted to lay heavy
    on cold bodies
y con el soplo caluroso de la vida
    con mi sarape áspero de lana
      la semilla estimulo
y mi sol[5] shines on
    to propagate
    the joy of our people
      and the pangs of our laughter
mi gente vibra y teje
    nuestro sarape
    versátil[6]
    and masterful
in the art of living to challenge
    death and the elements of opposition
to our self assertion
    to the radiance of our quilted heritage
a colores[7]
    electrifying warmth of somatic source
where the objects of from come
    la esencia de mi Raza es fundamental[8]
basic

*audience = chicanos*

*you = U.S.*

*lowercase + punctuation = fed up, angry*

*show that he knows what a strange poem looks like*

---

[3]And my clamor was not blood red
[4]But yellow crème and passive
[5]And with the warm breath of life / with my coarse wool serape / I incite the seed / and my sun . . .
[6]My people tremble and weave / our versatile serape
[7]In colors
[8]The essence of my race is fundamental

to the chromatic wheel of humanity
    free to compound in secondary colors
retaining the basic texture
    our <u>woolen</u> skin of color <u>bronze</u>

Sheep/
laṃbos

# Jimmy Santiago Baca

Jimmy Santiago Baca was born in Santa Fe, New Mexico, in 1952. He was abandoned by his parents at the age of two and placed in an orphanage after being under the care of one of his grandparents. Baca ended up living in the streets, and at twenty-one, he was convicted of drug possession and was incarcerated for six years, four of them in isolation. Baca used the time in prison to teach himself how to read and write, and began to write poetry. His books include *What's Happening* (1982), *Martín and Meditations on the South Valley* and *Immigrants in Our Own Land* (1987), *A Place to Stand: The Making of a Poet* (2001). Baca's other works include *Working in the Dark: Reflections of a Poet of the Barrio* (1992) and the screenplay *Bound by Honor*, for the film of the same name. He presently lives in Albuquerque, New Mexico.

## Martín III

Driving across the country
I thought back to my boyhood.
Those I'd known in New Mexico
came back to me again.

In Arkansas, on a fallen oak trunk,
half its limbs in the pond,
sat old one-armed Pepín.
"Martín, your father and I
were in the El Fidel cantina[1]

Primary works by Jimmy Santiago Baca: *What's Happening* (Willimantic: Curbstone Press, 1982); *Martín and Meditations on the South Valley* (NY: New Directions, 1987); *Immigrants in Our Own Land* (NY: New Directions, 1990); *A Place to Stand: The Making of a Poet* (NY: Grove Press, 2001); *Working in the Dark: Reflections of a Poet of the Barrio* (Santa Fe: Red Crane Books, 1992).

[1]Bar

with unas viejas[2] one afternoon.
Tú sabes, nos pusimos bien chatos.[3]
And then Sheri, your mamá, walks in.
I don't remember what she asked Danny,
but la vieja[4] that was with your father said,
*I thought your wife was a cripple.*
Sheri started crying and sin una palabra,[5]
She turned and went out."

In September Estella Gómez appeared.
She stood mid-air in a gust of wind,
blind, dressed in black and with a religious voice, said,
"92 years, m'ijito. ¿Qué pasó?[6] There was no more
beans to pick, no beans to load
on trains. Pinos Wells dried up, como mis manos.[7]
Everyone moved away to work.
I went to Estancia, con mi hijo,[8] Refugio.
Gavachos de Tejas,[9] we worked for them. Loading
alfalfa, picking cotton for fifty cents a row.
¿Y Danny? La borrachera.[10] ¿Y Sheri? La envidia.[11]
That's what happened, Martín, to your familia."[12]

Ohio, December 14th, great pines
crackled icicles to the forest floor,
jarring the air with explosions of sparkling flakes.
Wrapped in my serape, snow up to my knee,
at a bend in a dirt road.
When I reached the bend, Antonia Sánchez,
La Bruja[13] de Torreón, said to me,
ónde está tu mamá?[14] Safe from that madman

---

[2]Some women
[3]We got really drunk, you know
[4]The woman/old woman
[5]Without a word
[6]Son, what happened?
[7]Like my hands
[8]With my son
[9]Anglos from Texas
[10]The drunken state
[11]The envy
[12]Family
[13]The witch
[14]Where is your mother?

Se casó otra vez y tiene dos niños.[15]
No, no te puedo decir dónde viven."[16]

Four or five months later I moved.
to North Carolina
in a red brick house at the edge of Piedmont Woods.
Narrow red mud roads marked with tractor treads,
sultry air droning with insects and steamy
with harvest crops—
day after day in green dark shade I walked,
bending under briar riggings, my pole
with a blue rubber worm bait
dangling from 30 pound line, down deer trails,
skipping creek rocks, climbing over sagging
barbwire fences, until I found a secluded pond,
shores choked with bullrush I thrashed down,
as I tossed my line out into the sunset burning water,
big-mouth bass puckered, sending water rings
rippling through towering pines leaning over the water.
I fished until I could no longer see my bait
plop, until the far shore disappeared and the moon
bobbed in the black water
like a candle flame in a window against the night darkness.

One evening as I walked back
up a hill to the house,
I could hear all their voices
drifting through the trees—
I said aloud to myself
and the memories they lived in,
*I am leaving in the morning.*

Passing back through Tennessee
on the way to Albuquerque,
deep down a mountain dirt road bend,
walking barefoot on pebbles,
I see a woman talking with two men,
in the dark silence of the forest,
Señora Martínez walked toward me,
wavering like smoke in the cold air,

---

[15]She married again and has two children
[16]No, I can't tell you where they live

"Sheri was scared to go home for her purse.
So she sent me. Dios mío,[17]
I'll never forget that day, m'ijo.[18]
When I opened the closet door, there was Danny,
standing with a butcher knife raised high,
ready to kill."

April in Tennessee
Merlinda Griego appeared to me—she sat
on a rock, skirt raised to her knees, her bare toes
playing with petals floating in the creek.
"You cried a lot, Martín. Dios mío cómo llorabas.[19]
A veces your jefito[20] brought you to Las Flores Cantina
where I worked. He came to see me. You played on the floor
with empty whiskey bottles.
One day I was at El Parke, sitting like now, on a rock, my
feet in the water.
Your mother came up to me and started yelling
that I gave you mal de ojo,[21] and she dipped you
in the freezing water. I thought she was going to drown you
because of Danny seeing me. Quién sabe, m'ijo,[22]
all I remember is that she was jealous."

A week after I saw Merlinda, I was looking
through an old tobacco barn in a field.
In a corner with moldy gunney sacks
and rusting field tools, peeling an apple with his knife,
Pancho Garza sat, the retired manager of Piggly Wiggly
in Santa Fe.
"I gave her bruised fruit, old bread
and pastries. Once a week I gave her a sack of flour.
Danny drank up her pay check,
so I let her have a few things.
Besides she was a good checker."

It was June in Virginia.
One evening walking through the woods
I could see someone waiting for me

---

[17]My God
[18]My son
[19]My God, how you cried
[20]Dad/Daddy/boss
[21]Evil spell
[22]Who knows, son

her infant straddling her hip.
I thought of my boyhood in the South Valley
where women took summer evening walks,
their children fluttering like rose leaves
at their skirts.

Through the Texas panhandle
I remembered Estancia
where harvest dust smolders and insects whiff
empty crates and vegetable boxes
stacked against the produce stands.
Transparent wings of bees
wedge board bins, cracks sticky with chili mash.
Gorged flies buzz in tin pails and paper sacks
dropped on the sawdusted earthen floor,
their feet glazed with potato guck. And parked alongside
the stands at evening, rugged eight wheelers
simmer hot rubber and grease odors, their side board racks
oozing with crushed fruits.

Finally driving over the Sandía Mountains,
on the outskirts of Albuquerque,
I thought of you, mother—long ago
your departure uprooted me,
checked the green growing day,
hollowed out the core of my childhood—
whittled down
to keep me
in your rib crib
clothed in webs—
a doll in a cradle
in a barn loft in Willard.

Your absence
is a small burned area in my memory,
where I was cleared away
like prairie grass,
my identity smoldering under the blue sand of my soul—
my appearance dimmed to smoke,
in the glowing light somewhere
beyond your house each dusk.

Night now as I come into Albuquerque,
moon's rusty rings pass through one another

around me—
broken chain of events
decaying in black sand and ash
of the empty dark past
I dig through.

An embering stick
I call the past,
my dream of a mother existed in,
I breathed on to keep light
from extinguishing
like a star at dawn.
I come to inspect the old world,
those green years burned silvery with time,
by silence in the mind.

# Rafael Campo

Rafael Campo was born and raised in New Jersey. He is the eldest son of an immigrant father and an Italian mother. It is believed that Campo's bitter pride in Hispanic culture and language was instilled by his parents and through his grandfather's struggle as he was forced to flee Spain and Cuba under Batista. Campo attended Harvard Medical School to fulfill his parents' dreams of having their son become an exemplary American. When Campo was in medical school, he was forced to come to terms with his homosexuality. And it was at a workshop at Amherst College that he first was able to express himself on his sexuality and his identity as a Hispanic American. At that time, he considered abandoning his medical studies to dedicate to poetry. His poetry reflects well-crafted ideas that speak to the otherness that Hispanic Americans can experience while living in the United States.

## Belonging

I went to Cuba on a raft I made
From scraps of wood, aluminum, some rope.
I knew what I was giving up, but who
Could choose his comfort over truth? Besides,
It felt so sleek and dangerous, like sharks
Or porno magazines or even thirst—
I hadn't packed or anything, and when
I saw the sea gulls teetering the way

Primary works by Rafael Campo: *The Other Man Was Me* (Houston: Arte Público Press, 1994); *Diva* (Durham: Duke UP, 1999); *What the Body Told* (Durham: Duke UP, 1996); *Landscape with Human Figure* (Durham: Duke UP, 2002).

They do, I actually felt giddy. Boy,
It took forever on those swells of sea,
Like riding on a brontosaurus back
Through time. And when I finally arrived,
It wasn't even bloody! No beach of skulls
To pick over, nothing but the same damn sun,
Indifferent but oddly angry, the face
My father wore at dinnertime. I stripped
And sat there naked in an effort to
Attract some cannibals, but no one came;
I watched my raft drift slowly back to sea,
And wished I'd thought to bring a book
That told the history of my lost people.

## Lorna Dee Cervantes

Lorna Dee Cervantes was born in 1954 in the Mission District of San Francisco, and later moved to San Jose with her mother and brother. She began to write poetry at a young age. She edited, published, and printed a small-press journal, *Mango*, which successfully promoted other Chicano poets and helped establish their reputation. Her work began to receive national attention in the late 1970s. After spending nine months at the Fine Arts Workshop in Provincetown, Massachusetts, she completed *Emplumada* (1981), the title of which is an amalgamation of the participle *emplumado* ("feathered or in plumage") and the nouns *pluma* ("pen") and *plumada* ("a penstroke").

Her collection of poetry is divided into three sections dealing with the social environment, the class status of women, the poet's harmonious relationship with the world of nature, and the act of writing, among other things. Her latest collection is *From the Cables of Genocide: Poems of Love and Hunger* (1991).

### Refugee Ship

like wet cornstarch
I slide past *mi abuelita*'s[1] eyes
bible placed by her side
she removes her glasses
the pudding thickens

Primary works by Lorna Dee Cervantes: *Emplumada* (Pittsburgh: University of Pittsburgh, 1981); *From the Cables of Genocide: Poems on Love and Hunger* (Houston: Arte Público Press, 1989).

[1]My grandma's

*mamá* raised me with no language
I am an orphan to my spanish name
the words are foreign, stumbling on my tongue
I stare at my reflection in the mirror
brown skin, black hair

I feel I am a captive
aboard the refugee ship
a ship that will never dock
a ship that will never dock

*[handwritten: mad b/c not taught spanish]*

*[handwritten: repitition]*

# Lucha Corpi

Lucha Corpi was born in Mexico. She came to Berkeley, California, when she was nineteen. Her poetry is written in Spanish and her novels are written in English. Her work reflects her preoccupation with redefining stereotypes such as Malinche and La Llorona. She has a B.A. in comparative literature from the University of California, Berkeley, and an M.A. from San Francisco State University. She currently lives in Oakland, California, where she teaches English to adults in the Oakland Public Schools. She published two poetry books and five novels: *Palabras de mediodía/Noon Words* (1980); *Variaciones sobre una tempestad/Variations on a Storm* (1990); *Delia's Song* (1989); *Eulogy for a Brown Angel* (1992), which was selected as Best Fiction for 1993 by the Multicultural Publishers Exchange and introduced the first Chicana detective; *Cactus Blood* (1995); *Black Widow's Wardrobe* (1997); and *Crimson Moon* (2004).

## Marina Mother

They made her of the softest clay
and dried her under the rays of the tropical sun.
With the blood of a tender lamb
her name was written by the elders
on the bark of that tree
as old as they.

Steeped in tradition, mystic
and mute she was sold—
from hand to hand, night to night,
denied and desecrated, waiting for the dawn

Primary works by Lucha Corpi: *Delia's Song* (Houston: Arte Público Press, 1989); *Variaciones sobre una tempestad/Variations on a Storm* (1990); *Eulogy for a Brown Angel* (Houston: Arte Público Press, 1992); *Cactus Blood* (Houston: Arte Público Press, 1999); *Black Widow's Wardrobe* (Houston: Arte Público Press, 1999); *Palabras de mediodía/Noon Words* (Houston: Arte Público Press, 2001); *Crimson Moon* (Houston: Arte Público Press, 2004).

and for the owl's song
that would never come;
her womb sacked of its fruit,
her soul thinned to a handful of dust.

You no longer loved her, the elders denied her,
and the child who cried out to her "mama!"
grew up and called her "whore."

*(Translated by Catherine Rodríguez-Nieto)*

# Sandra María Esteves

Sandra María Esteves was born in 1948 in the Bronx, New York. She is the daughter of a Dominican mother and a Puerto Rican father. Raised by a single, Spanish-speaking, working-class mother and educated in the English-speaking environment of a Catholic boarding school, she was attracted to the ethnic and racial consciousness movements taking place around her in the 1960s and 1970s. She begin to read her works in public, along with other Nuyorican writers, in poetry cafés and university workshops. Her first collection, *Yerba Buena* (Good Herbs, 1980), was followed by *Tropical Rains: A Bilingual Downpour* (1984), and *Bluestown Mockingbird Mambo* (1990). Her ethnic awareness expanded in later works to encompass the struggles of Native Americans, African Americans, and Chicanos, and her approach became more woman-centered.

## Affirmations #3, Take Off Your Mask

Study the face behind it.
The one that has no flesh or bones.
The one that feels what the universe feels.

Take off the mask. Discard it.
Useless shell that it is.
An old skin. A cover.
Subject to weather distortions.

See for yourself
the you inside no one else can see.

Primary works by Sandra María Esteves: *Yerba Buena* (New York: Greenfield Review Press, 1980); *Bluestown Mockingbird Mambo* (Houston: Arte Público Press, 1990).

# Ray González

Ray González was born and raised in El Paso, Texas, a place that serves as the foundation for his poems and essays. His poems reflect the conflicting social forces around him as well as the historical and mythical implications of living in El Paso: a desert, a city, a border, a river, a bridge between two worlds. His ideas on writing are best expressed in his own words; "I want my writing to be read and perhaps have the reader see that the illumination of language is the light toward praising who we are as individuals. Of course, in the real world with its realities, my writing is also affected by my Mexican-American background and the place I was raised—the desert southwest of El Paso and the volatile U.S.–Mexican border."

## These Days

These years the border closes,
*mojados*[1] sent back to be found as bodies in the river,
or the cut-off head hanging in the tree.
The gang in the barrio where I work sprays
graffiti on my office door, symbols I don't understand.
The English and Spanish don't belong to me.
They vibrate in drive-by shootings,
boys gasping with laughter and the gun,
betting on who will get shot or dance in prison.

Inside a mountain,
a man gets up and wonders what happened to
the *cuento*[2] passed to him about madness
of a family who fled here, building a stone bridge
to hold water that saved them, made their corn grow.
Water seeps into the man's ears when he lies down.
It trickles into the room where he grows old,
water weeping out of the saguaro so he can cup his hands.

*marked*

---

Primary works by Ray González: *The Hawk Temple at Tierra Grande* (New York: BOA Editions, 2002); *Turtle Pictures* (Tucson: University of Arizona Press, 2000); *Cabato Sentora* (New York: BOA Editions, 1999); *The Heat of Arrivals* (New York: BOA Editions, 1996); *Railroad Face* (San Antonio: Chile Verde Press, 1995); *Twilights and Chants* (Colorado: James Andrews, 1987); *From the Restless Roots* (Houston: Arte Público Press, 1985); *The Underground Heart: Essays from Hidden Landscapes* (Tuscon: University of Arizona Press, 2002); *Memory Fever: A Journey Beyond El Paso del Norte* (Seattle: Broken Moon Press, 1993); *Circling the Tortilla Dragon: Short Fiction* (San Francisco: Creative Arts Books, 2002); *The Ghost of John Wayne* (Tucson: University of Arizona Press, 2001); *Luna: A Journal of poetry and translation* Volume 4, (May 2001); *Luna: A journal of poetry and translation* Volume 3, (October 2000), in *Muy Macho: Latino Men on Self-Identity* (New York: Anchor/Doubleday, 1996).

[1]Illegal immigrants
[2]Story

*[handwritten: Unmarked]*

The hills contain graves of <u>Mejicanos</u>,[3]
the rumor my father's ancestors were throat-cutting thieves
buried without markers on their graves.
I read about the psychic in the <u>Alamo</u> who encountered    *[handwritten: historical references]*
spirits of Mejicanos forced into <u>Santa Ana</u>'s army to die.
He contacts Bernardo y Juan Vargas, brothers trapped
<u>156 years</u> as tourists step on them,
soldiers revealing they want to rest in peace.
The psychic asks if the ghost of John Wayne dwells here.
The brothers tell him Wayne wanders among the dead,
never speaks because he can't find
the spirits of the Texas heroes.

I wave to the gang member we hired
to paint a mural on our center wall,
his arms finishing the blue and yellow feathers
on the Aztec face he created,
showing me how the man trapped in the mountain
can find his way out when I enter the old house to find
he is a muralist mixing color from
the burned mirrors under our familiar floors.

---

[3]Mexicans

---

# Víctor Hernández Cruz

Víctor Hernández Cruz was born in Aguas Buenas, Puerto Rico, in 1949. When he was five, he moved with his family to Spanish Harlem in New York. He is the Nuyorican most recognized and acclaimed by mainstream literary critics. His poetry begin to appear in *Evergreen Review,* the *New York Review of Books, Ramparts,* and other small magazines a few years after he graduated from high school. He published his first chapbook when he was sixteen and, at twenty, his first highly lauded collection, *Snaps* (1969). His poetry is considered Afro-Latin. He has developed as a consummate bilingual poet and experimenter who constantly explores the relationship of music to poetry in a multiracial, multicultural context. He has often been considered a jazz poet as a result of this and because he often reproduces salsa percussion rhythms. *Life* in April 1981 listed him as an outstanding American poet.

Primary works by Víctor Hernández Cruz: *Snaps* (New York: Random House, 1969); *Tropicalization* (San Francisco: Reed and Canon, 1976); *Rhythm, Content and Flavor* (Houston: Arte Público Press, 1989); *Red Beans* (Minneapolis: Coffee House Press, 1991).

# Loisaida

*To the memory of the original Nuyorican Poets
Cafe on Sixth Street—To Miguel Piñero who
lived it—To Tato Laviera who sings it—To Miguel
Algarín who knows it—To Chela, Flicha, Papote
Maggy and Cari my cousin named after Caridad
del Cobre and all the Saints that got me
Through in safety.*

By the East River
of Manhattan island
Where once the Iroquois
Canoed in style
Now the jumping
Stretch of Avenue D
housing projects
Where
Rican / Blacks
Johnny Pacheco / Wilson Pickett
Transistor
the radio night
Across the Domino sugar
sign
Red Neon on stage
It's the edge of Brooklyn

From heaven windows
megalopolis light
That's the picture
Into a lizard mind
Below the working
class jumps like frogs
Parrots with new raincoats
Swinging canes of bamboo
Like third legs
Strollers of cool flow
A didy-bop keeping step
time with the finest
Marching through
Red bricks aglow

Hebrew prayers
inside metals
Rolled into walls
Tenement relic
living in Museum
Home driven carts
arrive with the morning
slicing through the
curtains
Along with a Polish
English
Barking peaches and melons
The ice man sells
his hard water
Cut into blocks
Buildings swallowing
coals through their
Basement mouth

Where did the mountains
go
The immigrants ask
The place where houses
and objects went back
In history and entered
The roots of plants
And become eternal again
Now the plaster of Paris
The ears of the walls
The first utterances
in Spanish
Recalled what was left
behind

People kept arriving
as the cane fields dried
They came like flying bushes
from another planet
which had pineapples for moons
Fruits popping out of luggage
The singers of lament

into the soul of Jacob Riis
The Bible tongues
Santa María
Into the Torah
La liturgical lai le lo le
A Spanish never seen
before
Inside the gypsies
Parading through
Warsaw ghetto
Lower East Side
Rabinicals
Begin to vanish
into the economy
Left Loisaida
a skeleton
The works quarter

Orchard Street
garments
Falling off the torso
in motion down the avenue
It seems it could not hold
the cold back

The red Avenue B bus
disappearing down
The drain of Man
Hat on
Dissolving into the
pipes of lower Broadway
The Canals of streets
direct to the factories

After Foresite Park
Is the begining of Italy
Florence inside Mott
Street windows
Palmero eyes of Angie
Criss crossing these
mazes I would arrive

At Loudes home
With knishes she threw
next to red beans

Broome Street Hasidics
with Martian fur hats
Gone with their brims
Puerto Ricans with Pra
Pras
Atop faces with features
thrown out of some bag
Of universal racial
stew
Mississippi sharecroppers
through Avenue D black
Stories
All in exile from broken
Souths
The amapolas the daffodils
were cement tar and steel
Within architectural
gardens remembering
the agriculture of mountain
and field

From the guayava bushels
outside a town with a
Taíno name
I hear a whistle
In the aboriginal ear
With the ancient I
that saw Andalucía
Arrive on a boat
To distribute Moorish
eyes on the coast
Loisaida was faster
than the speed of light
A whirlpool within which
you had to grab on to something
It took off like a spauldine
hit by a blue broom stick

on 12th street
Winter time summer time
seasons of hallways
And roofs
Between pachanga[1] and duwap
Thousands of Eddies and Carmens
Stars and tyrants
Now gone
From the temporary station of
desire and disaster
The windows sucked them up
The pavement turned out to
be a mouth
Urban vanishment
Illusion
Henry Roth
Call it Sleep.

---

[1]Celebration/party

# Carolina Hospital

Carolina Hospital was born in Havana. She arrived in the United States, in Miami, Florida, in 1961. She teaches at Miami Dade Community College. Her poetry and fiction have been featured in *The Americas Review, Bilingual Review, Cuban Heritage Magazine, Linden Lane,* and *Looking for Home.* Hospital edited *Cuban American Writers: Los Atrevidos* (1989), where she explains that, to her, Cuban American writers of her generation are risk-takers who dared to belong to a future that acknowledges a new historical reality because they are forced to develop their artistic talents within two cultural and linguistic worlds. She argues that writers like them should be considered in both Cuban and North American literary traditions.

## The Hyphenated Man

Do you wake up each day
with an urge for a bagel
with café con leche?[1]
Do you flip back and forth

---

Primary works by Carolina Hospital: *A Little Love* (New York: Warner Books, 2001); ed., *Cuban American Writers: Los Atrevidos* (Princeton: Linden Lane Press, 1989); *The Child of Exile: A Poetry Memoir* (Houston: Arte Público Press, 2004).

[1]Coffee with milk

through *The Miami Herald* comparing every word
to *El Nuevo Herald*?
Do you circle around back alleys
trying to decide between McDonalds and
Pollo Tropical?
Do you feel guilty buying Cuban bread
at Publix,
while getting a cheesecake at Sedanos?
At Thanksgiving, do you creep into the kitchen
to put mojito[2] on the turkey,
and then complain at Christmas because
there's lechón[3] instead of turkey?
Do you find yourself Two-Stepping
to salsa beat and dancing güaracha[4]
to every other jazz beat?
Does your heart skip a beat for Sonia Braga
while longing wistfully for the days of Doris Day?
If so my friend,
then you are the hyphenated man.
Yes, H-Y-P-H-E-N.
The hyphenated man
lurks beneath that confident exterior
and it's time you consider
Hyphens Anonymous,
where the confused straddlers find refuge
and solace.
They meet once a week,
talk Spanglish to their heart's content,
eat mariquitas[5] with hot dogs, and
cuban coffee with Dunkin Donuts,
without explanations or alienations
Not the twelve step program,
but the three step dilemma.
Join today and
get off the see-saw,
jump off the fence,
slide down the hill,

---

[2]Cuban rum drink
[3]Pork
[4]Folkloric music
[5]Cuban food

cross the bridge,
get into the circle,
turn from the mirror.
Don't get off the wagon,
get on the hyphen.
Do not delay.
Hyphens Anonymous can help you forget
who you are
or better
who you wish you could be.

# Angela de Hoyos

Angela de Hoyos was born in Mexico but has lived for a number of years in San Antonio, Texas. She is a visual artist and a poet. She has published in English and Spanish. Roberta Fernández says Hoyos is "a verbal wizard, as she Hispanizes the English language to suit her particular needs, expanding beyond the linguistic limits of the monolingual writer." She has published several collections of poetry such as *Arise, Chicano, and Other Poems* (1975), *Chicano Poems: For the Barrio* (1975), *Poems/Poemas* (1975), *Selecciones* (1979), and *Woman, Woman* (1985). Her poetry has also been published in India, England, Switzerland, and Australia.

## Lesson in Semantics

Men, she said,
    sometimes
        in order to
           say it

it is
    necessary
        to spit
           the word.

Primary works by Angela de Hoyos: *Woman, Woman* (Houston: Arte Público Press, 1995); *Selected Poems: Selecciones* (San Antonio: Dezcalzo Press, 1979).

# Tato Laviera

Tato Laviera (Jesús Abraham "Tato" Laviera) was born in Santurce, Puerto Rico, in 1950. He migrated with his family to New York's Lower East Side in 1960. He is a poet, musician, dramatist, and songwriter whose works and performances reflect what has been called the Nuyorican modality. Although he had little academic training, he has produced a substantial body of work and has received critical recognition, including an invitation by President Carter in 1980 to read at a White House gathering of American poets. His first collection of poetry, *La Carreta Made a U-Turn* (1979), is a Puerto Rican response to René Márques's classic drama *La Carreta* (The Oxcart, 1953). Laviera's book gives voice to the millions of Puerto Ricans for whom permanent return to the island is impossible; nevertheless, in his poetry, those emigrants can still legitimately claim to be a valuable part of Puerto Rican culture. His skillful use of code switching, or Spanglish, reveals the linguistic dilemma of this population. The influence of music, particularly African rhythms, combined with a keen ear for street talk, double talk, and barrio dialect, make Laviera's works best appreciated in public presentations. His third collection, *AmeRícan* (1986), is a tribute to multiethnic identities and reflects his ongoing efforts to redefine Americanness apart from the mythological melting pot.

## AmeRícan[1]

we gave birth to a new generation,
AmeRícan, broader than lost gold
never touched, hidden inside the
puerto rican mountains.

*creating a new ethnicity*

we gave birth to a new generation,
AmeRícan, it includes everything
imaginable you-name-it-we-got-it
society.

we gave birth to a new generation,
AmeRícan salutes all folklores,
european, indian, black, spanish,
and anything else compatible:

Primary works by Tato Laviera: *La Carreta Made a U-Turn* (Houston: Arte Público Press, 1979); *Enclave* (Houston: Arte Público Press, 1981); *AmeRícan* (Houston: Arte Público Press, 1985).

[1]Combination of American and Puerto Rican

AmeRícan,    singing to composer pedro flores' palm
                trees high up in the universal sky!

AmeRícan,    sweet soft spanish danzas gypsies
                moving lyrics la española[2] cascabelling
                presence always singing at our side!

AmeRícan,    beating jíbaro[3] modern troubadours
                crying guitars romantic continental
                bolero[4] love songs!

AmeRícan,    across forth and across back
                back across and forth back
                forth across and back and forth
                our trips are walking bridges!

                it all dissolved into itself, the attempt
                was truly made, the attempt was truly
                absorbed, digested, we spit out
                the poison, we spit out the malice,
                we stand, affirmative in action,
                to reproduce a broader answer to the
                marginality that gobbled us up abruptly!

AmeRícan,    walking plena[5]-rhythms in new york,
                strutting beautifully alert, alive,
                many turning eyes wondering,
                admiring!

AmeRícan,    defining myself my own way any way many
                ways Am e Rícan, with the big R and the
                accent on the í!

AmeRícan,    like the soul gliding talk of gospel
                boogie music!

---

[2]The Spanish woman
[3]Peasant of Puerto Rico
[4]Love ballads
[5]Music composition of Puerto Rico

AmeRícan,   speaking new words in spanglish tenements,
             fast tongue moving street corner "que
             corta"[6] talk being invented at the insistence
             of a smile!

AmeRícan,   abounding inside so many ethnic english
             people, and out of humanity, we blend
             and mix all that is good!

AmeRícan,   integrating in new york and defining our
             own destino,[7] our own way of life,

AmeRícan,   defining the new america, humane america,
             admired america, loved america, harmonious
             america, the world in peace, our energies
             collectively invested to find other civilizations,
             to touch God, further and further,
             to dwell in the spirit of divinity!

AmeRícan,   yes, for now, for i love this, my second
             land, and i dream to take the accent from
             the altercation, and be proud to call
             myself american, in the u.s. sense of the
             word, AmeRícan, America!

---

[6]That cuts
[7]Destiny

# Pat Mora = girl

Pat Mora was born in El Paso, Texas. She has published several collections of poetry, among them *Chants* (1984), *Borders* (1986), *Communion* (1991), and *My Own True Name* (2000). Her poetry collections have won awards from the Border Regional Library Association, the National Chicano Studies Association, and the Southwest Council of Latin American Studies. She has received the Southwest Book Award twice and was elected to the Institute of Letters in 1987. Her collection of essays, *Nepantla*, was published in 1993, and her memoir, *House of Houses*, in 1997. She has also written several books for children, including *The Desert Is My Mother/El desierto es mi madre*.

---

Primary works by Pat Mora: *Chants* (Houston: Arte Público Press, 1984); *Borders* (Houston: Arte Público Press, 1986); *Communion* (Houston: Arte Público Press, 1991), *Nepantla: Essays from the Land in the Middle* (Albuquerque: University of New Mexico Press, 1993); *Agua Santa/Holy Water* (Boston: Beacon Press, 1995).

## Legal Alien

Bi-lingual, Bi-cultural,
able to slip from "How's life?"
to *"Me'stán volviendo loca,"*[1]
able to sit in a paneled office   ← setting
drafting memos in smooth English,
able to order in fluent Spanish
at a Mexican restaurant,
American but hyphenated,
viewed by Anglos as perhaps exotic,
perhaps inferior, definitely different,
viewed by Mexicans as alien,
(their eyes say, "You may speak
Spanish but you're not like me")
an American to Mexicans
a Mexican to Americans
a handy token
sliding back and forth
between the fringes of both worlds
by smiling
by masking the discomfort
of being pre-judged
Bi-laterally.

*Normal, educated & wants to be treated so.*

[1]You're driving me crazy

# Rosario Morales and Aurora Levins Morales

Rosario Morales and Aurora Levins Morales coauthored *Getting Home Alive* in 1986. Rosario Morales (1930) moved back to Puerto Rico after her marriage, and, in 1954, her daughter, Aurora, was born. The family returned to live in the United States when Aurora was a young girl. She and her mother have published both in collaboration and separately. *Getting Home Alive* is a collection of poetry, stories, vignettes of women who share the similarities of being Puerto Rican, mother, and daughter, but who are divided by generational differences and differing viewpoints regarding assimilation and cultural heritage.

Primary work by Aurora Levins Morales and Rosario Morales: *Getting Home Alive* (Ithaca, N.Y.: Firebrand Books, 1986).

# Ending Poem

I am what I am.
*A child of the Americas.*
A light-skinned mestiza of the Caribbean.
*A child of many diaspora, born into this continent at a crossroads.*
I am Puerto Rican. I am U.S. American.
*I am New York Manhattan and the Bronx.*
A mountain-born, country-bred, homegrown jíbara[1] child,
*up from the shtetl, a California Puerto Rican Jew*
A product of the New York ghettos I have never known.
*I am an immigrant*
and the daughter and granddaughter of immigrants.
*We didn't know our forbears' names with a certainty.*
They aren't written anywhere.
*First names only or mija,[2] negra,[3] ne, honey, sugar, dear*

I come from the dirt where the cane was grown.
*My people didn't go to dinner parties. They weren't invited.*
I am caribeña,[4] island grown.
*Spanish is in my flesh, ripples from my tongue, lodges in my hips,*
the language of garlic and mangoes.
*Boricua. As Bóricuas come from the isle of Manhattan.*
I am of latinoamérica,[5] rooted in the history of my continent.
*I speak from that body. Just brown and pink and full of drums inside.*

I am not African.
*Africa waters the roots of my tree, but I cannot return.*

I am not Taína.[6]
*I am a late leaf of that ancient tree,*
and my roots reach into the soil of two Americas.
*Taíno is in me, but there is no way back.*

I am not European, though I have dreamt of those cities.
*Each plate is different.*

---

[1]Peasant
[2]Daughter
[3]Black
[4]Caribbean woman
[5]Latin America
[6]Indain native to Puerto Rico

wood, clay, papier maché, metals, basketry, a leaf, a coconut shell.
*Europe lives in me but I have no home there.*

The table has a cloth woven by one, dyed by another,
*embroidered by another still.*
I am a child of many mothers.
*They have kept it all going*

All the civilizations created on their backs.
*All the dinner parties given with their labor.*

We are new.
*They gave us life, kept us going,*
brought us to where we are.
*Born at a crossroads.*
Come, lay that dishcloth down. Eat, dear, eat.
*History made us.*
We will not eat ourselves up inside anymore.

*And we are whole.*

# Miguel Piñero

Miguel Piñero was born in Puerto Rico in 1946. He came to the United States as a child and was raised in New York's Lower East Side, an area with a long immigrant history as well as a reputation for poverty, drug abuse, and social violence. His problems with the authorities began early: By the age of fifteen he had already been arrested for truancy, shoplifting, and drug possession; at age twenty-four the self-educated high school dropout was sent to Sing Sing prison for armed robbery. It was there that he caught the attention of a *New York Times* reporter in one of the theater workshops that he participated in. As a result, his play *Short Eyes* (1974) was produced first with a cast of convicts and ex-convicts. The play has been performed on Broadway and throughout the United States and abroad. For this play, Piñero received the New York Drama Critics' Circle Award and the Obie for best off-Broadway play of 1973–1974. He wrote several other plays and coedited a collection of poems, *Nuyorican Poetry* (1975), with Miguel Algarín, that introduced Nuyorican poets to a larger readership for the first time. His collection of poetry, *La Bodega Sold Dreams*, is an angry view of those who are marginalized in city life; it was published in 1980.

Primary works by Miguel Piñero: *Short Eyes* (New York: Hill and Wang, 1975); *La Bodega Sold Dreams* (Houston: Arte Público Press, 1980); *The Sun Always Shines for the Cool, Midnight Moon, at the Greasy Spoon, Eulogy for a Small Time Thief* (Houston: Arte Público Press, 1984); *Outrageous One Act Plays* (Houston: Arte Público Press, 1986).

# A Lower East Side Poem

Just once before I die
I want to climb up on a
tenement sky
to dream my lungs out till
I cry
then scatter my ashes thru
the Lower East Side.

So let me sing my song tonight
let me feel out of sight
and let all eyes be dry
when they scatter my ashes thru
the Lower East Side.

From Houston to 14th Street
from Second Avenue to the mighty D
here the hustlers & suckers meet
the faggots & freaks will all get
high
on the ashes that have been scattered
thru the Lower East Side.

There's no other place for me to be
there's no other place that I can see
there's no other town around that
brings you up or keeps you down
no food little heat sweeps by
fancy cars & pimps' bars & juke saloons
& greasy spoons make my spirits fly
with my ashes scattered thru the
Lower East Side . . .

A thief, a junkie I've been
committed every known sin
Jews and Gentiles . . . Bums and Men
of style . . . run away child
police shooting wild . . .
mother's futile wails . . . pushers
making sales . . . dope wheelers
& cocaine dealers . . . smoking pot
streets are hot & feed off those who bleed to death . . .

all that's true
all that's true
all that is true
but this ain't no lie
when I ask that my ashes be scattered thru
the Lower East Side.

So here I am, look at me
I stand proud as you can see
pleased to be from the Lower East
a street fighting man
a problem of this land
I am the Philosopher of the Criminal Mind
a dweller of prison time
a cancer of Rockefeller's ghettocide
this concrete tomb is my home
to belong to survive you gotta be strong
you can't be shy less without request
someone will scatter your ashes thru
the Lower East Side.

I don't wanna be buried in Puerto Rico
I don't wanna rest in long island cemetery
I wanna be near the stabbing shooting
gambling fighting & unnatural dying
& new birth crying
so please when I die . . .
don't take me far away
keep me near by
take my ashes and scatter them thru out
the Lower East Side . . .

# Alberto Álvaro Ríos

Alberto Álvaro Ríos was born in Nogales, Arizona, in 1952, in a place where, he has said, he could "put one foot in Mexico and one foot in the United States, at the same time." He was born to a Mexican father and an English mother; this influenced his writing. He earned an MFA in creative writing from the University of Arizona and has taught in the Creative Writing Program at Arizona State University since 1980. He received a Guggenheim Fellowship and a fellowship from the National Endowment for the Arts. *Whispering to Fool the Wind,* his first collection of poetry, won the Academy of American Poets Walt Whitman Award in 1981.

## Wet Camp

We have been here before, but we are lost.
The earth is black and the trees are bent
and broken and piled as if the game
of pick-up-sticks were ready and the children
hiding, waiting their useless turns.
The west bank of the river is burned
and the Santa Cruz has poured onto it.
The grit brown ponds
sit like dirty lilies in the black.
The afternoon is gone grazing
over the thin mountains.
The night is colder here without leaves.
Nothing holds up the sky.

Primary works by Alberto Ríos: *Whispering to Fool the Wind* (New York: Sheep Meadow Press, 1982); *Capirotada: A Nogales Memoir* (Albuquerque: University of New Mexico Press, 1999).

# Luis Omar Salinas

Luis Omar Salinas was born in Robstown, Texas, but moved with his family to Monterrey, Mexico, when he was young. When his mother died, Salinas moved to California, where he was raised by an uncle. He studied at several universities and was often plagued by nervous breakdowns. He began his career as a surrealistic poet in the Chicano Movement and continued to write until his death in the 1980s. Although he has received many awards for his writing, he has not become well known in mainstream poetry circles in the United States. His verses evidence the traditions of Chilean Pablo Neruda, Spanish Federico García Lorca, and Walt Whitman. His first widely praised book was *Crazy Gypsy* (1970), followed by *Afternoon of the Unreal* (1980) and *Prelude to Darkness* (1981). Arte Público Press published his collection *The Sadness of Days* in 1987.

## I Am America

It's a hell of a world.
I go like a schoolboy stepping

Primary work by Luis Omar Salinas: *Crazy Gypsy* (Santa Barbara: Orígenes Publication, 1970); *Darkness under the Trees; Walking behind the Spanish* (Berkeley: Chicano Studies Library Publications, 1982); *The Sadness of Days: Selected and New Poems* (Houston: Arte Público Press, 1987); *Prelude to Darkness* (San Jose: Mango Publications, 1981).

through the murderous countryside,
a bit off rhyme, a little drunk
with the wonderful juices of breasts,
and the magnificent
with their magician-like words
slipping into the voice of America.
I carry my father's coat,
some coins,
my childhood eyes in wonder—
the olive trucks plucky
in their brash ride
through the avenue,
the wino in a halo of freedom,
the shopkeepers of Democracy.

I am brave, I am sad
and I am happy with
the workers in the field,
the pregnant women
in ten dollar dresses,
the night air supping
and stopping to chat
like a wild romantic lady.
Children's voices and dogs,
the bar, the songs and fights.
I go ruminating in the brothels,
the ghettos, the jails.
Braggart, walking into early
cafés confessing naiveté
and love for the unemployed.
I'm a dream in the land
like the Black, Mexican, Indian,
Anglo and Oriental faces
with their pictures of justice.
I go gaudy into movie houses,
flamboyant spectator
of horse races.

I am not unloved, or unwanted
but I have seen the faces

of the rebel, the outcast,
I have touched the madness, all the terrible,
and I have seen the ghosts of the past.
I am a friend to all,
for I have touched everything,
even the empty plates of the poor.
I put on my clothes, my hat,
I visit everywhere—
I go to the market for bananas,
smoke the air,
breathe America.


I am wretched and mean,
I am kind and compassionate.
I remember catechism class,
the nuns and the priests,
my sister's wit,
and the neighbor's beautiful wife.
I am walking behind America,
suspicious, pie-eyed,
open-faced in the distance.
I am a father of prayers,
obedient,
I am a father of women,
a son of women.
I speak as the common man
and listen like the wise.
I am America,
and by hearts grown cold to me
I will be the seer of my intellect.
I will put an end to misery with
the bravado of the seeker,
drunken, reveling
in this American continent,
tight fisted,
exposed like a blue rose
to the night stars.

# Tino Villanueva

Tino Villanueva was born in San Marcos, Texas, in 1941. He is the founder of Imagine Publishers, Inc., and editor of *Imagine: International Chicano Poetry Journal*. He has a prolific writing career. Among his books are *Scene from the movie GIANT, Hay Otra Voz Poems, Shaking Off the Dark,* and *Crónica de mis años peores*. He teaches at Boston University.

## Chicano Dropout

Jesús.

In another world lo bautizaron,[1] *Jesse*—
    era el más chuco de todos.[2]

But no one, nadie
    (ni el más sabelotodo supo de su historia):[3]

*He doesn't bother participating in my history class.*
*He can't seem to verbalize in our speech class, you know.*
*Tino, just what's wrong with these Latin Americans?*

So Jesse,
    cuando era[4] junior, was pushed out into
    dirty-brown streets of his zip-coded barrio.

He left quietly,
    but on his desk he left carved his name: **CHUY**

---

Primary works by Tino Villanueva: *Chronicle of My Worst Years/Crónica de mis años peores* (Evanston: Northwestern Univ. Press, 1994); *Hay Otra voz: Poems* (1968–1971) (Staten Island: Editorial Mensaje, 1979); *Scene from the Movie GIANT* (Willimantic: Curbstone Press, 1993); *Shaking off the Dark* (Houston: Arte Público Press, 1984).

[1]They baptized him
[2]He was the coolest of all
[3]Nobody (not even the smartest knew his story)
[4]When he was

# PROSE

# Veronica Chambers

Veronica Chambers is of Panamanian descent. She has published since 1996, at which time her novel *Mama's Girl*, a memoir about growing up, was launched by Riverhead Books.

She then cowrote a book with John Singleton, *Poetic Justice: Filmmaking South Central Style*, in 2001. This led to the publication of several children books, including *Amistad Rising, The Harlem Renaissance, Quinceañera Means Sweet 15, Marisol and Magdalena,* and *Double Dutch: A Celebration of Jump Rope, Rhyme and Sisterhood.* She also writes for publications such as *The New York Times Magazine* where she has explored her African and Latino heritage.

## Secret Latina at Large

She's a *plátanos*[1]-frying, malta dukesa–drinking, salsa-dancing *mamacita*[2] —my dark-skinned Panamanian mother. She came to this country when she was twenty-one— her sense of culture intact, her Spanish flawless. Today, more than twenty years since she left her home country and became an American citizen, my mother still considers herself a Panamanian, checks "Hispanic" on the census form.

As a black woman in America, my Latina identity is murkier than my mother's. Without a Spanish last name or my mother's fluent Spanish at my disposal, I've often felt isolated from the Latin community. Latinos can be as racist as anybody else: there are pecking orders and hierarchies that favor blue-eyed blonde *rubios*[3] over *negritas*[4] like me. Sometimes, I feel that I put up with enough racism from white Americans, why should I turn to white Latinos for a second share? In much the same way that you can meet a person and not know if they are gay or straight, you could meet me and not know whether I was of Latin heritage. So I find myself making judgement calls—do I come out of the closet and when?

I was born in Panama to black Panamanian parents. My father's parents came from Costa Rica and Jamaica. My mother's family came from Martinique. I left Panama when I was two years old, we lived in England for three years, and I came to the U.S. when I was five. Having dark skin and growing up in Brooklyn in the '70's meant that I was black—period. I spent my childhood on Brooklyn streets that morphed, quickly, into worlds away. A stroll down Utica Avenue and the music or the smell of somebody's grandmother's cooking could transform a New York City corner into Santo Domingo, Kingston, Port-au-Prince. Long before I ever set out in search of the world, it found me. My friends, their families, and the histories they carried on their backs, kept me glued to the globe. I traced nations with my fingertips and knew that America was neither the beginning nor the end, just the crazy mixed-up right now that we all lived in. I also knew that we were only the latest wave of immigrants to make a home in our East Flatbush neighborhood. Every day after school, I rubbed my fingers across the Jewish mezuzah that ornamented our door frame. The super had painted over the

---

Primary works by Veronica Chambers: *Having it all?: Black Women and success* (New York: Doubleday, 2003); *Poetic Justice* with John Singleton (New York: Delta, 1993).

[1]Plantains
[2]Good-looking momma
[3]Blondes
[4]Black woman (diminutive)

Panama ≠ P.R.

mezuzahs, an ugly brown, but I never saw anyone ripping one off. I understood it to be out of respect, and I wondered how we would leave our mark.

Still, despite the international flavor of our neighborhood, I found it almost impossible to explain to my elementary school friends why my mother would speak Spanish at home. They asked me if I was Puerto Rican and I would tell them I was not. But Panama was a kind of nowhere to my young Brooklyn friends. They understood Puerto Ricans because there were so many of them and because of movies like *West Side Story* and groups like Menudo. Everybody knew where Jamaicans were from because of famous singers like Bob Marley. Panamanians had Rubén Blades and we loved him like royalty. But even if my friends knew who he was, because he sang in Spanish, they probably thought he was Puerto Rican too. So in my neighborhood, my brother and I were a sort of fish with feathers. We weren't so much Panamanians as much as we were assumed to be Jamaicans who spoke Spanish. An analogy that isn't without historical basis—Panama's black community was largely drawn to the country from all over the Caribbean as cheap labor for the Panama Canal.

My father didn't mind us considering ourselves black as opposed to Latino. He named my brother Malcolm X. If my mother hadn't put her foot down, I would've been called Angela Davis Chambers. It's not that my mother didn't admire Angela Davis, but you only have to hear how "Veronica Victoria" flows off of her Spanish lips to know that she was homesick for Panama and names that sang like *timbales*[5] on carnival day. So between my mother and my father, there was a black/Latin divide. Because of my father, we discussed and read books about black history and civil rights. Because of my mother, we ate Panamanian food, listened to salsa music and heard Spanish around the house.

I learned Spanish at home like a dog learns English, and understood mostly commands: "*¡Cállate la boca!*" ("Shut your mouth!") when I dared to interrupt grown-folk's talk. Or "*¡Baja la cabeza!*" ("Drop your head!") when my mother was braiding my hair and I kept looking up to see my favorite show on TV. My father was also Panamanian, but his mentality was simple. "You're in America," he ordered. "Speak English." It wasn't until my parents were divorced, when I was ten, that my mother tried to teach Malcolm and me to speak Spanish.

My mother was a terrible language teacher. She had no sense of how to explain the structure when we asked questions such as why we were supposed to say "*Toma café*"—literally, "He takes coffee"—instead of "He drinks coffee." Her answer to everything was "That's just the way it is." A few short weeks after our Spanish lessons began, my mother gave up and we were all relieved. I remained intent on learning my mother's language. Nosiness, mostly. What was she saying to her friends on the phone? But there was more to it than that. When my mother spoke Spanish, it was a fast current of words, a stream of language that was colorful, passionate fiery. I wanted to speak Spanish because I wanted to swim in the river of her words, her history, my history, too.

At Ditmas Junior High School, I had to petition the principal so I could take Spanish. All the other kids in the gifted and talented program were taking French. Apparently, to the

---

[5]Musical instrument (percussion)

language barrier

powers that were, French was more cultural, more intellectual. The principal approved my request to take Spanish and for two years, I dove into the language, matching what little I knew from home with all that I learned at school. I never asked my mother for help with my Spanish homework; she never asked me about my lessons. But one day when I was in the ninth grade, I felt confident enough to start speaking Spanish with my mother and it's been that way ever since.

My brother, who was born in England, never learned Spanish and still doesn't speak it. When I was younger, my Spanish became a point of pride, a typical case of sibling rivalry. Now, I know that my Spanish was also an important bond that I shared with my mother. When I was little, she used to watch astrologer Walter Mercado and *telenovelas*[6] on the Spanish language TV station. I would sit impatiently as she translated Mercado's horoscope for me or tried to explain what was going on in the latest installment of *La Tragedia de Lisette*. After I learned Spanish, I watched these programs with my mother—not needing translations, poking fun at the campiness of Spanish language TV. My mother and I would talk to each other in Spanish at our jobs or anywhere we needed some semblance of privacy.

When I spoke only English, I was the daughter, the little girl. As I began to learn Spanish, I became something more—an *hermanita*, a sister-friend, a Panamanian homegirl who could hang with the rest of them. I kissed *boricua* boys on my grandmother's porch and wondered when they whispered *prieta*[7] whether that meant they loved me more or loved me less. When Puerto Rican girls talked about me in front of my face, looking at my dark skin and assuming that I couldn't understand, I would playfully throw out, *"Oye, ¿sabes que yo entiendo?"*[8] Being *Latinegra*—black and Latin, has become a sort of a hidden weapon, something that you can't see at first glance. I know that many people look at my dark skin and don't expect me to be fluent in anything but homegirl.

After college, I put Panama on the back burner for seven years, traveling instead to Spain, Morocco, London, Paris, even China. Then last year, at the age of twenty-seven, I wrote my first young adult novel, *Marisol and Magdalena,* about a black Panamanian girl growing up in Brooklyn who goes to live with her grandmother in Panama. In many ways, the novel was a way for me to live a dream that never came true. When I was a young girl, my *abuela*[9] Flora came to live with us in New York. She was old, eighty-four, and sick, but we became fast friends. She told me stories about Panama, promising me that she and I would go together. My grandmother told me that she would make me a festive *pollera*[10] dress and I could dance in the carnival. She died when I was eleven but writing *Marisol and Magdalena* I imagined what all of those things would be like. Then I decided that it was finally time. With or without my grandmother, with or without my mother, I would have to make my way

---

[6]Soap operas
[7]Dark one
[8]Hey, you know that I understand?
[9]Grandmother
[10]Folkloric dress

*[handwritten note: Spanish brings her closer to her mother]*

home. The first thing I did was enlist my cousin, Digna. She was thrilled. *"¡Ay prima!"*[12] she exclaimed, calling me as she always does, by the Spanish word for cousin. "To visit our *patria* (homeland) together. We'll have so much fun." We planned our trip for the last week in February and made arrangements to stay with my godparents, whom I had never met.

Like Mardi Gras in New Orleans and the big carnivals in Brazil, carnival in Panama is the year's biggest event. We had no problem finding cheap fares. I flew from New York to Miami, where most of the flights to Panama depart from. Arriving in the Miami airport was like stepping into a huge family reunion. The waiting room was filled with hundreds of black Panamanians, speaking in Spanish and calling out the familiar greeting, *"¿Wappin?"* (It's short for "What's happening?") On the plane, I found myself seated next to a family friend from New York.

It's a narrow slither of a country. Panamanians like to say that is the only place in the world where you can swim in the Atlantic in the morning and backstroke across the Pacific in the afternoon. In Panama, the oceans are close—suburbs of each other. But for most of my life, the ocean has been a divide—separating me from my homeland. There were days, weeks, even years, when I could turn my back on the Atlantic, turn American and no one would know or care that there was another country that I called home. Other times, when I danced in dark Brooklyn basements to the rhythms of Celia Cruz and Tito Puente or sat at my aunt's kitchen table listening to the round rhythms of her Panamanian-accented English roll across the table like lucky dice, Panama seemed impossibly close.

When I was little and I told my friends that I was from Panama, they would invariably ask, "Were you born in the Canal?" And I would close my eyes for a second, and I would picture myself, a chocolate colored little girl, swaddled in pink, floating like the baby Moses down the Panama Canal. Then I would solemnly answer, "Yes, I was." I am not much of a swimmer. I am not even a water sign. But water is significant to me. There are days when I find myself longing to be near a river or a lake, to put my hand into water that stops with my touch then keeps on moving. Other days, in the midst of a crisis or a full-scale panic attack, I will sit in a bathtub full of warm water to clear my mind. As human beings, we are drawn to the water. But I think with me, there is another layer. If you could lift my soul, like a piece of parchment paper, and hold it to the light, you would see an *S*-like watermark in the shape of Panama. It is brown and green and blue along the edges. Even landlocked in New York City, there are days that my spirit awakens in the Atlantic and falls to sleep, dreaming in the Pacific. And on those days, I feel whole and secure. When the airplane touched down in Panama, bringing me home for the first time since I was two years old, I felt the same way.

My cousin Digna likes to say that women in Panama know how to be *mujeres de cache.*[13] I grew up in a world of Panamanian women who used cocoa butter to make their skin smooth and coconut oil to keep their hair soft, women who never went out without nail

---

[12]Oh cousin!
[13]Women of class

polish and immaculately pressed clothes. Even poor Panamanian women wear gold with the lavish indulgence that some women wear perfume: dripping from their arms and their ears, fourteen-karat trinkets glistening between their breasts. The first thing my godmother Olga did was book appointments for me and my cousin to get our eyebrows plucked and our nails and feet done with Panamanian-style manicures and pedicures with names like *Medialuna*[14] and *La Secretaria*.[15] "It's carnival," she said. "And you girls have to look your best." We just laughed. It was already feeling like home.

I know that I belong to many tribes. Sometimes, I see a dreadlocked girl on the subway reading a book or carrying a canvas and a bag from Lee's Art Supplies and I identify her as part of my artsy boho black girl tribe. Or I'll be out with a multi-culti group of friends and we'll see another group as wildly diverse as our own and identify them as fellow members of the Rainbow Tribe. In Panama, I went from being a lone black girl with a curious Latin heritage to being part of the *Latinegro* tribe or the *Afro-Antillanos*,[16] as we are officially called. On my first day in Panama, my godfather took me to a party for SAMAAP (Society of Afro-Antilliano People). I was thrilled to learn that there was actually a society for people like me; my only disappointment was that there was no secret handshake. Everyone was black, everyone spoke Spanish, and it could have been a fiesta on Flatbush Avenue because everyone danced the way they danced in Brooklyn, stopping only to chow down on the same smorgasbord of souse, rice with black-eyed peas, beef patties, empanadas[17] and codfish fritters. I immediately started to call my cousin Digna, "Pipa" because the whole trip she kept guzzling *agua de pipa* which is coconut water drunk straight from a ripe coconut.

In the *Afro-Antillano* museum, I took a quiet moment to explore my history. I was struck by the faces of the men who worked and died building the Panama canal. I thought of the feminist anthology that had changed my life in college, Editors Cherríe Moraga and Gloria Anzaldúa's *This Bridge Called My Back* and the phrase took on new meaning. The famous Panama canal which so efficiently linked the East and the West was built on the backs of my ancestors. The locks of the Canal were made strong with the gristle from their bones. My ancestors' tears filled two oceans. I had been taught to be proud of my heritage, but there is a difference between head knowledge and heart knowledge. Standing in the Afro-Antillano museum, I stood a little taller, knowing in my heart what my people had done. I looked at the pictures and I could feel the family connection in each of their eyes—they resembled my uncles, my grandfathers, the young men who were doing the *salsa con sabor*[18] right outside the museum door. So many of the objects in the museum, like the beautiful *molas* (Matisse-like prints made by Panamanian Indians) reminded me of things that I had grown

---

[14]Half-moon
[15]The secretary
[16]Afro-Antillians
[17]Turnover
[18]Salsa with flavor

up with in my mother's home. It was remarkable how comfortable I felt in Panama. There was none of the culture shock that I'd expected. I had my mother and my aunts to thank for that. Although we came to the U.S. with so little material possessions, somehow my family had managed to carry whole bushels of Panamanian culture in their bones and in their hearts.

The actual carnival was the all-night bacchanal that you might expect: elaborate floats, brilliantly colored costumes, live musicians and dancing. The black Panamanian community had a formal dance which felt like a real debutante ball for a long-lost native daughter like myself. My godmother took my cousin and me to a photo studio where we had our pictures taken in the traditional costume of Panama, the *pollera*. Suffice it to say, it was a real trip. After an hour of makeup, hair, and a rented costume, I looked like a Latin version of Scarlett in *Gone With the Wind.* But when I gave the photo to my mother, she almost cried. She says she was so moved to see me in a *pollera* because it was "such a patriotic thing to do." I had become so Americanized over the years, but when I reached out to Panama, it reached right back to me. On the flight back home, I felt a quiet sense of completeness. To paraphrase the Jamaican tourist ads, I had come back to Panama, my old island home.

A friend left a voice mail message for me once, calling me a "secret Latina-at-large." The message made me ridiculously happy. I saved it and played it again and again. He had hit on a perfect description for me. Ever since I was a little girl, I have wanted to be like my mother—a Latina with a proud sense of self. In one of my most vivid memories. I am seven or eight and my parents are having a party. Salsa music is blaring and the refrain, *"Wappin'* Colon? *Hola,* Panama," is bouncing off the walls. My mother is dancing and laughing. She sees me standing off in a corner, so she pulls me into the circle of grown-ups and tries to teach me how to dance to the music. Her hips are electric. She puts her hands on my sides and she says, "Move these," and I start shaking my hip bones like my life depends on it. Now I'm a grown woman, and I have hips and booty to spare. I can salsa. My Spanglish is flawless, and my Spanish isn't shabby. You may not look at me and know that I am Panamanian, that I am an immigrant, that I am both black and Latin. But like my homeland, I am a narrow being flanked by two oceans of heritage. I'm a secret Latina-at-large and that is more than enough for me.

Similie

# Judith Ortiz Cofer

Judith Ortiz Cofer was born in Puerto Rico. Her family moved to Paterson, New Jersey, as a result of her father's reassignment in the Navy. She received her B.A. in English from Augusta College and her M.A. from Florida Atlantic University. She received a fellowship from the English Speaking Union of America to spend a summer at Graduate School at Oxford University. She has published many collections of poetry, short stories, and novels, including *The Line of the Sun* (1989), *The Latin Deli* (1993), *Silent Dancing* (1990), *Terms of Survival* (1987), *Reaching for the Mainland* (1987), and *Peregrina* (1986). *Silent Dancing* received several awards including the PEN American/Albrand Special Citation in the category for best nonfiction by an American author in 1991; it also named to the "Best Books for the Teen Age." She teaches English and Creative Writing at the University of Georgia.

## Silent Dancing

*We have a home movie of this party. Several times my mother and I have watched it together, and I have asked question about the silent revellers coming in and out of focus. It is grainy and of short duration but a great visual aid to my first memory of life in Paterson at that time. And it is in color—the only complete scene in color I can recall from those years.*

We lived in Puerto Rico until my brother was born in 1954. Soon after, because of economic pressures on our growing family, my father joined the United States Navy. He was assigned to duty on a ship in Brooklyn Yard, New York City—a place of cement and steel that was to be his home base in the States until his retirement more than twenty years later.

He left the Island first, tracking down his uncle who lived with his family across the Hudson River, in Paterson, New Jersey. There he found a tiny apartment in a huge apartment building that had once housed Jewish families and was just being transformed into a tenement by Puerto Ricans overflowing from New York City. In 1955 he sent for us. My mother was only twenty years old, I was not quite three, and my brother was a toddler when we arrived at *El Building,* as the place had been christened by its new residents.

My memories of life in Paterson during those first few years are in shades of gray. Maybe I was too young to absorb vivid colors and details, or to discriminate between the slate blue of the winter sky and the darker hues of the snow-bearing clouds, but the single color washes over the whole period. The building we lived in was gray, the streets were gray with slush the first few months of my life there, the coat my father had bought for me was dark in color and too big. It sat heavily on my thin frame.

I do remember the way the heater pipes banged and rattled, startling all of us out of sleep until we got so used to the sound that we automatically either shut it out or raised our voices above the racket. The hiss from the valve punctuated my sleep, which has always been fitful, like a nonhuman presence in the room—the dragon sleeping at the entrance of my childhood. But the pipes were a connection to all the other lives being lived around us. Having come from a house made for a single family back in Puerto Rico—my mother's extended-family home—it was curious to know that strangers lived under our floor and above our heads, and that the heater pipe went through everyone's apartments. (My first spanking in Paterson came as a result of playing tunes on the pipes in my room to see if there would be an answer). My mother was as new to this concept of beehive life as I was,

Primary works by Judith Ortiz Cofer: *Terms of Survival* (Houston: Arte Público Press, 1987); *The Line of the Sun* (Athens: University of Georgia Press, 1989); *Silent Dancing; A Remembrance of a Puerto Rican Childhood* (Houston: Arte Público Press, 1990); *The Year of Our Revolution* (Houston: Arte Público Press, 1999).

but had been given strict orders by my father to keep the doors locked, the noise down, ourselves to ourselves.

It seems that Father had learned some painful lessons about prejudice while searching for an apartment in Paterson. Not until years later did I hear how much resistance he had encountered with landlords who were panicking at the influx of Latinos into a neighborhood that had been Jewish for a couple of generations. But it was the American phenomenon of ethnic turnover that was changing the urban core of Paterson, and the human flood could not be held back with an accusing finger.

"You Cuban?" the man had asked my father, pointing a finger at his name tag on the Navy uniform—even though my father had the fair skin and light brown hair of his northern Spanish family background and our name is as common in Puerto Rico as Johnson is in the U.S.

"No," my father had answered looking past the finger into his adversary's angry eyes. "I'm Puerto Rican."

"Same shit." And the door closed. My father could have passed as European, but we couldn't. My brother and I both have our mother's black hair and olive skin, and so we lived in El Building and visited our great-uncle and his fair children on the next block. It was their private joke that they were the German branch of the family. Not many years later that area too would be mainly Puerto Rican. It was as if the heart of the city map were being gradually colored in brown—*café-con leche*[1] brown. Our color.

*The movie opens with a sweep of the living room. It is "typical" immigrant Puerto Rican decor for the time: the sofa and chairs are square and hard-looking, upholstered in bright colors (blue and yellow in this instance, and covered in the transparent plastic) that furniture salesmen then were adept at making women buy. The linoleum on the floor is light blue, and if it was subjected to the spike heels as it was in most places, there were dime-sized indentations all over it that cannot be seen in this movie. The room is full of people dressed in mainly two colors: dark suits for the men, red dresses for the women. I have asked my mother why most of the women are in red that night, and she shrugs, "I don't remember. Just a coincidence." She doesn't have my obsession for assigning symbolism to everything.*

*The three women in red sitting on the couch are my mother, my eighteen-year-old cousin, and her brother's girlfriend. The "novia"[2] is just up from the Island, which is apparent in her body language. She sits up formally, and her dress is carefully pulled over her knees. She is a pretty girl but her posture makes her look insecure, lost in her full skirted red dress which she has carefully tucked around her to make room for my gorgeous cousin, her future sister-in-law. My cousin has grown up in Paterson and is in her last year of high school. She doesn't have a trace of what Puerto Ricans call "la mancha" (literally, the stain: the mark of the new immigrant—something about the*

---

[1] Coffee with milk
[2] Bride or girlfriend

*posture, the voice, or the humble demeanor making it obvious to everyone that that person has just arrived on the mainland; has not yet acquired the polished look of the city dweller). My cousin is wearing a tight red-sequined cocktail dress. Her brown hair has been lightened with peroxide around the bangs, and she is holding a cigarette very expertly between her fingers, bringing it up to her mouth in a sensuous arc of her arm to her as she talks animatedly with my mother, who has come to sit between the two women, both only a few years younger than herself. My mother is somewhere halfway between the poles they represent in our culture.*

It became my father's obsession to get out of the barrio, and thus we were never permitted to form bonds with the place or with the people who lived there. Yet the building was a comfort to my mother, who never got over yearning for *la isla.*[3] She felt surrounded by her language: the walls were thin, and voices speaking and arguing in Spanish could be heard all day. *Salsas* blasted out of radios turned on early in the morning and left on for company. Women seemed to cook rice and beans perpetually—the strong aroma of red kidney beans boiling permeated the hallways.

Though Father preferred that we do our grocery shopping at the supermarket when he came home on weekend leaves, my mother insisted that she could cook only with products whose labels she could read, and so, during the week, I accompanied her and my little brother to *La Bodega*—a hole-in-the-wall grocery store across the street from *El Building.* There we squeezed down three narrow aisles jammed with various products. Goya and Libby's— those were the trademarks trusted by her mamá, and so my mother bought cans of Goya beans, soups and condiments. She bought little cans of Libby's fruit juices for us. And she bought Colgate toothpaste and Palmolive soap. (The final *e* is pronounced in both those products in Spanish, and for many years I believed that they were manufactured on the Island. I remember my surprise at first hearing a commercial on television for the toothpaste in which Colgate rhymed with "ate.")

We would linger at La Bodega, for it was there that Mother breathed best, taking in the familiar aromas of the foods she knew from Mamá's kitchen, and it was also there that she got to speak to the other women of El Building without violating outright Father's dictates against fraternizing with our neighbors.

But he did his best to make our "assimilation" painless. I can still see him carrying a Christmas tree up several flights of stairs to our apartment, leaving a trail of aromatic pine. He carried it formally, as if it were a flag in a parade. We were the only ones in El Building that I knew of who got presents on both Christmas Day and on *Día de Reyes,*[4] the day when the Three Kings brought gifts to Christ and to Hispanic children.

Our greatest luxury in El Building was having our own television set. It must have been a result of Father's guilt feelings over the isolation he had imposed on us, but we were one of the first families in the barrio to have one. My brother quickly became an avid watcher of

[3]The island (usually refers to Puerto Rico)
[4]Kings' day, Epiphany

Captain Kangaroo and Jungle Jim. I loved all the family series, and by the time I started first grade in school, I could have drawn a map of Middle America as exemplified by the lives of characters in "Father Knows Best," "The Donna Reed Show," "Leave It to Beaver," "My Three Sons," and (my favorite) "Bachelor Father," where John Forsythe treated his adopted teenage daughter like a princess because he was rich and had a Chinese houseboy to do everything for him. Compared to our neighbors in El Building, we were rich. My father's Navy check provided us with financial security and a standard of life that the factory workers envied. The only thing his money could not buy us was a place to live away from the barrio—his greatest wish and Mother's greatest fear.

*In the home movie the men are shown next, sitting around a card table set up in one corner of the living room, playing dominoes. The clack of the ivory pieces is a familiar sound. I heard it in many houses on the Island and in many apartments in Paterson. In "Leave It To Beaver," the Cleavers played bridge in every other episode; in my childhood, the men started every social occasion with a hotly debated round of dominoes: the women would sit around and watch, but they never participated in the games.*

*Here and there you can see a small child. Children were always brought to parties and, whenever they got sleepy, put to bed in the host's bedrooms. Babysitting was a concept unrecognized by the Puerto Rican women I knew: a responsible mother did not leave her children with any stranger. And in a culture where children are not considered intrusive, there is no need to leave the children at home. We went where our mother went.*

Of my pre-school years I have only impressions: the sharp bite of the wind in December as we walked with our parents toward the brightly lit stores downtown, how I felt like a stuffed doll in my heavy coat, boots and mittens; how good it was to walk into the five-and-dime and sit at the counter drinking hot chocolate.

On Saturdays our whole family would walk downtown to shop at the big department stores on Broadway. Mother bought all our clothes at Penny's and Sears, and she liked to buy her dresses at the women's specialty shops like Lerner's and Diana's. At some point we would go into Woolworth's and sit at the soda fountain to eat.

We never ran into other Latinos at these stores or eating out, and it became clear to me only years later that the women from El Building shopped mainly at other places—stores owned either by other Puerto Ricans, or by Jewish merchants who had philosophically accepted our presence in the city and decided to make us their good customers, if not neighbors and friends. These establishments were located not downtown, but in the blocks around our street, and they were referred to generically as *La Tienda,*[5] *El Bazar,*[6] *La Bodega, La Botánica.*[7] Everyone knew what was meant. These were the stores where your face did not turn a clerk to stone, where your money was as green as anyone else's.

---

[5]The shop
[6]The bazaar
[7]The herb shop

On New Year's Eve we were dressed up like child models in the Sears catalogue—my brother in a miniature man's suit and bow tie, and I in black patent leather shoes and a frilly dress with several layers of crinolines underneath. My mother wore a bright red dress that night, I remember, and spike heels; her long black hair hung to her waist. Father, who usually wore his Navy uniform during his short visits home, had put on a dark civilian suit for the occasion: we had been invited to his uncle's house for a big celebration. Everyone was excited because my mother's brother, Hernán—a bachelor who could indulge himself in such luxuries—had bought a movie camera which he would be trying out that night.

Even the home movie cannot fill in the sensory details such a gathering left imprinted in a child's brain. The thick sweetness of women's perfume mixing with the ever-present smells of food cooking in the kitchen: meat and plantain *pasteles*,[8] the ubiquitous rice dish made special with pigeon peas—*gandules*—and seasoned with the precious *sofrito*[9] sent up from the island by somebody's mother or smuggled in by a recent traveler. *Sofrito* was one of the items that women hoarded, since it was hardly ever in stock at La Bodega. It was the flavor of Puerto Rico.

The men drank Palo Viejo rum and some of the younger ones got weepy. The first time I saw a grown man cry was at a New Year's Eve party. He had been reminded of his mother by the smells in the kitchen. But what I remember most were the boiled *pasteles*—boiled until the plantain or yucca rectangles stuffed with corned beef or other meats, olives, and many other savory ingredients, all wrapped in banana leaves. Everyone had to fish one out with a fork. There was always a "trick" pastel—one without stuffing—and whoever got that one was the "New Year's Fool."

There was also the music. Long-playing albums were treated like precious china in these homes. Mexican recordings were popular, but the songs that brought tears to my mother's eyes were sung by the melancholic Daniel Santos, whose life as a drug addict was the stuff of legend. Felipe Rodríguez was a particular favorite of couples. He sang about faithless women and brokenhearted men. There is a snatch of a lyric that has stuck in my mind like a needle on a worn groove: "De piedra ha de ser mi cama, de piedra la cabecera . . . la mujer que a mi me quiera . . . he de quererme de veras. Ay, Ay, corazón, ¿por qué no amas . . . ?".[10] I must have heard it a thousand times since the idea of a bed made of stone, and its connection to love, first troubled me with its disturbing images.

The five-minute home movie ends with people dancing in a circle. The creative filmmaker must have asked them to do that so that they could file past him. It is both comical and sad to watch silent dancing. Since there is no justification for the absurd movements that music provides for some of us, people appear frantic, their faces embarrassingly intense. It's as if you were watching sex. Yet for years, I've had dreams in the form of this home movie.

---

[8] Cakes/pies

[9] Puerto Rican spice

[10] Of stone must be my bed, of stone my pillow . . . the woman who loves me . . . should love me truly. Oh, oh, my darling, why don't you love . . . ?

In a recurring scene, familiar faces push themselves forward into my mind's eye, plastering their features into distorted close-ups. And I'm asking them: "Who is she? Who is the woman I don't recognize? Is she an aunt? Somebody's wife? Tell me who she is. Tell me who these people are."

"No, see the beauty mark on her cheek as big as a hill on the lunar landscape of her face—well, that runs in the family. The women on your father's side of the family wrinkle early; it's the price they pay for that fair skin. The young girl with the green stain on her wedding dress is *La Novia*—just up from the island. See, she lowers her eyes as she approaches the camera like she's supposed to. Decent girls never look you directly in the face. *Humilde,* humble, a girl should express humility in all her actions. She will make a good wife for your cousin. He should consider himself lucky to have met her only weeks after she arrived here. If he marries her quickly, she will make him a good Puerto Rican-style wife; but if he waits too long, she will be corrupted by the city, just like your cousin there."

"She means me. I do what I want. This is not some primitive island I live on. Do they expect me to wear a black *mantilla*[12] on my head and go to mass every day? Not me. I'm an American woman and I will do as I please. I can type faster than anyone in my senior class at Central High, and I'm going to be a secretary to a lawyer when I graduate. I can pass for an American girl anywhere—I've tried it—at least for Italian, anyway. I never speak Spanish in public. I hate these parties, but I wanted the dress. I look better than any of these *humildes* here. My life is going to be different. I have an American boyfriend. He is older and has a car. My parents don't know it, but I sneak out of the house late at night sometimes to be with him. If I marry him, even my name will be American. I hate rice and beans. It's what makes these women fat."

"Your *prima*[13] is pregnant by that man she's been sneaking around with. Would I lie to you? I'm your great-uncle's common-law wife—the one he abandoned on the island to marry your cousin's mother. I was not invited to this party, but I came anyway. I came to tell you that story that you've always wanted to hear about your cousin. Remember that comment your mother made to a neighbor that has always haunted you? The only thing you heard was your cousin's name and then you saw your mother pick up your doll from the couch and say: 'It was as big as this doll when they flushed it down the toilet.' This image has bothered you for years, hasn't it? You had nightmares about babies being flushed down the toilet, and you wondered why anyone would do such a horrible thing. You didn't dare ask your mother about it. She would only tell you that you had not heard her right and yell at you for listening to adult conversations. But later, when you were old enough to know about abortions, you suspected. I am here to tell you that you were right. Your cousin was growing an *americanito*[14] in her belly when this movie was made. Soon after she put something long and pointy into her pretty self, thinking maybe she could get rid of the problem before breakfast and still make it to her first class at the high school. Well, *Niña,*[15] her screams

---

[12]Shawl
[13]Female cousin
[14]Young American male
[15]Girl

could be heard downtown. Your aunt, her mamá, who had been a midwife on the Island, managed to pull the little thing out. Yes, they probably flushed it down the toilet, what else could they do with it—give it a Christian burial in a little white casket with blue bows and ribbons? Nobody wanted that baby—least of all the father, a teacher at her school with a house in West Paterson that he was filling with real children, and a wife who was a natural blond.

Girl, the scandal sent your uncle back to the bottle. And guess where your cousin ended up? Irony of ironies. She was sent to a village in Puerto Rico to live with a relative on her mother's side: a place so far away from civilization that you have to ride a mule to reach it. A real change in scenery. She found a man there. Women like that cannot live without male company. But believe me, the men in Puerto Rico know how to put a saddle on a woman like her. *La Gringa,*[16] they call her. ha, ha. ha. *La Gringa* is what she always wanted to be . . . "

The old woman's mouth becomes a cavernous black hole I fall into. And as I fall, I can feel the reverberations of her laughter. I hear the echoes of her last mocking words: ¡*La Gringa, La Gringa!* And the conga line keeps moving silently past me. There is no music in my dream for the dancers.

When Odysseus visits Hades asking to see the spirit of his mother, he makes an offering of sacrificial blood, but since all of the souls crave an audience with the living, he has to listen to many of them before he can ask questions. I, too, have to hear the dead and the forgotten speak in my dream. Those who are still part of my life remain silent, going around and around in their dance. The others keep pressing their faces forward to say things about the past.

My father's uncle is last in line. He is dying of alcoholism, shrunken and shriveled like a monkey, his face is a mass of wrinkles and broken arteries. As he comes closer I realize that in his features I can see my whole family. If you were to stretch that rubbery flesh, you could find my father's face, and deep within *that* face—mine. I don't want to look into those eyes ringed in purple. In a few years he will retreat into silence, and take a long, long time to die. *Move back, Tío,*[17] I tell him. *I don't want to hear what you have to say. Give the dancers room to move, soon it will be midnight. Who is the New Year's Fool this time?*

---

[16]The Anglo woman
[17]Uncle

# Américo Paredes

Américo Paredes was born in Brownsville, Texas in 1915. In 1934, one of his early poems won first place in the Texas state contest sponsored by Trinity College in San Antonio, a prize that possibly led to his later publication of poetry in *La Prensa*. His interest on border folklore led to the 1958 publication of *With His Pistol in His Hand: A Border Ballad and Its Hero*, a book-length study on "The Ballad of Gregorio Cortez" for his dissertation for the

University of Texas at Austin. In 1989 he was awarded the Charles Frankfel Prize by the National Endowment for the Humanities for "outstanding contributions to the public's understanding of the texts, themes and ideas of the humanities." His publications include *George Washington Gómez* and *The Hammon in the Beans*.

# The Hammon and The Beans

Once we lived in one of my grandfather's houses near Fort Jones. It was just a block from the parade grounds, a big frame house painted a dirty yellow. My mother hated it, especially because of the pigeons that cooed all day about the eaves. They had fleas, she said. But it was a quiet neighborhood at least, too far from the center of town for automobiles and too near for musical, night-roaming drunks.

At this time Jonesville-on-the-Grande was not the thriving little city that it is today. We told off our days by the routine on the post. At six sharp the flag was raised on the parade grounds to the cackling of the bugles, and a field piece thundered out a salute. The sound of the shot bounced away through the morning mist until its echoes worked their way into every corner of town. Jonesville-on-the-Grande woke to the cannon's roar, as if to battle, and the day began.

At eight the whistle from the post laundry sent us children off to school. The whole town stopped for lunch with the noon whistle, and after lunch everybody went back to work when the post laundry said that it was one o'clock, except for those who could afford to be old-fashioned and take the siesta. The post was the town's clock, you might have said, or like some insistent elder person who was always there to tell you it was time.

At six the flag came down, and we went to watch through the high wire fence that divided the post from the town. Sometimes we joined in the ceremony, standing at salute until the sound of the cannon made us jump. That must have been when we had just studied about George Washington in school, or recited "The Song of Marion's Men" about Marion the Fox and the British cavalry that chased him up and down the broad Santee. But at other times we stuck out our tongues and jeered at the soldiers. Perhaps the night before we had hung at the edges of a group of old men and listened to tales about Aniceto Pizaña and the "border troubles," as the local paper still called them when it referred to them gingerly in passing.

It was because of the border troubles, ten years or so before, that the soldiers had come back to old Fort Jones. But we did not hate them for that; we admired them even, at least sometimes. But when we were thinking about the border troubles instead of Marion the Fox, we hooted them and the flag they were lowering, which for the moment was theirs alone, just as we would have jeered an opposing ball team, in a friendly sort of way. On these occasions even Chonita would join in the mockery, though she usually ran home at the stroke of six. But whether we taunted or saluted, the distant men in khaki uniforms went about their motions without noticing us at all.

---

Primary works by Américo Paredes: *Between Two Worlds* (Houston: Arte Público Press, 1990); *George Washington Gómez* (Houston: Arte Público Press, 1990); *The Hammon and the Beans* (Houston: Arte Público Press, 1994).

The last word from the post came in the night when a distant bugle blew. At nine it was all right because all the lights were on. But sometimes I heard it at eleven when everything was dark and still, and it made me feel that I was all alone in the world. I would even doubt that I was me, and that put me in such a fright that I felt like yelling out just to make sure I was really there. But next morning the sun shone and life began all over again, with its whistles and cannon shots and bugles blowing. And so we lived, we and the post, side by side with the wire fence in between.

The wandering soldiers whom the bugle called home at night did not wander in our neighborhood, and none of us ever went into Fort Jones. None except Chonita. Every evening when the flag came down she would leave off playing and go down toward what was known as the "lower" gate of the post, the one that opened not on main street but against the poorest part of town. She went into the grounds and to the mess halls and pressed her nose against the screens and watched the soldiers eat. They sat at long tables calling to each other through food-stuffed mouths.

"Hey bud, pass the coffee!"

"Give me the ham!"

"Yeah, give me the beans!"

After the soldiers were through, the cooks came out and scolded Chonita, and then they gave her packages with things to eat.

Chonita's mother did our washing, in gratefulness—as my mother put it—for the use of a vacant lot of my grandfather's which was a couple of blocks down the street. On the lot was an old one-room shack which had been a shed long ago, and this Chonita's father had patched up with flattened-out pieces of tin. He was a laborer. Ever since the end of the border troubles there had been a development boom in the Valley, and Chonita's father was getting his share of the good times. Clearing brush and building irrigation ditches, he sometimes pulled down as much as six dollars a week. He drank a good deal of it up, it was true. But corn was just a few cents a bushel in those days. He was the breadwinner, you might say, while Chonita furnished the luxuries.

Chonita was a poet too. I had just moved into the neighborhood when a boy came up to me and said, "Come on! Let's go hear Chonita make a speech."

She was already on top of the alley fence when we got there, a scrawny little girl of about nine, her bare dirty feet clinging to the fence almost like hands. A dozen other kids were there below her, waiting. Some were boys I knew at school; five or six were her younger brothers and sisters.

"Speech! Speech!" they all cried. "Let Chonita make a speech! Talk in English, Chonita!"

They were grinning and nudging each other except for her brothers and sisters, who looked up at her with proud serious faces. She gazed out beyond us all with a grand, distant air and then she spoke.

"Give me the hammon and the beans!" she yelled. "Give me the hammon and the beans!"

She leaped off the fence and everybody cheered and told her how good it was and how she could talk English better than the teachers at the grammar school.

I thought it was a pretty poor joke. Every evening almost, they would make her get up on the fence and yell, "Give me the hammon and the beans!" And everybody would cheer and make her think she was talking English. As for me, I would wait there until she got it over with so we could play at something else. I wondered how long it would be before they got tired of it all. I never did find out because just about that time I got the chills and fever, and when I got up and around, Chonita wasn't there anymore.

In later years I thought of her a lot, especially during the thirties when I was growing up. Those years would have been just made for her. Many's the time I have seen her in my mind's eye, in the picket lines demanding not bread, not cake, but the hammon and the beans. But it didn't work out that way.

One night Doctor Zapata came into our kitchen through the back door. He set his bag on the table and said to my father, who had opened the door for him, "Well, she is dead."

My father flinched. "What was it?" he asked.

The doctor had gone to the window and he stood with his back to us, looking out toward the lights of Fort Jones. "Pneumonia, flu, malnutrition, worms, the evil eye," he said without turning around. "What the hell difference does it make?"

"I wish I had known how sick she was," my father said in a very mild tone. "Not that it's really my affair, but I wish I had."

The doctor snorted and shook his head.

My mother came in and I asked her who was dead. She told me. It made me feel strange but I did not cry. My mother put her arm around my shoulders. "She is in Heaven now," she said. "She is happy."

I shrugged her arm away and sat down in one of the kitchen chairs.

"They're like animals," the doctor was saying. He turned round suddenly and his eyes glistened in the light. "Do you know what that brute of a father was doing when I left? He was laughing! Drinking and laughing with his friends."

"There's no telling what the poor man feels," my mother said.

My father made a deprecatory gesture. "It wasn't his daughter, anyway."

"No?" the doctor said. He sounded interested.

"This is the woman's second husband," my father explained. "First one died before the girl was born, shot and hanged from a mesquite limb. He was working too close to the tracks the day the Olmito train was derailed."

"You know what?" the doctor said. "In classical times they did things better. Take Troy, for instance. After they stormed the city they grabbed the babies by the heels and dashed them against the wall. That was more humane."

My father smiled. "You sound very radical. You sound just like your relative down there in Morelos."

"No relative of mine," the doctor said. "I'm a conservative, the son of a conservative, and you know that I wouldn't be here except for that little detail."

"Habit," my father said. "Pure habit, pure tradition. You're a radical at heart."

"It depends on how you define radicalism," the doctor answered. "People tend to use words too loosely. A dentist could be called a radical, I suppose. He pulls up things by the roots."

My father chuckled.

"Any bandit in Mexico nowadays can give himself a political label," the doctor went on, "and that makes him respectable. He's a leader of the people."

"Take Villa, now . . . " my father began.

"Villa was a different type of man," the doctor broke in.

"I don't see any difference."

The doctor came over to the table and sat down. "Now look at it this way," he began, his finger in front of my father's face. My father threw back his head and laughed.

"You'd better go to bed and rest," my mother told me. "You're not completely well, you know."

So I went to bed, but I didn't go to sleep, not right away. I lay there for a long time while behind my darkened eyelids Emiliano Zapata's cavalry charged down to the broad Santee, where there were grave men with hoary hairs. I was still awake at eleven when the cold voice of the bugle went gliding in and out of the dark like something that couldn't find its way back to wherever it had been. I thought of Chonita in Heaven, and I saw her in her torn and dirty dress, with a pair of bright wings attached, flying round and round like a butterfly shouting, "Give me the hammon and the beans!"

Then I cried. And whether it was the bugle, or whether it was Chonita or what, to this day I do not know. But cry I did, and I felt much better after that.

# Patricia Preciado Martín

Patricia Preciado Martín is from Arizona. Her books are emblematic of the combination of oral traditions and writing. She writes charming stories that blend songs, letters, and prayers. Her books attest to the delicious mixing of modern sensibility and folk wisdom. She has published extensively with the University of Arizona Press.

## Dichos

Proverbs

It's no fair. My mamá sends me downtown every Saturday on the Old Pueblo bus line to visit my great-grandmother, Mamanina Agrippina. There is no arguing, neither, and that's that, no matter how much I act la chipeleada[1] and pout.

---

Primary works by Patricia Preciado Martín: *Amor Eterno: Eleven Lessons in Love* (Tucson: University of Arizona Press, 2000); *Songs My Mother Sang to Me* (Tucson: University of Arizona Press, 1993); *Days of Plenty, Days of Want* (Tucson: University of Arizona Press, 1999); *El Milagro and Other Stories (Camino del Sol)* (Tucson: University of Arizona Press, 1996).

[1]The spoiled one

All of my friends are off having a good time after chores, going to the early afternoon matinee at the Fox Theater—getting to stand in line and flirt with the boys, getting to see Roy Rogers and Dale Evans or a Zorro movie and the Mickey Mouse cartoon. But not me. Rain or shine, I'm on that bus and don't talk back neither.

No use pleading with my papá. He mostly minds his own business and says that Mamá es la jefita.[2] And he's always busy anyway, a cigarette dangling from his lips, his forehead furrowed in thought, fixing the leak on the roof or the leak under the sink or the leak under the hood of his car or the leak in the garden hose so he can water the street to keep the dust down.

So there it is. And here I am, sitting on my usual seat on the rickety bus, my legs sticking to the torn plastic seats, watching through the dust-streaked cracked windows for anything of interest so I don't die of boredom or have (as Sister Francisca warns me with her warm minty breath) impure thoughts.

And wouldn't you know it—the bus goes clanking down Congress Street just about the time the movie theater opens its doors for the twelve o'clock show. So I feel all worse, seeing my friends, Martita and Concha and Blanca, all dressed up fit to kill and wearing lipstick and face powder and eye shadow behind their mothers' backs. They're chewing gum and pushing and shoving in the line with the eighth-grade boys and acting so great.

I slouch down so they don't see me. It's just my luck, too—that cute guy Chuy Ramírez is there. He sits behind me in math and religion, and sometimes I think he likes me because he asks me to do his homework. But there he is, holding hands on the sly with la María Elena, who thinks she's so big because she has green eyes and wears a training bra. Blanca told me that he buys her a cherry coke and popcorn with real butter before the show. I haven't got a chance.

And me, in all my glory, what a square, with pigtails and saddle shoes and a hand-me-down dress that's a size too big, in the company of every old maid, widow, tía and abuelita from a hundred miles around. They've come to do their shopping at the Grand Central Market on Stone Avenue because Saturday is double-green-stamp day and the day los chinos[3] bring in their fresh vegetables and flowers from their milpas[4] along the river.

The viejitas[5] are dressed almost exactly the same: shapeless dark dresses down to their ankles; black priest shoes; thick cotton stockings; big old-fashioned earrings that make their lobes hang down; a huge gold medal with La Virgen de Guadalupe[6] or El Sagrado Corazón[7]; and all of them carrying enormous black leather purses that are bulging with Lord knows what. They look so ancient and frail that I can't figure out how they carry those heavy bolsas,[8] but they do, and they spring off the bus without missing a step when it comes to a creaking stop in front of the Grand Central Market.

---

[2]Mother is the boss
[3]The Chinese
[4]Cultivated fields
[5]Old ladies
[6]Virgin of Guadalupe
[7]The Sacred Heart
[8]Purses /bags

And me dragging my butt and feeling like a martyr. I have a list and some dollar bills that Mamá gave me crumpled up in my dress pocket. The list is always the same, more or less: a couple cans of Campbell soup of one kind or another (Mamanina told me once that she thought the Campbell Soup Kid looked like El Santo Niño,[9] but she worried that he had las paperas y sarampión);[10] a package of manzanilla[11] tea; fideo;[12] frijoles;[13] arroz;[14] flour; lard; a couple chops of beef or pork; and cilantro, onion, chile, and tomato, unless they're in season in Mamanina's garden, which they usually are.

It's just a few blocks from the Grand Central Market to Barrio El Hoyo where my Mamanina lives. The house my Tatanino built, you couldn't miss it in a thousand years even if you try. For one thing, it's painted bright blue with yellow windowsills crowded with red and pink geraniums blooming in rusty Folgers coffee cans. And another thing, she trims all her front-yard hedges in the shapes of animals: a rooster, a peacock, a burro, a pig, a bull, a turkey, a cat, a dog. Never mind that they're all the same size. She says they remind her of her ranchito[15] in Jalisco, and they're a lot easier to take care of because she doesn't have to feed them or clean up after them.

If that's not enough, she has this big old shrine that my Tatanino made her from river stones before he died. The nicho—well, it looks like a crowded bus stop if you ask me, with all those statues and pictures of every virgin and saint and every Santo Niño of this or that under the sun. Some I'll bet you've never ever heard of like Los Santos Cuates,[16] who if you pray to them, they keep visitors away; or San Expedito, who keeps them from staying too long; or San Lázaro, who will burn your house or car up if you don't keep your manda;[17] or San Antonio, who helps you find things—sometimes even a husband or boyfriend. All the good he has done me.

My Mamanina has the shrine all decorated with plastic ferns and flowers from El Kresge's, and fresh flowers, too, and some from last year's velación[18] that are all dried up; and pretty pebbles and driftwood from the Santa Cruz River; and seashells and starfish that relatives brought her from California; and Christmas bells and balls and tinsel garlands; and a candle that is always burning; and two or three strings of multicolored, blinking Christmas lights that she keeps lit all year round because, she says, "Every day should be like Christmas."

You won't believe it, neither, when I tell you that I'll bet every single flower growing in my Mamanina's garden around that nicho[19] is named after Saint Somebody-or-Other, like the Barritas de San José[20] or San Miguelito or Lirios del Sagrado Corazón[21] or Lágrimas de

---

[9]The Sacred Boy
[10]Mumps and measles
[11]Chamomile
[12]Vermicelli
[13]Beans
[14]Rice
[15]Small ranch
[16]The saintly friends
[17]Promise
[18]Vigil
[19]Niche, recess
[20]San José's little bars
[21]Sacred Heart irises

María[22] or Cornetas del Ángel Gabriel[23] or Rosas guadalupanas[24] or Trompillos del Ángel de la Guardia[25] or Flor de Santa Catarina.[26]

I tell you, I get in a better mood the minute I turn the corner and see that shrine.

She's waiting for me, so brown and small, in the doorway under the porch like she knows the exact time I'm going to arrive. She's wearing this big old apron with gigantic pockets that's made out of old flour sacks—"La Piña"[27] it says today, and on other days it's "La Azteca"[28] or "La Rosa."[29] She's so glad to see me, like always, and she gives me this big old hug and pulls a treat for me, a saladito,[30] out of one of the pockets. Sometimes it's a pan dulce[31] or membrillo[32] or a piece of gum. I never know what's going to come out of those pockets.

I help her put away the groceries in the kitchen. It smells so good because she's always cooking something on her wood-burning stove. I settle into the little chair she keeps for me by the big black stove, and I watch her while she pours flour into a mound in a big clay bowl so she can make tortillas. She adds the baking powder and the salt in the form of a cross, "to bless the bread," she says solemnly. I watch while she rolls the tortillas out perfect and round like a Communion host, and she gives me one right off the comal,[33] all warm and bubbly with melting butter. I am waiting hungrily for the guiso[34] in the simmering pot to be done.

I have to talk to her in Spanish because she never learned any English, only a few words like "enough is too many." Besides, she says, "What for? No one in this old barrio speaks English anyway, and I'm going back to my ranchito in Mexico someday." Sometimes I can't think of a word, or I pronounce something funny or use the wrong verb, and she corrects me but never criticizes.

"Oh, Mamanina," I sigh, "esta tortilla está tan sabrosa."[35]

She smiles. "Cuando hay hambre, no hay mal pan," she says all humble-like. And all the time she's pat-pat-patting and rolling out tortillas, she's keeping her eye on the simmering pot and stirring with a big wooden spoon or adding a pinch of this or that.

I am taking big bites out of the tortilla and gulping it down, and the butter is running down my arm, but she doesn't scold.

"To tell you the truth, Mamanina," I confide in my halting Spanish, "I didn't have a very good week."

"De la olla a la boca a todos se le cae la sopa,"[36] she consoles.

"Sister Francisca, she picks on me. She said I was passing notes and talking in history class, and she scolded me, and I didn't do nothing, I swear. The trouble is, I talked back and

---

[22]Mary's tears
[23]Archangel Gabriel's trumpets
[24]Guadalupe's roses
[25]Guardian angel's spinning tops
[26]Saint Catarina's flower
[27]The Pineapple
[28]The Aztec
[29]The Rose
[30]Name of a candy
[31]Sweet bread
[32]Quince
[33]Grill
[34]Cooked dish
[35]This tortilla is so tasteful.
[36]Everyone is capable of making mistakes.

said, 'It's no fair. I didn't do it,' so I got double time in detention and a note sent home to Mamá and Papá."

"En boca cerrada no entra mosca,"[37] she chides gently.

"It's that María Elena," I say enviously. "She thinks she's so great. She's a teacher's pet, and she shows off and wears a new outfit to school every week."

"No jusgues el hombre por su vestido; Dios hizo el uno, el sastre el otro,"[38] she opines soothingly as she spoons out steaming ladles of the guiso into two clay bowls.

"My friends, they're lucky. They get to go to the movies every week and sometimes to the roller-skating rink."

"Luz de la calle, obscuridad de la casa,"[39] she warns.

"And they never invite me," I whine.

"Al nopal van a ver nomás cuando tiene tunas,"[40] she comforts.

We are sitting at her small kitchen table now under the brown limpid gaze of the apostles at the Last Supper. I am tearing off pieces of tortillas and making little scoops to eat the guiso with. Mamá doesn't let me do that at home; she says it is muy ranchero[41] to sopear.[42]

"Anyway, Mamanina," I announce, to soften my litany of complaints, "next year when I'm in the ninth grade and in high school I'm going to try harder, and it will all be better, you'll see."

"Poco a poco se anda lejos,"[43] she answers encouragingly as she wipes one of my spills on the red-and-white oilcloth with her napkin.

The afternoon wears on. I help with the dishes, the sweeping and the dusting, the changing of the bed, and the washing in that old wringer washer out on the back porch. I hang the clothes out on the clothesline to dry because the day is sunny. Before I know it, it's time for me to hurry so I can catch the last cross-town bus.

I give her a hug as I say goodbye, "Hasta la semana que entra."[44] I run out of the house, slamming the screen door in my haste.

I'm running down the street, and I turn to look back before I turn the corner. I see her with her hand lifted up in a blessing. She's so small, so small, framed in her doorway like one of those faded little old saints in her shrine.

My panza[45] is full of that blessed bread.

The breeze is in my face. I have wings on my feet and angles at my back.

No se puede repicar y en la procesión andar.[46]

---

[37]Silence is golden.

[38]Do not judge a book by it's cover; God created one, and a tailor created the other.

[39]A person who is willing to do things in a public environment that they will not do at home.

[40]People are only interested in you whenever they can get something from you.

[41]Very cowboy

[42]Act of eating with tortillas

[43]You can get far by taking small steps.

[44]See you next week.

[45]Stomach

[46]One cannot complain if one does not want to change.

# Tomás Rivera

Tomás Rivera was born in Crystal City, Texas, in 1935. He graduated from Southwest Texas Junior College and from Southwest Texas State University in 1958, earning an M.Ed. in administration in 1964. In 1969 Rivera received a Ph.D. in Romance languages and literatures from the University of Oklahoma. At the time of his death in 1984, he was chancellor of the University of California at Riverside. Rivera was a poet, novelist, short-story writer, literary critic, college administrator, and educator. His novel *. . . y no se lo tragó la tierra* (1971) tells the story of a young man's coming of age. The character's memories convey the migrant experience in the United States through vignettes and stories. Rivera, in much of his work, showed his belief that memory brings people and the land together in a struggle for selfhood and identity against formidable odds.

## Zoo Island

Jose had just turned fifteen when he woke up one day with a great desire of taking a census count, of making a town and making everybody in it do what he said. All this happened because during the night he had dreamed that it was raining and, since they would not be working in the fields the next day, he dreamed about doing various things. But when he awoke, it hadn't rained at all. Anyway, he still had the desire.

The first thing he did when he got up was to count his family and himself—five. "We're five," he thought. Then he went on to the other family that lived with his, his uncle's—"Five more, and that's ten." Next he counted the people living in the chicken coop across the way. "Manuel and his wife and four more—that's six." And, with the ten he already had—"that's sixteen." Then he took into account the coop where Manuel's uncle lived, where there were three families. The first one, Don Jose's family, had seven, so now there were twenty-three. He was about to count the second family, when they told him to get ready to go to the fields.

It was still dark at five-thirty in the morning, and that day they would have to travel some fifty miles to reach the field overgrown with thistle that they had been working on. And as soon as they finished it, they would have to continue searching for more work. It would be way after dark by the time they got back. In the summertime, they could work up to eight o'clock. Then add an hour on the road back, plus the stop at the little store to buy something to eat . . . "We won't get back to the farm till late," he thought. But now he had something to do during the day while they were pulling up thistle. During the day, he could figure out exactly how many there were on that farm in Iowa.

---

Primary works by Tomás Rivera: *The Complete Works*, ed. Julián Olivares, 2nd ed. (Houston: Arte Público Press, 1995), *. . . y no se lo tragó la tierra/ . . . And the Earth Did Not Devour Him* (Houston: Arte Público Press, 1996).

"Here come those sonsabitches."

"Don't say bad words in front of the kids, Pa. They'll go around saying 'em all the time. That'd really be something, then, wouldn't it?"

"I'll bust them in the mouth if I hear them swearing. But here come those Whities. They don't leave a person in peace, do they? Soon as Sunday comes, and they come riding over to see us, to see how we live. They even stop and try to peek inside our chicken coops. You saw last Sunday how that row of cars passed by here. Them all laughing and laughing, and pointing at us. And you think they care about the dust they raise? Hell no. With their windows closed, why, they go on by just as fine as you please. And here we are, just like a bunch of monkeys in that park in San Antonio—Parkenrich."

"Aw, let 'em be, Pa. They're not doing nothing to us, they're not doing any harm—not even if they was gypsies. Why you get all heated up for?"

"Well, it sets my blood a boiling, that's all. Why don't they mind their own business? I'm going to tell the owner to put a lock on the gate, so when they come they can't drive inside."

"Aw, let it go, it's nothing to make a fuss over."

"It sure is."

\* \* \*

"We're almost to the field. Pa, you think we'll find work after we finish here?"

"Sure, son, there's always a lot of work. They don't take us for a bunch of lazy-bones. You saw how the boss' eyes popped out when I started pulling out all that thistle without any gloves on. Huh, they have to use gloves for everything. So, they're bound to recommend us to the other landowners. You'll see how they'll come and ask us if we want another field to work."

\* \* \*

"The first thing I'll do is jot down the names on a list. Then, I'll use a page for each family, and that way I won't lose anybody. And for each bachelor, too, I'll use a page for each one, yeah. I'll also write down everybody's age. I wonder how many men and women there are on this farm, anyway? We're forty-nine field hands, counting the eight and nine-year-olds. Then, there's a bunch of kids, and then there's the two grandmothers that can't work anymore. The best thing to do is to get Jitter and Hank to help me with the counting. They could go to each coop and get the information, then we could gather up all the numbers. Too, it would be a good idea to put a number on each coop. Then, I could paint the number above each door. We could even pick up the mail from the box and distribute it, and that way the folks could even put the number of their coop on the letters they write. Sure, I bet that would make them feel better. Then we could even put up a sign at the farm gate that'll tell the number of people that live here, but . . . what would we call the farm? It doesn't have a name. I gotta think about that."

It rained the next day, and the following day as well. Therefore, Jose had the time and the opportunity to think over his plan. He made his helpers, Jitter and Hank, stick a pencil behind their ear, strap on a wrist watch—which they acquired easily enough—and shine their shoes. They also spent a half day reviewing the questions they would put to each household head and to each bachelor. The folks became aware of what the youngsters were up to and were soon talking about how they were going to be counted.

"These kids are always coming up with something . . . just ideas that pop into their heads or that they learn in school. Now, what for? What're they going to get out of counting us? Why, it's just a game, plain tomfoolery."

"Don't think that, comadre,[1] no, no. These kids nowadays are on the ball, always inquiring about something or other. And you know, I like what they're doing. I like having my name put on a piece of paper, like they say they're gonna do. Tell me, when's anybody ever asked you your name and how many you got in the family and then write it all down on paper. You better believe it! Let them boys be, let 'em be, leastways while the rain keeps us from working."

"Yeah, but, what's it good for? I mean, how come so many questions? And then there's some things a person just doesn't say."

"Well, if you don't want to, don't tell 'em nothin.' But, look, all they want to know is how many of us there are in this grove. But, too, I think they want to feel like we're a whole lot of people. See here, in that little town where we buy our food there're only eighty-three souls, and you know what? They have a church, a dance hall, a filling station, a grocery store and even a little school. Here, we're more than eighty-three, I'll bet, and we don't have any of that. Why, we only have a water pump and four out-houses, right?"

* * *

"Now, you two are going to gather the names and the information. Ya'll go together so there won't be any problems. After each coop, you'll bring me the information right back. Ya'll jot it down on a sheet of paper and bring it to me, then I'll make a note of it in this notebook I got here. Let's start out with my family. You, Hank, ask me questions and jot down everything. Then you give me what you wrote down so that I can make a note of it. Do ya'll understand what we're going to do? Don't be afraid. Just knock on the door and ask. Don't be afraid."

It took them all afternoon to gather and jot down the details, then they compiled all the figures by the light of an oil lamp. Yes, it turned out that there were more fieldhands on the farm than there were people in the town where they bought their food. Actually, there were eighty-six on the farm, but the boys came up with a figure of eighty-seven because two women were expecting and they counted them for three. They gave the exact number to the rest of the folks, explaining the part about the pregnant women. Everyone was pleased to know that the farm settlement was really a town and bigger than the one where they bought their groceries every Saturday.

The third time the boys went over the figures they realized that they had forgotten to go over to Don Simon's shack. They had simply over looked it because it was on the other side of the grove. When old Don Simon had gotten upset and fought with Stumpy, he asked the owner to take the tractor and drag his coop to the other side of the grove, where no one would bother him. The owner did this right away. There was something in Don Simon's eyes that made people jump. It wasn't just his gaze but also the fact that he hardly ever spoke. So, when he did talk everybody listened up so as not to lose a single word.

It was already late and the boys decided not to go see him until the next day, but the fact of the matter was they were a little afraid just thinking that they would have to go and ask him something. They remembered the to-do in the field when Don Simon got fed up with Stumpy's needling him and chased Stumpy all over the field with his onion knife. Then

---

[1]Godmother (a term used between close female friends)

Stumpy, even though he was much younger, tripped and fell, tangling himself in the tow-sacks. Right then, Don Simon threw himself on Stumpy, slicing at him with his knife. What saved Stumpy were the tow-sacks. Luckily, Stumpy came out of it with only a slight wound in his leg; nonetheless, it did bleed quite a bit. When the owner was told what had happened, he ran Stumpy off. But Don Simon explained that it wasn't much to make a fuss over, so he let Stumpy stay but the owner did move Don Simon's coop to the other side of the grove, just like Don Simon wanted. So, that's why the boys were a little afraid of him. But, like they told themselves, just not riling him, he was good folk. Stumpy had been riling Don Simon for some time about his wife leaving him for somebody else.

> "Excuse us, Don Simon, but we're taking up the farm census, and we'd like to ask you a few questions. You don't have to answer them if you don't want to."
>
> "All right."
>
> "How old are you?"
>
> "Old enough."
>
> "When were you born?"
>
> "When my mother born me."
>
> "Where were you born?"
>
> "In the world."
>
> "Do you have a family?"
>
> "No."
>
> "How come you don't talk much?"
>
> "This is for the census, right?"
>
> "No."
>
> "What for, then? I reckon ya'll think you talk a lot. Well, not only ya'll but all the folks here. What ya'll do most of the time is open your mouth and make noise. Ya'll just like to talk to yourselves, that's all. I do the same, but I do it silently, the rest of you do it out loud."
>
> "Well, Don Simon, I believe that's all. Thanks for your cooperation. You know, we're eighty-eight souls here on this farm. We're plenty, right?"
>
> "Well, you know, I kinda like what ya'll are doing. By counting yourself, you begin everything. That way you know you're not only here but that you're alive. Ya'll know what you oughta call this place?"
>
> "No."
>
> "Zoo Island."

The following Sunday just about all the people on the farm had their picture taken next to the sign the boys had made on Saturday afternoon and which they had put up at the farm gate. It said: **Zoo Island, Pop. 88½.** One of the women had given birth.

And every morning Jose would no sooner get up than he would go see the sign. He was part of that number, he was in Zoo Island, in Iowa, and like Don Simon said, in the world. He didn't know why, but there was a warm feeling that started in his feet and rose through his body until he felt it in his throat and in all his senses. Then this same feeling made him talk, made him open his mouth. At times it even made him shout. The shouting was something the owner never managed to understand. By the time he arrived sleepy-eyed in the morning, the boy would be shouting. Sometimes he thought about asking him why he shouted, but then he'd get busy with other things and forget all about it.

# Nelly Rosario

Nelly Rosario was born in the Dominican Republic and raised in Brooklyn, New York. She received an M.F.A. in fiction from Columbia University. Fab Serignese claims that Rosario in her novel, *Song of the Water Saints* manages to capture the essence of three generations of Dominican women as they engage issues of freedom, sexuality, and rebellion within themselves. Through these observations, Rosario is believed to problematize the mentality of the colonized as she takes readers to the Dominican Republic of the twentieth century and to an urban ghetto in 1990, in this way, Rosario proves that racism remains throughout the years. Another issue that is a constant in her work is black Latinos and the way in which they identify or define themselves. She is currently an adjunct assistant professor at Columbia University and lives in Brooklyn.

3rd person

## On Becoming

A woman born in the Dominican Republic and raised in Brooklyn, New York, is expecting her first child. Having lingered in many communities but remaining firmly rooted in none, having named and renamed herself, she is like a stamped travel trunk. She needs to constantly rub the compass in her belly and look within for her true North. This woman has flat feet. Always a nauseous feeling of vertigo, disoriented on the land where she feels both native and foreign.

Balance is often difficult for this woman, but she keeps traveling. Sometimes she sits in her Brooklyn apartment horrified that she lives in a country where scientists fiddle with genes and black men are still dragged to their deaths. Other times she finds herself exhausted on a plane back from a summer stay in Santo Domingo, glad (and surprised she is glad) to finally see the island of her birth shrink away through the window. Where's home for this woman? She can't completely control the world around her; she herself must become home.

Shift to 1st person

After twenty-seven years it's still hard for me to believe that I am that buoying woman full of new life, flat-footed, wanting the right shoe to keep balance and walk my own path. Who the hell am I, really, I ask all the time, and with more probing, who do I want to ultimately become?

To become anything involves a process of gradual transformation from one state of being to another. Caterpillars become butterflies. Children become adults. I spend most of my life in a state of constant transformation. My views of the world change with the calendar dates. One year I like my wardrobe, the next year I'm disgusted. I'm not satisfied with myself for too long, wanting new beginnings: a new haircut, a change of address, more schooling, increased spir-

Primary work by Nelly Rosario: *Song of the Water Saints* (New York: Pantheon Books, 2002).

itual growth. So I fumble through life in this haze of changes, leaving a trail of discarded husks. Occasionally, in moments of intense reflection (and writing), I go back to one of these husks to sniff it, to see if some of my original essence is still there. I'll try one on for size, maybe take pieces of it to graft onto the newer me. Still, many times I feel outside of myself, as if I live my life in third person, the struggle being to turn the "she" into "I."

This struggle's not a simple matter of replacing pronouns. It's the tough process of breaking through the outer shell and inwardly becoming that "I." The fact that I was born at roughly 23°30' north longitude 30°30' west latitude and was raised at 38° north longitude 97° west latitude easily generates a laundry list of who I'm supposed to be: a "Dominican-York" in spandex, probably raised in Washington Heights, a spitfire Latina torn between "Old World" submission and "New World" rebellion, a Hispanic American sponsored by Budweiser. The list could be longer if I only paid more attention.

But I don't. Ironically, it's in the very country that has generated this list (and fiddled with genes and dragged black men to their deaths) where I feel I have the luxury of becoming "I." These United States, where individualism is Word, has allowed me the privilege of breaking away from that woman who was supposed to live with her parents until marriage (virgin), who was supposed to study at a local college instead of going away, who was supposed to keep her hair long and ultra relaxed.

For a long time I fiercely fought the idea that I'd become American (a term itself so slippery, so transitory, that no geography, no anthropology, no obsessive essay can stuff it into a neat category). Living all my life in a country where anyone with a dose of melanin is considered marginal, I have willingly, if not defiantly, used many other cultural/racial labels for myself outside of the mainstream. I've labeled myself a Dominican woman, an Afro-Dominicana, Latina, Afro-Latina, black woman, Caribbean woman, woman of African descent, woman of the African Diaspora, woman of color.

I used and still use these labels before resorting to "American" or the oh-so-dreaded hyphen, "Dominican-American." My resistance to "American" also has roots in the efforts various ethnic groups historically put into obliterating their own culture, to fit into mainstream (white) United States.

Okay, I've done my share of frantic Dominican flag-waving worthy of a Fifth Avenue parade in mid-August: Goddammit I'm Dominican, baby! I am merengue. I like *plátanos*[1] and fried cheese. My Spanish is song. I like sand between my toes. I love drama. I love parties. Visit my home and I'll offer you a million beverages. I'm sun-drenched and superstitious. I'm obsessive-compulsive. I'm beautiful. I'm hardworking and self-reliant. I'll die without family. I'll die without jokes. I have a martyr complex. I'm political, Raunchy. Resilient. *Dios, patria, libertad!*[2]

Again I've become a list.

Where does Dominican end and "I" begin? Sure, within each culture there are differences. This combination of qualities is not solely Dominican (though some may say

---

[1]Plantains
[2]God, Homeland, Freedom!

label ≠ identity

it's pretty damn close), but I do wonder where stereotypes end and the heterogeneous identity or self begins. Then within each family there are differences. So what is there to be said for national psyche and personal idiosyncrasy? Though I've lived here since I was three months old, I became a naturalized citizen at the age of twenty-two. I was born in 1972 in Santo Domingo, Dominican Republic. I was conceived and raised in Brooklyn, New York.

Papi came to New York in 1962, a year after the end of Rafael Trujillo's thirty-year dictatorship. The opportunity to travel abroad opened up to those beyond the rich, and Papi grabbed it with hopes of improving the economic lot of his parents, his siblings, and himself. Mami arrived five years later, leaving behind a rural upbringing for a shot at better work, and maybe an education. They met each other here, and despite the drudgery of sweatshops and odd jobs, managed to begin a life together.

Twenty-three and pregnant with her first child in a country she was still adjusting to, my mother later went to spend her last months of pregnancy with her mother-in-law in the Dominican Republic. As the last of my organs developed, she sat eating mangoes in the shade of my grandmother's porch, always with too much spit in her mouth. Now in my last weeks of pregnancy and with less spit in my mouth, I wonder how she must have felt away from the chill of New York, knowing that once she had me she would have to return. I've never bothered to ask her who she imagined she would become in the United States, who her children would become. Mami, what went through your mind as you held your three-month-old baby in your lap and the island shrank away through the airplane window?

Soon we were four siblings being raised in a predominantly working-class Latino neighborhood on the Southside of Brooklyn. Like many immigrants and their children, we lived in two worlds. Each of us in the family found individual ways to navigate between the varying degrees of our Dominican and American selves—including my parents. During tax season it's Papi who does the taxes for folks for whom English is still a nightmare. My siblings' music collections include bachata, hip-hop, reggae, merengue, R&B, and salsa. My mother has read Danielle Steel, V.C. Andrews, Jackie Collins, and some American classics—in Spanish. My own eyes cross when I'm looking from both Dominican and American perspectives. The vertigo comes from being simultaneously nearsighted and farsighted, a feeling of seasickness, my compass awry. Even my parents' vision of this land has changed.

My parents' American Dream in the '90s is fresher and more proactive than their dream during the '70s. Making lots of money here and returning to the Dominican Republic to build a house and live happily ever after has been replaced by investing in the well-being of their family here in this country. They've sweat thick drops to channel resources toward their children's education, and service in our Brooklyn community. The United States is their present reality and priority. As naturalized citizens, they're still helping steer the gears of America. They—we—are here to stay.

But where else would I be? I've lived here all my life. I've studied and worked here, and even conceived new life here. I will not cheat myself of an America I'm continuously helping to shape.

My race politics, to many a Dominican stateside and abroad, are amusingly American: African-American, in particular. A quickness to embrace blackness or African heritage is in direct opposition to Dominican pride in hybridity. "We are a mulatto nation," says current president Leonel Fernández with a comfort that comes from not having to prove whiteness or accept blackness. Though the Dominican Republic is a racially heterogeneous nation, its strong African presence can't be simply dismissed with deflated statistics and powerful hair relaxers.

Having been raised in the United States has allowed me the legacy of black consciousness left behind by past generations. Like every other person of color, I grew up colonized: "bad hair" complexes, trying not to smile too widely to keep my nose "in check," taunting my brother with the darker skin. Whiteness and blackness were relative, their meaning changing as I got older. Growing up, we Dominicans were the blacks and Puerto Ricans the whites in a Latino community that replicated the United States' racial polarities. White status came with lighter skin, automatic American citizenship, and English fluency, sometimes at the expense of Spanish.

In the United States "culture" and "race" seem to be Siamese twins. High school peer and intellectual-bully-on-the-down-low Dana Hale forced me to reconfigure what I identified as. Dana herself was a contradiction. She preached blackness à la Malcolm X in green contacts lenses and peroxide hair. I wasn't Dominican, she maintained with authority, I was black—our only difference being that our slave owner spoke different languages. Black not only meant race but also culture (the Siamese twins), whereas for me black referred to race, not necessarily culture. I considered myself Dominican, not black in the sense of African-American. "Latino" and "black" didn't have to be such oxymorons. I refused to accept blackness on African-American terms, as if they had a patent on the concept.

"See, that American imperialistic streak is where they're just like their white counterparts," I'd say to Pan-African friends in college. Dominicans—or more specifically "black folks who speak Spanish"—were an anomaly to many African-Americans. In my dorm room I hung a Dominican flag, as did other children of immigrants, not only to remember but also to educate. I gravitated toward the black diaspora on campus instead of the Latino groups, which were really cliques of Latin American's well-to-dos who wouldn't be bothered with either Chicanos, Nuyoricans, or any other American derivative thereof. I wanted to simultaneously share my urbanness, my blackness, my Latinaness, my Dominicanness, and all the other "nesses" I was still discovering. In addition to a heavy workload freshman year, I further splintered myself as a member of the Black Student Union, the Caribbean Club, the Hispanic Society of Professional Engineers, and any Pan-African group activities. I'm sure this country's fixation on racial/ethnic categories contributes to making many a poor soul suffer from multiple personality disorder.

Returning to my Brooklyn neighborhood after college, I found myself having assimilated very American idiosyncrasies. I didn't feel as "Latina" with a prestigious white college degree under my arm and a very Afrocentric view of the world. At the local bodegas I was sometimes spoken to in English, then met with surprise when I answered in as Dominican a Spanish as I could muster. I was reactive at family gatherings when I heard slurs worthy of David Duke. My words had little credibility. Who gave a damn that I was in defense of our own blackness? Who cared that the black struggle in this country has allowed us fairly comfortable bus rides and somewhat reduced the number of times a cop's club grazes our heads? I was just this Americanized post-college kid with too many black friends and other imported ideas in her kinky head.

Some of the other imported ideas in my kinky head took away a lot of my "femininity." I was literally too headstrong. Love of books and sports and going places and an appetite for learning were not "girlie" enough for most of my extended family. A part of me, though, was very much subservient—the well-behaved. A student who never challenged authority figures. Summer trips to Dominican Republic—where the cultivation of feminity can be almost clownish—has made me most aware of how the United States has shaped my idea of feminity.

My cousins (the "hair and nail cousins" as coined by writer Julia Alvarez) hated the slackness of my jeans or my refusal to wear my hair straight. Well, I hated having to be accompanied by a male relative or acquaintance wherever we went past sundown. I hated having to limit my comments on politics in conversation with men. I hated the incessant "pssssst" coming even from the mouths of ten-year-olds. I hated the rigorous exhibition of our bodies for foreign consumption. I hated claustrophobic discussions with other women about clothing, hair, men, men, and men. I hated the complacent martyrdom of women humiliated by their husbands' infidelities. I hated constant questions about boyfriends and marriage and children. I hated male chest thumping, for everything from driving a car to eating a piece of fruit. I hated to hate.

Being raised here, then, has brought me into conflicts with my parents. Though they raised me to be educated and hence, independent, the result later proved to go against their own traditions. They were uncomfortable with my wanting to study away from home, to travel, to have boyfriends (premarital sex), to move out on my own. Along the way they've eventually supported my decisions, but I was always left with a feeling of guilt, of having betrayed them and broken from tradition. For them, American women aged before their time because they lived wordly lives. "There's a difference between being liberated (*la libertad*) and being a 'libertine' [*el libertinaje*]," my father would say, shaking his index finger at me, the specter of illicit sex always hovering.

Well, with delightfully illicit sex now behind me (and, hopefully, still more ahead of me), I'm entering the realm of motherhood. In a few weeks, I'll bring a new soul to this world. Will I be an

"American" mother or a "Dominican" mother or both? Which elements of each woman will I draw from? Whether or not I choose to be the one to wash dishes and cook and clean is of consequence. The name my partner and I choose for our child is of consequence. It may determine whether this soul will be defined by the double hyphens, Dominican-Puerto Rican-American, or whether American will be a sufficient term to contain her or his rich cultural and racial background. Every action in my life responds to where I have placed myself—including my writing.

The very language of this essay is an eye-cross. Not simply English, but English with American idioms and conventions. My writing has many times been a struggle to find the right word, the right turn of phrase to articulate an idea, emotion, or experience that may have originally occurred to me in Spanish, or emerged out of a very Dominican place in me.

I shuttle the world in my head from Spanish to English and vice versa. Spanish to English has helped me find more interesting phrasing for my work, consequently filling my writing with enough hiccups to keep an editor's knuckles cracking. English to Spanish has helped me fill in the parts of my Spanish that haven't matured beyond high school composition. Consequently my Spanish, however fluent, is littered with Anglicisms.

I can't say I'm fully comfortable in either language. When speaking to native Spanish speakers, I hold my breath after blurting out a word fashioned out of English when its Spanish equivalent fails me. I don't feel my Spanish is "educated" enough. My relationship to the language is not academic as it is social and religious, and very much a part of my childhood. I've been told that in Spanish my voice takes on a softer, pleasant, sometimes subservient timbre. The language does represent for me love and constraint, passion, warmth, and at times self-oppression. Self-oppression from obligatory Sunday mass, from parents with many rules for children growing up in New York, from a country where children and women are told too often to shut up.

English, on the other hand, feels so much more liberating, cruder. I curse more, demand more, invent more. Though the language to me is colder, not always as colorful, it's more elastic. Black English, in particular, allows for more movement and expression. Yet around those who chew English like gum, I still find myself faltering. There are so many words in my vocabulary with which I am intimate as a reader but not as a speaker. I understand the meaning of "episiotomy," yet my pronunciation of it is phonetic, and the discreet listener will repeat the word properly for me before taking another sip of calcium-rich juice at the birthing center.

With my siblings I speak English. Spanish used to be a way of tattletaling. "Alex, *no digas malas palabras.*"[3] With our friends, too, English is the language of choice. Spanish used to be for us too right-off-the-boat, not hip enough. Spanish meant trousers and pointy shoes instead of Lees and fat-laced Pumas.

Lees and fat-laced Pumas were the cornerstones of hip culture for us. As we get older, the meaning of culture and what we choose as our culture becomes more complicated than clothing and music. We are all in transition, becoming something else, giving birth to new

---

[3]Don't say bad words

selves. Now is a time to nurse new life. It's a time for me to soak my feet and calibrate my compass. I'm still at 38° north longitude 97° west latitude.

The real question for me isn't "Have I become American?" but "Is this discussion already passé?"

*[handwritten: no longer cool?]*

# Rosaura Sánchez

*[handwritten: born in America / Spanish speaker]*

Rosaura Sánchez was born in San Angelo, Texas. She was raised in a working-class environment in which she grew up speaking Spanish and where racism was present. She moved to California to attend the university. She states that she writes in Spanish because it is her native tongue and because "I believe that politically, it is important to write in Spanish." Her stories are a legacy for future generations. She is a professor in the Department of Literature at the University of California in San Diego.

## Dallas

*[handwritten: Who's 'em?]*

*[handwritten: POV: Car = symbol for U.S.]*

I got picked to take them to the Guerreros' house. When we got there they left me there next to the curb, so from where I was I could barely hear what was going on over near the front door. What I do know is that they were arguing with the old man who opened the door and that afterwards two kids—eleven or twelve years old or so—showed up behind him. Then they had the kids pile in and we then headed down the road toward the station—except that they changed their mind about it and we headed back, stopping at the Seven-Eleven. That's where they made me stop. There were two riding in the front and another two in back. One of the policemen was driving and the other one was sitting in back with one of the two kids. That's where they started getting into it—about whether the boys had stolen the watches, or whether they hadn't, about where they had hidden them—the standard stuff. I mean, I was already pretty used to these scenes, pretty tired of the whole thing of riding out from one side of town to another picking up drunks, potheads, all sorts of perps from armed robbers to murderers, and once in a while some dumb jerk who was in the wrong place at the wrong time. Like I said, I was pretty used to transporting all types, but this was the first time that they'd brought two kids on board. But I better slow down and tell this right so that you'll have a better idea of what went down. *[handwritten: you're right]*

What I did manage to hear from the curb where the cops left me before going up to the Guerreros' house was that there'd been a robbery at the Seven-Eleven on Houston Street and

Primary works by Rosaura Sánchez: *He Walked In and Sat Down and Other Stories* (Albuquerque: University of New Mexico Press, 2000); ed., *Who Would Have Thought It?* (Houston: Arte Público Press, 1995); ed. *The Squatter and the Don* (Houston: Arte Público Press, 1992); *Conflicts of Interest: The Letters of María Amparo Ruiz de Burton* (Houston: Arte Público Press, 2001).

*[handwritten: driver of police vans?]*

that some watches that were in a glass case on the counter had been stolen. According to the manager at the Seven-Eleven, when he came back to the counter from the storeroom, he'd seen the backs of two Mexican boys running from the store. That's when he realized that the watches were missing from the case. He figured that the boys must have come in while he was in the back of the store putting up a shipment he'd just gotten in. That's more or less what I understood had taken place, although I missed bits and pieces of the conversation when the traffic noise got real loud. Anyway, the police were there arguing with old man Guerrero, who apparently was the kids' grandfather, and they then carted the two boys off. Like I said, the guy at the store couldn't ID them—but because the boys lived right near the store, he suspected them right away. Of course, it could have been anybody. Anyway, like I was saying, they brought them out of the house and hauled them in. Man, sometimes I really hate this job; but I'm stuck with it, having to cart around all these suspects, drunks, delinquents and whores. Sometimes I'd get to thinking about it and I'd try to convince myself that suffering at least I was in direct contact with the nitty-gritty side of life, the way things really are— the belly of the beast. Still, sometimes—when they have me hauling ass from one place to the other or taking a turn faster than I should—I have to sort of put myself on automatic overdrive and try to take my mind off it all. I'll start thinking and dreaming to get away from all the disgusting shit that's going on around me, because, let me tell you, sometimes it gets really bad. Man, the stories I could tell you about the stuff that goes down, including all the shit police you find out about the cops themselves—anyway, it's better that you don't get me started on brutality that. Stuff like you wouldn't believe! So, like I said, lots of times I needed to dream or something to get away from it all and I'd keep telling myself that maybe someday something good would come out from all the shit I saw around me, you know, maybe like some enormous cancer or something would start eating away at all the rottenness and get rid of it once and for all. wrong That night though, I was more freaked than usual, considering the two kids in the back and to have all. I'd never had two kids on board like that. But like I was saying, the cops started to question boys the boys as soon as we started down the road, but the kids just kept on saying that they didn't have anything to do with it. To tell you the truth, I thought we'd be taking them back home any minute. Besides, I kept on thinking about how worried the grandpa must be by now. But the cops just kept at it, going on and on about how the kids had done it and about how they'd better 'fess up to it. Finally, one of the cops, a real S.O.B., pulled out his revolver. This was right there in front of the Seven-Eleven store. This guy was a real bastard and I'd seen him act off the dick wall before, but never like that night. Right then and there he whipped out his gun and started playing with it, threatening to shoot the older kid unless they both confessed to the robbery. As he pulled back on the trigger the cylinder started to spin and I felt this shiver go right though me, right down to my pistons. When I heard the hammer come down, all I could think of was getting away from there, of being somewhere—anywhere—else, where I wouldn't have to hear, or feel or be there to see what was going down. But there wasn't anything I could do. The shot rang out and right afterwards I heard the cries of his little brother. By the time I got to the emergency room, the kid was dead.

Riding back to the station with the two policemen, I thought of flipping over and I even tried to drive off a cliff to do away with these two criminals, but I couldn't manage it. The

lots of assumptions going on.

damn driver had me too much under his control. Yeah, I know that nothing much would change if somebody was to put a bomb under the hood to blow away these vermin. And I know that there are hundreds like these two out there in patrol cars in cities all over the world. Still. . . sometimes I have this dream about how someday people will do something about it. That's at least what keeps me going.

*(Translated by Beatrice Pita)*

# Michele Serros

Michele Serros published her first book of poetry and short stories, *Chicana Falsa and Other Stories of Death, Identity and Oxnard,* while she was still a student at Santa Monica City College. She is an award-winning poet and commentator for National Public Radio (*Morning Edition, Weekend All Things Considered*). She released a spoken-word CD with Mercury Records. This CD allowed her to tour nationally with Lollapalooza as a Road Poet and The Getty Research Institute selected her and the Poetry Society of America to have her poetry placed on MTA buses throughout Los Angeles County. She has been a featured contributor for the *Los Angeles Time's* children's fiction section. *How to Be a Chicana Role Model,* Serros's new collection of fiction (Riverhead Books, 2000), instantly reached the *Los Angeles Times* bestseller list. In 2002, Serros lived in Los Angeles, where she wrote for the ABC sitcom *The George Lopez Show.* "An opportunity," she says, "that hopefully, with my contribution, opens the door for a wider representation of Latinos in the mass media."

## Senior Picture Day

Sometimes I put two different earrings in the same ear. And that's on a day I'm feeling preppy, not really new wave or anything. One time, during a track meet over at Camarillo High, I discovered way too late that I'd forgot to put on deodorant and that was the worst 'cause everyone knows how snooty those girls at Camarillo can be. Hmmm. Actually the worst thing I've ever forgotten to do was take my pill. That happened three mornings in a row and you can bet I was praying for weeks after that.

So many things to remember when you're seventeen years old and your days start at six A.M. and sometimes don't end until five in the afternoon. But today of all days there's one thing I have to remember to do and that's to squeeze my nose. I've been doing it since the seventh grade. Every morning with my thumb and forefinger I squeeze the sides of it, firmly pressing my nostrils as close as they possibly can get near the base. Sometimes while I'm waiting for the tortilla to heat up, or just when I'm brushing my teeth, I squeeze. Nobody ever notices. Nobody ever asks. With all the other shit seniors in high school go through,

Primary works by Michele Serros: *Chicana Falsa and Other Stories of Death, Identity, and Oxnard* (New York: Riverhead Books, 1998); *How to Be a Chicana Role Model* (New York: Riverhead Books, 2000).

squeezing my nose is nothing. It's just like some regular early-morning routine, like yawning or wiping the egg from my eyes. Okay, so you might think it's just a total waste of time, but to tell you the truth, I do see the difference. Just last week I lined up all my class pictures and could definitely see the progress. My nose has actually become smaller, narrower. It looks less Indian. *I* look less Indian and you can bet that's the main goal here. Today, when I take my graduation pictures, my nose will look just like Terri's and then I'll have the best picture in the yearbook. I think about this as Mrs. Milne's Duster comes honking in the driveway to take me to school.

Terri was my best friend in seventh grade. She came from Washington to Rio Del Valle Junior high halfway through October. She was the first girl I knew who had contact lenses and *four* pairs of Chemin de Fers. Can you believe that? She told everyone that her daddy was gonna build 'em a swimming pool for the summer. She told me that I could go over to swim anytime I wanted. But until then, she told me, I could go over and we could play on her dad's CB.

"Your dad's really got a CB?" I asked her.

"Oh, yeah," she answered, jiggling her locker door. "You can come over and we can make up handles for ourselves and meet lots of guys. Cute ones."

"Whaddaya mean, handles?" I asked.

"Like names, little nicknames. I never use my real name. I'm 'G.G.' when I get on. That stands for Golden Girl. Oh, and you gotta make sure you end every sentence with 'over.' You're like a total nerd if you don't finish with 'over.' I never talk to anyone who doesn't say 'over.' They're the worst."

Nobody's really into citizen band radios anymore. I now see 'em all lined up in pawnshops over on Oxnard Boulevard. But back in the seventh grade, everyone was getting them. They were way better than using a phone 'cause, first of all, there was no phone bill to bust you for talking to boys who lived past The Grade and second, you didn't have your stupid sister yelling at you for tying up the phone line. Most people had CBs in their cars, but Terri's dad had his in the den.

When I showed up at Terri's to check out the CB, her mama was in the front yard planting some purple flowers.

"Go on in already." She waved me in. "She's in her father's den."

I found Terri just like her mama said. She was already on the CB, looking flustered and sorta excited.

"Hey," I called out to her, and plopped my tote bag on her dad's desk.

She didn't answer but rather motioned to me with her hands to hurry up. Her mouth formed an exaggerated, "Oh, *my* God!" She held out a glass bowl of Pringles and pointed to a glass of Dr Pepper on the desk.

It turned out Terri had found a boy on the CB. An older *interested* one. He was fifteen, a skateboarder, and his handle was Lightning Bolt.

"Lightning Bolt," he bragged to Terri. "Like, you know, powerful and fast. That's the way I skate. So," he continued, "where do you guys live? Over."

"We live near Malibu." Terri answered. "Between Malibu and Santa Barbara. Over."

"Oh, excuse me, fan-ceee. Over."

"That's right." Terri giggled. "Over."

We actually lived in Oxnard. Really, in El Rio, a flat patch of houses, churches, and schools surrounded by lots of strawberry fields and some new snooty stucco homes surrounded by chain-link. But man, did Terri have this way of making things sound better. I mean, it *was* the truth, geographically, and besides it sounded way more glamorous.

I took some Pringles from the bowl and thought we were gonna have this wonderful afternoon of talking and flirting with Lightning Bolt until Terri's dad happened to come home early and found us gabbing in his den.

"What the . . . !" he yelled as soon as he walked in and saw us hunched over his CB. "What do you think this is? Party Central? Get off that thing!" He grabbed the receiver from Terri's hand. "This isn't a toy! It's a tool. A tool for communication, you don't use it just to meet boys!"

"Damn, Dad," Terri complained as she slid off her father's desk. "Don't have a cow." She took my hand and led me to her room. "Come on, let's pick you out a handle."

When we were in her room, I told her I had decided on Cali Girl as my handle.

"You mean, like California?" she asked.

"Yeah, sorta."

"But you're Mexican."

"So?"

"So, you look like you're more from Mexico than California."

"What do you mean?"

"I mean, California is like, blond girls, you know."

"Yeah, but I *am* Californian. I mean, real Californian. Even my great-grandma was born here."

"It's just that you don't look like you're from California."

"And you're not exactly golden," I snapped.


We decided to talk to Lightning Bolt the next day, Friday, right after school. Terri's dad always came home real late on Fridays, sometimes even early the next Saturday morning. It would be perfect. When I got to her house the garage door was wide open and I went in through its side door. I almost bumped into Terri's mama. She was spraying the house with Pine Scent and offered me some Hi-C.

"Help yourself to a Pudding Pop, too," she said before heading into the living room through a mist of aerosol. "They're in the freezer."

Man, Terri's mama made their whole life like an afternoon commercial. Hi-C, Pringles in a bowl, the whole house smelling like a pine forest. Was Terri lucky or what? I grabbed a Pudding Pop out of the freezer and was about to join her when I picked up on her laugh. She was already talking to Lightning Bolt. Dang, she didn't waste time!

"Well, maybe we don't ever want to meet you," I heard Terri flirt with Lightning Bolt. "How do you know we don't already have boyfriends? Over."

"Well, you both sound like foxes. So, uh, what *do* you look like? Over."

"I'm about five-four and have green eyes and ginger-colored hair. Over."

Green? Ginger? I always took Terri for having brown eyes and brown hair.

"What about your friend? Over."

"What about her? Over."

Oh, this was about me! I *had* to hear this. Terri knew how to pump up things good.

"I mean, what does she look like?" Lightning Bolt asked. "She sounds cute. Over."

"Well . . . " I overheard Terri hesitate. "Well, she's real skinny and, uh . . . "

"I like skinny girls!"

"You didn't let me finish!" Terri interrupted. "And you didn't say 'over.' Over."

"Sorry," Lightning Bolt said. "Go ahead and finish. Over."

I tore the wrapper off the Pudding Pop and continued to listen.

"Well," Terri continued. "She's also sorta flat-chested, I guess. Over."

*What?* How could Terri say that?

"Flat-chested? Oh yeah? Over." Lightning Bolt answered.

"Yeah. Over."

Terri paused uncomfortably. It was as if she knew what she was saying was wrong and bad and she should've stopped but couldn't. She was saying things about a friend, things a real friend shouldn't be saying about another friend, but now there was a boy involved and he was interested in that other friend, in me, and her side was losing momentum. She would have to continue to stay ahead.

"Yeah, and she also has this, this nose, a nose like . . . like an *Indian*. Over."

"An Indian?" Lightning Bolt asked. "What do ya mean an Indian? Over."

"You know, *Indian*. Like powwow Indian."

"Really?" Lightning Bolt laughed on the other end. "Like Woo-Woo-Woo Indian?" He clapped his palm over his mouth and wailed. A sound I knew all too well.

"Yeah, just like that!" Terri laughed. "In fact, I think she's gonna pick 'Li'l Squaw' as her handle!"

I shut the refrigerator door quietly. I touched the ridge of my nose. I felt the bump my mother had promised me would be less noticeable once my face "filled out." The base of my nose was far from feminine and was broad like, well, like Uncle Rudy's nose, Grandpa Rudy's nose, and yeah, a little bit of Uncle Vincente's nose, too. Men in my family who looked like Indians and here their Indian noses were lumped together on me, on my face. My nose made me look like I didn't belong, made me look less Californian than my blond counterparts. After hearing Terri and Lightning Bolt laugh, more than anything I hated the men in my family who had given me such a hideous nose.

I grabbed my tote bag and started to leave out through the garage door when Terri's mama called out from the living room. "You're leaving already?" she asked. "I know Terri would love to have you for dinner. Her daddy's working late again."

I didn't answer and I didn't turn around. I just walked out and went home.

And so that's how the squeezing began. I eventually stopped hanging out with Terri and never got a chance to use my handle on her dad's CB. I know it's been almost four years since she said all that stuff about me, about my nose, but man, it still stings.

During freshman year I heard that Terri's dad met some lady on the CB and left her mama for this other woman. Can you believe that? Who'd wanna leave a house that smelled like a pine forest and always had Pudding Pops in the freezer?

As Mrs. Milne honks from the driveway impatiently, I grab my books and run down the driveway, squeezing my nose just a little bit more. I do it because today is Senior Picture Day and because I do notice the difference. I might be too skinny. My chest might be too flat. But God forbid I look too Indian.

# Piri Thomas

Piri Thomas was the first mainland-born Puerto Rican writer to achieve national, mainstream recognition in the United States. His autobiographical work, *Down These Mean Streets* (1967), chronicles Thomas's difficult life in the streets of Spanish Harlem from the Depression era to the early 1960s. Thomas was born in New York City in 1928 to a light-skinned Puerto Rican mother and a dark-skinned Cuban father. His experiences as a child in the barrio and as a teenager in an Italian section of East Harlem and later in Babylon, Long Island, forced him to confront issues of racial and ethnic identity. Thomas had to decide whether to consider himself a Puerto Rican based on language and family origin or to accept society's label of African American based on skin color. The autobiography traces his early initiation into gangs, violence, drugs, and sex, as well as time spent in a maximum-security prison after his conviction for armed robbery. It ends with his reintegration into the community and ultimate personal redemption after his parole at the age of twenty-eight. The novel is continued in the sequels *Savior, Savior Hold My Hand* (1972) and *Seven Long Times* from which we include the Prologue (1975).

## Prologue to *Seven Long Times*

Like I'm standing here and nuttin's happening. Diggit, man, what's in this here world for me? Except I gotta give, give, give. I'm tired of being a half-past nuttin'. I've come into this stone world of streets with all its living, laughing, crying, and dying. A world full of backyards, rooftops, and street sets, all kinds of people and acts, of hustles, rackets, and eye-dropper drugs. A world of those who is and those who ain't. A world of name-calling, like "nigger sticks" and "*mucho* spics."

I'm looking at me and no matter how I set my face, rock-hard or sullen-soft, I still feel the me inside rumbling low and crazy-like, like I'm mad at something and don't know what it is. Damn it, it's the craps of living every day afraid and not diggin' what's in tomorrow. What's the good of living in a present that's got no future, no nuttin', unless I make some-

Primary works by Piri Thomas: *Down These Mean Streets* (New York: Knopf, 1967); *Stories from El Barrio* (New York: Knopf, 1992); *Seven Long Times* (Houston: Arte Público Press, 1995).

thing. I fell into this life without no say and I'll be a mother-jumper if I live it without having nuttin' to say.

I know this world is on a hustle stick and everybody's out to make a buck. This I can dig, 'cause it's the same here on the street. I gotta hustle, too, and the only way to make it is on a hard kick. I dig that—copping is the main bit and having is the main rep. You see, I'm really trying to understand and see where you're at.

How many times have I stood on my street corner, looking out at your blippy world full of pros? At all you people who made it and got to be great, a real bunch of killer-dillers. I know about you. I've gone to the big school, too. I've dug how to live, too.

Are you willing to learn about me and what makes me click? Well, let me run it to you nice and easy.

Have you ever sensed the coming danger as on a bop you go? A rumbling of bravery, of *puro corazón,* [1] and gusto to the *n*th degree? Have you ever punched a guy in the mouth with a ripped-off garbage can handle, or spit blood from jammed-up lips? Have you ever felt the pain from a kick in the balls? Have you ever chased in victory in a gang fight supreme or run in tasteless defeat with all the heart you can muster? Have you felt the bond of belonging when with your boys you went down?

Tell me, did you ever make out in dark hallways with wet kisses and fumbling hands? Did you ever smother a frightened girl's rejections and force a love from her? Did you fill your dreams with the magic of what you wanted to be only to curse the bitchin' mornings for dragging you back on the scene? Did you ever smoke the blast of reefers and lose your freakin' mind? Did you ever worry about anything at all—like a feeling of not belonging? Did you ever lover-dubber past this way?

Did you ever stand on street corners and look the other way from the world of *muchos ricos* [2] and think, *I ain't got a damn*?

Did you ever count the pieces of garbage that flowed down dirty gutters, or dig the backyards that in their glory were a garbage dump's dream? Did you ever stand on rooftops and watch nighttime cover the bad below? Did you ever put your hand round your throat and feel your pulse beat say, *I do belong and there's not gonna be nobody can tell me I'm wrong*?

Say, did you ever mess with the hard stuff—that cocaine, heroin? Have you ever filled your nose with the wild kick coke brought or pushed a needle full of the other poison and felt the sharp-dull burning as it ate away your brain? Did you ever feel the down-gone-high as the drug took effect? And feel all your yearnings become sleepy memories and reality become illusion—and you are what you wanted to be?

Did you ever stand, small and a little quiet-like, and dig your mom's and pop's fight for lack of money to push off the abundance of wants? Did you ever stand with outstretched hands and cop a plea from life and watch your mom's pride on bended knees ask a welfare investigator for the needed welfare check while you stood there getting from nothing and

---

[1] True heart
[2] Many wealthy

resenting it just the same? Did you ever feel the thunder of being thrown out for lack of money to pay the rent, or walk in scared darkness—the light bill unpaid—or cook on canned heat for a bunch of hungry kids—no gas—unpaid?

Did you ever sneak into the movies and dig a crazy set where everybody's made it on that wide wild screen? They ride in long, down shorts, like T-Birds, Continentals, Caddies. Such *viva*[3] smoothies, with the vines—the clothes—like you never ever saw. And, oh, man, did you ever then go out of that world to sit on hard stoops and feel such cool hate and ask yourself, "Why, man? Why does this gotta be for me?"

Have you ever known the coldness of getting busted . . . the scared, hollow feeling of loneliness as you're flung into a prison cell?

Have you ever heard voices inside you screaming, *Don't bitch about being busted, turkey—you done broke the law and that's wrong,* and had that truth eased off by another voice saying, *Don't fret, little brother. How could you ever have done it right when everything out there in them streets was so goddamn wrong?*

So carry the burden with *mucho corazón* and try like hell to make the shadows of the prison bars go away by closing your eyes to the weight of time.

Hard days, long nights. Without a name, a number instead. Your love of color blighted by a sea of monotonous blues and grays. Warmth replaced by cold steel bars. Tiny, bleak cells surrounded by chilly, concrete, mountain-high prison walls. Within is lost the innocence of a smile. . . . The tears that flow are unsalted and the laughter is unreal. The days that eventually turn into long years are each terrible in themselves;

*You don't want to hear me. I'll make you hear me.*
*You don't want to see me. I'll make you see me.*

---

[3]Alive

---

# Helena María Viramontes

Helena María Viramontes was born in East Los Angeles in 1954 to a family of nine children. She earned a B.A. in English literature from Immaculate Heart College in 1975. She published her first collection of fiction, *The Moths and Other Stories*, in 1985, and in 1995 she published her first novel, *Under the Feet of Jesus*. In many works of Chicana narrative the voices are those of young girls; *The Moths* contains powerful stories that focus on girls and women and attack the patriarchal values that pervade Latino culture.

## Birthday

(At the moment, there are only two things I am sure of: my name is Alice and all I want to do is sleep. I want to sleep so badly that I am angry at their conspiracy to keep me awake.

Primary works by Helena María Viramontes: *The Moths and Other Stories* (Houston: Arte Público Press, 1985); *Under the Feet of Jesus* (New York: E. P. Dutton Press, 1996); *Their Dogs Came with Them* (New York: E. P. Dutton Press, 2000).

Why so early? I want to knot myself into a little ball and sleep. I will knot myself into a little ball and sleep. I will. I will become you, knotted stomach.)

*finally bonded drifting afloat i become, and how much i love it. craft cradles me drifting far. far away. the waves rock me into an anxious sleepless sleep, and i love it—God, how much i love it. brimming baptism roll. swell. thunder. reaching up to vastness. calm. i relax beneath the fluids that thicken like jelly. Thickening. i am transparent and light, ounceless. spinning with each breath you exhale. i move closer and closer to the shore and i love it.*

I rub my stomach because it aches. (Would I like to stay Alice, or become a mama?) I rub my stomach again as I sit on the couch (perhaps unconsciously hoping the rubbing will unknot my . . . my baby? No, doesn't sound right. Baby-to-be? Isn't the same. Isn't.) I sit, my arms folded, on a vinyl plastic couch which squeaks every time I cross or recross my legs. One of my legs swings back and forth. My breath is misty and I exhale hard to watch it form into smoke. Unfolding my arms, I lift my hands to my face and my fingers massage my eyelids. Blurred. Slowly focusing the room. A living room converted into a waiting room. Across from me a small fireplace. An off-white wall supports a single picture of snow and church. Dusty. Everything is dusty. In an isolated corner, a wire chair stands. Big room; practically empty. One dirty window pasted with announcements.

"I don't know *why,* that's all." And that was all it had come to. "Now will you please stop bugging me?" Her voice became thorny with these last words, and she was now more annoyed than hurt. How many times had she asked herself that same question which became implanted in her mind and soon germinated into a monstrous sponge, leaving no room for an answer?

He finally lifted his eyes off the lawn and shifted his glance to her face. Slowly, he continued, "It's the twentieth century . . . " Again he shook his head in disbelief and his eyes glanced over her shoulder and into nothing. "Why weren't you taking anything? You know better . . . " He paused, wet his lips and sighed. "You're a girl. You're supposed to know those things."

"Don't. Don't. I don't know why." She felt sorry for him and her voice became increasingly soft. "What do you think we ought to do?" He looked down at the blotches of dirt and grass, staring hard, as if the answer laid beneath.

"You'll have to get an abort . . . "

"Wait." She couldn't breathe and she held her hand to his lips so that the word would not be mentioned out loud and therefore made a real possibility. "Let's . . . we gotta think this over." There was a long pause between them. The wind blew weak leaves off the tree they sat under, and, she thought, weak leaves enjoy the moment of freedom faster, but they die sooner. She realized now, suffering from this heaviness on her heart, that the decision was ultimately hers and hers alone. Her eyes, that had first pleaded desperately under the tree, now looked upon him as a frightened child.

"Alice." She turned to him and a reassuring smile appeared on her face. She hugged him tenderly and whispered, "You're just making it worse for both of us." Hers. The wind blew a colder breeze and they comforted themselves with an embrace.

A girl with long stringy hair enters the room followed by a chilly draft that slaps me on the back (I hope I don't look *that* bad). She sits on the lonely wire chair. I smile at her with lazy lips, but the encouraging gesture is not returned. (Oily hair. Looks like she used mayonnaise for shampoo.) I belch out a giggle. (Alice—now's not the time to joke.) I keep swinging my legs until my heart swells and I choke—Oh my God . . .

My God, what am I doing here? Alone and cold. And afraid. Damn, dammit. I should have stayed a virgin. STUPID, stupid! Virgins have babies, too. Enough Alice. Keep warm, Alice. No sex, Alice. Punishing me. For loving, God? Fucking, Alice. Fucking Alice. Stop it, Alice. Grow up, not out.

Alice.

God isn't pregnant.

Alice.

"Alice. Alice Johnson."

"Me." I nod my head and smile. I think I'm going to win.

"Then *you* must be Cynthia Simmons." The girl with the mayonnaise hair barely nods her head. "It sure is cold in here . . . " I smile in agreement. I don't feel like small talk. "My name is Kathy." She resembles a small elf. A petite and skinny girl wearing an orange dress and white tights that gather at her bony knees. " . . . Follow me, please . . . " We follow her like zombies into another larger room. On one side, test tubes, desk lights, bottles; on the other, desks and telephones. The room was probably a kitchen before. Cabinets, like Terry's kitchen.

"How do I realize these things? Y'know the feeling. I was a whole invisible. I felt so light, I automatically took everything lightly. The responsibility of having a child didn't fit into my scheme of loving. To me, to me, Terry . . . " She paused to take another sip of jasmine tea. The light of the kitchen made a round, bright ring on the table where Alice put her cup down. " . . . love was satisfaction, happiness, and all that other bullshit, not babies." Terry gestured mocking amazement with a dull smirk which impelled Alice to defend herself. "Babies, yea, sure, but not in the real sense. Not me."

Terry sat across from her and munched on graham crackers throughout the evening. Alice searched for some evidence of sympathetic understanding from her, but all Terry seemed to do was munch slowly on a cracker, once in a while dipping it into her tea.

"Relax, Alice. My God, you would think it was the end of the world." She said it with such an air of nonchalance that Alice became angry, and yet comforted by her words. (Tell me what to do.) "How does Mike feel about it?"

"I haven't really told him . . . I mean, nothing definite. This is all so unreal." She tried to hide the tears from Terry. A moment later Terry stood up from the table. Alice's eyes followed her to the living room. She picked up her phone book and, with the slowness of thick molasses, returned to her chair. She opened the book. "Here, take this number down . . ."

"What's this? Dial-A-Prayer?" Neither of them laughed. Alice copied the number down, hesitating to ask her what place it belonged to, but nonetheless trusting Terry's experience and age. She thought of Terry as an experienced woman at twenty-one. She was a big-boned female with high cheekbones that did not give her face away to any genre of feeling. Yet,

Terry was sensuously beautiful. She was her own best friend and took responsibility for her actions. Her coolness in the hottest situations always troubled Alice. She knew Terry concealed all her emotions behind a facade, an almost perfect unbreakable mask, and she hoped to see the day her flowing warmth would turn into blazes unchecked.

Terry was Alice's best friend.

"It's to the Woman's Abortion Referral Center, in case . . . " and that was all it had come to.

"Why are you so sure I want an abortion?"

"You don't?"

"I just haven't made up my mind yet." Terry picked up a cracker and munched on it. Alice knew what was coming.

"We both know you can't have a child. You're young and dreamy. That won't help you or your child any. Look, you'll stew and brood and feel pitiful and pray until your knees chap, but in the end, you'll decide on the abortion. So why not cut out all this silliness."

"I wish it were all that easy. But you wouldn't know how it feels. I wish it were . . . " Alice couldn't finish the sentence. Instead she watched Terry's silent flowing stream of mascara crack the cheeks of her face. She reached down to get Alice's hand and patted it gently.

"I do know, Alice."

(Terry, I hear your voice floating on and on and on. It was my decision that seemed already decided for me. I don't have to go through it. But here I am now, bringing out the money to pay. Lack of sleep, so early. That's why I don't feel good.)

" . . . and here is your receipt. Now that we have the business over with, I want you girls to fill out these forms . . . " I make neat "X's" in the boxes next to the word "no." The girl sitting next to me begins to redden and her eyes melt. I don't know what to do so I smile and she returns it. Kathy enters again with some lemonade and wheat crackers. (Good, all I had this morning was a hershey bar.)

I sit on the toilet seat with a paper cup under me. Damn cold, and early. At last. (AH! The trickling of today's morning water.) The warmth of my urine makes my stomach turn. As I walk out with my warm paper cup, I glance at the waiting room. There are many girls now sitting and waiting.

The lid of the university opens up. Watercolored people slowly emerge, moving endlessly about the thick cemented walls. I want so much to disappear. I sit under the tree with my pile of books and look at the quiet people; they float like balloons. I hope everything will be better when he comes. Arrived as expected. No kiss, a simple smile. Sits next to me. For a moment, I feel resentment towards him. We begin a conversation and I feel myself replying but instantly forgetting what I say or hear. Sometimes I feel myself giggling at his remarks, while other times my head automatically nods in agreement to whatever he says. Then by the expression on his face, by the pounding of his heart that buries all other sounds, by the watercolors fusing into nothing, I realize I've told him I am pregnant.

"I don't know *why*, that's all." And that was all it had come to. "Alice."

Alice

"Alice. Alice Johnson."

"Me."

"My, that *is* a pretty dress. The name's Sharon and I'll be assisting the doctor in the procedure." I smile. I follow her into a small doctor's office. Clean and white with silver objects that reflect my face in distortion. (Oh, God, my God, forgive me for I have sinned.)

"Shall I take off my dress?" "No, no need to." I remove my clean underwear and place my feet on the stirrups with great caution. The thick paper under me crinkles. It is so cold. Kathy enters the room while Sharon prepares the vacuum-like machine.

"Would you like me to stay with you? You *are* the first of the morning, y'know. (I know) I nod. She's a nice girl. She pulls my dress up a little more and removes my slip. Sharon is moving a utility table near the stirrups as the little elf begins to rub my thighs. The doctor enters the room. Cold. Her hands are very cold. "Relax. Think of something that you love." Kathy continues rubbing my thighs. "Relax," Sharon reasures me. "Relax," the doctor demands.

"Tell me, Alice, so what are you taking up in school . . . *finally bonded drifting afloat i become, and how much i love it. Cold hands. Forgive me, Father, for I have . . .* Music. How nice! Are you into Classical or . . . *craft cradles me drifting farther away; and how much i love it.* The operation takes about 5 minutes. Now the doctor will insert . . . *the waves rock me into an anxious sleepless sleep. And i love. No! I don't love you, not you, God, knotted ball. I hate you, Alice.* What other instruments do you play? *brimming baptism waters roll. swell. thunder.* Relax, Alice, and try not to move again. *reaching up to the vastness. calm. i relax under the fluids that thicken like jelly.* i am still; my body is transparent and light, ounceless.

---

# Richard Yáñez

Richard Yáñez was born and raised in El Paso, Texas. He graduated from New Mexico State University and Arizona State University. His first book is *El Paso del Norte: Stories on the Border* in which he explores the life of people, young and old, men and women, who must face life in a world filled with dualities.

## Desert Vista

The mud balls appeared the day I kissed Ana Garza.

Wet dirt from the nearby canal clung like brown hands to the front windows, garage doors, tile roof. Our house—covered in Frisbee-sized chocolate chips—looked good enough to eat.

I didn't mind that I had to wash and scrub instead of being free to shoot baskets when I came home after school. And when I drank from the mouth of the hose, I thought of how Ana Garza's lips had been pressed on mine. My tongue had touched hers.

Primary work by Richard Yáñez: *El Paso del Norte: Stories on the Border* (Nevada: Univ. of Nevada Press, 2003).

It might've been the inside of her bottom lip. But who cared? We'd kissed.

That evening, while my dad interrogated me and my older brother, I suckled a mango. This was after I'd tried a peach and a nectarine. When my mom said, "I thought you didn't like fruit," I shook my head and continued to kiss the orange flesh hidden inside the spotted, yellow-green skin.

I wanted to ask my brother, who I knew had kissed more than one girl, if I had done it right. When I nudged him, sitting next to me on the den sofa, I saw that all he and my dad were interested in was who might've used our house for target practice. I flicked dried mud off my corduroys and wondered if we had any more mangoes. My dad marched off and left me and my brother in front of a rerun on TV.

"Maybe it's those guys you flipped off," I said, pretending to care about the other big news earlier today. "Remember when they were scoping out your car?"

"Naw, those guys were older. These are kids."

"Kids?" I said, licking the sweet off my lips. "What makes you think there was more than one?"

"Man, did you see all those mud balls? There were about a hundred."

"Thirty-three," I said and nodded.

Judging from my brother's tone, he appeared to have taken this very personal. And since he and I rarely talked anymore, I made the most out of this opportunity.

"Maybe it's *cholos,*"[1] I said.

"Cholos?" he asked curiously. "What do you know about cholos?"

"I know cholos." I liked the way "cholos" sounded and how it opened my mouth, like if I was blowing a bubble.

An image of a cholo strutted into my mind: a brown-skinned boy wearing a hairnet and a starched T-shirt and khakis, with a neatly folded bandanna drooping out of his back pocket.

"How do you know?" My brother swatted the top of my head, something our dad used to do when we were little.

"There's this guy in my English class. Antonio. Tony. Tony Ayala. He flipped the teacher off one time."

"And that makes him a cholo?"

"Doesn't it? And he writes it too."

"Writes what?"

"Those cool letters. The thin, curvy ones." I moved my index finger in the space between us. "Like on the Declaration of Independence."

My brother was cracking up, so I kept going.

"When I gave Tony Ayala some paper, he wrote out my name, El Ruly, and called me an *'es-say.'*"

"You mean *'ése,'*"[2] he said and again swatted my head. "Don't you know Spanish?"

"I didn't know that's what cholos talked," I said.

---

[1]Homeboys
[2]Brother/man

Before falling asleep, I thought about how clean our house was when we first moved here from La Loma less than a year ago. A yard full of grass. Tall mulberries. And like every house in Desert Vista—"Best View in East El Paso," as advertised on billboards—our four-bedroom house was beige stucco. Our front doors were the only things different from any of the other homes. My dad bought ours across the Border. After sanding the pine, he painted them Oaxaca Blue.

With my family's move, I also transferred to my first public school, Desert Vista Junior High. When my brother said he was glad that he wouldn't have to wear a uniform, I lied and said I'd also hated the blue-and-gray-plaid shirts and shiny loafers we wore at Father Yermo.

From the stories I'd heard from my cousins, who all went to public school, I had many expectations. Bigger hallways, my own locker, sports teams, a cafeteria with better snack machines. None of these was the first thing I noticed at Desert Vista Junior High. As soon as I arrived at the school, I saw "the writing on the wall," an expression I heard on TV.

It was hard not to notice the graffiti scrawled all over the buildings. The letters were curved and bent like the ironwork of houses in Juárez. I wondered if the words and phrases were there to make my transition easier. Since I only really used Spanish the few times we visited my grandparents in La Loma, much of the graffiti was foreign to me. And given that I couldn't make out all the ornate letters, it might as well have been in another language altogether. I know I certainly felt that way when a note appeared in my locker.

VATO[3] WATCH YOUR SORRY ASS
WE DONT KNOW WERE YOU FROM
PUTO[4] YOUR NOT FROM HERE
PONTE TRUCHA[5] WERE CHECKING
YOU OUT DONT THINK WE CANT
MESS YOU UP ESE
El Sapo[6] VLK
c/s

And like that, the words I tried to ignore in the hallways, all over desks, and on bathroom stalls had found their way into my hands.

That day, which was during my first month at Desert Vista Junior High, I was only able to decipher the note's shorter words. After studying it alone in my bedroom, afraid to show it to anyone, I put most of it together. When I found out that "VLK" stood for "Varrio Los Kennedys," one of the baddest gangs around, I wished I hadn't worked so hard to read the note.

For weeks I walked around scared. I knew of gangs, but I didn't know anyone who'd been threatened by one, much less someone who was a part of one.

I carried and read the note all the time. During morning announcements. In the lunch line. At PE. I didn't know why. Maybe if I read it enough, I thought, it might lose its threat.

---

[3]Man/Dude
[4]Bugger
[5]Be alert
[6]The frog

Every day that I came home from school not messed up, the note became less and less intimidating. I finally tucked the worn sheet of paper in the back of my sock drawer, where I also kept my communion rosary and a *TV Guide* cover of Wonder Woman.

I decided it must've been someone playing a joke or some kind of initiation. Though every time I saw the letters VLK freshly spray-painted around school, I made sure to look over my shoulder. And I always knew El Sapo could be any one of the cholos who cruised the hallways before, during, and after class.

As I walked to catch the bus the next morning, I paused at the end of our street. The mud balls had left me suspicious of where we lived. In the time since we'd moved to Desert Vista, a barrier of wooden posts and metal rails with a NO PASSING sign had been put up. County workers planted it right where the sidewalk ended, in front of an empty lot.

When I asked my parents why the neighborhood association wanted to split up Nottingham Drive, they said, "You'll be safer. We all will." I hadn't felt unsafe in Desert Vista, but I didn't say anything. I trusted my parents.

Santiago Reyes lived on the other side of the barrier. He was my new friend. After the cholo note, I'd made an effort to make friends. We took bus #12 to and from school, and when I saw him carrying a basketball, I started sitting next to him. I invited him over to my house to shoot baskets in the driveway.

I'd wanted to try out for the school's basketball team, "the Mighty Giants," when I transferred to Desert Vista Junior High, but I was afraid I wasn't good enough.

Santiago said he would've tried out but that Coach Tapia didn't like him. When I asked why, he said he'd called Coach a *joto*.[7] I laughed along with Santiago as he faked left and ducked in to make a layup. "Joto," I repeated. While I wasn't exactly sure what "joto" meant in English, I also enjoyed the way "joto" blew out of my mouth. It rhymed with "cholo."

"Why does your mom keep looking out the window?" Santiago asked after I fouled him on a jump shot. "She think you run away?"

"Naw, she's watching for cholos."

"Cholos?" Santiago asked, catching his breath. "What are you talking about?"

"Nothing, ignore her."

"C'mon, aren't we friends, ése?" His smile stretched into a wide u.

"Okay, but let me ask you something," I said.

"Go for it." He spun the ball on his index finger.

"Do you know any cholos?"

"My brothers were," he said while he aimed a free throw shot, "but now they're roofers. Like our father." *Swish*.

I ended up telling Santiago how, in addition to mud-balling our house, someone had toilet-papered the houses closest to the barrier. The neighborhood association had another meeting. When my dad came home, he said, "That's it." I wanted to ask what "it" was but I didn't.

---

[7] Faggot

I told Santiago that I thought it was probably some older kids horsing around. Of his six brothers, two attended Ysleta High along with my brother.

As my best friend and I played game after game of HORSE—him beating me more times by making a basket for each letter—we both agreed that high school was probably way more fun than stupid junior high.

Tired and thirsty, I invited Santiago inside for a snack. At the kitchen table, I savored a mango while he finished a peanut butter sandwich in three bites. When he caught me kissing the mango, I got nervous.

"You want some?" I asked, hoping he didn't.

"Naw, they make my mouth itch."

We were about to go mess with my brother's stuff when my mom entered the kitchen. I was too busy eating my mango and forgot to introduce Santiago. My mom looked him over.

"He's my friend," I said, wiping my chin with the back of my hand. "We ride the bus together."

My mom kept staring as if she knew him from somewhere other than through the window. "Do you live in that big house with the birdbath out front?"

Santiago shook his head. "We don't have but one bath. And my brothers leave it full of hairs."

My mom laughed. I laughed. Santiago smiled.

"I'm going to start supper, so," my mom said and motioned for us to leave the kitchen, her favorite part of the new house, I'd heard her tell my dad.

Santiago said he'd better go and do some homework. We both hated homework, so I knew he was lying. I worried that my mom might've said something wrong.

When I walked him down Nottingham Drive, I decided he would be the first one I told about Ana Garza. Feathered, pecan-pie-brown hair. Eyes like my favorite shooties. No pimples. How we'd kissed at her locker and before PE. The second time, I put my hands on her waist. "Her hips?" Santiago asked, "Yeah, her hips," I corrected myself. We both agreed that I was lucky to be kissing.

I instinctively stopped before we got to the barrier.

Although I'd ridden my bike up and down Nottingham Drive when we first moved here, I now saw it differently. As two sides. And I wondered if Santiago was also aware of this other side.

We shook hands in the long way that only best friends had. And then I watched him climb over the barrier like Spider-Man before I turned and ran home.

News of me and Ana Garza kissing bounced through Desert Vista Junior High faster than the story of my house being mud-balled. Many of the guys gave me a hard time—asking if we'd *Frenched,* when was she gonna give me a *hickey,* and if I'd touched her *chi chis.* Like graffiti and cholos, I learned, kissing had its own vocabulary.

At lunch while I scrambled for the ball on the blacktop, I made sure that Ana Garza was watching. She whistled each time I made a basket. I wanted to get called out, so I could go over and kiss her. But the truth was that I wasn't brave enough to do that in front of the whole school.

One of Ana Garza's friends, Gracie Levario, came over when I went for a drink of water. I would've thought Gracie was pretty if I wasn't kissing Ana Garza. Gracie handed me a note. When I saw Ana Garza's handwriting—thick and slanted—I couldn't wait to read it. I didn't get a chance because the bell rang. I stopped by my locker and hurried to English.

As Mrs. Harris went over some homework assignment, I thought of how public school was better than Catholic school. It wasn't all about long assemblies, parent-teacher conferences, and weekly confessions. Kissing had changed all that. Ana Garza and I went from planning to bump into each other between fourth and fifth periods to holding hands as we waited in the lunch line. And now she had written me a note saying that she wanted me to go to Western Playland Amusement Park. She and her friends were going, and I had to go. Yes, I had to. No matter what.

When I saw Mrs. Harris walking my way, I tucked the note in my corduroys and opened my journal. I counted the check marks on the inside cover. Kissing for the ninth time was as good, if not better, as the first time. That was for sure. If it had been up to me, I would've written about the sweetness of kissing, not "How I See Myself in Ten Years." I'd been writing in my journal almost every day, and English was becoming my favorite subject.

Ever since my bike was stolen, I'd been taking bus #12 home from school. I had no clue who took my bike from our front yard. I suspected El Sapo—whichever cholo he was—since it disappeared around the time I got the threatening note. I'd written in my journal how he might've converted my BMX to one of those lowrider bikes I'd seen at Ascarate Park. All chrome and mirrors. Candy-apple red. *Low and slow.*

It didn't matter, anyway. I liked the bus. Boys and girls' voices in Spanish and English—and a mouthwatering combination of the two, like a gordita[8] and burrito plate—echoed inside the cavernous metal body. On the bus ride to and from school, I'd gaze out the windows as we drove along North Loop Road. The rows of cotton fields reminded me of my brown corduroys, and the chile fields blurred by me like the green lines on notebook paper. I'd gotten A's and B's on my essays but D's in penmanship. "You think faster than you can write," Mrs. Harris wrote on my paper. "Stay within the lines."

On the bus, I told Santiago about going to Western Playland. I was surprised that he was interested. I thought he'd say that riding the El Bandido Roller Coaster and the Matador Twister was dumb. I guessed why he wanted to go. Before we split up at the barrier, he made sure to ask about Ana Garza and her friend Letty Sida. "Yeah, for sure they're going," I said. When Santiago smiled, his mouth stayed slightly open as if in anticipation. Pretty soon, we both might be kissing.

One day after school, when Santiago had to help his father shingle a roof, I came home to find another boy in our driveway. I was more surprised to see my mom home so early than to see her clutching a broom next to the boy holding our water hose.

"What are——" I started to say.

"Get inside," my mom said, her eyes fixed on the boy. "I'll be in soon."

For a second I thought she was addressing the boy. When she repeated herself—"Get inside now, Raul Luis."—I registered her tone, not to mention her use of my two first names, and I rushed inside.

---

[8]Type of Mexican food.

From my brother's bedroom window, I peeked outside. After the boy sprayed water where my mom pointed, he dried each window with one of my dad's old T-shirts. He had to jump to reach the higher windows.

While I didn't recognize the boy, I didn't think of him as a stranger. Face, hair, eyes— all brown—like most at Desert Vista Junior High.

I wanted to question him. Do you have a hairnet? How about a bandanna? I decided he wasn't a cholo when I noticed his pants weren't creased, no sharp lines running down his legs like fences.

When I saw him run toward the barrier, I figured that's what side he lived on. I couldn't spend any more time thinking about it. My mom came in the house. I raced to my room and took out my language arts book. The "C-" on my last report card was enough for my mom to say that she and my dad had "their eye on me." Although I'd also heard this expression followed by laughter on TV, it still made me nervous.

I didn't tell my parents why homework no longer mattered. Math, science, history, all boring compared to Ana Garza, cholos, bus rides. I hoped that they wouldn't make me confess any of it.

At dinner that night, we made it through half of a meat loaf, most of the instant mashed potatoes, and two cans of cream corn before my mom said anything.

"Don't you think you should tell your father?" She sat in the chair across from me.

I raised my eyes from my plate and swallowed. "Huh?" A chunk of meat loaf didn't slide down as easily as the potatoes.

"You know what I mean." She kept her eye on me while my dad and brother kept theirs on their plates.

I shook my head and reached for my bottle of Mr. PiBB.

"Maybe this will help you remember." She pulled something from her lap and tossed it on the table like Mrs. Seymour returning the science test I failed. The square of loose-leaf paper landed between a plate of Wonder Bread and a bowl of homemade salsa.

I stared at the note folded in eighths. I wanted to snatch it up, roll it into a ball, and swallow it. I quickly studied the situation. Everything led back to the boy from earlier. Could he have been El Sapo? Did the mud balls spell some kind of message? What did "c/s" mean?

My brother reached for the note, but my mom was quicker. She put it back in her pocket, saving the evidence for later.

The sun was setting behind our house, where minutes away the Rio Grande separated us from another country. Light swam through our wallpapered kitchen and made it even more orange. I would've given almost anything to be somewhere else at that moment.

"C'mon, let's have it, whatever it is," my dad said, raking his fork through the mashed potatoes.

"Okay, but it's not my fault," I said and put both elbows on the table for some balance. "There are these guys at school. VLK. They're a gang."

I took a breath and saw that my brother appeared as excited as when we watched Mil Máscaras, our favorite wrestler, on Mexican TV.

"They wanted to mess me up," I continued, "but nothing happened."

I craved hearing something other than dogs barking outside, so I kept talking. "I found the note in my locker. And at first I couldn't read it—it's written in cholo—but I figured it out. I understand now."

My brother smacked me on the head. "You and that cholo stuff. I told you it was dumb, menso."[9]

"Hey." My dad punctuated his only word by spearing a rectangle of meat loaf.

"And I don't know the boy you caught. He's not El Sapo, is he?" I said to my mom, who hadn't eaten very much off her plate.

"What boy?" my dad said before biting into his meat loaf.

"The one mom made wash windows." I sat up in my chair, happy that I was the only one with answers.

My dad and brother simultaneously turned to my mom.

"He—has—a—girlfriend." There were long pauses between each of my mom's words. As much was said in the silence as in the joining of consonants and vowels.

She might as well have hit me with a broom. Across the head. On my butt. A blow to my stomach.

I burped and tasted salsa. Although I knew it wouldn't help things, all I could do was chew another slice of Wonder Bread. No stories about cholos or mud balls could hide my secret. Ana Garza and I were kissing.

That night, with my ear to the wall, I listened as my mom told my dad about the note she'd found in my pants. She went on and on how I was too young to be kissing girls. How maybe I should go back to Father Yermo. How I was still her "m'ijito."[10] From a recent conversation I'd eavesdropped on, I remembered her saying the same thing after a trip to Kmart. She'd been upset that I'd asked her to wait in the car while I shopped for school clothes on my own.

My stomach grumbled when I heard her mention my low grades. They agreed that I would be grounded.

I also heard my mom tell my dad about the boys mud-balling our house. She'd intended to scare them off with the broom. Running barefoot, she was so mad that she managed to catch the slowest one. When she asked him why they did it, he said nothing. She even questioned him in Spanish. *Nada*[11]—the boy wasn't giving anything up.

I might've tried my cholo vocabulary, the one I'd been studying off walls and on the bus. "C'mon, don't be a pinche.[12] Why you messing up our house, ése?"

The next day at school I searched the hallways, cafeteria, playground, and even the detention room for the boy my mom had caught. I was bigger than he was. I could get him to confess. I would offer my mom his answers as a bribe to let me go to Western Playland.

---

[9]Dumb

[10]Baby son/dear son

[11]Nothing

[12]Damn

When I didn't find the boy, I described him to Santiago, making sure to mention that his khakis weren't creased. Santiago said that he sounded like every boy on his side of the barrier.

After the mud balls, my mom finding the note, and my grounding, I tried not to get in any more trouble. Days went by without me seeing much of Ana Garza. When she asked why I couldn't go to Western Playland, I said my mom was sick. I didn't like lying, but I didn't want to tell Ana Garza that my mom had found out we were kissing.

Santiago also stopped coming to my house after I told him about my mom's use of a broom. I assured him that it didn't hurt, remembering the swats I'd gotten for asking about a Spanish word I'd read on the school bus. While I still wasn't sure what *"pendejo"*[13] meant in English, I crowded my mouth with *o*'s. Cholo. Joto. Pendejo.

I would've preferred that my mom hit me again, rather than keep me grounded. I made sure to wash the dishes without being told. Even on nights when it was my brother's turn. I almost hoped I would catch someone throwing mud balls at our house, so I could prove that I was on her side. I made sure to keep the front curtains open, the glass Windexed.

One evening, after I'd hurried home and done my homework, I went to see what my mom was making for dinner. Since I'd been spending all my free time shooting baskets, I hadn't helped her like I used to. In our La Loma home, I'd learned how to clean the beans before you put them in the pot, how much cilantro to put in arroz,[14] and which chiles were the hottest, and best, for salsa.

Without saying anything, I began grating cheese while she diced onions for red enchiladas. We stood right next to each other—hip to hip. Her favorite novela,[15] *Semillas de Amor y Dolor*,[16] played on the TV in the other room. The voices in Spanish were much more dramatic than anything I understood on the school bus. When I heard my mom sniffle, I checked to see if she was crying. She pointed to the onions. We smiled.

"Do you have a lot of homework this weekend?" she asked, adding the onions to the rice.

I wanted to ask why but said, "Not so much."

"Good. There's a company picnic," she said as she took out a pan. The flame of the burner went from blue to orange. Melted lard sizzled when she dropped a spoonful of beans.

I imagined a park filled with old people eating bologna sandwiches and potato salad. When I didn't say anything, she said, "It's at Western Playland. You can bring your friend. What's his name?"

"Santiago." I grinned and inhaled the heavy smell of refried beans. Hungrier than I'd been in weeks, I thought about checking for mangoes but snatched a palmful of Jack cheese instead. I swished the mini orange ball into my mouth.

With things at home back to normal, I tried to do the same with my life at school. I was ready to tell Ana Garza the whole story. From the mud balls to me and my mom

---

[13]Stupid

[14]Rice

[15]Soap opera

[16]Seeds of love and pain

making up. I wrote it out in my journal, taking my time to stay within the lines, and hoped that it would get me and Ana Garza kissing again. That's what I wanted more than anything.

When I opened my locker the next day, I found a note, I hesitated unfolding it, but the letters were round cursive, not stilted print. Ana Garza's, not a cholo's. I read the note while I made my way outside the school building. The last bell let me know that I'd missed my bus.

"Do you mean it?" These were the first words I said when I met Ana Garza outside by the portable classrooms. She brushed her hair back and avoided eye contact. I dropped my gym bag and tried to take her hand. She slipped it in her rear pocket.

"Yeah, I'm pretty sure."

"Why? Because I didn't walk you to your bus?"

No matter how many steps I moved forward, she kept dancing back.

"No. Not just that—"

"What? What did I do?"

Before she could answer, I started blabbering. Not from the beginning straight to the present like I'd prepared in my journal. My spinning thoughts mixed up my neatly written sentences. "This boy—my mom had a broom—the barrier—do you know El Sapo?—she's not mad anymore—he's a cholo—wanna go to a picnic?"

The words poured out of my mouth like a mudslide. I couldn't escape.

Ana Garza lifted her head. Although she looked in my eyes for the first time, something far away had her attention.

That's when I knew, I just did. The way she kept her hips out of reach. The way she turned her shoulders. The way she sucked in her lips.

Even in her paper-soft voice, the news was bad. She left nothing out. How he put his arm around her. On the El Bandido Roller Coaster. How he kissed her. In the Haunted House. How it just happened. At Western Playland. How I shouldn't be mad.

Mad? I wasn't mad. I wasn't anything. My body was numb. Jell-O. My heart, the fruit trapped inside.

When Ana Garza breathed his name, I wanted to swallow the syllables that grazed her lips. There wasn't a kiss big enough.

Before she could say "Santiago" again, I grabbed my gym bag and took off. My feet pumped under me and my arms flailed at my sides. I ran fast, like I'd imagined I would if a cholo ever came after me.

I sprinted down North Loop Road, a dust devil racing me. The wind smelled like yellow chile. The sun was a giant Spalding beginning its descent.

I crossed Zaragoza Road and kept running. When I reached the canal that ran behind my house, I thought about throwing my gym bag—filled with books, my journal, Ana Garza's note, a mango, and half a peanut butter sandwich—in the algae-colored water, but its weight kept me anchored to the caliche road. I didn't stop running till I arrived at Desert Vista. Even then, I walked fast through our neighborhood with my head tilted back. I couldn't open my mouth wide enough to replace all the air escaping my lungs.

Through the front windows of my house, I saw my mom in the kitchen. She moved her hips side to side. I thought she might've been dancing, like they often did on her novelas, but I realized she was sweeping. I considered going in, grabbing the broom, and telling her I was chasing a cholo.

Like when I'd discover a note in my locker, my heart began running a hundred-yard dash. Blood rushed through my arms and legs. When I ran out of sidewalk, I climbed the graffiti-covered barrier for the first time. Straddling the top rail, I hesitated. When I glanced back, I couldn't tell which was my house. They all appeared the same. I took a deep breath and jumped to the other side.

Busted Big Wheels. Crooked swing sets. Kids in diapers. The houses on this side weren't much different than the ones on the other side except that there seemed to be more things out front. No basketball courts. No birdbaths. No mulberry trees.

I expected to see the boy my mom had caught. I wasn't mad at him, but I knew that I could easily hit him. The fists I carried were heavy.

After going up and down unfamiliar streets—waving to Mary Rodarte, who was in my history class, smelling caldo de res[17] from an open window, hearing a TV switch from Spanish to English to Spanish—I gave up trying to find the right house. I was almost glad that I didn't know where Santiago lived. Although I wasn't sure what I would say, I did know that I wanted to foul him, like if he was going in for a layup. Hard enough so that he would know how bad it felt to not be kissing Ana Garza.

I was resting under a stop sign, worrying that I should get home before it got dark, when a truck drove by. The Chevy was faded green, made lots of noise, and a ladder hung out the back. None of these was what drew me.

REYES ROOFING. The red letters painted across the doors lifted me off the ground. I followed the truck. My calves were sore, and my gym bag weighed my shoulders down as I ran.

I stopped outside the front gate where the truck had parked. In the driveway, there was a beat-up car. An engine hung by a chain over an open hood, a gaping mouth ready to swallow. A toolbox, wrenches, and sockets—scattered like puzzle pieces—also sat in the oil-stained driveway.

Even with a basketball court and trimmed bushes, this wouldn't have compared to my house. One side of the roof was missing shingles and appeared ready to cave in. The front door was more rust than any color of paint. I couldn't tell where the cement driveway ended and the grassless yard began. Trash and tumbleweeds clenched the chainlink fence.

Before I realized what I was doing, I jumped over the fence and landed in the yard. On my hands and knees, I couldn't remember Santiago saying whether they had dogs.

A few seconds passed. I stood. Looked around. No one.

Still not sure what I was doing, I unzipped my gym bag and reached inside.

I pictured this house like someone—a stranger, a cholo, an ex-best friend—had pictured ours: as a target.

Like kissing Ana Garza for the first time, I knew that if I thought about it too much I would chicken out.

---

[17]Meat stew

I planted my feet. I inhaled.
I lifted my arm. I focused.
I twisted my hips. I couldn't miss.

As I leaned forward and released, a stream of air brushed my face. On Santiago's front door bloomed the ripe kiss of a mango.

---

# ESSAY

## Cherríe Moraga

Cherríe Moraga was born in California in 1952. She is a poet, essayist, and playwright. She has given a voice to the Latina lesbian experience in the groundbreaking anthology she coedited with Gloria Anzaldúa, *This Bridge Called My Back: Writings by Radical Women of Color* (1981), as well as in her book *Loving in the War Years: lo que nunca pasó por sus labios* (*what never passed through her lips*, 1983). In 1977 she moved from Los Angeles to the San Francisco Bay area, where she participated in a women's writing group and immersed herself in the increasingly political atmosphere of the late 1970s.

*This Bridge Called My Back,* which consists of stories, poetry, and essays, helped to define a perspective on feminism that incorporates issues of race, culture, and class as well as those of gender and sexuality. It provided a counterbalance to white Anglo feminist perspectives by bringing together writings by Latina, African American, Native American, and Asian American women.

### La Güera[1]

*It requires something more than personal experience to gain a philosophy or point of view from any specific event. It is the quality of our response to the event and our capacity to enter into the lives of others that help us to make their lives and experiences our own.* — Emma Goldman*

---

Primary works by Cherríe Moraga: *Loving in the War Years: Lo que nunca pasó por sus labios* (Boston: South End Press, 1983); *Heroes and Other Plays* (Albuquerque: West End Press, 1994).

[1]The blond one/fair-skinned

---

*Alix Kates Shulman, "Was My Life Worth Living?" *Red Emma Speaks.* (New York: Random House, 1972), p. 388.

I am the very well-educated daughter of a woman who, by the standards in this country, would be considered largely illiterate. My mother was born in Santa Paula, Southern California, at a time when much of the central valley there was still farm land. Nearly thirty-five years later, in 1948, she was the only daughter of six to marry an anglo, my father.

*Oral traditions*

I remember all of my mother's stories, probably much better than she realizes. She is a fine story-teller, recalling every event of her life with the vividness of the present, noting each detail right down to the cut and color of her dress. I remember stories of her being pulled out of school at the ages of five, seven, nine, and eleven to work in the fields, along with her brothers and sisters; stories of her father drinking away whatever small profit she was able to make for the family; of her going the long way home to avoid meeting him on the street, staggering toward the same destination. I remember stories of my mother lying about her age in order to get a job as a hat-check girl at Agua Caliente Racetrack in Tijuana. At fourteen, she was the main support of the family. I can still see her walking home alone at 3 A.M., only to turn all of her salary and tips over to her mother, who was pregnant again.

The stories continue through the war years and on: walnut-cracking factories, the Voit Rubber factory, and then the computer boom. I remember my mother doing piecework for the electronics plant in our neighborhood. In the late evening, she would sit in front of the T.V. set, wrapping copper wires into the backs of circuit boards, talking about "keeping up with the younger girls." By that time she was already in her mid-fifties.

Meanwhile, I was college-prep in school. After classes, I would go with my mother to fill out job applications for her, or write checks for her at the supermarket. We would have the scenario all worked out ahead of time. My mother would sign the check before we'd get to the store. Then, as we'd approach the checkstand, she would say— within earshot of the cashier— "oh honey, you go 'head and make out the check," as if she couldn't be bothered with such an insignificant detail. No one asked any questions.

I was educated, and wore it with a keen sense of pride and satisfaction, my head propped up with the knowledge, from my mother, that my life would be easier than hers. I was educated; but more than this, I was "la güera"—fair-skinned. Born with the features of my Chicana mother, but the skin of my Anglo father, I had it made.

No one ever quite told me this (that light was right), but I knew that being light was something valued in my family (who were all Chicano, with the exception of my father). In fact, everything about my upbringing (at least what occurred on a conscious level) attempted to bleach me of what color I did have. Although my mother was fluent in it, I was never taught much Spanish at home. I picked up what I did learn from school and from over-heard snatches of conversation among my relatives and mother. She often called other lower-income Mexicans "braceros,"[2] or "wet-backs," referring to herself and family as "a different class of people." And yet, the real story was that my family, too, had been poor (some still are) and farmworkers. My mother can remember this in her blood as if it were yesterday. But this is something she would like to forget (and rightfully), for to her, on a basic economic level,

---

[2]Migrant workers

being Chicana meant being "less." It was through my mother's desire to protect her children from poverty and illiteracy that we became "anglocized"; the more effectively we could pass in the white world, the better guaranteed our future.

From all of this, I experience, daily, a huge disparity between what I was born into and what I was to grow up to become. Because, (as Goldman suggests) these stories my mother told me crept under my "güera" skin. I had no choice but to enter into the life of my mother. *I had no choice.* I took her life into my heart, but managed to keep a lid on it as long as I feigned being the happy, upwardly mobile heterosexual.

When I finally lifted the lid to my lesbianism, a profound connection with my mother reawakened in me. It wasn't until I acknowledged and confronted my own lesbianism in the flesh, that my heartfelt identification with and empathy for my mother's oppression—due to being poor, uneducated, and Chicana—was realized. My lesbianism is the avenue through which I have learned the most about silence and oppression, and it continues to be the most tactile reminder to me that we are not free human beings.

You see, one follows the other. I had known for years that I was a lesbian, had felt it in my bones, had ached with the knowledge, gone crazed with the knowledge, wallowed in the silence of it. Silence *is* like starvation. Don't be fooled. It's nothing short of that, and felt most sharply when one has had a full belly most of her life. When we are not physically starving, we have the luxury to realize psychic and emotional starvation. It is from this starvation that other starvations can be recognized—if one is willing to take the risk of making the connection—if one is willing to be responsible to the result of the connection. For me, the connection is an inevitable one.

What I am saying is that the joys of looking like a white girl ain't so great since I realized I could be beaten on the street for being a dyke. If my sister's being beaten because she's Black, it's pretty much the same principle. We're both getting beaten any way you look at it. The connection is blatant; and in the case of my own family, the difference in the privileges attached to looking white instead of brown are merely a generation apart.

In this country, lesbianism is a poverty—as is being brown, as is being a woman, as is being just plain poor. The danger lies in ranking the oppressions. *The danger lies in failing to acknowledge the specificity of the oppression.* The danger lies in attempting to deal with oppression purely from a theoretical base. Without an emotional, heartfelt grappling with the source of our own oppression, without naming the enemy within ourselves and outside of us, no authentic, non-hierarchical connection among oppressed groups can take place.

When the going gets rough, will we abandon our so-called comrades in a flurry of racist/heterosexist/what-have-you panic? To whose camp, then, should the lesbian of color retreat? Her very presence violates the ranking and abstraction of oppression. Do we merely live hand to mouth? Do we merely struggle with the "ism" that's sitting on top of our heads?

The answer is: yes, I think first we do; and we must do so thoroughly and deeply. But to fail to move out from there will only isolate us in our own oppression—will only insulate, rather than radicalize us.

To illustrate: a gay white male friend of mine once confided to me that he continued to feel that, on some level, I didn't trust him because he was male; that he felt, really, if it ever came down to a "battle of the sexes," I might kill him. I admitted that I might very well. He wanted to understand the source of my distrust. I responded. "You're not a woman. Be a woman for a day. Imagine being a woman." He confessed that the thought terrified him because, to him, being a woman meant being raped by men. He *had* felt raped by men; he wanted to forget what that meant. What grew from that discussion was the realization that in order for him to create an authentic alliance with me, he must deal with the primary source of his own sense of oppression. He must, first, emotionally come to terms with what it feels like to be a victim. If he—or anyone—were to truly do this, it would be impossible to discount the oppression of others, except by again forgetting how we have been hurt.

And yet, oppressed groups are forgetting all the time. There are instances of this in the rising Black middle class, and certainly an obvious trend of such "capitalist-unconsciousness" among white gay men. Because to remember may mean giving up whatever privileges we have managed to squeeze out of this society by virtue of our gender, race, class, or sexuality.

Within the women's movement, the connections among women of different backgrounds and sexual orientations have been fragile, at best. I think this phenomenon is indicative of our failure to seriously address ourselves to some very frightening questions: How have I internalized my own oppression? How have I oppressed? Instead, we have let rhetoric do the job of poetry. Even the word "oppression" has lost its power. We need a new language, better words that can more closely describe women's fear of and resistance to one another; words that will not always come out sounding like dogma.

What prompted me in the first place to work on an anthology by radical women of color was a deep sense that I had a valuable insight to contribute, by virtue of my birthright and my background. And yet, I don't really understand first-hand what it feels like being shitted on for being brown. I understand much more about the joys of it—being Chicana and having family are synonymous for me. What I know about loving, singing, crying, telling stories, speaking with my heart and hands, even having a sense of my own soul comes from the love of my mother, aunts, cousins . . .

But at the age of twenty-seven, it is frightening to acknowledge that I have internalized a racism and classism, where the object of oppression is not only someone *outside* my skin, but the someone *inside* my skin. In fact, to a large degree, the real battle with such oppression, for all of us, begins under the skin. I have had to confront the fact that much of what I value about being Chicana, about my family, has been subverted by anglo culture and my own cooperation with it. This realization did not occur to me overnight. For example, it wasn't until long after my graduation from the private college I'd attended in Los Angeles, that I realized the major reason for my total alienation from and fear of my classmates was rooted in class and culture.

Three years after graduation, in an apple-orchard in Sonoma, a friend of mine (who comes from an Italian Irish working class family) says to me, "Cherríe, no wonder you felt like such a nut in school. Most of the people there were white and rich." It was true. All along I had felt the difference, but not until I had put the words "class" and "race" to the experience, did my feelings make any sense. For years, I had berated myself for not being as "free" as my classmates. I completely bought that they simply had more guts than I did—to rebel against their parents and run around the country hitch-hiking, reading books and studying "art." They had enough privilege to be atheists, for chrissake. There was no one around filling in the disparity for me between their parents, who were Hollywood filmmakers, and my parents, who wouldn't know the name of a filmmaker if their lives depended on it (and precisely because their lives didn't depend on it, they couldn't be bothered). But I knew nothing about "privilege" then. White was right. Period. I could pass. If I got educated enough, there would never be no telling.

Three years after that, I had a similar revelation. In a letter to a friend, I wrote:

> I went to a concert where Ntosake Shange was reading. There, everything exploded for me. She was speaking in a language that I knew—in the deepest parts of me—existed, and that I ignored in my own feminist studies and even in my own writing. What Ntosake caught in me is the realization that in my development as a poet, I have, in many ways, denied the voice of my own brown mother—the brown in me. I have acclimated to the sound of a white language which, as my father represents it, does not speak to the emotions in my poems—emotions which stem from the love of my mother.
>
> The reading was agitating. Made me uncomfortable. Threw me into a week-long terror of how deeply I was affected. I felt that I had to start all over again. That I turned only to the perceptions of white middle-class women to speak for me and all women. I am shocked by my own ignorance.

Sitting in that auditorium chair was the first time I had realized to the core of me that for years I had disowned the language I knew best—ignored the words and rhythms that were the closest to me. The sounds of my mother and aunts gossiping—half in English, half in Spanish— while drinking cerveza[3] in the kitchen. And the hands—I had cut off the hands in my poems. But not in conversation; still the hands could not be kept down. Still they insisted on moving.

The reading had forced me to remember that I knew things from my roots. But to remember puts me up against what I don't know. Shange's reading agitated me because she spoke with power about a world that is both alien and common to me: "the capacity to enter into the lives of others." But you can't just take the goods and run. I knew that then, sitting in the Oakland auditorium (as I know in my poetry), that the only thing worth writing about is what seems to be unknown and, therefore, fearful.

The "unknown" is often depicted in racist literature as the "darkness" within a person. Similarly, sexist writers will refer to fear in the form of the vagina, calling it "the orifice of death." In contrast, it is a pleasure to read works such as Maxine Hong Kingston's *Woman Warrior,* where fear and alienation are depicted as "the white ghosts." And yet, the bulk of literature in this country reinforces the myth that what is dark and female is evil. Consequently, each of us—whether dark, female, or both—has in some way *internalized* this oppressive imagery. What the oppressor often succeeds in doing is simply *externalizing* his fears, projecting them into the bodies of women, Asians, gays, disabled folks, whoever seems most "other."

call me
roach and presumptuous
nightmare on your white pillow

---

[3]Beer

your itch to destroy
the indestructible
part of yourself

    —Audre Lorde*

But it is not really difference the oppressor fears so much as similarity. He fears he will discover in himself the same aches, the same longings as those of the people he has shitted on. He fears the immobilization threatened by his own incipient guilt. He fears he will have to change his life once he has seen himself in the bodies of the people he has called different. He fears the hatred, anger, and vengeance of those he has hurt.

This is the oppressor's nightmare, but it is not exclusive to him. We women have a similar nightmare, for each of us in some way has been both oppressed and the oppressor. We are afraid to look at how we have failed each other. We are afraid to see how we have taken the values of our oppressor into our hearts and turned them against ourselves and one another. We are afraid to admit how deeply "the man's" words have been ingrained in us.

To assess the damage is a dangerous act. I think of how, even as a feminist lesbian, I have so wanted to ignore my own homophobia, my own hatred of myself for being queer. I have not wanted to admit that my deepest personal sense of myself has not quite "caught up" with my "woman-identified" politics. I have been afraid to criticize lesbian writers who choose to "skip over" these issues in the name of feminism. In 1979, we talk of "old gay" and "butch and femme" roles as if they were ancient history. We toss them aside as merely patriarchal notions. And yet, the truth of the matter is that I have sometimes taken society's fear and hatred of lesbians to bed with me. I have sometimes hated my lover for loving me. I have sometimes felt "not women enough" for her. I have sometimes felt "not man enough." For a lesbian trying to survive in a heterosexist society, there is no easy way around these emotions. Similarly, in a white-dominated world, there is little getting around racism and our own internalization of it. It's always there, embodied in someone we least expect to rub up against.

When we do rub up against this person, *there* then is the challenge. *There* then is the opportunity to look at the nightmare within us. But we usually shrink from such a challenge.

Time and time again, I have observed that the usual response among white women's groups when the "racism issue" comes up is to deny the difference. I have heard comments like, "Well, we're open to *all* women; why don't they (women of color) come? You can only do so much . . . " But there is seldom any analysis of how the very nature and structure of the group itself may be founded on racist or classist assumptions. More importantly, so often the women seem to feel no loss, no lack, no absence when women of color are not involved; therefore, there is little desire to change the situation. This has hurt me deeply. I have come to believe that the only reason women of a privileged class will dare to look at *how* it is that

---

*From "The Brown Menace or Poem to the Survival of Roaches," *The New York Head Shop and Museum* (Detroit: Broadside, 1974), p. 48.

*they* oppress, is when they've come to know the meaning of their own oppression. And understand that the oppression of others hurts them personally.

The other side of the story is that women of color and white working-class women often shrink from challenging white middle-class women. It is much easier to rank oppressions and set up a hierarchy, rather than take responsibility for changing our own lives. We have failed to demand that white women, particularly those that claim to be speaking for all women, be accountable for their racism.

The dialogue has simply not gone deep enough.

In conclusion, I have had to look critically at my claim to color, at a time when, among white feminist ranks, it is a "politically correct" (and sometimes peripherally advantageous) assertion to make. I must acknowledge the fact that, physically, I have had a *choice* about making that claim, in contrast to women who have not had such a choice, and have been abused for their color. I must reckon with the fact that for most of my life, by virtue of the very fact that I am white-looking, I identified with and aspired toward white values, and that I rode the wave of that Southern California privilege as far as conscience would let me.

Well, now I feel both bleached and beached. I feel angry about this—the years when I refused to recognize privilege, both when it worked against me, and when I worked it, ignorantly, at the expense of others. These are not settled issues. This is why this work feels so risky to me. It continues to be discovery. It has brought me into contact with women who invariably know a hell of a lot more than I do about racism, as experienced in the flesh, as revealed in the flesh of their writing.

I think: what is my responsibility to my roots: both white and brown, Spanish-speaking and English? I am a woman with a foot in both worlds. I refuse the split. I feel the necessity for dialogue. Sometimes I feel it urgently.

But one voice is not enough, nor two, although this is where dialogue begins. It is essential that feminists confront their fear of and resistance to each other, because without this, there *will* be no bread on the table. Simply, we will not survive. If we could make this connection in our heart of hearts, that if we are serious about a revolution—better—if we seriously believe there should be joy in our lives (real joy, not just "good times"), then we need one another. We women need each other. Because my/your solitary, self-asserting "go-for-the-throat-of-fear" power is not enough. The real power, as you and I well know, is collective. I can't afford to be afraid of you, nor you of me. If it takes head-on collisions, let's do it. This polite timidity is killing us.

As Lorde suggests in the passage I cited earlier, it is looking to the nightmare that the dream is found. There, the survivor emerges to insist on a future, a vision, yes, born out of what is dark and female. The feminist movement must be a movement of such survivors, a movement with a future.

September 1979

# Benjamín Alire Sáenz

Benjamín Alire Sáenz is a former Wallace E. Stegner Fellow in poetry at Stanford University. His first book of poems, *Calendar of Dust*, was awarded an American Book Award in 1991; his second collection, *Dark and Perfect Angels*, won a Southwest Book Award. In 1992 he was awarded a Lannan Literary Fellowship. His third book of poems, *Elegies in Blue* (2002), delves into a series of themes that deal with living on the border, between two world economies where working-class people are overlooked. Sáenz also published a collection of short stories, *Flowers for the Broken*, and two novels, *Carry Me Like Water* and *The House of Forgetting*. Alire Sáenz currently teaches at UT El Paso.

## Exile

That morning—when the day was new, when the sun slowly touched the sky, almost afraid to break it—that morning I looked out my window and stared at the Juárez Mountains. Mexican purples—burning. I had always thought of them as sacraments of belonging. That was the first time it happened. It had happened to others, but it had never happened to me. And when it happened, it started a fire, a fire that will burn for a long time.

As I walked to school, I remember thinking what a perfect place Sunset Heights was: turn-of-the-century houses intact; remodeled houses painted pink and turquoise; old homes tastefully gentrified by the aspiring young; the rundown Sunset Grocery store decorated with the protest art of graffiti on one end and a plastic-signed "Circle K" on the other.

This was the edge of the piece of paper that was America, the border that bordered the University—its buildings, its libraries; the border that bordered the freeway—its cars coming and going, coming and going endlessly; the border that bordered downtown—its banks and businesses and bars; the border that bordered the border between two countries.

The unemployed poor from Juárez knocking on doors and asking for jobs—or money—or food. Small parks filled with people whose English did not exist. The upwardly mobile living next to families whose only concern was getting enough money to pay next month's rent. Some had lived here for generations, would continue living here into the next century; others would live here a few days. All this color, all this color, all this color beneath the shadow of the Juárez Mountains. Sunset Heights; a perfect place with a perfect name, and a perfect view of the river.

After class, I went by my office and drank a cup of coffee, sat and read, and did some writing. It was a quiet day on campus, nothing but me and my work—the kind of day the mind needs to catch up with itself, the kind of uneventful day so necessary for living. I started walking home at about three o'clock, after I had put my things together in my torn backpack. I made a mental note to sew the damn thing. *One day everything's gonna come tumbling out— better sew it.* I'd made that mental note before.

Primary works by Benjamín Alire Sáenz: *Dark and Perfect Angels* (El Paso: Cinco Puntos Press, 1995); *Carry Me Like Water* (New York: Harper-collins, 1996); *Sammy and Juliana in Hollywood* (El Paso: Cinco Puntos Press, 2004); *Flowers for the Broken* (Seattle: Broken Moon Press, 1992); *The House of Forgetting* (New York: HarperCollins, 1997); *Elegies in Blue: Poems* (El Paso: Cinco Puntos Press, 2002).

Walking down Prospect, I thought maybe I'd go for a jog. I hoped the spring would not bring too much wind this year. The wind, common desert rain; the wind blew too hard and harsh sometimes; the wind unsettled the desert—upset things, ruined the calmness of the spring. My mind wandered, searched the black asphalt littered with torn papers; the chained dogs in the yards who couldn't hurt me; the even bricks of all the houses I passed. I belonged *yes!* here, yes. I belonged. Thoughts entered like children running through a park. This year, maybe the winds would not come.

I didn't notice the green car drive up and stop right next to me as I walked. The border patrol interrupted my daydreaming: "Where are you from?" *Fuck 5-0*

I didn't answer. I wasn't sure who the agent, a woman, was addressing.

She repeated the question in Spanish, "*¿De dónde eres?*"[1]

Without thinking, I almost answered her question—in Spanish. A reflex. I caught myself in midsentence and stuttered in a nonlanguage.

"*¿Dónde naciste?*"[2] she asked again.

By then my mind had cleared, and quietly I said: "I'm a U.S. citizen."

"Were you born in the United States?"     *interesting way to put it*

She was browner then I was. I might have asked her the same question. I looked at her for awhile—searching for something I recognized.

"Yes," I answered.

"Where in the United States were you born?"     *she's so suspicious...*

"In New Mexico."     *bitch.*

"Where in New Mexico?"

"Las Cruces."

"What do you do?"

"I'm a student."

"And are you employed?"

"Sort of."

"Sort of?" She didn't like my answer. Her tone bordered on anger. I looked at her expression and decided it wasn't hurting anyone to answer her questions. It was all very innocent, *is it?* just a game we were playing.

"I work at the University as a teaching assistant."

She didn't respond. She looked at me as if I were a blank. Her eyes were filling in the empty spaces as she looked at my face. I looked at her for a second and decided she was finished with me. I started walking away. "Are you sure you were born in Las Cruces?" she asked again.

I turned around and smiled, "Yes, I'm sure." She didn't smile back. She and the driver sat there for awhile and watched me as I continued walking. They drove past me slowly and then proceeded down the street.

I didn't much care for the color of their cars.

---

[1]Where are you from?

[2]Where were you born?

*[handwritten: yes.]*

*[handwritten: exactly my reaction to her.]*

"Sons of bitches." I whispered, "pretty soon I'll have to carry a passport in my own neighborhood." I said it to be flippant; something in me rebelled against people dressed in uniforms. I wasn't angry—not then, not at first, not really angry. In less than ten minutes I was back in my apartment playing the scene again and again in my mind. It was like a video I played over and over—memorizing the images. Something was wrong. I was embarrassed, ashamed because I'd been so damned compliant like a piece of tin foil in the uniformed woman's hand. Just like a child in the principal's office, in trouble for speaking Spanish. "I should have told that witch exactly what I thought of her and her green car and her green uniform."

I lit a cigarette and told myself I was overreacting. "Breathe in—breathe out—breathe in—breathe out—no big deal—you live on a border. These things happen—just one of those things. Just a game . . . " I changed into my jogging clothes and went for a run. At the top of the hill on Sunbowl Drive, I stopped to stare at the Juárez Mountains. I felt the sweat run down my face. I kept running until I could no longer hear *Are you sure you were born in Las Cruces?* ringing in my ears.

*[handwritten: torture.]*

\* \* \*

School let out in early May. I spent the last two weeks of that month relaxing and working on some paintings. In June I got back to working on my stories. I had a working title, which I hated, but I hated it less than the actual stories I was writing. It would come to nothing; I knew it would come to nothing.

From my window I could see the freeway. It was then I realized that not a day went by when I didn't see someone running across the freeway or walking down the street looking out for someone. They were people who looked not so different from me—except that they lived their lives looking over their shoulders.

One Thursday, I saw the border patrol throw some men into their van—*[handwritten: emphasis]* throw them— as if they were born to be thrown like baseballs, like rings in a carnival ring toss, easy inanimate objects, dead bucks after a deer hunt. The illegals didn't even put up a fight. They were aliens from somewhere else, somewhere foreign, and it did not matter that the "somewhere else" was as close as an eyelash to an eye. What mattered was that someone had once drawn a line, and once drawn, that line became indelible and hard and could not be crossed.

*[handwritten left margin: great comp. tears]*

The men hung their heads so low that they almost scraped the littered asphalt. Whatever they felt, they did not show; whatever burned did not burn for an audience. I sat at my typewriter and tried to pretend I saw nothing. *What do you think happens when you peer out windows? Buy curtains.*

I didn't write the rest of the day. I kept seeing the border patrol woman against a blue sky turning green. I thought of rearranging my desk so I wouldn't be next to the window, but I thought of the mountains. No, I would keep my desk near the window, but I would look only at the mountains.

*[handwritten: as opposed to a run]*

\* \* \*

Two weeks later, I went for a walk. The stories weren't going well that day; my writing was getting worse instead of better; my characters were getting on my nerves—I didn't like them—no one else would like them either. They did not burn with anything. I hadn't show-more setting

ered, hadn't shaved, hadn't combed my hair. I threw some water on my face and walked out the door. It was summer; it was hot; it was afternoon, the time of day when everything felt as if it were on fire. The worst time of the day to take a walk. I wiped the sweat from my eyelids; it instantly reappeared. I wiped it off again, but the sweat came pouring out—a leak in the dam. Let it leak. I laughed. A hundred degrees in the middle of a desert afternoon. Laughter poured out of me as fast as my sweat. I turned the corner and headed back home. I saw the green van. It was parked right ahead of me.

A man about my height got out of the van and approached me. Another man, taller, followed him. *¿Tienes tus papeles?*[3] he asked. His gringo accent was as thick as the sweat on my skin. *ref. footnote*

"I can speak English," I said. I started to add: *I can probably speak it better than you,* but I stopped myself. No need to be aggressive, no need to get any hotter.

"Do you live in this neighborhood?"

"Yes."

"Where?"

"Down the street."

"Where down the street?"

"Are you planning on making a social visit?"

— again w/ the eta

He gave me a hard look—cold and blue—then looked at his partner. He didn't like me. I didn't care. I liked that he hated me. It made it easier.

I watched them drive away and felt as hot as the air, felt as hot as the heat that was burning away the blue in the sky. heated

There were other times when I felt watched. Sometimes, when I jogged, the green vans would slow down, eye me. I felt like prey, like a rabbit who smelled the hunter. I pretended not to notice them. I stopped pretending. I started noting their presence in our neighborhood more and more. I started growing suspicious of my own observations. Of course, they weren't everywhere. But they *were* everywhere. I had just been oblivious to their presence, had been oblivious because they had nothing to do with me; their presence had something to do with someone else. I was not a part of this. I wanted no part of it. The green cars and the green vans clashed with the purples of the Juárez Mountains. Nothing looked the same. I never talked about their presence to other people. Sometimes the topic of the *Migra*[4] would come up in conversations. I felt the burning; I felt the anger would control it. I casually referred to them as the Gestapo, the traces of rage carefully hidden from the expression on my face— and everyone would laugh. I hated them. → damn

When school started in the fall, I was stopped again. Again I had been walking home from the University. I heard the familiar question: "Where are you from?"

"Leave me alone."

"Are you a citizen of the United States?"

"Yes."

---

[3]Do you have your papers?
[4]Border patrol

*he's getting fed up.*

"Can you prove it?"

"No. No, I can't."

He looked at my clothes; jeans, tennis shoes, and a casual California shirt. He noticed my backpack full of books.

"You a student?"

I nodded and stared at him.

"There isn't any need to be unfriendly—"

"I'd like you to leave me alone."

"Just doing my job," he laughed. I didn't smile back. *Terrorists. Nazis did their jobs. Death squads in El Salvador and Guatemala did their jobs, too.* An unfair analogy. An unfair analogy? Yes, unfair. I thought it; I felt it; it was no longer my job to excuse—someone else would have to do that, someone else. The Juárez Mountains did not seem purple that fall. They no longer burned with color.

In early January I went with Michael to Juárez. Michael was from New York, and he had come to work in a home for the homeless in South El Paso. We weren't in Juárez very long—just looking around and getting gas. Gas was cheap in Juárez. On the way back, the customs officer asked us to declare our citizenship. "U.S. citizen," I said. "U.S. citizen," Michael followed. The customs officer lowered his head and poked it in the car.

"What are you bringing over?"

"Nothing."

He looked at me. "Where in the United States were you born?"

"In Las Cruces, New Mexico."

He looked at me a while longer. "Go ahead," he signaled.

*racism*

I noticed that he didn't ask Michael where he was from. But Michael had blue eyes; Michael had white skin. Michael didn't have to tell the man in the uniform where he was from.

\* \* \*

That winter, Sunset Heights seemed deserted to me. The streets were empty like the river. One morning, I was driving down Upson Street toward the University, the wind shaking the limbs of the bare trees. Nothing to shield them—unprotected by green leaves. The sun burned a dull yellow. In front of me, I noticed two border patrol officers chasing someone, though that someone was not visible. One of them put his hand out, signaling me to slow down as they ran across the street in front of my car. They were running with their billy clubs in hand. The wind blew at their backs as if to urge them on, as if to carry them.

In late January, Michael and I went to Juárez again. A friend of his was in town, and he wanted to see Juárez. We walked across the bridge, across the river, across the line into another country. It was easy. No one there to stop us. We walked the streets of Juárez, streets that had seen better years, that were tired now from the tired feet that walked them. Michael's friend wanted to know how it was that there were so many beggars. "Were there always so many? Has it always been this way?" I didn't know how it had always been. We sat in the Cathedral and in the old chapel next to it and watched people rubbing the feet of statues; when I touched

*his friend made an assumption*

a statue, it was warmer than my own hand. We walked to the marketplace and inhaled the smells. Grocery stores in the country we knew did not have such smells. On the way back we stopped in a small bar and had a beer. The beer was cold and cheap. Walking back over the bridge, we stopped at the top and looked out at the city of El Paso. "It actually looks pretty from here, doesn't it?" I said. Michael nodded. It did look pretty. We looked off to the side— down the river—and for a long time watched the people trying to get across. Michael's friend said it was like watching the *CBS Evening News*.  — horrible

As we reached the customs building, we noticed that a border patrol van pulled up behind the building where the other green cars were parked. The officers jumped out of the van and threw a handcuffed man against one of the parked cars. It looked like they were going to beat him. Two more border patrol officers pulled up in a car and jumped out to join them. One of the officers noticed we were watching. They straightened the man out and walked him inside—like gentle-men. They would have beat him. They would have beat him. But we were watching. *he hates them*

My fingers wanted to reach through the wire fence, not to touch it, not to feel it, but to break it down, to melt it down with what I did not understand. The burning was not there to be understood. Something was burning, the side of me that knew I was treated different, would always be treated different because I was born on a particular side of a fence, a fence that separated me from others, that separated me from a past, that separated me from the country of my genesis and glued me to the country I did not love because it demanded some-thing of me I could not give. Something was burning now, and if I could have grasped the source of that rage and held it in my first, I would have melted that fence. Someone built that fence; someone could tear it down. Maybe I could tear it down; maybe I was the one. Maybe then I would no longer be separated.

\* \* \*

The first day in February, I was walking to a downtown Chevron station to pick up my car. On the corner of Prospect and Upson, a green car was parked—just sitting there. A part of my landscape. I was walking on the opposite side of the street. For some reason, I knew they were going to stop me. My heart clenched like a fist; the muscles in my back knotted up. *Maybe they'll leave me alone. I should have taken a shower this morning. I should have worn a nicer sweater. I should have put on a pair of socks, worn a nicer pair of shoes. I should have cut my hair; I should have shaved . . .*

The driver rolled down his window. I saw him from the corner of my eye. He called me over to him—*whistled me over*—much like he'd call a dog. I kept walking. He whistled me over again. *Here, boy.* I stopped for a second. Only a second. I kept walking. The border patrol officer and a policeman rushed out of the car and ran toward me. I was sure they were going to tackle me, drag me to the ground, handcuff me. They stopped in front of me.

"Can I see your driver's license?" the policeman asked.

"Since when do you need a driver's license to walk down the street?" Our eyes met. "Did I do something against the law?"

The policeman was annoyed. He wanted me to be passive, to say: "Yes, sir." He wanted me to approve of his job.

"Don't you know what we do?"   *assholes!*

"Yes, I know what you do."

"Don't give me a hard time. I don't want trouble. I just want to see some identification."

I looked at him—looked, and saw what would not go away: neither him, nor his car, nor his job, nor what I knew, nor what I felt. He stared back. He hated me as much as I hated him. He saw the bulge of my cigarettes under my sweater and crumpled them.

I backed away from his touch. "I smoke. It's not good for me, but it's not against the law. Not yet, anyway. Don't touch me. I don't like that. Read me my rights, throw me in the can, or leave me alone." I smiled.

"No one's charging you with anything."

My eyes followed them as they walked back to their car. Now it was war, and *I had won this battle.* Had I won this battle? Had I won?

*     *     *

This spring morning, I sit at my desk, wait for the coffee to brew, and look out my window. This day, like every day, I look out my window. Across the street, a border patrol van stops and an officer gets out. So close I could touch him. On the freeway—this side of the river— a man is running. I put on my glasses. I am afraid he will be run over by the cars. I cheer for him. *Be careful. Don't get run over.* So close to the other side he can touch it. The border patrol officer gets out his walkie-talkie and runs toward the man who has disappeared from my view. I go and get my cup of coffee. I take a drink slowly, it mixes with yesterday's tastes in my mouth. The officer in the green uniform comes back into view. He has the man with him. He puts him in the van. I can't see the color in their eyes. I see only the green. They drive away. There is no trace that says they've been there. The mountains watch the scene and say nothing. The mountains, ablaze in the spring light, have been watching—and guarding—and keeping silent longer than I have been alive. They will continue their vigil long after I am dead.

The green vans. They are taking someone away. They are taking. Green vans. This is my home, I tell myself. But I am not sure if I want this to be my home anymore. The thought crosses my mind to walk out of my apartment without my wallet. The thought crosses my mind that maybe the *Migra* will stop me again. I will let them arrest me. I will let them warehouse me. I will let them push me in front of a judge who will look at me like he has looked at the millions before me. I will be sent back to Mexico. I will let them treat me like I am illegal. But the thoughts pass. I am not brave enough to let them do that to me.

Today, the spring winds blow outside my window. The reflections in the pane, graffiti burning questions into the glass: *Sure you were born . . . Identification . . . Do you live? . . .* The winds will unsettle the desert—cover Sunset Heights with green dust. The vans will stay in my mind forever. I cannot banish them. I cannot banish their questions: *Where are you from?* I no longer know.

*This is a true story.*

# DRAMA

*born in U.s.*

# Luis Valdez

Luis Valdez was born in 1940 to a family of migrant workers in Delano, California. He founded El Teatro Campesino (Theater of the Farmhand), a mixture of art and politics that received acclaim around the country for its grassroots activism. He has written, produced, and directed twenty dramas, beginning with *The Shrunken Head of Pancho Villa* (1963), produced while he was still a student at San Jose State College and *I Don't Have to Show You No Stinking Badges*, produced in Los Angeles in 1986. He is also a television and film director of films such as *Zoot Suit* and *La Bamba*. As the first Chicano drama to reach beyond the Chicano community, *Zoot Suit* was a breakthrough production; it played to sold-out houses for ten months, won the Los Angeles Critics Circle Award for distinguished production, and was nominated for a Golden Globe Award.

## Los Vendidos[1]

*1967-setting*

*Characters:*
Honest Sancho: *owner of models*
Secretary
Farmworker: *sombrero*
Pachuco: *knife*
Revolucionario: *sombrero, bullet belt, rifle*
Mexican-American

*Scene:* HONEST SANCHO's *Used Mexican Lot and Mexican Curio Shop. Three models are on display in* HONEST SANCHO's *shop. To the right, there is a* REVOLUCIONARIO, *complete with sombrero, carrilleras and carabina[2] 30–30. At center, on the floor, there is the* FARM-WORKER, *under a broad straw sombrero. At stage left is the* PACHUCO, *filero[3] in hand.* HONEST SANCHO *is moving among his models, dusting them off and preparing for another day of business.*

Primary works by Luis Valdez: *Luis Valdez: Early Works* (Houston: Arte Público Press, 1990); *Zoot Suit and Other Plays* (Houston: Arte Público Press, 1990).

[1]The sellouts
[2]Bullet belts and rifle
[3]Slang for knife

_Comedy_

SANCHO: Bueno, bueno, mis monos, vamos a ver a quién vendemos ahora, ¿no?[4] (_To audience._) ¡Quihúbo![5] I'm Honest Sancho and this is my shop. Antes fui contratista, pero ahora logré tener mi negocito.[6] All I need now is a customer. (_A bell rings offstage._) Ay, a customer!

SECRETARY: (_Entering._) Good morning, I'm Miss Jimenez from . . .

SANCHO: Ah, una chicana! Welcome, welcome Señorita Jiménez.

SECRETARY: (_Anglo pronunciation._) JIM-enez.

SANCHO: ¿Qué?[7]    U.S. Latino

SECRETARY: My name is Miss JIM-enez. Don't you speak English? What's wrong with you?

SANCHO: Oh, nothing, Señorita JIM-enez. I'm here to help you.

SECRETARY: That's better. As I was starting to say, I'm a secretary from Governor Reagan's office, and we're looking for a Mexican type for the administration.

SANCHO: Well, you come to the right place, lady. This is Honest Sancho's Used Mexican Lot, and we got all types here. Any particular type you want?

SECRETARY: Yes, we were looking for somebody suave . . .

SANCHO: Suave.

SECRETARY: Debonaire.

SANCHO: De buen aire.

SECRETARY: Dark.

SANCHO: Prieto.

SECRETARY: But of course, not too dark.

SANCHO: No muy prieto.

SECRETARY: Perhaps, beige.

SANCHO: Beige, just the tone. Así como cafecito con leche, ¿no?[8]

SECRETARY: One more thing. He must be hard-working.

SANCHO: That could only be one model. Step right over here to the center of the shop, lady. (_They cross to the_ FARMWORKER.) This is our standard farmworker model. As you can see, in the words of our beloved Senator George Murphy, he is "built close to the ground." Also, take special notice of his 4-ply Goodyear huaraches,[9] made from the rain tire. This wide-brimmed sombrero is an extra added feature; keeps off the sun, rain and dust.

SECRETARY: Yes, it does look durable.

SANCHO: And our farmworker model is friendly. Muy amable.[10] Watch. (_Snaps his fingers._)

FARMWORKER: (_Lifts up head._) Buenos días, señorita.[11] (_His head drops._)

SECRETARY: My, he is friendly.

---

[4]Well, well, my mannequins, let's see who we sell today, no?

[5]Hello

[6]Before I was a contractor, but now I manage to have my own small business.

[7]What?

[8]Something like coffee with milk, right?

[9]Sandals

[10]Very kind

[11]Good morning, miss

SANCHO:  Didn't I tell you? Loves his patrones![12] But his most attractive feature is that he's hard-working. Let me show you. (*Snaps fingers.* FARMWORKER *stands.*)

FARMWORKER:  ¡El jale![13] (*He begins to work.*)

SANCHO:  As you can see he is cutting grapes.

SECRETARY:  Oh, I wouldn't know.

SANCHO:  He also picks cotton. (*Snaps.* FARMWORKER *begins to pick cotton.*)

SECRETARY:  Versatile, isn't he?

SANCHO:  He also picks melons. (*Snaps.* FARMWORKER *picks melons.*) That's his slow speed for late in the season. Here's his fast speed. (*Snap.* FARMWORKER *picks faster.*)

SECRETARY:  Chihuahua . . . [14] I mean, goodness, he sure is a hardworker.

SANCHO:  (*Pulls the* FARMWORKER *to his feet.*) And that isn't the half of it. Do you see these little holes on his arms that appear to be pores? During those hot sluggish days in the field when the vines or the branches get so entangled, it's almost impossible to move, these holes emit a certain grease that allows our model to slip and slide right through the crop with no trouble at all.

SECRETARY:  Wonderful. But is he economical?

SANCHO:  Economical? Señorita, you are looking at the Volkswagen of Mexicans. Pennies a day is all it takes. One plate of beans and tortillas will keep him going all day. That, and chile. Plenty of chile. Chile jalapeños, chile verde, chile colorado.[15] But, of course, if you do give him chile, (*Snap.* FARMWORKER *turns left face. Snap.* FARMWORKER *bends over.*) then you have to change his oil filter once a week.

SECRETARY:  What about storage?

SANCHO:  No problem. You know these new farm labor camps our Honorable Governor Reagan has built out by Parlier or Raisin City? They were designed with our model in mind. Five, six, seven, even ten in one of those shacks will give you no trouble at all. You can also put him in old barns, old cars, riverbanks. You can even leave him out in the field over night with no worry!

SECRETARY:  Remarkable.

SANCHO:  And here's an added feature: every year at the end of the season, this model goes back to Mexico and doesn't return, automatically, until next Spring.

SECRETARY:  How about that. But tell me, does he speak English?

SANCHO:  Another outstanding feature is that last year this model was programmed to go out on STRIKE! (*Snap.*)

FARMWORKER:  ¡Huelga! ¡Huelga! Hermanos, sálganse de esos files.[16] (*Snap. He stops.*)

SECRETARY:  No! Oh no, we can't strike in the State Capitol.

SANCHO:  Well, he also scabs. (*Snap.*)

FARMWORKER:  Me vendo barato, ¿y qué?[17] (*Snap.*)

---

[12]Bosses
[13]The work!
[14]Darn it; literally, the name of a state in Mexico
[15]Chile peppers, green chile, red chile
[16]Strike! Strike! Brothers, come out of those fields.
[17]I sell myself cheap, so what?

*[handwritten note:]* asks the question: what makes Latinos desireable?

SECRETARY: That's much better, but you didn't answer my question. Does he speak English?

SANCHO: Bueno . . . no, pero he has other . . .

SECRETARY: No.

SANCHO: Other features.

SECRETARY: No! He just won't do!

SANCHO: Okay, okay, pues.[18] We have other models.

SECRETARY: I hope so. What we need is something a little more sophisticated.

SANCHO: Sophisti-qué?

SECRETARY: An urban model.

SANCHO: Ah, from the city! Step right back. Over here in this corner of the shop is exactly what you're looking for. Introducing our new 1969 JOHNNY PACHUCO model! This is our fast-back model. Streamlined. Built for speed, low-riding, city life. Take a look at some of these features. Mag shoes, dual exhausts, green chartruese paint-job, dark-tint windshield, a little poof on top. Let me just turn him on. (*Snap.* JOHNNY *walks to stage center with a* PACHUCO *bounce.*)

SECRETARY: What was that?

SANCHO: That, señorita, was the Chicano shuffle.

SECRETARY: Okay, what does he do?

SANCHO: Anything and everything necessary for city life. For instance, survival: he knife fights. (*Snaps.* JOHNNY *pulls out a switchblade and swings* at SECRETARY. SECRETARY *screams.*) He dances. (*Snap.*)

JOHNNY: (*Singing.*) "Angel Baby, my Angel Baby . . . " (*Snap.*)

SANCHO: And here's a feature no city model can be without. He gets arrested, but not without resisting, of course. (*Snap.*)

JOHNNY: En la madre, la placa.[19] I didn't do it! I didn't do it! (JOHNNY *turns and stands up against an imaginary wall, legs spread out, arms behind his back.*)

SECRETARY: Oh no, we can't have arrests! We must maintain law and order.

SANCHO: But he's bilingual.

SECRETARY: Bilingual?

SANCHO: Simón que yes.[20] He speaks English! Johnny, give us some English. (*Snap.*)

JOHNNY: (*Comes downstage.*) Fuck-you!

SECRETARY: (*Gasps.*) Oh! I've never been so insulted in my whole life!

SANCHO: Well, he learned it in your school.

SECRETARY: I don't care where he learned it.

SANCHO: But he's economical.

SECRETARY: Economical?

SANCHO: Nickels and dimes. You can keep Johnny running on hamburgers, Taco Bell tacos, Lucky Lager beer, Thunderbird wine, yesca[21] . . .

---

[18]Then
[19]Oh shoot, the police
[20]Of course
[21]Drugs

SECRETARY: Yesca?

SANCHO: Mota.[22]

SECRETARY: Mota?

SANCHO: Leños . . . marijuana. (*Snap.* JOHNNY *inhales on an imaginary joint.*)

SECRETARY: That's against the law!

JOHNNY: (*Big smile, holding his breath.*) Yeah.

SANCHO: He also sniffs glue. (*Snap.* JOHNNY *inhales glue, big smile.*)

JOHNNY: Tha's too much man, ése.

SECRETARY: No, Mr. Sancho, I don't think this . . .

SANCHO: Wait a minute, he has other qualities I know you'll love. For example, an inferiority complex (*Snap.*)

JOHNNY: (*To* SANCHO.) You think you're better than me, huh, ése? (*Swings switchblade.*)

SANCHO: He can also be beaten and he bruises. Cut him and he bleeds, kick him and he . . . (*He beats, bruises and kicks PACHUCO.*) Would you like to try it?

SECRETARY: Oh, I couldn't.

SANCHO: Be my guest. He's a great scape goat.

SECRETARY: No really.

SANCHO: Please.

SECRETARY: Well, all right. Just once. (*She kicks PACHUCO.*) Oh, he's so soft.

SANCHO: Wasn't that good? Try again.

SECRETARY: (*Kicks* PACHUCO.) Oh, he's so wonderful! (*She kicks him again.*)

SANCHO: Okay, that's enough, lady. You'll ruin the merchandise. Yes, our Johnny Pachuco model can give you many hours of pleasure. Why, the LAPD just bought 20 of these to train their rookie cops on. And talk about maintenance. Señorita, you are looking at an entirely self-supporting machine. You're never going to find our Johnny Pachuco model on the relief rolls. No, sir, this model knows how to liberate.

SECRETARY: Liberate?

SANCHO: He steals. (*Snap.* JOHNNY *rushes to* SECRETARY *and steals her purse.*)

JOHNNY: ¡Dame esa bolsa, vieja![23] (*He grabs the purse and runs. Snap by* SANCHO, *he stops.* SECRETARY *runs after* JOHNNY *and grabs purse away from him, kicking him as she goes.*)

SECRETARY: No, no, no! We can't have any more thieves in the State Administration. Put him back.

SANCHO: Okay, we still got other models. Come on, Johnny, we'll sell you to some old lady. (SANCHO *takes* JOHNNY *back to his place.*)

SECRETARY: Mr. Sancho, I don't think you quite understand what we need. What we need is something that will attract the women voters. Something more traditional, more romantic.

a game

---

[22]Marijuana

[23]Gimme me your purse, old woman!

SANCHO: Ah, a lover. (*He smiles meaningfully.*) Step right over here, señorita. Introducing our standard Revolucionario and/or Early California Bandit type. As you can see, he is well-built, sturdy, durable. This is the International Harvester of Mexicans.

SECRETARY: What does he do?

SANCHO: You name it, he does it. He rides horses, stays in the mountains, crosses deserts, plains, rivers, leads revolutions, follows revolutions, kills, can be killed, serves as a martyr, hero, movie star. Did I say movie star? Did you ever see Viva Zapata? Viva Villa, Villa Rides, Pancho Villa Returns, Pancho Villa Goes Back, Pancho Villa Meets Abbott and Costello?

SECRETARY: I've never seen any of those.

SANCHO: Well, he was in all of them. Listen to this. (*Snap.*)

REVOLUCIONARIO: (*Scream.*) ¡Viva Villaaaaa!

SECRETARY: That's awfully loud.

SANCHO: He has a volume control. (*He adjusts volume. Snap.*)

REVOLUCIONARIO: (*Mousey voice.*) Viva Villa.

SECRETARY: That's better.

SANCHO: And even if you didn't see him in the movies, perhaps you saw him on TV. He makes commercials. (*Snap.*)

REVOLUCIONARIO: Is there a Frito Bandito in your house?

SECRETARY: Oh yes, I've seen that one!

SANCHO: Another feature about this one is that he is economical. He runs on raw horsemeat and tequila!

SECRETARY: Isn't that rather savage?

SANCHO: Al contrario,[24] it makes him a lover. (*Snap.*)

REVOLUCIONARIO: (*To* SECRETARY.) Ay, mamasota, cochota, ven pa 'ca![25] (*He grabs* SECRETARY *and folds her back, Latin-lover style.*)

SANCHO: (*Snap.* REVOLUCIONARIO *goes back upright.*) Now wasn't that nice?

SECRETARY: Well, it was rather nice.

SANCHO: And finally, there is one outstanding feature about this model I know the ladies are going to love: he's a genuine antique! He was made in Mexico in 1910!

SECRETARY: Made in Mexico?

SANCHO: That's right. Once in Tijuana, twice in Guadalajara, three times in Cuernavaca.

SECRETARY: Mr. Sancho, I thought he was an American product.

SANCHO: No, but . . .

SECRETARY: No, I'm sorry. We can't buy anything but American made products. He just won't do.

SANCHO: But he's an antique!

---

[24]On the contrary

[25]Oh momma, sexy momma, come closer!

SECRETARY:  I don't care. You still don't understand what we need. It's true we need Mexican models, such as these, but it's more important that he be American.

SANCHO:  American?

SECRETARY:  That's right, and judging from what you've shown me, I don't think you have what we want. Well, my lunch hour's almost over, I better . . .

SANCHO:  Wait a minute! Mexican but American?

SECRETARY:  That's correct.

SANCHO:  Mexican but . . . (*A sudden flash.*) American! Yeah, I think we've got exactly what you want. He just came in today! Give me a minute. (*He exits. Talks from backstage.*) Here he is in the shop. Let me just get some papers off. There. Introducing our new 1970 Mexican-American! Tara-ra-raaaa! (SANCHO *brings out the* MEXICAN-AMERICAN *model, a clean-shaven middle class type in a business suit, with glasses.*)

SECRETARY:  (*Impressed.*) Where have you been hiding this one?

SANCHO:  He just came in this morning. Ain't he a beauty? Feast you eyes on him! Sturdy U.S. Steel frame, streamlined, modern. As a matter of fact, he is built exactly like our Anglo models, except that he comes in a variety of darker shades: naugahide, leather or leatherette.

SECRETARY:  Naugahide.

SANCHO:  Well, we'll just write that down. Yes, señorita, this model represents the apex of American engineering! He is bilingual, college educated, ambitious! Say the word "acculturate" and he accelerates. He is intelligent, well-mannered, clean. Did I say clean? (*Snap.* MEXICAN-AMERICAN *raises his arm.*) Smell.

SECRETARY:  (*Smells.*) Old Sobaco, my favorite.

SANCHO:  (*Snap.* MEXICAN-AMERICAN *turns toward* SANCHO.) Eric? (*To* SECRETARY.) We call him Eric García. (*To* ERIC.) I want you to meet Miss JIM-enez, Eric.

MEXICAN-AMERICAN:  Miss JIM-enez, I am delighted to make your acquaintance. (*He kisses her hand.*)

SECRETARY:  Oh, my, how charming!

SANCHO:  Did you feel the suction? He has seven especially engineered suction cups right behind his lips. He's a charmer all right!

SECRETARY:  How about boards, does he function on boards?

SANCHO:  You name them, he is on them. Parole boards, draft boards, school boards, taco quality control boards, surf boards, two by fours.

SECRETARY:  Does he function in politics?

SANCHO:  Señorita, you are looking at a political machine. Have you ever heard of the OEO, EOC, COD, WAR ON POVERTY? That's our model! Not only that, he makes political speeches.

SECRETARY:  May I hear one?

SANCHO:  With pleasure. (*Snap.*) Eric, give us a speech.

MEXICAN-AMERICAN:  Mr. Congressman, Mr. Chairman, members of the board, honored guests, ladies and gentlemen. (SANCHO *and* SECRETARY *applaud.*) Please, please. I come before you as a Mexican-American to tell you about the problems of the Mexican. The problems of the Mexican stem from one thing and one thing only: he's stupid. He's uneducated. He needs to stay in school. He needs to be ambitious, foward-looking, harder-working. He needs to think American, American, American, American, American! God bless America! God bless America! God bless America! (*He goes out of control.* SANCHO *snaps frantically and the* MEXICAN-AMERICAN *finally slumps forward, bending at the waist.*)

SECRETARY:  Oh my, he's patriotic too!

SANCHO:  Sí, señorita, he loves his country. Let me just make a little adjustment here. (*Stands* MEXICAN-AMERICAN *up.*)

SECRETARY:  What about upkeep? Is he economical?

SANCHO:  Well, no, I won't lie to you. The Mexican-American costs a little bit more, but you get what you pay for. He's worth every extra cent. You can keep him running on dry Martinis, Langendorf bread . . .

SECRETARY:  Apple pie?

SANCHO:  Only Mom's. Of course, he's also programmed to eat Mexican food at ceremonial functions, but I must warn you, an overdose of beans will plug up his exhaust.

SECRETARY:  Fine! There's just one more question. How much do you want for him?

SANCHO:  Well, I tell you what I'm gonna do. Today and today only, because you've been so sweet, I'm gona let you steal this model from me! I'm gonna let you drive him off the lot for the simple price of, let's see, taxes and license included, $15,000.

SECRETARY:  Fifteen thousand dollars? For a Mexican!!!!

SANCHO:  Mexican? What are you talking about? This is a Mexican-American! We had to melt down two pachucos, a farmworker and three gabachos[26] to make this model! You want quality, but you gotta pay for it! This is no cheap run-about. He's got class!

SECRETARY:  Okay, I'll take him.

SANCHO:  You will?

SECRETARY:  Here's your money.

SANCHO:  You mind if I count it?

SECRETARY:  Go right ahead.

SANCHO:  Well, you'll get your pink slip in the mail. Oh, do you want me to wrap him up for you? We have a box in the back.

SECRETARY:  No, thank you. The Governor is having a luncheon this afternoon, and we need a brown face in the crowd. How do I drive him?

SANCHO:  Just snap your fingers. He'll do anything you want. (SECRETARY *snaps.* MEXICAN-AMERICAN *steps forward.*)

MEXICAN-AMERICAN:  ¡Raza querida, vamos levantando armas para liberarnos de estos desgraciados gabachos que nos explotan! Vamos . . . [27]

SECRETARY:  What did he say?

---

[26]Anglos

[27]Dear brothers, let's raise our arms so that we can free ourselves of the wretched Anglos who abuse us. Let's . . .

SANCHO:  Something about taking up arms, killing white people, etc.

SECRETARY:  But he's not supposed to say that!

SANCHO:  Look, lady, don't blame me for bugs from the factory. He's your Mexican-American, you bought him, now drive him off the lot!

SECRETARY:  But he's broken!

SANCHO:  Try snapping another finger. (SECRETARY *snaps.* MEXICAN-AMERICAN *comes to life again.*)

MEXICAN-AMERICAN:  Esta gran humanidad ha dicho basta! ¡Y se ha puesto en marcha! ¡Basta! ¡Basta! ¡Viva la raza! ¡Viva la causa! ¡Viva la huelga! ¡Vivan los brown berets! ¡Vivan los estudiantes![28] ¡Chicano power! (*The* MEXICAN-AMERICAN *turns toward the* SECRETARY, *who gasps and backs up. He keeps turning toward the* PACHUCO, FARMWORKER *and* REVOLUCIONARIO, *snapping his fingers and turning each of them on, one by one.*)

PACHUCO:  (*Snap. To* SECRETARY.) I'm going to get you, baby! ¡Viva la raza!

FARMWORKER:  (*Snap. To* SECRETARY.) ¡Viva la huelga! ¡Viva la ¡huelga! ¡Viva la huelga!

REVOLUCIONARIO:  (*Snap. To* SECRETARY.) ¡Viva la revolución![29] (*The three models join together and advance toward the* SECRETARY, *who backs up and runs out of the shop screaming.* SANCHO *is at the other end of the shop holding his money in his hand. All freeze. After a few seconds of silence, the* PACHUCO *moves and stretches, shaking his arms and loosening up. The* FARMWORKER *and* REVOLUCIONARIO *do the same.* SANCHO *stays where he is, frozen to his spot.*)

JOHNNY:  Man, that was a long one, ése. (*Others agree with him.*)

FARMWORKER:  How did we do?

JOHNNY:  Pretty good, look at all that lana,[30] man! (*He goes over to* SANCHO *and removes the money from his hand.* SANCHO *stays where he is.*)

REVOLUCIONARIO:  En la madre, look at all the money.

JOHNNY:  We keep this up, we're going to be rich.

FARMWORKER:  They think we're machines.

REVOLUCIONARIO:  Burros.[31]

JOHNNY:  Puppets.

MEXICAN-AMERICAN:  The only thing I don't like is how come I always get to play the goddamn Mexican-American?

JOHNNY:  That's what you get for finishing high school.

FARMWORKER:  How about our wages, ése?

JOHNNY:  Here it comes right now. $3,000 for you, $3,000 for you, $3,000 for you and $3,000

---

[28]This great humanity now says stop! And it has begun to march! Stop! Stop! Hooray for our race! Hooray for our cause! Hooray for the strike! Hooray for the Brown Berets! Hooray for the students!

[29]Hooray for the revolution!

[30]Money (figuratively); wool (literally)

[31]Asses

for me. The rest we put back into the business.

MEXICAN-AMERICAN:  Too much, man. Heh, where you vatos[32] going tonight?

FARMWORKER:  I'm going over to Concha's. There's a party.

JOHNNY:  Wait a minute, vatos. What about our salesman? I think he needs an oil job.

REVOLUCIONARIO:  Leave him to me. (*The* PACHUCO, FARMWORKER *and* MEXICAN-AMER-ICAN *exit, talking loudly about their plans for the night. The* REVOLUCIONARIO *goes over to* SANCHO, *removes his derby hat and cigar, lifts him up and throws him over his shoulder.* SANCHO *hangs loose, lifeless. To audience.*) He's the best model we got! ¡Ajúa! (*Exit.*)

---

[32]Dudes/homeboys

# Exile and Immigration

The literature of exile and immigration shares this basic tenet: Latinos and Latinas who migrate to the United States do so with the intention of returning to their native homelands. Although many are never allowed to return due to the controlling governments, some make their way back, with the exception of Cubans who are still kept from the Island by Fidel Castro's government.

Both categories, seen as one in *U.S. Latino Literature Today*, part from the idea that Latinos assume, or believe, they are living in the United States just for the time being and that eventually they will return home. In this way, we can visualize and understand why literary expressions in this category are a reflection on *allá*—the home that was left behind. In the case of exile literature, there is a strong effort to influence the host country to become involved in the problems that the exile's country may be experiencing. For example, writers such as Marjorie Agosín, Alicia Partnoy, and José María Heredia write clear depictions of the problems they are facing or have faced in their countries. Their literature provides a forum for discussing venues through which the United States can become involved.

The authors' task or primary responsibility in this category is to represent or voice information that will raise awareness in the host country so that their country's problems are no longer obscured and are present in the minds of those who have the power to help. More recently, and particularly now that the Latino community is the largest minority group in the United States, this awareness is significant. Through their votes, the Latino community in the United States can demand that the U.S. government become more involved in helping people whose governments, (some Latino activists and writers contend), the U.S. helped destroy, or countries whose security, some assert, may have been compromised by U.S. involvement. Latino writers and activists are also concerned about the affects that trade agrements, such as NAFTA (North American Free Trade Agreement), may have on the citizens of their own native countries.[1]

---

[1] For more information on this topic, please refer to Juan Gonzalez's book *Harvest of Empire* (New York: Penguin, 2000).

Another role assumed by writers in this category is to send a message to compatriots about preventing acculturation, the Americanization of Latin immigrants. Immigrants and exiles believe in a return to their homeland; however, circumstances more often than not prevent the long-awaited return. Many believe that their message should be to warn those who were thinking of migrating not to do so. Their target audience is those who were about to make the trip to *El Norte*, as Alicia Alarcón does in "All I Thought About Was Disneyland." In this instance, exile and immigrant literature differ in that immigrant literature maintains a register appropriate for mass culture and not one that pertains to an elite audience. We witness an example of this when English, Spanish, and neologisms such as "jamenegs" (ham and eggs) or "tokinglish," (talk English) as well as regional dialects, appear in one text. Exiles, on the other hand, do not succumb to cultural changes; their preoccupation is with their ties to the land left behind, and they have a diminishing interest in becoming American. They are not in the United States to stay; they are here until their country changes and is liberated from whatever power or control expelled the exile. Therefore, acculturation is not a possibility for them, and it is not something that the exile community is threatened by.

Exile literature, in this respect, tries to appeal to a community that would perceive the author and his or her ideas worthy of an educated person. For that reason, in their writing, such authors respect all grammar rules and use one language to communicate their ideas: English or Spanish. Whenever a term is cited in another language, it is done with the correct spelling. This demonstrates their language/writing skills and proves that they are worthy of their readers' attention. Their target audience is any group or organization in the host country with enough power to execute changes and provide any possible aid. José María Heredia's poem, for example, "Hymn of Exile" follows a traditional format that is also concerned with a careful selection of language to entice compatriots and sympathizers to join the cry for help in Cuba's independence from Spain.

An additional strategy employed in exile and immigrant literature is the imagery of the United States as hell and the homeland as paradise. In this way, any person who comes to live in the United States is faced with all sorts of temptations that beguile him or her to lose their identity. This idea is especially useful in immigration literature, where authors and characters are almost enchanted and are not capable of abstaining from giving in to American ways. Some go to the extreme of changing their names from the traditionally Latin, such as María, to Mary to break ties with their Latino identity.[2] Authors

---

[2] A practice that was common in literary sketches (*crónicas*) published in Spanish newspapers in the United States during the early part of the twentieth century.

perceive this act as treason because those who change their names are breaking the strongest tie to their homeland; their names provide them with an identity, one that is exchanged and replaced in the United States. These ideas foster the creation of small communities such as "México de afuera," in Texas, California and Los Angeles; "Trópico en Manhattan," in New York; and "La Pequeña Habana," in Miami in which people learn to isolate their traditions, religion, and language from Americanization as well as the clear depiction of the United States as Paradise Lost or its comparison to Babel and Sion, where citizens are lost and are searching for the place they belong.

Of the many reasons for departure from the native homeland, it is probably safe to say most can be categorized as political or economic. Forced migration is a process that does not discriminate: All social classes are represented, from the elite—those who are university educated—to those who have never gone to school or had any money. Each class claims nostalgia for the homeland, especially if they have been expelled. As immigrants try to maintain their celebrations in an effort to keep their ties to their place of origin, exiles are soon disillusioned by the state of their countries. They often realize that they cannot do much to create change in their native lands; many have to go back and join battles or work on projects that aid the recreation of the country into what they envision, for example, José Martí went back to Cuba and died in a battle fighting oppression.

The characters in these works are tools that allow authors to present messages to the readers. In this way, exile literature uses heroes—epic, tragic, and classic figures, who are endowed with powers that make them superior to all—because there is an interest in establishing a clear association among those who battle for what they believe and are willing to sacrifice their lives for it, as Martí did for Cuban independence. Until the 1970s, most of the characters were men.

Immigrant literature involves characters who represent the audience: working-class men and women who are mistreated and abused by people who prey on the innocent, and provincial characters who are not accustomed to life in the United States. Pochos[3] and any character who is believed to reject and deny his or her Latino heritage are also present, as are women who are easily seduced by life in America because they can access rights and privileges that are not available in their native homeland. Such women come to be known as *Evas* or *pelonas* (Eves, short-haired women in the likes of the roaring twenties).

---

[3] Derogatory term used for people of Hispanic descent who have Americanized and can no longer speak Spanish correctly or no longer follow traditions.

The themes that surge from this literature are, in the first instance, those of the lost soul that cannot find a place in the United States, although it is forced to be here. In later literary expressions, generational conflicts lead in that families are forced to remain in the United States, which translates into having their children attend U.S. schools where they learn values that do not correspond with those of the first generation of immigrants. Therefore, lack of communication between generations occurs, and even if there were communication, there is no understanding because families—parents and children—no longer share values, and neither is willing to compromise. The same occurs culturally between recent arrivals to the United States and those who have been here longer. A lot of tension is expressed regarding what is truly Latino or Latin American and what is not. This is probably the deciding factor for many who later reclaim or claim their rights as citizens of the United States, citizens of North America. "El Súper," by Iván Acosta, portrays some of these themes and characters.

The concept of not belonging and the extent to which each community goes to abstain from Americanization make these categories significant to Latino literature in the United States because it demonstrates the process of negotiating identities in order to reclaim/claim their sense of place in America. The selections that follow demonstrate each author's efforts to present a clear message to their readers: Urge action or persuade soon-to-be migrants not to migrate. Great care was taken to create in this section a chorus of voices that speak to the experience of migrating to the United States.

# POETRY

## Marjorie Agosín

Marjorie Agosín was born in Bethesda, Maryland, to Chilean parents. She is a human-rights activist, a teacher, and a poet. She received her Ph.D. from Indiana University and has been a professor of Latin American Literature for many years at Wellesley College. Among the awards and prizes that she has received are the Jeanetta Rankin Award for human rights and the Good Neighbor Award from the Conference of Christians and Jews. She has published extensively; her works include *Conchanlí* (1981), *Zones of Pain* (1988), *Brujas y algo más/Witches and Other Things* (1984), *Women of Smoke* (1988), *Sargasso* (1993), *Hogueras/Bonfires* (1990), *Circles of Madness: Mothers of the Plaza de Mayo* (1992), and *La Felicidad/Happiness* (1993). Her writing has received critical acclaim worldwide.

## United States

*[handwritten: exile]*

United States,
I do not take your name
in vain,
nor do I accuse you for   *[handwritten: rape]*
deflowering so many stars
I only follow
your immense lonely spaces
and I understand it's not your fault
that you invented ready-made
life *[circled]*
or the golden sundowns
of Miss Monroe.   *[handwritten: tone change]*
But confess
that you enjoyed the sad sickness
of meek peoples
and you crept up to the Andes
to load up on copper, chromosomes, guns,
but thinking it all through,
I make my way down through Managua, El Salvador,
down the Avenida Providencia in Santiago de Chile
and we're all wearing cowboy boots
in a deafened dialogue of rock and roll.

*[handwritten: surprises w/ line changes]*

*(Translated by Naomi Lindstrom)*

# Claribel Alegría

Claribel Alegría was born in Estelí, Nicaragua, in 1924, to a Nicaraguan father and a Salvadoran mother. Alegría grew up in El Salvador, and, in 1943, she moved to the United States, where she graduated from George Washington University with a B.A. in phi-

Primary works by Marjorie Agosín: *An Absence of Shadows* (Fredonia: White Pine Press, 1998); *Alfareras Women in Disguise* (Falls Church: Azul Editions, 1996); *The Alphabet in my Hands* (New Brunswick: Rutgers, 2000); *Amigas: Letters of Friendship and Exile* (Austin: Univ. of Tx Press, 2001); *Brujas y algo más/Witches and Other Things* (Pittsburgh: Latin American Literary Review Press, 1984); *Felicidad* (Fredonia: White Pine Press, 1993); *Women, Gender, and Human Rights* (New Brunswick: Rutgers, 2001).

losophy and letters. She is a significant voice in the struggle for liberation in El Salvador and Central America. She is associated with the Sandinistas Liberation Front, the left-wing guerilla movement that took control of the Nicaraguan government in 1979 after the overthrow of Anastasio Somoza Debayle. She states, "In the middle 1970s, lots of people, not only from my country but throughout Latin America, were being murdered or disappeared, including some of my friends. I felt that I had a niche in my heart for each one of them, and it is because of them I called myself a cemetery." Her writing reflects the literary movement that emerged in Central America in the mid-1950s and early 1960s that came to be known as *la generación comprometida*, or "the committed generation." Aside from writing about the civil war, Alegría also writes urging women to break free from oppressive patriarchy. She has written thirteen volumes of poetry, several novels, and a collection of children's stories. *Sobrevivo*, one of her poetry books, won the prestigious Casa de las Américas Prize. *Fugues* is her most recent collection in English.

## Nocturnal Visits

I think of our anonymous boys
of our burnt-out heroes
the amputated
the cripples
those who lost both legs
both eyes
the stammering teen-agers.
At night I listen to their phantoms
shouting in my ear
shaking me out of lethargy
issuing me commands
I think of their tattered lives
of their feverish hands
reaching out to seize ours.
It's not that they're begging
they're demanding

Primary works by Claribel Alegría: *Death of Somoza* with Darwin J. Flakoll (Willimantic: Curbstone Press, 1996); *Fugues* trans. D. J. Flakoll (Willimantic: Curbstone Press, 1993); *Luisa in Realityland* trans. D. J. Flakoll (Willimantic: Curbstone Press, 1987); *Woman of the River* trans. D. J. Flakoll (Pittsburgh: Univ. of Pittsburgh Press, 1989); edited, *On the Front Line: Guerrilla Poems* trans. D. J. Flakoll (Willimantic: Curbstone Press, 1989); *Saudade/Sorrow* trans. Carolyn Forché (Willimantic: Curbstone Press, 1999); *Umbrales/Thresholds: Poems* trans. D. J. Flakoll (Willimantic: Curbstone Press, 1996).

they've earned the right to order us
to break up our sleep
to come awake
to shake off once and for all
this lassitude.

*(Translated by Darwin J. Flakoll)*

# Richard Blanco

Richard Blanco was "made in Cuba, assembled in Spain, and imported to the United States," according to the biography included in his first book of poetry, *City of a Hundred Fires*. He has a diverse resume that includes stints as a professional engineer, translator, furniture designer, YMCA volunteer, underwater photographer, bongo player, and salsa dancer. He has been featured as a guest poet on the National Public Radio's *All Things Considered*. Blanco is characterized as builder of poems and bridges, since he holds degrees in engineering and creative writing from Florida International University. Blanco lives in Miami, where he works as a consultant engineer while he writes.

## América

### I.

Although Tía Miriam boasted she discovered
at least half a dozen uses for peanut butter—
topping for guava shells in syrup,
butter substitute for Cuban toast,
hair conditioner and relaxer—
Mamá never knew what to make
of the monthly five-pound jars
handed out by the immigration department
until my friend, Jeff, mentioned jelly.

---

Primary work by Richard Blanco: *City of a Hundred Fires* (Pittsburgh: Univ. of Pittsburgh Press, 1998).

## II.

There was always pork though,
for every birthday and wedding,
whole ones on Christmas and New Year's Eve,
even on Thanksgiving day—pork,
fried, broiled, or crispy skin roasted—
as well as cauldrons of black beans,
fried plantain chips, and yuca con mojito.[1]
These items required a special visit
to Antonio's Mercado on the corner of Eighth Street
where men in guayaberas[2] stood in senate
blaming Kennedy for everything—"¡Ese hijo de puta!"[3]
the bile of Cuban coffee and cigar residue
filling the creases of their wrinkled lips;
clinging to one another's lies of lost wealth,
ashamed and empty as hollow trees.

## III.

By seven I had grown suspicious—we were still here.
Overheard conversations about returning
had grown wistful and less frequent.
I spoke English; my parents didn't.
We didn't live in a two-story house
with a maid or a wood-panel station wagon
nor vacation camping in Colorado.
None of the girls had hair of gold;
none of my brothers or cousins
were named Greg, Peter, or Marcia;
we were not the Brady Bunch.
None of the black and white characters
on Donna Reed or on the Dick Van Dyke Show
were named Guadalupe, Lázaro, or Mercedes.
Patty Duke's family wasn't like us either—
they didn't have pork on Thanksgiving,
they ate turkey with cranberry sauce;
they didn't have yuca, they had yams
like the dittos of Pilgrims I colored in class.

---

[1]Yucca with seasoning
[2]Short-sleeved shirts common in the Caribbean
[3]That son of a bitch!

## IV.

A week before Thanksgiving
I explained to my abuelita[4]
about the Indians and the Mayflower,
how Lincoln set the slaves free;
I explained to my parents about
the purple mountain's majesty,
"one if by land, two if by sea,"
the cherry tree, the tea party,
the amber waves of grain,
the "masses yearning to be free,"
liberty and justice for all, until
finally they agreed:
this Thanksgiving we would have turkey,
as well as pork.

## V.

Abuelita prepared the poor fowl
as if committing an act of treason,
faking her enthusiasm for my sake.
Mamá set a frozen pumpkin pie in the oven
and prepared candied yams following instructions
I translated from the marshmallow bag.
The table was arrayed with gladiolas,
the plattered turkey loomed at the center
on plastic silver from Woolworth's.
Everyone sat in green velvet chairs
we had upholstered with clear vinyl,
except Tío Carlos and Toti, seated
in the folding chairs from the Salvation Army.
I uttered a bilingual blessing
and the turkey was passed around
like a game of Russian Roulette.
"DRY," Tío Berto complained, and proceeded
to drown the lean slices with pork fat drippings
and cranberry jelly—"esa mierda roja,"[5] he called it.
Faces fell when Mamá presented her ochre pie—

[4]Grandma
[5]That red shit

pumpkin was a home remedy for ulcers, not a dessert.
Tía María made three rounds of Cuban coffee
then Abuelo[6] and Pepe cleared the living room furniture,
put on a Celia Cruz LP and the entire family
began to merengue over the linoleum of our apartment,
sweating rum and coffee until they remembered—
it was 1970 and 46 degrees—
in América.
After repositioning the furniture,
an appropriate darkness filled the room.
Tío Berto was the last to leave.

---

[6]Grandfather

# Tomás Borge

Tomás Borge is known worldwide as a political leader; he is a former Minister of the Interior of Nicaragua, where he directed the security forces that subverted the counter-revolutionaries' battle plans in the cities. He is the only surviving founder of the FSLN, the Sandinista National Liberation Front. An anthology of essays, poems, and stories, *Have You Seen a Red Curtain in My Weary Chamber?* was the first publication of his US writings. In 1990 he published his autobiography, *The Patient Impatience.*

## Nicaragua

I love you from here, volcano
cracked vase of clay
canoe amidst flesh-eating fish

From my loneliness I love you
whirlwind, mirror
bashed in the valley of thunder

I love the lineal thighs
of your eyes baring teeth

---

Primary works by Tomás Borge: *Have You Seen a Red Curtain in My Weary Chamber?* (Willimantic: Curbstone Press, 1989); *Women and the Nicaraguan Revolution* (Atlanta: Pathfinder Press, 1991); *Nicaragua: The Sandinista People Revolution* (Atlanta: Pathfinder Press, 1985); *The Patient Impatience: From Boyhood to Guerilla: A Personal Narrative of Nicaragua's Struggle for Liberation* (Willimantic: Curbstone Press, 1992).

weeping pyrotechnics
I love your poets, famous and sad
your joyful dead
who refuse to die.

*(Translated by Russell Bartley, Kent Johnson and Sylvia Yoneda)*

# Pablo Antonio Cuadra

Pablo Antonio Cuadra was born in Managua, Nicaragua, in 1912 and died in 2002. He was born into a home filled with politics and literature. Cuadra participated in the avant-garde movement in Nicaragua, working on political and historic cultural issues. *Poemas nicaragüenses* were written between 1930 and 1933 and published in Chile in 1934. His works are testaments to his love for his homeland and for Mexico, where he worked late in his life, and his appreciation and passion for other countries in America and Spain. He had the ability to make poetry and reality a theme that could be shared by all.

## The Campesinos[1] Go Down the Roads

Two by two,
ten by ten,
by hundreds
and thousands,
the campesinos go barefoot
with their bedrolls and their rifles.

Two by two the sons have left,
hundreds of mothers have cried,
thousands of men have fallen
and turned to dust forever
dreaming on their bedrolls
about the life that was their rifle.

The abandoned ranch,
the lonely fields of corn,
the fields of beans destroyed by fire.

---

Primary works by Pablo Antonio Cuadra: *The Birth of the Sun: Selected Poems, 1935–1985* (Greensboro: Unicorn Press, 1987); *Songs of Cifar and the Sweet Sea: Selections from the* Songs of Cifar, *1967–1977* (New York: Columbia UP, 1979).

[1]Farm workers

The birds flying over mute stalks
and the heart crying
its naked tears.

Two by two,
ten by ten,
by hundreds and thousands
the campesinos are leaving
barefoot with their bedrolls and their rifles.

Two by two,
ten by ten,
by hundreds
and thousands
the campesinos go down the roads
to fight the civil war!

# Martín Espada  / *Puerto Rican*

Martín Espada was born in Brooklyn, New York, in 1957. He is the author of several books
of poems, including *The Immigrant Iceboy's Bolero*, *Trumpets from the Islands of their Evic-
tion*, *Rebellion Is the Circle of Lover's Hands/Rebelión es el giro de manos del amante*, and *City
of Coughing and Dead Radiators*. He has received many awards, including two National
Endowment for the Arts (NEA) fellowships, a Massachusetts Artist Fellowship, and the
PEN/Revson Fellowship, as well as the Paterson Poetry Prize for *Rebellion Is the Circle of
Lover's Hands*. He worked as a tenant lawyer for six years, but he is currently a professor of
English at the University of Massachusetts at Amherst.

## Federico's Ghost

The story is
that whole families of fruitpickers
still crept between the furrows
of the field at dusk,
when for reasons of whiskey or whatever
the cropduster plane sprayed anyway,
floating a pesticide drizzle

Primary works by Martín Espada: *The Immigrant Iceboy's Bolero* (Maplewood: Waterfont Press, 1986); *Trumpets from the Islands of their
Eviction* (Tempe: Bilingual Press, 1994); *Rebellion Is the Circle of Lover's Hards/Rebelión es el giro de manos del amante* (Willimantic:
Curbstone Press, 1990); *City of Coughing and Dead Radiators* (New York: W. W. Norton, 1993); *Alabanta: New and Selected Poems,
1982–2002* (New York: W.W. Norton, 2003).

over the pickers
who thrashed like dark birds
in a glistening white net,
except for Federico,
a skinny boy who stood apart
in his own green row,
and, knowing the pilot
would not understand in Spanish
that he was the son of a whore,
instead jerked his arm
and thrust an obscene finger.

The pilot understood.
He circled the plane and sprayed again,
watching a fine gauze of poison
drift over the brown bodies
that cowered and scurried on the ground,
and aiming for Federico,
leaving the skin beneath his shirt
wet and blistered,
but still pumping his finger at the sky.

After Federico died,
rumors at the labor camp
told of tomatoes picked and smashed at night,
growers muttering of vandal children
or communists in camp,
first threatening to call Immigration,
then promising every Sunday off
if only the smashing of tomatoes would stop.

Still tomatoes were picked and squashed
in the dark,
and the old women in camp
said it was Federico,
laboring after sundown
to cool the burns on his arms,
flinging tomatoes
at the cropduster
that hummed like a mosquito
lost in his ear,
and kept his soul awake.

## Revolutionary Spanish Lesson

*[handwritten: retaliation/revenge poem]*

Whenever my name
is mispronounced,
I want to buy a toy pistol,
put on dark sunglasses,
push my beret to an angle,   *[handwritten: ← Latino gangster]*
comb my beard to a point,
hijack a busload
of Republican tourists
from Wisconsin,
force them to chant
anti-American slogans
in Spanish,
and wait
for the bilingual SWAT team
to helicopter overhead,
begging me
to be reasonable

*[handwritten: enjambed]*

*[handwritten: Marxism b/c taking power back]*

*[handwritten: no ending punctuation]*

*[handwritten: imagery]*

*[handwritten: verbs]*

# Isaac Goldemberg

Isaac Goldemberg was born in Chepén, Perú, in 1945. He emigrated to the United States in 1964 and returned to Perú to write his first novel, *La vida a plazos de don Jacobo Lerner*. The uncomfortable reality of his Peruvian-Jewish experience is present in his writing. He evidences a search for identity and meaning in an effort to synthesize his cultural and experiential parts—the Peruvian, the Jew, the immigrant to the United States. He currently teaches at Eugenio María de Hostos Community College in CUNY.

## Self-Portrait

I and my Jew on my back
observing ourselves from behind
and yet
ear to ear

---

Primary works by Isaac Goldemberg: *El nombre del padre/The Name of the Father* (Madrid: Alfaguara, 2002). *The Fragmented Life of Don Jacobo Lerner*, trans. Robert S. Piccioto (New York: Persea, 1976), *Hombre de paso/Just Passing Through* (Hanover, N.H.: Ediciones del Norte, 1981), *La vida al contado* (Lima: Lluvia Editores, 1989).

he, imperturbable
disdainful of death, one would say
tolling the bell against time
on his mission of roaming
through the abyss of history
he, his youthful countenance
lagging behind in mirrors
tattooed from sole to soul
I and my Jew on my back
indelibly marked up to my crooked nose
that we are wearing out
smelling the Kingdom of this Earth

# Victor Montejo

Victor Montejo was born in 1952 of Jakaltek Mayan parents in rural Guatemala. He attended Maryknoll school, where he learned Spanish and earned a teaching degree. He is the author of *The Bird Who Cleans the World,* one of the first collections of its type to be published in the United States. Currently he is a professor of anthropology at the University of California-Davis.

## The Dog

Near the military barracks
a stray dog was shot;
it was a skinny cur, flea-ridden
which the military commanders

Primary works by Victor Montejo: *The Bird who Cleans the World and Other Mayan Fables* trans. Wallace Kaufman (Willimantic: Curbstone Press, 1991); *Popol Vuh: A Sacred Book* trans. David Unger (Toronto: Douglas & McIntyre, 1999); *Sculpted stones/Piedras labradas* trans. Victor Perera (Willimantic: Curbstone Press, 1995); *Testimony: Death of a Guatemalan Village* trans. Victor Perera (Willimantic: Curbstone Press, 1987); *Voices from Exile: Violence and Survival in Modern Maya History* (Norman: U of OK, 1999).

believed to be a defiant guerrilla
who changed into a dog
and urinated on their tents.

People say in the countryside
that the soldiers kill dogs
because they are sure the guerrillas
with their "nahuals" can turn themselves
into sticks, stones, or dogs;
and that is why so few guerrillas
are ever killed in combat.

Poor miserable dogs
who suffer the fate of their owners,
who a eat a tortilla or two a day
and who are beaten to a pulp
if they wander into the kitchen
overcome by hunger.
Not even in dreams do they ever eat meat,
like the fat foreign dogs do!

Wretched dog riddled with bullets,
he was not a top guerrilla commander,
he was just a dog, a stray mongrel
like many others who walk the dusty streets
and who without evil intent
stop to raise a leg and urinate
on the barracks posts of the frightened colonels.

*(Translated by Victor Perera)*

# José María Heredia

José María Heredia was born in Santiago de Cuba in 1803. In 1823, a month before his twentieth birthday, after participating in revolutionary activities, he was forced to flee to the United States. He lived in New York, Connecticut near New Haven, and Philadelphia for two years before departing to Mexico. Heredia is a key figure in the establishment of the literary exile community of the 1820s and 1830s. During this time he wrote patriotic poetry, a diary, and founded a newspaper.

Like José Martí, for political reasons, Heredia spent little of his adult life in his beloved Cuba. He went back there in 1836, but the following year he returned to Toluca, Mexico, where he died in 1839.

## Hymn of the Exile (Himno del desterrado)

The sun is shining and the serene waves
Are cut by the triumphant prow,
and a deep trail of brilliant foam
the ship leaves in its wake.
Land-ho! is the cry; anxious, we look
at the border of the calm horizon
and in the distance discover a mountain . . .
I know it . . . Cry, my sad eyes!

It is the Pan . . . In its outskirts breathe
the kindest and most constant friend,
the beloved women of my life, my lover . . .
What treasures of love have I there!
And more distant, my sweet sisters
and my mother, my beloved mother,
by silence and sorrow surrounded,
consumes her life crying for me.

Cuba, Cuba, what life you gave me,
sweet land of light and beauty,
how many dreams of fate and glory
have I tied to your happy soil!
I look at you again . . . ! How heavily
the harshness of my luck weighs upon me!
Oppression threatens me with death
in the fields where to the world I was born.

What does it matter if the tyrant thunders?
Poor yes, but free am I,

Primary works by José María Heredia: *Poesías completas* (Miami: Ediciones Universal, 1970); *El laúd del desterrado*, ed. Matías Montes-Huido-bro (Houston: Arte Público Press, 1995).

only the soul of the soul is the center:
what is gold without glory or peace?
Although I am banished and forced to
        wander,
and severe destiny weighs upon me,
for the scepter of the Iberian despot
I would not trade my fate.

Since I lost the vision of joy,
give me, oh glory, your divine breath.
Dare I curse my destiny,
when I can still conquer or die?
There must still be hearts in Cuba
that envy my martyr's fate,
and prefer a splendid death
to their bitter, difficult life.

Surrounded by a sea of evils,
the patriot is immutable and steadfast,
and either meditates upon the future,
or spends his time in contemplation of
        the past.
Like the Andes, inundated with light,
serenity, in excelsis above the clouds.
listening to thunder and lightning
loudly resound at his feet.

Sweet Cuba! on your breast are seen
in the highest and most profound degree,
the beauties of the physical world,
the horrors of the moral world.
Heaven made you earth's fairest flower,
but you ignored your strength and destiny,
and by adoring the despot of Spain,
you learned to worship the blood-demon
        of evil.

What does it matter now that, you reach out
        to heaven
dressed in your verdure of perennial green,
or that you offer your palm-crowded forehead
to the ardent kisses of the sea.

if the clamor of the insolent tyrant,
the pitiful groan of the slave,
and the crack of the terrible whip
only resound on your plains?

Opressed by the weight of insolent vice,
virtue falters and faints,
and the law is sold for gold,
and power is at the service of crime,
and a thousand fools, who believe
        themselves great
because they have purchased honors from
        the Crown
idolize the tyrant, and prostrate themselves
before the sacrilegious throne.

Let life's very breath oppose the abuse
        of power,
and death avenge death;
constancy determines fate,
and he who knows how to die, conquers.
Let us weave a glorious name
for all the fleeing centuries:
let us raise our eyes to heaven,
and to the years that have yet to come.

It is worthier to present
a fearless chest to the enemy's sword,
than to languish in pain on our deathbed
and a thousand deaths suffer in dying.
May glory in battle foster
the ardor of the loyal patriot,
and circle with a brilliant halo
the happy moment of his death.

You shrink at blood . . . ? In battle
it is better spilt in torrents
than hauled in torpid canals
amid vices, agonies and horror.
What do you have . . . ? Not even a safe
        sepulcher
in that unhappy Cuban soil!

Doesn't our blood serve the tyrant
to fertilize the soil of Spain?

If it is true that people cannot
exist but in hardened chains,
and that a ferocious heaven condemns
    them
to ignominy and eternal oppression,
then my heart abjures the fatal truth,
the melancholy horror,
to pursue the sublime lunacy
of Washington and Brutus and Cato.

Cuba! At last you'll see yourself free and
    pure
like the air of light that you breathe,
like the boiling waves you watch
kiss the sand on your shores.
Although vile traitors serve
the tyrant, rage is useless;
it is not in vain that 'twixt Cuba and Spain
the broad sea tends its waves.

# Gustavo Pérez Firmat

Gustavo Pérez Firmat was born in Havana, Cuba, in 1949. He and his family left Cuba in 1960, when he was eleven. Bilingualism is a constant in his writing, poetry, prose, and literary criticism, as is biculturalism, primarily in a Cuban American context. Through his writing, Pérez Firmat discusses the problems that immigrants and exiles face as they try to survive "life on the hyphen."

## Bilingual Blues

Soy un ajiaco de contradicciones.[1]
I have mixed feelings about everything.

---

Primary works by Gustavo Pérez Firmat: *Tongue Ties: Logo: Eroticism in Anglo-Hispanic Literature* (New York: Palgrave Macmillan, 2003); *Life on the Hyphen: The Cuban-American Way* (Austin: University of Texas Press, 1994); *Next Year in Cuba: A Cuban's Coming of Age in America* (New York: Doubleday, 1995); *Anything But Love: A Novel* (Houston: Arte Público Press, 2000).

[1] I am a combination of contradictions

Name your tema,[2] I'll hedge;
name your cerca,[3] I'll straddle it
like a cubano.[4]

I have mixed feelings about everything.
Soy un ajiaco de contradicciones.   *rep.*
Vexed, hexed, complexed,
hyphenated, oxygenated, illegally alienated,
psycho soy, cantando voy:[5]
You say tomato,
I say tu madre;[6]
You say potato,
I say Pototo.
Let's call the hole
un hueco,[7] the thing
a cosa,[8] and if the cosa goes into the hueco,
consider yourself en casa,[9]
consider yourself part of the family.

Soy un ajiaco de contradicciones,   *humor*
un potaje de paradojas:[10]
a little square from Rubik's Cuba
que nadie nunca acoplará.[11]
(Cha-cha-chá.)

---

[2]Theme
[3]Fence
[4]Cuban male
[5]I am psycho, singing I go
[6]Your mother
[7]A hole
[8]A thing
[9]At home
[10]A jumble of paradoxes
[11]That no one will ever set in place

# Salomón de la Selva

Salomón de la Selva was born in Nicaragua in 1893. He left his home and family when he was eleven with a scholarship to study in the United States. He began teaching Spanish and French at Williams College in Massachusetts in 1916 and became a member of the

Northeastern literati. He loved the United States, despite his being torn by US interventions in his homeland, and he hoped to enlist in the US Army during World War I; however, he was not allowed to do so, because he was not a citizen of the United States, and he would not renounce his Nicaraguan citizenship. At that time, he wrote the first of a number of books, *Tropical Town and Other Poems* (1918). Shortly thereafter, de la Selva left to join the British Army. After the war, he returned to Nicaragua, where he became an important literary figure.

## A Song for Wall Street   — protest

In Nicaragua, my Nicaragua,
    What can you buy for a penny there?—
A basketful of apricots,                      exaggeration
    A water jug of earthenware,
A rosary of coral beads
    And a priest's prayer.

And for two pennies? For two new pennies?—          nostalgia
    The strangest music ever heard              — apricots
All from the brittle little throat              — bird
    Of a clay bird,                             — river
And, for good measure, we will give you
    A patriot's word.

And for a nickel? A bright white nickel?—
    It's lots of land a man can buy,
A golden mine that's long and deep,
    A forest growing high,
And a little house with a red roof
    And a river passing by.

But for your dollar, your dirty dollar,
    Your greenish leprosy,          greed
It's only hatred you shall get
    From all my folks and me;
So keep your dollar where it belongs
    And let us be!

Primary works by Salomón de la Selva: *Tropical Town and Other Stories* (Houston: Arte Público Press, 1999); *Antología poética* (Managua: Editora Mundial, 1969).

# PROSE

## Alicia Alarcón — Mexican

Alicia Alarcón was born in Jacotepec, Mexico. Her parents moved the family to Mexicali in search of better opportunities for the children when Alarcón was in grade school. Alarcón has worked as a journalist with *La Opinión*, Univisión, and Radio CNN in Spanish in Los Angeles. She currently works as a radio broadcaster for Radio Única in Los Angeles, where she hosts a program for Spanish-speaking immigrants. Her collection of testimonials, *La Migra me hizo los mandados*, was published in 2002; in it, she presents the stories of twenty-nine people who made it across the Rio Grande into the United States after long days of sacrifice and fright.

## All I Thought about Was Disneyland

It's a small world after all
It's a small world after all
It's a small world after all
It's a smaaall, smaaall wooorld!

They dragged him from his house. The boy cried. His bare feet made S's on the ground. His mother called out for help but no one came to her aid. "Ay! Ay! They're taking my son! They're going to kill him! For the love of God, just let him go!"

Without letting go of the young boy, one of the two officials responded to her with indifference, "It's the law. He must present himself for military service."

"But, sir, he's only twelve years old! He's still a boy!"

"He'll be a man soon enough, ma'am," replied one of the officials. They stopped in front of an armored truck. One of them opened the backdoor and, like a sack of potatoes, they threw the young man inside.

"Murderers! Swine! They're taking my son off to his death!" Like a banshee, Doña Regina, my neighbor from across the street, ran after the truck as it turned the corner.

That was the day when my mother made the decision to leave El Salvador along with my seventeen-year-old brother. Two months had gone by since then. The situation grew worse. The clashes between the army and the guerilla soldiers had become more frequent.

I was one year away from finishing high school. One day I was a student and the next, in my mother's absence, I had become the woman of the house, at eighteen years of age. I had to cook, clean, iron and attend to my dad and my five year-old little sister.

\* \* \*

Primary works by Alicia Alarcón: *La Migra me hizo los mandados* (Houston: Arte Público Press, 2002); *The Border Patrol Ate My Dust* (Houston: Arte Público Press, 2004).

When my father broke the news to my little sister, her eyes opened wide. Her cheeks blushed red and she began to jump for joy. Her dreams were coming true. "You and your sister are going to Disneyland." My father's eyes sparkled, and he smiled as if convinced that we were going to meet Pluto and Mickey Mouse.

My little sister couldn't stop laughing. I imagined her in Disneyland, scanning her eyes over the figures of Snow White and the Seven Dwarves. Trembling with fits of joy when meeting with Mimi and Pocahontas. Television had been responsible for convincing us that Disneyland was a magical paradise.

My father tried to convince me that I needed to leave El Salvador. "Look," he told me. "Remember how they dragged away Doña Regina's son? You know that they would have come for your brother, too. Go, take your little sister with you. It's too dangerous for you two here," he said with a calculating voice.

I couldn't sleep that night. I went out onto the patio of the house with only my nightshirt on. The moon illuminated the passageway and the ferns hanging from the walls. I breathed in the fragrance of the geraniums, roses and spikenards. At the end of the patio, there were two izotes, whose white flowers scrambled with eggs gave us something to eat in August. It was my mom's favorite little plant. Would there be any izotes in the United States?

I was a year away from graduating from high school and entering into the university. The violence in El Salvador couldn't go on forever. The end must be near. It was a nation that had been bombarded, broken-down, divided, treaded upon, but populated by people who tried to be keep happy in the middle of so much suffering. Who was going to care for the geraniums?

My father was a merchant and, during the week, he traveled to neighboring towns to purchase toys and clothes. On one of those business trips, he disappeared for a number of days. When he returned, he wasn't the same. At night, he was terrorized with nightmares. He showed up barefoot and without a shirt on. He had dried, coagulated blood clots stuck to his temples. He had lost many teeth in a week. His arms and legs were so purple it was as if someone had beaten him mercilessly. His body was full of bruises, and it appeared as if two bracelets had been branded onto his wrists with a hot iron. He spent days in silence but, at night, bits and pieces of what had happened to him escaped from his damaged throat.

"Talk, you son of a bitch! When did you get in from Cuba?"

I would place coldwater compresses on him during his bouts with delirium. I imagined the sinister torturer who interrogated him. "How many of them are there? What's their address?" I thought about his brutal beating. His body hanging from the ceiling, his wrists bound in handcuffs. "Talk, you son of a bitch, or you'll die in here. Where do they keep their weapons?" My father was very close to being one of the thousands of missing persons. Only once did he explain how he saved himself.

"They threw me out thinking that I was dead. They stole all of my merchandise." That was the reason why he had decided to send us to the United States.

"We're going to go to Disneyland! Yippieee!" The memory of my little sister's cries of joy stirred me from my thoughts.

It isn't easy to say goodbye to your country, much less to leave a father who had aged ten years in a week. I was encouraged by the promise that we would all soon be reunited. The farewell was brief. My little sister, excited to see Disneyland, quickly said goodbye. My father took us to the house of the man with whom we would travel. He was a short, thin dark-skinned man with his head mostly shaved. There were many other people there. He gave us instructions about what we should say in case they stopped us along the way. "Tell them that you came on your own. And when you get off the plane, don't say anything to anyone. Is that clear?" he directed his words to me.

"Yes, sir," I replied.

The airport in Tijuana seemed very small to me. For being such a famous city, every-thing looked so crowded. The short, dark-skinned man took all of us to a room in a nearby hotel. There, we suffered our first deception. The man opened the door and the smell of caca and peepee almost made me want to throw up. The worst of all was that they had charged us extra money for the quality of the room. He left us all there. Locked up, crowded. Practi-cally sticking to each other. I smiled at my little sister who looked at me with her very big, and very frightened eyes. "From here, they're going to come and take us to Disneyland."

Hours went by, long hours full of anguish and anxiety. I peeked out the window. I could make out the hotel marquee: Hotel Catalina. It was beginning to get dark when another man, who was younger than the first but had some gray hair around his temples and his hair almost down to his shoulders, appeared. His gaze left me petrified. He had the look of a lecherous animal. He took us to a house. It smelled just as bad as, or maybe even worse than, the hotel room. It was an ugly, abandoned house, very close to the fence separating Mexico from the United States. We stayed there for the rest of the night. The man with gray hair left then came back with some torta[1] sand-wiches that had more chile on them than anything else. My little sister ate it without complain-ing. All that I had in my stomach were the candy and nuts that they had given us on the plane.

The noises from the street passed through the cracks in the really ugly house. Howling dogs and wailing police sirens sounded like they were very close. My blood began to race through my veins. I propped myself up against the wall and sat my little sister on my lap. I dozed all night long. I saw myself among the geraniums and the spikenards in my house in El Salvador. The ring of ferns covering my shoulders. My battered father, treating his injuries, illuminated by the round, milky moon. I hadn't left El Salvador. I was in my bed, preparing myself to enter the university. This wasn't happening.

I opened my eyes. My little sister was asleep. My legs had gone numb. I looked at her. Her curls fell onto her forehead. The red lath that held her hair in place this morning had now fallen onto her shoulders. A shout startled her. Two figures in the doorway. One of them was coming in our direction. "C'mon, you bunch of lazy bums, wake up," he said with indifference. There was no emotion in his voice. I could make him out better. Where there wasn't gray, his hair was dark brown, his eyes very black with very long eyelashes. Thin lips, he wouldn't stop staring at me.

The man who had been with us since El Salvador was also looking at me. As I woke up my little sister, he approached me. He sat on an imaginary bench with his elbows on top of his knees. "Stay by my side at all times." He spoke in a gentle, paternal tone.

---

[1]Mexican sandwiches

It was starting to get dark when we left the house. How ugly! They took us to this far off place. It was like an open field, but there weren't any trees. They made us walk toward the mountains. I had never walked so much in my life. I worked hard to keep myself close to the man who had spoken to us with such a fatherly voice. We had been walking for a number of hours. The swelling on my feet demonstrated that it must have been many hours.

Out of the shadows, a group of motorcyclists jumped out and surrounded us. It was a large circle. The lights from the motorcycle riders blinded us momentarily: zzzooooommmm, zzzzooooommmm. The circle closed around us. They looked like rabid dogs circling their prey. They drove their motorcycles with dexterity. They dodged the shrubs with precision. My little sister clung onto my legs. Who were those men with hate in their eyes? Their clothing was just like in the movies. Black jackets, black gloves that showed their naked fingers. I looked all around. It was as if we had climbed to the top of the mountain. The tension was growing. The one on the lead motorcycle said something to our "guides." Without delay, the younger one handed him a paper bag. Without turning off his motorcycle, he made a sign and they all returned to the shadows from whence they came. Everything happened so fast that I still wonder if it all wasn't just a dream.

We crossed a ravine when I felt the hand of the man with graying hair on my little sister's shoulder. I looked at him surprised. He apologized saying that he just wanted to help me with my little sister. I hesitated before letting her go. It was his first friendly gesture toward me. He hugged my little sister. I walked along next to her, holding her hand. Forcefully, the man panted and stared at me in a strange manner. A cold sweat began to run down my spine. The hike became harder and longer. I asked him to give her back to me. I was going to take her by the hand. I had her next to me when somebody yelled, "The Border Patrol!"

I felt my blood race through my veins. Everyone took off running. Without letting go of my little sister's hand, I hid behind some shrubs. A shadow approached and I reached for my little sister. I thought I was going to go crazy. When I came out, I couldn't see her anywhere. Twenty minutes went by. They were the longest twenty minutes of my life. The immigration officers hadn't seen us. Everyone was coming out from their hiding places except for the man who had helped me with my little sister. I was about to scream when he came out from some shrubs with her. I embraced her and we both started to cry. At that moment, the "coyote"[2] with black eyes and graying hair told the man who had taken us out of El Salvador, "The young lady and the little girl are coming with me."

I peed on myself I was so scared. There were thirty of us in the group.

"They're coming with me, right?"

I went silent.

"The only person who's going to go with you is your fucking mama," the other one replied.

Upon hearing this, the Mexican coyote let loose on the Salvadoran and whacked him with a punch. He fell on his back. I felt a pit in my stomach. The Salvadoran coyote got back

---

[2]Illegal alien smuggler

to his feet and went after him with such rage that the Mexican coyote screamed, "Chill out, dumb ass, because if you don't, you can go to hell!"

"I guess we can go together," replied the Salvadoran.

The two looked at each other like rabid dogs. They exchanged blows. Finally, the Mexican coyote said, "You can just die here, for all I care. But I'm warning you: I'm not going to help them. You have five minutes to make it across that open space and reach the other side of the highway." His black eyes had swollen up on him from the beating.

We waited for the sign for all of us to start running. When the man who had defended us wasn't looking, the Mexican coyote drew his rough face up to mine. "You and your little sister aren't going to make it." My pulse accelerated. At the top of his voice, the coyote yelled, "Now run!"

We all started to run. I wouldn't let go of my little sister's hand. It all turned into a race full of obstacles, declines, narrow passageways, until we came to an esplanade with few trees. No way! Everything was so ugly! There, they ordered us to lie down on the ground. My little sister and I shook from head to toe. After quite a while, the sound of a car could be heard. It was a van. They shoved us inside in such a hurry that they threw my little sister inside as if she was some kind of inanimate object. We were sitting one on top of the other. They took us to a house in San Diego. I realized that all of the houses that the coyotes used had the same smell: urine, excrement and vomit. They told us to sleep on the floor. The Mexican coyote stared at me and licked his lips with a mocking smile. There were two other women waiting in that house. Now there were more than thirty of us.

Sitting down, with my back straight, sore, up against the wall, with my little sister sleeping on top of my legs, I closed my eyes. I saw the volcanoes, the passageway full of ferns and I breathed in the fragrance of the spikenards. The man who had taken care of us noticed that I was awake. He sat down beside me. He spoke to me quietly, "Remember, your father sent you here so that you could have a better life. And your little sister, too. Very early tomorrow morning we leave for Los Angeles. The hard part is all over." I thanked him for having looked after us. He told me about all of the nice things in the United States. "People obey the law here, my dear. For running a stop sign, they fine you about the equivalent of 500 colones."

Days later we were greeted by cloudy skies in Los Angeles. My little sister, disconcerted, asked, "Are we in Disneyland yet?"

# Julia Alvarez

Julia Alvarez was born in New York City in 1950. Her family moved to the Dominican Republic right after her birth, and Alvarez spent her childhood there. In 1960, her family immigrated to the United States, fleeing the Dominican Republic because of her father's involvement with an attempt to overthrow the Trujillo dictatorship. In high school, Alvarez realized that she wanted to pursue a career as writer. She earned a B.A. from Middlebury College in 1971, graduating summa cum laude, and she received her M.F.A. in 1975 from the Bread Loaf School of English. Her writing bridges the realms of Latina and American culture. Her stories are often traced to her Dominican roots, but they also contain much of the human experience.

## Snow, from *How the García Girls Lost their Accents*

### YOLANDA

Our first year in New York we rented a small apartment with a Catholic school nearby, taught by the Sisters of Charity, hefty women in long black gowns and bonnets that made them look peculiar, like dolls in mourning. I liked them a lot, especially my grandmotherly fourth grade teacher, Sister Zoe. I had a lovely name, she said, and she had me teach the whole class how to pronounce it. *Yo-lan-da*. As the only immigrant in my class, I was put in a special seat in the first row by the window, apart from the other children so that Sister Zoe could tutor me without disturbing them. Slowly, she enunciated the new words I was to repeat: *laundromat, corn flakes, subway, snow*.

Soon I picked up enough English to understand holocaust was in the air. Sister Zoe explained to a wide-eyed classroom what was happening in Cuba. Russian missiles were being assembled, trained supposedly on New York City. President Kennedy, looking worried too, was on the television at home, explaining we might have to go to war against the Communists. At school, we had air-raid drills: an ominous bell would go off and we'd file into the hall, fall to the floor, cover our heads with our coats, and imagine our hair falling out, the bones in our arms going soft. At home, Mami and my sisters and I said a rosary for world peace. I heard new vocabulary: *nuclear bomb, radioactive fallout, bomb shelter*. Sister Zoe explained how it would happen. She drew a picture of a mushroom on the blackboard and dotted a flurry of chalkmarks for the dusty fallout that would kill us all.

The months grew cold, November, December. It was dark when I got up in the morning, frosty when I followed my breath to school. One morning as I sat at my desk daydreaming out the window, I saw dots in the air like the ones Sister Zoe had drawn—random at first, then lots and lots. I shrieked, "Bomb! Bomb!" Sister Zoe jerked around, her full black skirt ballooning as she hurried to my side. A few girls began to cry.

But then Sister Zoe's shocked look faded. "Why, Yolanda dear, that's snow!" She laughed. "Snow."

Primary works by Julia Alvarez: *Before We Were Free* (New York: A. Knopf, 2002); *A Cafecito Story* (White River Junction: Chelsea Green Pub., 2001); *Cry Out: Poets Protest the War* (New York: G. Braziller with Northshire Bookstore, 2003); *How the García Girls Lost their Accents* (Chapel Hill: Algonquin Books, 1991); *In the Name of Salomé* (Chapel Hill: Algonquin Books, 2000); *In the Time of Butterflies* (Chapel Hill: Algonquin Books, 1994); *The Other Side/El Otro Lado* (New York: Plume Book, 1995); *Something to Declare* (Chapel Hill: Algonquin Books, 1998); *Yo!* (Chapel Hill: Algonquin Books, 1997).

"Snow," I repeated. I looked out the window warily. All my life I had heard about the white crystals that fell out of American skies in the winter. From my desk I watched the fine powder dust the sidewalk and parked cars below. Each flake was different, Sister Zoe had said, like a person, irreplaceable and beautiful.

---

# Arturo Arias

Arturo Arias was born in Guatemala City, Guatemala, in 1950. He is the director of Latin American Studies at the University of Redlands and has published several novels and research projects. Arias coauthored the screenplay for the film *El Norte*. He wrote *After the Bombs* (1979), *Itzam Na* (Casa de las Américas Award, 1981), *Jaguar en llamas* (Ana Seghers Prize, 1990), *Los caminos de Paxil* (1991), *Cascabel* (1998), *Sopa de caracol* (2002) and *The Rigoberta Menchú Controversy* (2001). He is also the author of three books of literary criticism. Arias has dedicated most of his research to ethnic issues and subaltern identity.

## Toward Patzún

The road twisted so many times that I thought I would soon reach the top of the mountain. The cool, dense wind had now ceased picking up the road dust and was being enriched by the soft aroma from the rows of pines.

I had walked the whole morning and expected to reach Patzún before nightfall.

The long rows of pines at the borders of the deep ravines caused my heart to swell. I smiled with that involuntary smile that surges up like a jet of water whose drops burn into us unexpectedly when we contemplate the beauty of a landscape that at first seems alien to our nature but is then suddenly felt to be shot through with our own being. I stopped to listen for a moment and heard only the breeze among the leaves. I sighed. The humidity of the atmosphere was overloaded and I anticipated that within a short time thick drops of water would begin to shake me. I pushed ahead, trying to find the zig-zags of the shortcut without wavering.

It was then that I perceived a woman in the distance walking along the same path, going in the same direction as mine. With a graceful, playful step she was advancing rapidly through the trees, though not in a straight line, but in a roundabout way. It seemed as though she would run into the trees on one side and disappear, and then I would see her among those of the opposite side. With her head erect and proud she radiated a perfect harmony with all that was around her.

Primary works by Arturo Arias: *After the Bombs* trans. Asa Zatz (Willimantic: Curbstone Press, 1990); *Rattlesnake* (Willimantic: Curbstone Press, 2003); Ed. *The Rigoberta Menchú Controversy* (Minnesota: Univ. of Minnesota Press, 2001).

In the distance that separated us and given the angle from which the intense light of the sun bathed her, her skin seemed of pure gold. I imagined her as quite refined in her shape and manner of being. Slender, she was doubtless modest and restrained in her speech. Her black hair was well pulled back over her head and fell in two braids down her back. She was dressed in a typical huipil,[1] a blouse from Patzún. It was bright red, loose and flowing over her waist. The fabric was a heavy stuff with green and yellow fringes.

I followed her with my eyes, turning my neck in order to keep from losing her. She walked at such a rapid pace that she rather appeared to be gliding between the branches.

The sky, which so recently had been perfectly limpid, unfolding luminously with a blue so blue that its very clarity dazzled, began to be covered with black clouds. Nonetheless, the leaves on the chichicaste nettle bushes still flashed intensely white.

I hastened my step still more. Allowing a sigh to escape, I matched my step with hers and continued on my way, maintaining the same distance behind her. All of a sudden the path was smooth before heading down into a gorge and from there beginning the last ascent that would take us almost to the town.

Swiftly, lightly, vaguely or densely, sometimes shining and bright, brisk and clear, thirty years of recollections went through my mind. That woman ahead of me, with her huipil filtering reddish bursts of light over the growing clouds, lighting up the air with a soft blaze of golden color spread palely toward the black clouds, embodied the perfume of the fragrant carnations, the resinous aroma of the conifers of my childhood. I had spent it happily far away in Antigua, that colonial city with cobbled streets. In those days everything was simpler. There were mountains, valleys, streams. I used to climb the mountains, wander through the valleys, sit down on the riverbanks. I would liken the hilltops to the breasts of wild turkeys, the rocks to calves. With curious eyes I sought to discover the wisdom that seemed to me hidden everywhere. And when from the peak of the Agua volcano I spied the white dots that comprised the former capital, my eyes opened even wider, my breast quivered, and I begged for that luminosity never to end: that intense greenness, the tranquillity of a breeze as soft and transparent as a crystalline drop of water. The kindliness, the beauty of my country at that moment seemed vast, infinite, and incapable of being matched. I saluted each peak, each star, as if they existed for me alone and would dissolve into smiles when they saw me, and on the cold, damp afternoons when it rained I would lie down on a blanket made thin by use in order to contemplate the flames of the chimney for uncountable hours, watching the white smoke given off by the firewood twisting around as if it wanted to avoid going out into the cold outside. The fire would burn with the sound of a satisfied cat spreading its warm breath throughout the whole room. It projected its tremulous light in the shape of a fan over the floor, frightening the shadows and forcing them to take refuge in the coldest and most distant corners. In that period, darkness was not safe anywhere, and I would hum the saddest songs with cheerful, harmonious sounds that lasted for a long while.

---

[1] Blouse common to Central American

Now we were in tormented times. The sky was unrelenting, gray and clouded over. Cold bursts of wind beginning to descend in swirls from the sierra peaks seemed driven mad and were advancing blindly, crashing as often into the cornfields as into the slender cypresses, giving voice to howls like those of a wounded coyote. The mountainous countryside, whitened suddenly by the cold rain, lost all its depth. The stream that I had been hearing for some time now at the bottom of the gorge was bellowing, crazed and furious. The wind laden with drops of water flung them at my face as if they were whips.

Forced to nearly shut my eyes, I would try to guess where the path was. My only fear, in the midst of this sudden cold, was losing the woman from my sight. It seemed to me I could hear her shouts, and I was able to make out two or three children's voices. Strident shouts that bothered me, that made my hopes vacillate.

Anxiety gripped me. I felt dragged down into the darkest depths by the beating of the wind. I tried to open my eyes slightly, to understand the significance of this sudden violence over so gentle a nature; I trembled in distress because of its effect on the woman and the children who were obviously accompanying her. Grief was suffocating me and I became violently upset.

I started to run. Through the curtain of water it seemed to me I could make out three or four silhouettes almost floating amid all the mud. A little higher up the woman was running, shouting some words and lifting her arms toward what was even higher yet. When I saw her I felt as if cool water were running through me and, letting a profound sigh escape, I allowed my mouth to be transformed into a fleeting smile. Up there, higher up on the path, the red color of her huipil stood out over the brown ribbon of the path and above the green leaves.

She had scarcely disappeared over the hilltop when the three or four mud-covered silhouettes were rushing up behind her. One could see they were attempting to move much more rapidly than they were able to.

After the gorge where, struggling with the wind and rain, I was unable to prevent the mud from covering my lower legs, the ascent began again. It was a steep path that passed under the menacing shadow of the howling cypresses all covered with slippery dead leaves. I made all possible haste, furiously pushing my hands down on my knees in order to help my legs straighten out. My breath began to fail.

In a few moments I sensed I was drawing closer to the woman and the children. I could hear their voices through the trees.

Soon I reached a section still narrower and more torturous. I tried to move still faster and felt myself being invaded by an unknown calm, an artificial, treacherous peace, in keeping with the way the rain was getting gentler and the wind was abating its force. I thought I heard the steps of the woman and the children just in front of me, crushing the dry leaves, but the sounds seemed unusually strong, as if they belonged to some large animal.

It was a lengthy deliberation that had finally convinced me to walk to Patzún. I was no longer able to bear the melancholy that had gotten into me; I felt embittered by the surrounding situation.

In a slight clearing of the vegetation, I was able to see the woman's face for a single instant, up above mine. There was a point where the path went up in the form of a hook and I felt the reflection of her overwhelming proximity. Her large black eyes were severe, as if some disturbing fluids might any moment burst out of their long-suffering, dark depths. But what impressed me most was the coldness of her expression, so markedly indifferent that I instantly knew I would never dare to address a word to her. She seemed to have lost even the strength to turn her face down to look at me.

She vanished as quickly as she had appeared. For a moment I contemplated the shaded place where the apparition had been. It seemed to me I could hear a light sound of footsteps, almost abusively excessive, in the distance. I recalled again my childhood vista from the peak of Agua volcano, and, rejecting with an angry gesture the vision of the face that had so wounded me, I was unable to prevent bitter tears of rage and impotence from escaping my eyes.

I felt my body was empty. I lost the notion of time. I was unable to think anymore. Exhausted, I slowed my pace until I was almost dragging my feet over the dry leaves. Pressing my lips tightly together, I repressed the nostalgic need for coolness, serenity. Violently I yanked a branch from a bush and covered my eyes with it, as if this way I would be able to generate a state of mind in which everything might blend together harmoniously, like washing out the inside of my head with pure water which as it rinsed would leave nothing behind but a mollifying sweetness.

It was at that moment that I heard the shouts. They were the same as before but now they sounded desperate, heartrending, as if a tremendous squall had suddenly removed all the vegetation. The screams penetrated the thickest tree trunks and filtered through the earth by means of the same invisible cracks into which the water used to disappear. The screaming ceased and a silence as cold as it was brief began, like the grating calm of a big frost. And then I heard, with a knot in my stomach and an immediate weakening of my legs, a burst of machine-gun fire. And following that came another scream, still stronger, more cutting, a thousand times more heartrending.

I didn't know whether to run toward the point where the screaming came from or whether to hide in the underbrush. There was a sudden looseness in my intestines and a strange shuddering in my stomach. I was standing, very pale, leaning against a fragrant-smelling pine tree, shivering so that it seemed to me the very tree trunk itself was trembling and that some of its branches were knocking against the others.

The previous cycle was repeated once more. The screams, the icy silence, a new burst from the machine gun. The only thing different was the intense whimpering of the children, whose number seemed fewer with each burst.

It was so insanely inconceivable that I was unable to think of the woman in the red huipil, of the three or four silhouettes as muddy as my own legs, except with a superstitious horror. Suddenly losing my balance, or my strength, or my mind, I fell to my knees with the knowledge that now there was not a single probable certainty in life, not a single rational confidence, not a single human surety. Why kill them? Why? Why? Did it have to be this way inevitably?

And once again the screams, the silence, the new burst of gunfire.

A prisoner of panic, I burst into the underbrush, away from the path, and ran uphill headlong, paying no attention to the branches thrusting at me, the tears in my clothing, the stumbling, the thorns. I ran uphill with my mouth open, panting, like a desperate person who has run out of oxygen, as if appealing to the most brutal of means hoping to quell those screams, the inevitable gunfire, the muffled despair.

Not knowing how, with my feet unsteady, temples pounding, hands dripping blood, I reached the base of a large rock that seemed to mark the highest point of the hill. I wanted to go around it in order to pursue my violent and reckless flight, when I was stopped suddenly, absolutely jolted, and threw myself backward with such violence that my wrist struck hard against the rock. I let myself fall to the ground, weeping and cursing at once.

From that point I was able to observe what was happening. A military patrol had stopped the woman and the children. They were pointing their machine guns at them. Trembling like a leaf, the officer was swinging his arms back and forth like someone insane. His voice was hoarse.

"Where is he, you bitch? Tell us where he is!"

The woman screamed and shouted in her own tongue. For me, at least, it was impossible to decipher her words.

"You don't want to speak, is that it? Kill another one!"

Then I saw one of the mud-covered silhouettes, screaming with terror, being pulled around by a soldier. The woman tried to rush toward him but the officer grabbed her by the wrist. The woman attempted a slap toward his face with her free hand but the officer ducked it agilely and twisted her arm behind her back and forced her to fall to her knees. The other soldier threw the muddy silhouette to the ground and, almost in the same instant, fired.

"Let's see if you'll talk now, you turd-colored Indian!"

I let myself fall against the ground, sinking my face into the dry leaves. Again I clutched at my humble desire to love and be loved, howling pitiably like a dog recently beaten. At once my whole body relaxed and remained there on the ground, overcome. The dark dampness, the longing, the sorrow were interrupted only by the indecipherable screams, the quite clear "kill another one," the yells, the burst of machine-gun fire, while my body got accustomed to a strange laxity, a calm desperation, an insensibility that little by little was becoming adjusted to the shadow of affliction.

I felt like a captive wandering fruitlessly in darkness and monotony, never arriving any place, eternally alone, with the daily deaths of my compatriots as my only consolation and company.

Finally I heard the final sentence:

"Now there's only you. Are you finally going to talk or not? Where is he?"

Again the unintelligible shouting, this time without the chorus of whimpering anymore. And in the midst of the tormented crumbling away of lives, it seemed to me that once I heard her say in bad Spanish, "But I really don't know, I already told you he went away more than two years ago." As if in a half-dozing state, in the middle of a dream more terrifying even than reality itself, with its nebulous images of a life that has ceased being so, I heard perfectly when the officer said, almost disdainful and bored, "Let's finish her off once and for all." I made out the screams, the noise of a body being thrown violently into the weeds, the final deafening burst of gunfire of the day. Then the footsteps indicating a gradual withdrawal, and finally, of course, the reign of silence.

I remained in the same position for a long time, until the cold began to shoot through me and I started to feel achy and feverish. Only then did I get to my feet.

I saw the bodies clearly some distance away. And for a brief instant I shivered with fright on seeing there, stretched out in their midst, my own bleeding body. I could not take my eyes away from the place, as if the only way to drive away the image was to engrave it in my mind like a tattoo, down to the last detail of that macabre scene. In that way, before my own family eliminated with such impunity, I found a hopeless astonishment over my own destiny. I ran my hand over my hair and then lowered it to my mouth, kissing it with the serene generosity of feeling myself still temporarily unsure whether I was alive or dead. Then I hesitated an instant and lowered my eyes. Immediately I went down on my knees and, filled with anguished distress shot through with fierce hatred, I lowered my bare head utterly, respectfully, and wished for once not to have been born engulfed in this immense sea of misfortunes that used to be the most beautiful country in the world, while I felt for the bullet holes perforating my body.

*(Translated by Leland H. Chambers)*

# Aurora Levins Morales — Puerto Rican

Aurora Levins Morales spent most of her early life in Indiera, a coffee-farming community in the western mountains of Puerto Rico, where she was born. When she was thirteen, her family moved to Chicago. Levins Morales started writing when she was very young. She went to college in New Hampshire, and in 1976 moved to the San Francisco Bay Area. She received her Ph.D. in Women's Studies and Puerto Rican history from The Union Institute. With her mother, Rosario Morales, Levins Morales published a collection of poetry and prose that is hailed as the most important book to come out of the Puerto Rican Diaspora, *Getting Home Alive*, in 1986. Levins Morales also published a collection of fiction, *A Remedy for Heartburn and Other Medicine Stories* and *Remedios: Lives of Puerto Rican Women*, which retells Puerto Rican history through prose-poetry stories on the lives of women.

Primary works by Aurora Levins Morales: *Medicine Stories: History, Culture, and the Politics of Integrity* (Boston: South End Press, 1998); Cherríe Moraga and Gloria Anzaldúa, eds., *This Bridge Called My Back: Writings by Radical Women of Color* (Watertown, MA: Persephone Press, 1981).

# Immigrants

For years after we left Puerto Rico for the last time, I would wake from a dream of something unbearably precious melting away from my memory as I struggled desperately to hold on, or at least to remember that I had forgotten. I am an immigrant, and I forget to feel what it means to have left. What it means to have arrived.

There was hail the day we got to Chicago and we joked that the city was hailing our arrival. The brown brick buildings simmered in the smelly summer, clenched tight all winter against the cold and the sooty sky. It was a place without silence or darkness, huddled against a lake full of dying fish whose corpses floated against the slime-covered rocks of the south shore.

Chicago is the place where the slack ended. Suddenly there was no give. In Indiera there was the farm: the flamboyan tree, the pine woods, the rainforest hillsides covered with alegría,[1] the wild joyweed that in English is called impatiens. On the farm there were hideouts, groves of bamboo with the tiny brown hairs that stuck in your skin if you weren't careful. Beds of sweet-smelling fern, drowsy-making under the sun's heat, where the new leaves uncurled from fiddleheads and tendrils climbed and tangled in a spongy mass six feet deep. There were still hillsides, out of range of the house, where I could watch lizards hunt and reinitas[2] court, and stalk the wild cuckoos, trying to get up close. There were mysteries and consolations. There was space.

Chicago was a wasteland. Nowhere to walk that was safe. Killers and rapists everywhere. Police sirens. Ugly, angry looks. Bristling hostility. Worst of all, nowhere to walk. Nowhere to go if it was early morning and I had to get out. Nowhere to go in the late afternoon or in the gathering dusk that meant fireflies and moths at home. Nowhere to watch animal life waking into a new day. The animal life was rats and dogs, and they were always awake because it never got dark here: always that sickly purple and orange glow they call sky in this place. No forest to run wild in. Only the lot across 55th Street with huge piles of barren earth, outlines of old cellars, and a few besieged trees in a scraggly row. I named one of them Ceres, after the goddess of earth and plenty who appeared in my high school production of *The Tempest*. Bounteous Ceres, queen of the wasteland. There were no hills to race down, tumbling into heaps of fern, to slide down, on a slippery banana leaf: no place to get muddy. Chicago had grime, but no mud. Slush, but no slippery places of the heart, no genuine moistness. Only damp alleyways, dank brick, and two little humps in the middle of 55th Street over which grass had been made to grow. But no real sliding, no slack.

*There are generations of this desolation behind me, desolation, excitement, grief, and longing all mixed in with the dirty air, the noise, seasickness, and the strangeness of wearing a winter coat.*

My grandmother Lola was nineteen the day she married my grandfather and sailed away to Nueva York in 1929. She had loved someone else, but his family disapproved and he obeyed their orders to leave for the States. So her family married her to a son of a neighboring family

---

[1] Happiness
[2] Queen bees

because the family store was doing poorly and they could no longer support so many children. Two months after her first love left, she found herself married and on the boat. She says: "I was a good Catholic girl. I thought it was my duty to marry him, that it was for the good of my family." I have pictures of her, her vibrant beauty wrapped up but not smothered in the winter coats and scarves, in my grandfather's violent possessiveness and jealousy. She is standing in Central Park with her daughters, or with her arms around a friend or cousin. Loving the excitement. Loving the neighbors and the hubbub. In spite of racist landlords. In spite of the girdle factory. In spite of Manolin's temper and the poverty and hunger. Now, retired to Manolin's dream of a little house in Puerto Rico with a yard and many plants to tend, she longs for New York or some other U.S. city where a woman can go out and about on her own, live among many voices speaking different languages, out of the stifling air of that house, that community, that family.

*My mother, the child in that Central Park photo, grew up an immigrant child among immigrants. She went to school speaking not a word of English, a small Puerto Rican girl scared out of her wits, and learned fast: learned accentless English in record time, the sweet cadence of her mother's open-voweled words ironed out of her vocabulary, the edges flattened down, made crisp, the curls and flourishes removed. First generation.*

The strangeness. The way time worked differently. The way being on time mattered. Four second bells. Four minutes of passing time between classes. A note from home if you were ten minutes late, which you took to the office and traded for a late pass. In Indiera the classroom emptied during coffee season, and they didn't bother to send the inspector up unless we were out for longer than four or five weeks. No one had a clock with a second hand. We had half days of school because there were only four rooms for six grades. Our room was next to the bakery, and the smell of the warm pan de agua[3] filled our lungs and stomachs and mouths. Things happened when they were read or "cuando Dios quiere."[4] The público[5] to town, don Paco's bread, the coffee ripening, the rain coming, growing up.

The stiffness. The way clothing mattered with an entirely different kind of intensity. In Indiera, I wore the same wine-colored jumper to school each day with the same white blouse, and only details of the buttons or the quality of the cloth or the presence or absence of earrings, only the shoes gave information about the homes we left at dawn each day, and I was grateful to be able to hide my relative wealth. In Chicago, there were rituals I had never heard of. Kneesocks and plaid skirts and sweaters matching each other according to a secret code I didn't understand. Going steady and wearing name tags. First date, second date, third date, score. The right songs to be listening to. The right dances. The coolness.

In the middle of coolness, of stiffness, of strangeness, my joyful rushing up to say, "I come from Puerto Rico, a nest of beauty on the top of a mountain range." Singing "beauty, beauty, beauty." Trying to get them to see in their minds' eyes the perfect edge of a banana leaf against a tropical blue sky, just wanting to speak of what I longed for. Seeing embarrassed faces turning away, getting the leering voices, singing "Puerto Riiiico, my heart's devotion ... let it sink into the ocean!" Learning fast not to talk about it, learning excruciatingly slowly how to dress, how to act, what to say, where to hide.

---

[3]Water,bread, typical of Puerto Rico
[4]Whenever God wants
[5]Bus

The exuberance, the country-born freshness going quietly stale. Made flat. Made palatable. Made unthreatening. Not different, really. Merely "exotic."

*I can remember the feelings, but I forget to give them names. In high school we read novels about immigrant families. In college we discussed the problems of other first generations, talked about displacement, talked about families confused and divided, pride and shame. I never remembered that I was an immigrant, or that both my parents are the first U.S.-born generations of their families.*

My father is the First American Boy. His mother, Ruth, was born in Russia. Took the boat with her mother, aunt, and uncle when she was two. My grandfather Reuben was the second son of Lev Levinsky, the first one born in the new country, but born into the ghetto. Lev and the first son, Samuel, were orthodox, old-country Jews, but Reuben and his younger brother Ben went for the new. They worked three or four jobs at once. They ran a deli in shifts and went to law school in their free hours. So Rube grew up and out of the immigrant poverty, still weak and bent from childhood hungers, still small and vulnerable. The sicker he got, the harder he worked to safeguard his wife and sons, adding on yet another job, yet another project until he worked himself to death at the age of forty-six.

My father was the First American Boy: the young genius, the honors student, the Ph.D. scientist. Each milestone recorded in home movies. His letters and report cards hoarded through the decades, still exhibited to strangers. The one who knew what was what. The expert. The one who carried the family spark, the one to boast about. The one with the weight of the family's hope on his shoulders. First generation.

*And what am I?*

The immigrant child of returned immigrants who repeated the journey in the second generation. Born on the island with firsthand love and the stories of my parents' Old Country—New York; and behind those, the secondhand stories of my mother's father, of the hill town of his long ago childhood, told through my mother's barrio childhood. Layer upon layer of travel and leaving behind, an overlay of landscapes, so that I dream of all the beloved and hated places, and endlessly of trains and paths and roads and ships docking and leaving port and a multitude of borders and officials waiting for my little piece of paper.

I have the passport with which my great-grandmother Leah, traveling as Elisavieta, and her sister Betty (Rivieka) and her brother Samuel and her mother Henke and my grandmother Riva, a round two-year-old to be known all her life as Ruth, and a neighbor who traveled with them as a relative, all came together into New York. I touch the seal of Russia, the brown ink in which their gentile names were recorded, the furriness of the old paper, the place where the date is stamped: June 1906. My great-grandfather Abe had come alone, fleeing the draft, by way of England and Canada, two years earlier.

I don't know what it looked like, the Old Country they left, the little farm in the Ukraine. I will never know. The town of Yaza was utterly destroyed in two gory days in 1942, eight thousand shot and buried in long trenches. My aunt Betty was unable to speak by the time I wanted to ask her: What was it like, a girl of fifteen, to come from that countryside to New York, to suddenly be working ten hours a day in a factory? I have the tiniest fragments, only the dust clinging to their shoes. The dreamy look on my great-grandmother's face one morning when I was ten, watching me play jacks. "There was a game we used to play on the farm, just like that, but with round little stones from the river, tossed from the fronts to the backs of our hands: how many times before they fall?" Pop's, my great-grandfather's painting of the farm he grew up on, and a dozen pages he left in phonetic yiddishy English about the place he grew up in, the horses, the pumpkins, the potatoes, the family decision for him to marry, to flee to New York, where you had to use *tsikolodzi* (psychology) to stay on top.

My grandmother Ruth unexpectedly answering my questions about her earliest memories with a real story, one whole, shining piece of her life: "*Dancing. We were on the boat from Russia. The sun was shining. The place we slept was smelly, stuffy, dark, so all the people were out on the deck as much as possible, sharing food, talking, laughing, playing music. Some of the other passengers were playing accordions and riddles and I began to dance in the middle of the deck. I danced and danced and all the people around me were laughing and clapping and watching me as I spun round and round in my short skirts. It was the happiest moment of my life!*"

My children will be born in California. It's not strange anymore, in this part of the world, in this time, to be born a thousand miles from the birthplace of your mother. My children will hear stories about the coquís[6] and coffee flowers, about hurricanes and roosters crowing in the night, and will dig among old photographs to understand the homesick sadness that sometimes swallows me. Living among these dry golden hills, they will hear about rain falling for months, every afternoon at two o'clock, and someday I'll take them there, to the farm on the top of Indiera, redolent of my childhood, where they can play, irreverent, in the ruins of my house. Perhaps they will lie in bed among the sounds of the rainforest, and it will be the smell of eucalyptus that calls to them in their dreams.

*[handwritten: doesn't want her children to feel like immigrants]*

---

[6]Small frogs common to Puerto Rico

# Victor Montejo

Victor Montejo was born in 1952 of Jakaltek Mayan parents in rural Guatemala. He attended Maryknoll school, where he learned Spanish and earned a teaching degree. He is the author of *The Bird Who Cleans the World*, one of the first collections of its type to be published in the United States. Currently he is a professor of anthropology at the University of California-Davis.

## Prelude from *Testimony: Death of a Guatemalan Village*

Tzalalá is a remote village in the northwest of Huehuetenango Department in Guatemala, Central America. There are no movie houses nor theaters, television, electric

Primary works by Victor Montejo: *The Bird who Cleans the World and Other Mayan Fables* trans. Wallace Kaufman (Willimantic: Curbstone Press, 1991) *Popol Vuh: A Sacred Book* trans. David Unger (Toronto: Douglas & McIntyre, 1999); *Sculpted stones/Piedras labradas* trans. Victor Perera (Willimantic: Curbstone Press, 1995); *Testimony: Death of a Guatemalan Village* trans. Victor Perera (Willimantic: Curbstone Press, 1987); *Voices from Exile: Violence and Survival in Modern Maya History* (Norman: U of OK, 1999).

light, drinking water or highways. The only access to this community is by narrow twisting roads that cross streams and deep gullies as they climb high into the craggy uplands.

The thatched roofs of the village begin to emit smoke at four in the morning, when the women rise to prepare the *nixtamal*[1] and tortillas for their men, who very early make their way to the fields they have worked since the time of their earliest ancestors.

The women remain behind to weave their meager dreams of subsistence on their looms, and after nightfall they lie on their mats to ruminate in Mayan about their poverty and plan their yearly journeys to work as migrants on the coastal plantations.

That is how life has been and still goes on in this community, whose only hope is the *milpas* or cornfields they are able to scratch out of the rocky hillsides.

In the ten years since I'd arrived in the village as schoolmaster, time in the village had flown by, as the children I had the first years in my classroom grew into youths who sought marriage and made dates by the well, where the young women in their lovely native dress go to fetch water in their clay jars.

Very few of the villagers finish their sixth grade of schooling, as the great majority abandon classes after their third or fourth grades—not because they do not like schoolwork but because they must accompany their parents on their migration to the distant coastal plantations. This is the community's way of life. The native peoples know how to live in peace and harmony, which normally is only broken during the elections.

One such occasion was a Friday in February 1978, when several politicians arrived in the village, rabble rousing and pretending concern for the villagers' most urgent needs, beginning with the roads, which were in miserable condition. The leader of the delegation spoke his pledge in a booming voice:

"WHEN WE GAIN THE PRESIDENCY, SAN JOSÉ, TZALALÁ WILL HAVE ITS HIGHWAY, AND AS A GUARANTEE OF THIS YOU ARE TO MAKE AN X OVER THE SYMBOL OF OUR PARTY."

The villagers went to the voting booth with the hope that with their ballots they would win the promised assistance in completing the road they themselves had begun some months back with pickaxes, shovels and hoes.

After the voting, the politicians who gained good posts in the government rapidly forgot their promises.

Three years later the politicians insisted the project would be completed before long if the villagers voted again for their official candidate in the next election, so the new government could carry out the offers the previous one did not.

The community gave up expecting any results from politicians.

But what most worried the community was the formation of "civil patrols" in July of 1982.

One Sunday the military commander summoned all the head men of the surrounding villages, and there he set forth his intention to form the so-called civil defense patrols.

The entire community protested this unexpected measure, insisting they had no desire to bear arms, as this was the army's function.

---

[1] Corn used to make tortillas

The commander grew angry and declared that everyone in the village had to unite and defend themselves against subversion. The people responded that they preferred to organize a labor team to carry out a project of communal benefit, such as the roads that were needed in the village and its surrounding hamlets.

The commander realized he could not convince the villagers and accepted their proposal to form a work detachment.

That is how the village and its hamlets formed into separate work groups. Once they were formed, however, the commander again summoned the heads of each group and advised them that since they were already organized into civilian detachments, they would have to go on military patrol. Those who protested this deceit by the commander were threatened with prison and were told that to oppose these measures was to be an enemy of the government.

That is how all these communities became subject to the will of the military and liable to sanctions or punishment if they disobeyed orders.

From that time on, civil patrols were in operation in Tzalalá, and they included youths of fourteen as well as old men of seventy. Under the constant pressure from the army, all the neighbors had to carry their clubs or *garrotes* in place of rifles and were under orders to attack any foreign elements that entered the community.

That is the background of the terrible events of September 9, 1982, when the civil patrol of Tzalalá mistook an army detachment dressed in olive fatigues for guerrillas.[2]

## The Attack from *Testimony: Death of a Guatemalan Village*

Friday the 9th of September dawned bright and clear. The air was crystalline after a week of heavy rains. I rose very early that day and unhurriedly gathered a few things in the *morral*[4] which I used because rucksacks of any color were too dangerous to carry around. Only the army was considered to have the right to use them, and their counterparts, the guerrillas, also carried them. I wrapped a week's used clothing in a plastic bag, next to a few bananas I'd bought from an Indian woman who travels from village to village.

Every Friday, when I returned to town, my children looked into my morral[3] first thing to discover what presents I brought them. For that reason I always carry some sweets and something else for my wife and children, who always awaited my return near the outskirts of town.

I put away my cot and prepared my breakfast. I began eating at seven and by seven-fifteen I set out for the schoolhouse to begin the day's teaching. Friday has always been a happy day for me, full of the anticipation of reuniting with my family in the town, several kilometers from the village.

---

[2]Armed insurrection groups
[3]Sack

After our morning hygiene exercises and a quick benediction I began classes as usual. For the past several days I'd been helping the upper grades prepare some observances for Independence Day ceremonies, to be celebrated the following week. Manuelito, the most mischievous boy in the class, asked me to sing the ditty of the "Indito" or little Indian, which goes like this:

> A little Indian I saw
> as he danced the trot
> how well he moved his feet
> touching his own heart.
> I asked, How do you do it?
> Do tell me please
> And he said, you just dance
> the same as I do.

I realized the song was discriminatory because the questioner uses the familiar "vos"[4] (in a vulgar sense) and the little Indian replies in a respectful USTED.[5] For the rural child all songs taught in school are equally discriminatory, or at least alienating, because their true intention is to condition them to the requirements of the *patrón* or boss, and thereby to perpetuate the Indian's inferior status.

Manuelito insisted on singing the song, so I corrected the usages to make them the same. In the middle of our exercise the head of the civil patrol of the village burst in out of breath and gave the alarm at the top of his voice:

"The guerrillas are approaching the village. Everyone get ready!"

While he continued to shout, another member of the patrol began to ring the bell of the chapel, which signalled imminent danger.

Out of curiosity I stepped to the door and saw the villagers, or rather the first company of the civil patrol, take up their clubs, stones, slingshots and machetes and run to the aid of the front lines which guarded the entrance to the village.

The mobilization was carried out rapidly to the uninterrupted tolling of the bronze bell of the Catholic chapel.

I consulted my watch and saw it was eleven in the morning. At almost the same instant I heard the first shot fired. Behind it came a volley of machinegun fire. The peaceful community broke into confusion. The women wept and prayed to God to protect their husbands and older sons who had been forced to join the civil patrol.

I ordered the students to stretch out on the floor and barred the door and windows with old broomsticks. The invaders had encircled the village and the hills echoed the furious explosions of grenades and the sputter of bullets that whistled past the corrugated tin roof of the schoolhouse.

---

[4]You (informal use)
[5]You (formal use)

"Don't make a sound," I ordered my children. Some began to weep and others trembled with fear. Their fathers were in the midst of that gunfire, armed only with sticks, stones and slingshots and the children were fully aware of the danger they were in.

"Pray—pray for your fathers and don't raise your heads—" I insisted. It was twelve noon and the thunderous blasts of the rifles and submachineguns continued without a pause. From time to time we heard the voice of a patrol leader who shouted in Mayan: "Keep on, *compañeros*,[6] don't be afraid of the sons of bitches. They'll soon run out of ammunition . . . Attack!"

The voice of the patrol leader was heard on the eastern side of the schoolhouse, toward the windows. Flattened against the wall I peered under the slits of the window to locate the patrols or the attackers, but my vision was blocked and I could not see beyond a few meters. I squinted to look in all directions but could see nothing. The coffee arbor and the trees back of the school impeded my vision.

My pupils were growing restless and stretched to exercise their limbs, but I forbade them to move.

"Flatten yourselves against the floor," I ordered again as the blasts of the machineguns came closer and closer. The students obeyed and remained quiet under their desks, and I threw myself down on the floor beside them.

Immediately afterward I heard footsteps in the school patio, coming toward the door. It was a woman who began to shout for her son.

"Pascual, Pascualito my son, where are you? Pascual my son, come home with me."

I approached the barred door and shouted at the woman, "Your son is safe here, return to your home please and look after your other children without endangering yourself."

The woman grew angry and shouted at me: "If something happens to my son I will hold you responsible."

I paid no heed to the woman and told her son Pascual to lie down on the floor—his mother's cries had made him rise to his feet and expose himself to gunfire.

Another hour went by. It was one in the afternoon and the gunblasts were closer and louder. I began to suspect that the patrol members may have committed a grave mistake. After the mother returned to her home, I once again heard running steps in the patio. I peered through the keyhole and saw several older men running toward their homes. They too were reluctant members of the civil patrol. A military officer had forced them to join and had threatened to kill them if they refused. This officer was the same lieutenant who ordered the execution of two villagers apprehended by the patrol and who warned that anyone who refused to join the civil patrol would be considered an enemy of the government. On August 30th, exactly ten days before, the patrol had been forced to club the two men to death. The lieutenant's voice was still fresh in the minds of the villagers: "You

---

[6]Comrades

must all look after yourselves and stop being sissies. Don't let the communist bandits into your village. Do you understand me?"

"Yes, Commander," the neighbors had shouted in unison.

"We shall see now if it's true. Kill these two motherfuckers that you yourselves apprehended."

"No," the villagers replied. "We are not accustomed to killing."

"Well, then, you will now become accustomed to it. Do it at once, or I will do it for you."

On August 30th the villagers had carried out their first execution.

It should not surprise anyone that even the old men and adolescents joined the patrol to escape the lieutenant's grave threats.

The old men I saw running away were in charge of guarding the school and fled for their lives when the gunfire got too close. The school and the chapel are located in the village plaza, and between them is a basketball court with an earthen floor.

I looked at my watch and saw it was 2 p.m. I felt sorry for the children stretched out on the floor. They were praying because it was all that they could do.

Fifteen minutes passed, and I was startled to hear the frantic ringing of the bell in the chapel of the village's patron saint, directly across from the school.

I peered through the keyhole once again and felt a shiver on seeing a man in olive green leading twelve patrol members with their hands tied behind them. Two other men similarly dressed pointed rifles at them. I recognized at once that the rifles they bore were Galils, of Israeli manufacture. I knew these rifles by name because the military detachment had used them in my hometown to cut down innocent people who were accused of being guerrillas.

Although the bell rang, no one approached the chapel. On other occasions the ringing of the bell would bring all the men of the village to the plaza, carrying clubs in their callused hands, and stones in their pouches for their rubber slingshots. As no one heeded the bell, the civil defender who rang it was ordered by the armed man to call at the top of his lungs and summon the villagers to gather in the school patio.

The defender filled his lungs and shouted in his own language to the villagers:

"Come close, brothers, don't be afraid. It is the army that is among us. Come quickly."

The women who had hidden in neighbors' homes when the shooting began were the first to approach. They were anxious to see if their husbands or sons were among the bound captives.

The hail of gunfire had finally ceased, and I instructed my students to rise from the floor. They sat on their desks while I opened the door and went out to the corridor to find out what was happening.

Doña Elena, who was waiting for me, approached as I left the school and began to plead with me. "I beg of you, inquire about my husband so they will release him; I don't speak Spanish and I'm afraid to speak with them."

When I saw her crying, I too felt a desire to weep, but I did not allow my tears to flow. I girded myself up and slowly approached the armed men who held the patrol members captive. I greeted them cordially and identified myself as the village schoolmaster.

The sergeant who led the captives responded in poor Spanish. By his torturous manner of speaking I deduced he was also an Indian, a native of Sololá or Totonicapán.

With an expression smeared with rage he stared at me and replied:

"Well, look here you, these bastards attacked us. We're army men and I think all these people are guerrillas."

I confirmed at first sight that they were indeed soldiers. I had begun to suspect as much when I heard the sound of their weapons. It was the same coughing noise of Galil rifles I remembered hearing when they massacred two communities on the northern trunk road, not far from the village of Tzalalá. It was the same familiar gunblasts heard when they carry out their counter-insurgency operations and sow panic in the communities they invade.

I again attempted to reason with the man, although I was aware that I was playing with fire.

"Gentlemen, these men you have bound with ropes belong to the civil patrol. They have strict orders to finish off any guerrillas that show themselves here, and that is what they mistook you for."

"Then why didn't they take notice of our rifles?"

"No doubt they failed to take notice of them, but their worst error was over the olive green uniforms you are wearing. The patrol is more familiar with the speckled camouflage fatigues commonly worn by the army."

"Wait for the lieutenant, and he will decide what to do with all of you." Saying this, the man turned his back on me.

I returned to the school and ordered my students to head directly for their homes. More soldiers leading other bound captives were arriving. Some of the patrol members were bleeding; the rest were sweating and disoriented.

When I dismissed the class and told them to go home, each of them fled like a deer out the door and raced to find their parents.

I shut the door of the school and once again I approached the civil defenders, as their women continued to weep. I felt pity for all of them, but there was very little to be done under the circumstances.

More members of the patrol arrived with their uniformed captors. They looked as if they had fled from an insane asylum. Some had broken arms from the bullets, and others had their ribs crushed from the blows of rifle butts and repeated falls. The defenders suffered in silence, without letting go the clubs they clutched in trembling hands, while the soldiers spat out curses as they shoved and kicked the villagers and rounded them all up in the patio.

# Alicia Partnoy

Alicia Partnoy was born in Argentina in 1955. She was one of the many political activists who "disappeared" after the military junta came to power in 1976. After three years of imprisonment, she was forced to leave Argentina. During her years as a political prisoner, her stories were smuggled out of prison and published anonymously in human rights journals. Her testimony was quoted in the final report of the Argentine Commission for the Investigation of Disappearance. Since her arrival in the United States, she has lectured extensively at the invitation of Amnesty International, religious organizations, and universities. She edited *You Can't Drown the Fire: Latin American Women Writing in Exile*, and wrote *The Little School: Tales of Disappearance and Survival in Argentina*.

## The One-Flower Slippers from *The Little School*

That day, at noon, she was wearing her husband's slippers; it was hot and she had not felt like turning the closet upside down to find her own. There were enough chores to be done in the house. When they knocked at the door, she walked down the ninety-foot corridor, *flip-flop, flip-flop*. For a second she thought that perhaps she should not open the door; they were knocking with unusual violence . . . but it was noon time. She had always waited for them to come at night. It felt nice to be wearing a loose house dress and his slippers after having slept so many nights with her shoes on, waiting for them.

She realized who was at the door and ran towards the backyard. She lost the first slipper in the corridor, before reaching the place where Ruth, her little girl, was standing. She lost the second slipper while leaping over the brick wall. By then the shouts and kicks at the door were brutal. Ruth burst into tears in the doorway. While squatting in the bushes, she heard the shot. She looked up and saw soldiers on every roof. She ran to the street through weeds as tall as she. Suddenly the sun stripped away her clothing; it caught her breath. When the soldiers grabbed her, forcing her into the truck, she glanced down at her feet in the dry street dust; afterward she looked up: the sky was so blue that it hurt. The neighbors heard her screams.

---

Primary works by Alicia Partnoy: *Revenge of the Apple/Venganza de la manzana* trans. Richard Schaaf, Regina Kreger, and Alicia Partnoy (Pittsburgh: Cleis Press, 1992); Ed., *You Can't Drown the Fire: Latin American Women Writing in Exile* (Pittsburgh: Cleis Press, 1992); *The Little School: Tales of Disappearance and Survival in Argentina* (Pittsburgh: Cleis Press, 1998).

The floor of the truck was cool, but the tiles at Army Headquarters were still cooler. She walked that room a thousand times from one end to the other until they came to take her. Through a peep hole under her blindfold she could see her feet on the tiny black and white tiles, the stairs, the corridor. Then came the trip to the Little School.

At the concentration camp kitchen they made a list of her belongings. "What for, if you are going to steal them all?" she asked.

"A wedding ring, a watch . . . dress color . . . bra . . . she doesn't wear one . . . shoes . . . she doesn't have any."

"She doesn't? It doesn't matter, she won't have to walk much." Loud guffaws.

She was not paying attention to what they were saying. She did try to guess how many of them there were. When she thought the interrogation session was about to begin, they took her to a room. She walked down a tiled corridor, then an old wooden floor. After arriving at the wretched bed assigned to her, she discovered a ragged blanket. She used it to cover her feet and did not feel so helpless.

The following morning someone tapped her on the shoulder and made her stand up. Someone had re-tied her blindfold during the night. The peep hole was smaller but still big enough for her to be able to see the floor: blood on the tiles next to a spot of sky blue. They made her walk on the bloodstains; she tried not to avoid them so they would not notice that she could see.

While they opened the iron grate into the corridor, she thought for a minute of the sky blue spot. She could have sworn that it was a very familiar color, like the sky blue color of her husband's pants. It was the same sky blue of his pants; it *was* him, lying on the hall floor, wounded. Her heart shrank a little more until it was hard as a stone. "We must be tough," she thought, "otherwise they will rip us to shreds." Fear carved an enormous hole in her stomach when she stepped down onto the cement floor of the "machine" room and saw the side of the metal framed bed like those used for torture.

She does not remember exactly the day it all happened. In any event, she already knew by then something about the pace of life at the Little School. She knew, for example, that after mealtimes, if they were allowed to sit for a short while on the edge of the bed, she could, without being caught, whisper a few words out of the side of her mouth to Vasquita, who was in the bunk next to hers. She chose the words.

"Vasca," she called out.

"Yes . . ."

"They gave me some slippers with only one flower."

"At last."

"Did you understand me? Just one flower, two slippers and just one flower."

Vasca stretched her neck and lifted up her face to peek under her blindfold. The flower, a huge plastic daisy, looked up at them from the floor. The other slipper, without flower, was more like them. But that one-flowered slipper amid the dirt and fear, the screams and the torture, that flower so plastic, so unbelievable, so ridiculous, was like a stage prop, almost obscene, absurd, a joke.

Vasca smiled first and then laughed. It was a nervous and barely restrained laughter. If she were caught laughing, it was going to be very hard to explain what was so funny. Then blows would come, with or without explanations.

She shuffled the daisy around for more than a hundred days, from the latrine to the bed, from the bed to the shower. Many times she blindly searched under the bed for the daisy in between the guards' shouts and blows.

The day she was transferred to prison, someone realized that she should be wearing "more decent" shoes. They found her a pair of tennis shoes three sizes too big. The one-flowered slippers remained at the Little School, disappeared . . .

# Virgil Suárez — cuban

Virgil Suárez was born in Havana, Cuba. He knew he wanted to write at the young age of twelve. His family was forced into exile in 1974; that same year, he moved to the United States with his parents. His focus has been to write to remember an experiences of exile, putting into words the pain, anguish, fears, and passion he felt. Suárez received a B.A. in creative writing at California State University at Long Beach and an M.F.A. from Louisiana State University in Baton Rouge in creative writing and contemporary American literature. He has published extensively in numerous literary journals, including the *New England Review, New Orleans Review, American Literary Review*, and *Shenandoah*. His works include *Infinite Refuge* (2002), *The Cutter* (1998), *Spared Angola: Memories of a Cuban-American Childhood* (1997), and *Welcome to the Oasis and Other Stories* (1992). Also, he coedited *Little Havana Blues: A Cuban-American Literature Anthology* (1996) and *Iguana Dreams: New Latino Fiction* (1993). In 2002, he received the G. MacCarthur Poetry Prize and a National Endowment of the Arts award for Poetry. Suárez is a professor of creative writing and Latino/a literature at Florida State University.

Primary works by Virgil Suárez: *Latin Jazz* (New York: William Morrow, 1989); *The Cutter* (Houston: Arte Público Press, 1997); *Welcome to the Oasis* (Houston: Arte Público Press, 1992); *Going Under* (Houston: Arte Público Press, 1996); *Spared Angola* (Houston: Arte Público Press, 1998); and *Infinite Refuge* (Houston: Arte Público Press, 2002).

# Spared Angola

After a twenty-year absence, my grandmother, Donatila, flies from Havana to Miami for a visit. Waiting for her in the crowded and noisy lobby of Miami International Airport, I am struck by memories of my childhood in the arms of this woman who, except for vague moments, is a perfect stranger. To my mother she is Tina of the constant aches and headaches, of the bouts with rheumatism, of the skin disease that spotted her face and neck with pink blotches, of the hair the color of smoke and straw. Abuela Tina. Twenty years before this moment caught in the restless humdrum of waiting, this woman about to visit showed me many things: how to feed leftover rice to chickens, tie my shoelaces, brew the kind of watery coffee I like to drink with toasted bread. She kept my behind from feeling the wrath of my father's belt on numerous occasions; she stayed with me while I took a shower in the room by the side of the clapboard house because I was terrified of the bullfrogs that sought the humidity trapped there. She told me stories, most of which I've forgotten, except for the one about the old hag who would wait for a man to come by on horseback to cross the old bridge. The hag would jump on the horse and spook the animal and the rider. The horsemen knew never to look back or risk spooking themselves crazy. "Never look back," she said, "as you cross your bridges." The flight arrives and the waiting intensifies. My mother sinks her nails into my flesh as she holds my hand. My father every so often retrieves a handkerchief from his back pocket (he's never used one) and wipes his forehead and under his eyes. The first few passengers come out the glass doors of Customs and are greeted by relatives who have never forgotten these tired and worn faces, frail bodies. Parents, sisters, brothers, sons, daughters, all now looking thirty-six years older. "Time," my father says, "is a son of a bitch." Finally, I spot my aunt (I have not seen her for as long as I have not seen my grandmother), my father's sister who'd gotten cancer. She is holding on to my grandmother, and I realize my memory has served me better than I am willing to admit. Grandmother Tina looks the same except for the patches of the skin disease which have completely taken over her face. My mother screams and lets go of my hand and runs to the arms of her mother. My father to his sister. I stand back and brace myself. After the hugs and the kisses, my mother says, "There he is! Your grandson, Mamá!" She walks toward me and I find I cannot move, for I cannot believe in movement; I am still stuck in time. She comes toward me. "*¿No te acuerdas de mí?*"[1] she says, her Spanish the necessary tug. I lean into her arms, for she is small and frail, and we stand there in the middle of the lobby. I tell her that I do remember. I remember everything. Slowly now we make our way out of the terminal to the parking lot, into the car, onto the freeway, home to my parents', up the stairs and into the living room of an apartment in which I've spent so very little time. All this time everybody has been talking except me; I've

---

[1] Don't you remember me?

been driving and listening, bewildered by all the catching up. In the living room now, waiting for refreshments, my grandmother comes over to where I sit and she holds my face between her hands. She looks into my eyes. Can I? Can I remember this woman? My grandmother Donatila. She's an apparition, I think, but don't say it. She says, "You must tell me about you, all that the distance has taken from us." I tell her I am happy to see her, after so much time. "*¿Sabes?*"[2] she says. "You are a lucky young man. Your parents did the right thing. When they took you out of Cuba, your parents spared you. Yes, you were spared. Spared Angola."

---

[2]You know?

*[handwritten: theme = protection makes the abuela happy]*

# ESSAY

# Claribel Alegría

Claribel Alegría was born in Estelí, Nicaragua, in 1924, to a Nicaraguan father and a Salvadoran mother. Alegría grew up in El Salvador, and, in 1943, she moved to the United States, where she graduated from George Washington University with a B.A. in philosophy and letters. She is a significant voice in the struggle for liberation in El Salvador and Central America. She is associated with the Sandinistas Liberation Front, the left-wing guerilla movement that took control of the Nicaraguan government in 1979 after the overthrow of Anastasio Somoza Debayle. She states, "In the middle 1970s, lots of people, not only from my country but throughout Latin America, were being murdered or disappeared, including some of my friends. I felt that I had a niche in my heart for each one of them, and it is because of them I called myself a cemetery." Her writing reflects the literary movement that emerged in Central America in the mid-1950s and early 1960s that came to be known as *la generación comprometida*, or the "committed generation." Aside from writing about the civil war, Alegría also writes urging women to break free from oppressive patriarchy. She has written thirteen volumes of poetry, several novels and a collection of children's stories. *Sobrevivo*, one of her poetry books, won the prestigious Casa de las Américas Prize. *Fugues* is her most recent collection in English.

---

Primary works by Claribel Alegría: *Death of Somoza* with Darwin J. Flakoll (Willimantic: Curbstone Press, 1996); *Fugues* trans. D. J. Flakoll (Willimantic: Curbstone Press, 1993); *Luisa in Realityland* trans. D. J. Flakoll (Willimantic: Curbstone Press, 1987); *Woman of the River* trans. D. J. Flakoll (Pittsburgh: Univ. of Pittsburgh Press, 1989); edited, *On the Front Line: Guerrilla Poems* trans. D. J. Flakoll (Willimantic: Curbstone Press, 1989); *Saudade/Sorrow* trans. Carolyn Forché (Willimantic, Curbstone, 1999); *Umbrales/Thresholds: Poems* trans. D. J. Flakoll (Willimantic: Curbstone Press, 1996).

# The Politics of Exile

Exile has long been one of the accepted occupational hazards of writers, professionals and politicians throughout Central America: a likelihood, under the military dictatorships that have existed in the area for the greater part of the 20th century, that is roughly equal to the chances of coming down with malaria.

In my own case, I was born in Nicaragua but grew up as a Salvadoran because my father, a medical doctor and Nicaraguan Liberal, was driven into exile by the U.S. Marines when I was only nine years old. He could never return, except clandestinely, because the Somoza dynasty placed a price on his head, and he died, forty years later, still in exile.

A good many years ago, I left El Salvador, but not as an exile. I went abroad to study, to learn other languages, to see the world. I never again resided in my country, but every year or so I would return for a few months to visit family and friends, to regain the essential contact with my roots. It was not until seven years ago that I learned I could not go back to El Salvador. Or, to be exact, I could return, but from what I was told, the chances of leaving with a whole skin were not encouraging. So yes, that makes me an authentic exile.

Since then, I have lived almost permanently in Nicaragua, which is also my motherland: a land of warm, generous people where I feel very much at home. Naturally, it is painful not to be able to return to El Salvador whenever I feel like it, to be unable to feast my eyes on its incredible gamut of greens, to be prohibited from contemplating the giant *ceiba*[1] tree that adopted me when I was a little girl, or from listening to the everyday speech of my people. But I realize that my anger, my resentment, is subjective, and that I would be falsifying if I told you I feel "exiled" in Nicaragua. Because of that, instead of speaking about my own experience, which is unimportant, I would like to talk about the true political exiles of my country: the refugees, the displaced, the dispossessed.

Today, twenty percent of my fellow countrymen fall into those categories. At least one million Salvadorans have fled the country or have been driven out in fear for their lives. There are 500,000 of them in the United States alone, where the Reagan administration is making intensive efforts, under a new, restrictive immigration law, to round them up and return them to El Salvador where they face internment in the army's new concentration camps, or death. More thousands are scattered throughout Canada, Mexico, the other Central American republics, and Europe.

---

[1]Silk-cotton tree

Two years ago I talked with some of the new flood of exiles in a Sanctuary center in San Francisco, where there is an underground colony of some 300,000 Salvadorans, nearly all of them undocumented, and where an average of 300 per week were, even at that time, being hunted down by the *migra*—the immigration authorities—and deported.

The figures boggle the imagination, and the only protection these people have is the sheer weight of their numbers and their social invisibility in largely Chicano communities. So, let me focus on a single case—a typical story which I learned secondhand—a tale that you can multiply in your mind by a factor of hundreds of thousands. Let me tell you about Pastora, the child poet of Colomoncagua, a refugee camp in Honduras a few miles from the Salvadoran border.

Pastora is twelve, perhaps thirteen years old by now, and she told her story to my daughter, Patricia, who visited the camp as a member of a human rights delegation two years ago. Until she was eight, Pastora lived in the Salvadoran department of San Vicente, which is a disputed zone in the current civil war.

The National Guard swept through one day, in a typical "search and destroy" operation, and caught her entire family in their peasant hut. One of the soldiers knocked her mother unconscious with his rifle butt, another shot her father through the head and then killed her two small brothers, who were screaming, while Pastora, huddling in a corner under the bed, watched the carnage.

She and her mother managed to escape, hiding in a *tatus*, or manmade cave, until the last of the Guards had passed through. Little by little, other survivors of the massacre came out of their hiding places and, without burying their dead, commenced their exodus at night-fall. Their flight, in single file, toward the Lempa River which forms the border between Honduras and El Salvador in that region, was a nightmare that has been repeated thousands of times since then. It is known, with typical Salvadoran black humor, as *la guinda*, which means, "as easy as picking cherries."

When babies cried, their mothers would stop their mouths so the Guards wouldn't hear them, or offer them their dry breasts to stop their whimpering from hunger, thirst and fright. One small boy would not stop screaming until his father, in desperation, stuffed a handkerchief in his mouth, and he died of asphyxiation. During four terror-filled days and arduous nights of forced marching, they followed the banks of the Lempa, nourishing themselves on roots and leaves and an occasional wild berry. During the days of hiding, helicopter gunships patrolled overhead, firing rockets at anything that moved. At night, the adults took turns carrying the wounded in makeshift litters.

On the morning of the fifth day, a detachment of Guards appeared ahead of them, cutting off their retreat, and they were forced to cross the river into Honduras. Those who could, swam across. The others clung to rotting logs, and someone had brought an inner tube and a rope for such an eventuality. There were more deaths at the crossing: a number of small children, some of the wounded and one pregnant woman.

It has been five years now since Pastora arrived at Colomoncagua. A schoolteacher at the camp taught her and the other children to read, and she in turn taught her mother and is now teaching smaller children and adults the elements of literacy. As if that were not enough, Pastora developed the poetic itch. She writes poems about her dead father and brothers, about the importance of learning to read (the illiteracy rate in the encampment has dropped from eighty to less than thirty percent), about the threatened resettlement in El Salvador that the refugees dread. She began to write rhymed verse without anyone teaching her, and when she writes about the New Society, her words take on a prophetic ring.

She sent me half a dozen of her poems with Patricia—a fraternal gesture from one poet to another—and I had them published in a Managua literary supplement. Much, much later, Patricia wrote me that another human rights delegate had personally delivered the published poems to Pastora, who was delighted—as any poet would be—at her early recognition.

A few months after Patricia recorded Pastora's story, a company of Honduran soldiers burst into the Colomoncagua encampment on a mission of terror and intimidation. The attack took place at 3:00 p.m. on August 29, 1985, and I have read the detailed eyewitness accounts of the atrocity, disseminated by the El Salvador Commission on Human Rights on September 5, 1985.

I can only imagine that Pastora must have witnessed this second nightmare from another hiding place. According to multiple accounts from international observers in the camp, there were five Salvadoran soldiers and one North American Green Beret guiding the Honduran troops in a hunt for specific victims. I will not go into the gory details, graphically described in the testimony. Two people were killed, one of them a two-month-old baby who was kicked to death by a Honduran soldier. Thirteen were seriously wounded by gunfire, and twenty-five others were savagely beaten with rifle butts. Two women—one of them the schoolteacher—were repeatedly raped in the schoolhouse, and ten men and boys were captured and led away to a waiting helicopter, never to be seen again.

This is typical of the human suffering resulting from what the U.S. Pentagon laconically calls the Doctrine of Low Intensity Conflict. The "low intensity" presumably refers to its minimal effects on U.S. and international public opinion. But for Pastora and her fellow victims, the intensity is maximal and mortiferous.

The Salvadoran army is waging total war against its own people, with the expert advice of hundreds of U.S. military advisors and the logistical and economic support of the Reagan administration. The same holds true for its next-door neighbor, Guatemala, except that the military advisors there are Israelis. These are quiet little wars that have dragged on for years without receiving much attention in the international news media. There are no body bags being shipped back to the United States with the remnants of

American boys inside them. Congress can be counted on to give President Reagan any amount he says he needs to continue the war, now that the deathsquad killings have dropped to about one a day and the Salvadoran military have President José Napoleón Duarte as their civilian front man.

Perhaps few have heard about Operation Phoenix, which took place little more than a year ago in the Guazapa area of El Salvador.

Operation Phoenix: the name has macabre overtones since the Vietnam War, when it was the code name for a CIA terrorist operation, run by former CIA director William Colby, that slaughtered 30,000 civilians who were suspected of being Vietcong sympathizers. This new Operation Phoenix used ten percent of the Salvadoran army, including three elite battalions and the Salvadoran air force, to kill or drive the civilian population out of a 1500 square kilometer area covering Suchitoto, Aguilares and Guazapa. The soldiers applied "scorched earth" tactics to the entire area, killing civilians, burning huts, destroying animals and crops. The air force rained a ton of bombs daily for more than a month on the densely-populated area, and the army troops followed with a "mopping up" operation to clear the area of all signs of life. An undetermined number of civilians were killed and some 500 were captured and taken off to relocation camps.

What is the strategic objective of these Phoenix-type operations, which have taken place at regular intervals for the past five years? In counter-insurgency parlance, they are aimed at "taking the water away from the fish"—that is, taking the civilian population away from the guerrilla forces to deprive the latter of support. After a guerrilla zone has been properly "scorched" and depopulated, the government plans to resettle it with concentration camps containing displaced persons from other zones of the country who have been investigated, cleared and issued identification documents which they must carry at all times. The army controls all aspects of life and seeds the camps with informants to report on suspected guerrilla sympathizers.

This Orwellian militarization of society has worked better in Guatemala than it has thus far in El Salvador. The illiterate indigenous population of the Guatemala highlands is less politicized than the wily Salvadoran peasant, and the so-called Guatemalan "poles of development" are reportedly packed with the widows and children of men who were slaughtered in the savage counter-insurgency operations that Ríos Montt launched in 1982.

In El Salvador, however, with its dense population, the "water"—the people—stubbornly flows back to surround the "fish." The *guinda* has become a way of life for the people of Guazapa, who have survived approximately twenty such army forays during the past five years. The civilian population melts away before the army advance, each column of refugees led by guerrillas who know the direction of the army's thrust, and circle around it to wait until the armed forces have completed their work of devastation before flowing back into their ravaged territory to start rebuilding and replanting.

Displacement camps and exile are a deliberate strategy of the doctrine of low intensity warfare. The Guazapa peasants are intermittent refugees on the very land they till. Pastora has been exiled for five years within a few kilometers of her own country. As for the 500,000 Salvadoran exiles being hounded out of the United States under President Reagan's new immigration law, I have only this to say.

When they refurbished the Statue of Liberty in New York harbor recently, I hope someone had the common decency to take down the bronze plaque engraved with Emma Lazarus' poem:

> Send me your wretched and your poor,
> your huddled masses yearning to be free . . .

Lady Liberty may be holding high her torch "beside the Golden Door," but in her other hand, these days, she holds something that looks suspiciously like a whip.

# José Martí

José Martí was born in Havana, Cuba, in 1853. At sixteen he was arrested for sedition by the Spanish colonial authorities and was sentenced to several months of hard labor. In 1871, he was deported to Spain, where he began his studies in law and continued to fight for the liberation of Cuba. When he returned to Havana, he became involved in activities that landed him in prison. This led to his opportunity to travel through New York and several Central and South American countries. He returned to New York to live; there he worked as a journalist while he conspired against Spain. Some of his publications include *Ismaelillo* (1882) and *Simple Verses* (1891).

## Our America

The villager fondly believes that the world is contained in his village, and he thinks the universal order good if he can be mayor, humiliate the rival who stole his sweetheart, or add to the savings in his sock—unaware of the giants with seven-league boots who can crush

Primary works by José Martí: *Major Poems: A Bilingual Edition*, ed. Philip S. Foner, trans. Elinor Randall (New York: Holmes and Meier, 1982); *On Art and Literature: Critical Writings*, ed. Philip S. Foner, trans. Elinor Randall, Luis A. Baralt, Juan de Onís, and Roslyn Held Foner (New York: Monthly Review Press, 1982); *Simple Verses*, trans. Manuel A. Tellechea (Houston: Arte Público Press, 1997); *The America of José Martí: Selected Writings* (New York: Noonday Press, 1953).

him under foot, or the strife in the heavens between comets, which streak through space, devouring worlds. What remains of the parochial in America must awake. These are not times for sleeping in a nightcap, but rather with weapons for a pillow, like the warriors of Juan de Castellanos: weapons of the mind, which conquer all others. Barricades of ideas are worth more than barricades of stone.

There is no prow that can cleave a cloud-bank of ideas. An energetic idea, unfurled in good season before the world, turns back a squadron of ironsides with the power of the mystic banner of the judgement day. Nations that do not know one another should make haste to do so, as brothers-in-arms. Those who shake their fists at each other, like jealous brothers who covet the same land, or the cottager who envies the squire his manor, should clasp hands until they are one. Those who allege the sanction of a criminal tradition to lop off the lands of their brother, with a sword dipped in his own blood, had best return the lands to the brother punished far beyond his due, if they do not want to be called thieves. The honorable do not seek money in satisfaction of debts of honor, at so much a slap. We can no longer be a people like foliage, living in the air, heavy with blossoms, bursting and fluttering at the whim of light's caress, or buffeted and tossed by the tempest: the trees must form ranks so the giant with seven-league boots shall not pass! It is the hour of muster and the united march. We must advance shoulder-to-shoulder, one solid mass like the silver lodes in the depths of the Andes.

Only the seven-month birthling will lack the courage. Those who do not have faith in their country are seven-month men. They cannot reach the first limb with their puny arms, arms with painted nails and bracelets, arms of Madrid or Paris; and they say the lofty tree cannot be climbed. The ships must be loaded with these destructive insects, who gnaw the marrow of the country that nourishes them. If they are Parisians or Madrilenians, let them stroll along the Prado under the lamplights, or take sherbet at Tortoni's. These carpenter's sons who are ashamed of their father for his trade! These American sons who are ashamed of the mother that loves them because she wears an Indian apron, and disown their sick mother, the scoundrels, abandoning her on her sick bed! Well, who is the man worthy of the name? The one who stays with his mother to nurse her in her sickness, or the one who puts her to work out of the sight of the world and lives off her labors in the decadent lands, affecting fancy cravats, cursing the womb that carried him, displaying the sign of traitor on the back of his paper cassock? These children of our America, which will be saved by its Indians, and goes from less to more, these deserters who take up arms in the armies of North America, which drowns its Indians in blood, and goes from more to less! These delicate beings, who are men but do not want to do the work of men! The Washington who forged this land, did he go to live with the English, to live with them during the years in which he saw them coming against his own country? These *incroyables* of their honor, who trail it through alien lands, like their counterparts in the French Revolution, with their dancing, their affectations, their drawling speech!

For in what lands can a man take greater pride than in our long-suffering republics of America, raised up from among the mute Indian masses by the bleeding arms of a hundred apostles to the sounds of battle between the book and the thurible. Never in history have such advanced and unified nations been forged in less time from such disordered elements. The fool in his pride believes that the earth was created to serve him as a pedestal because words flow easily from his pen, or his speech is colorful, and he charges his native land with being worthless and beyond salvation because its virgin jungles do not provide him with means to travel continuously abroad, driving Persian ponies and lavishing champagne, like a tycoon. The incapacity does not lie with the nascent country, which seeks suitable forms and greatness that will serve, but with those who attempt to rule nations of a unique character, and singular, violent composition, with laws that derive from four centuries of operative liberty in the United States, and nineteen centuries of French monarchy. A decree by Hamilton does not halt the charge of the *llanero*'s[1] pony. A phrase of Sièyes does nothing to quicken the stagnant blood of the Indian race. One must see things as they are, to govern well; the good governor in America is not one who knows how government is conducted in France or Germany, but who knows the elements of which his country is composed and how they can be marshaled so that by methods and institutions native to the country the desirable state may be attained wherein every man realizes himself, and all share in the abundance that Nature bestowed for the common benefit on the nation they enrich with their labor and defend with their lives. The government must be the child of the country. The spirit of the government must be the same as that of the country. The form of government must conform to the natural constitution of the country. Good government is nothing more than the true balance between the natural elements of the nation.

For that reason, the foreign book has been conquered in America by the natural man. The natural men have vanquished the artificial, lettered men. The native-born half-breed has vanquished the exotic Creole. The struggle is not between barbarity and civilization, but between false erudition and nature. The natural man is good. He respects and rewards superior intelligence, as long as his submission is not turned against him, or he is not offended by being disregarded, a thing the natural man does not forgive, prepared as he is to regain by force the respect of whoever has wounded his pride or threatened his interests. Tyrants in America have risen to power serving these scorned natural elements, and have fallen the moment they betrayed them. Republics have paid in tyrannies for their inability to recognize the true elements of their countries, to derive from them the proper form of government, and govern accordingly. To be a governor of a new country means to be a creator.

In nations of cultured and uncultured elements, the uncultured will govern, because it is their habit to strike and resolve all doubts by force, whenever the cultured prove inca-

---

[1]Plainsman

pable in office. The uncultured mass is lazy, and timid in matters of the mind. It asks only to be well-governed. But if the government hurts it, it rebels and governs itself. How can the universities be expected to produce governors, if there is not one university in America that teaches the rudimentary in the art of government, which is the analysis of the elements peculiar to America? Young men go out into the world wearing Yankee or French spectacles, and hope to govern by guesswork a nation they do not know. In the political race, all entries should be scratched who do not demonstrate a knowledge of the political rudiments. The prize in literary contests should go not to the best ode, but to the best study of the political factors in one's country. Newspapers, universities, and schools should foment the study of their country's dynamic factors. They have only to be stated, straightforward and in plain language. For whoever disregards any portion of the truth, whether by ignorance or design, is doomed to fall; the truth he lacked grows in the negligence and brings down whatever was erected without it. It is easier to determine the elements and attack the problem, than to attack the problem without knowing the elements. The natural man arrives, indignant and strong, and topples the authority based on books because he was not governed according to the obvious realities of the country. Knowledge holds the key. To know one's country, and govern it with that knowledge, is the only alternative to tyranny. The European university must give way to the American university. The history of America, from the Incas to the present, must be taught until it is known by heart, even if the Archons of the Greeks go by the board. Our Greece must take priority over the Greece that is not ours: we need it more. Nationalist statesmen must replace cosmopolitan statesmen. Let the world be grafted on our republics; but the trunk must be our own. And let the vanquished pedant hold his tongue: for there are no lands in which a man can take greater pride than in our long-suffering American republics.

With the rosary as our guide, our head white and our body mottled, both Indian and Creole, we intrepidly entered the community of nations. We set out to conquer liberty under the standard of the Virgin. A priest, a handful of lieutenants, and a woman raised the Mexican Republic on the shoulders of the Indians. A few heroic students instructed in French liberty by a Spanish cleric, raised Central America against Spain under a Spanish general. In the oriflammed habits of monarchy, Venezuelans and Argentinians set out, from north to south, to deliver nations. When the two heroes collided, and the continent almost rocked, one, and not the lesser, turned back. But when the wars ended, heroism, by being less glorious, became rarer; it is easier for men to die with honor than to think with order. It was discovered that it is simpler to govern when sentiments are exalted and united, than in the wake of battle when divisive, arrogant, exotic, and ambitious ideas emerge. The forces routed in the epic conflict sought, with the feline cunning of their species, and utilizing the weight of realities, to undermine the new structure, which embraced at once the rude and singular provinces of our half-breed America, and the cities of silken hose and Parisian frock coat, beneath the unfamiliar flag of reason and liberty, borrowed from nations skilled in the arts of government. The hierarchical constitution of the colonies resisted the democratic organization of the republics. The capitals of stock and collar kept the countryside of horse-hide boots cooling its heels in the vestibule. The cultured leaders did not realize that the revolution had triumphed because their words had unshackled the soul of the nation, and that they had to govern with that soul, and not against it or without it. America began to suffer, and still suffers, from the effort of trying to find an adjustment between the discordant and hostile elements it inherited from a despotic and perverse colonizer, and the imported ideas and forms which have retarded the logical government because of their lack of local reality. The continent, disjointed by three centuries of a rule that denied men the right to use their reason, embarked on a form of government based on reason, without thought or reflection on the unlettered hordes which had helped in its redemption; it was to be the reason of all in matters of general concern, not the reason of the university over the reason of the province. The problem of the Independence was not the change in forms, but the change in spirit.

It was necessary to make common cause with the downtrodden, to secure the new system against the interests and habits of rule of the oppressors. The tiger, frightened off by the powder flash, returns at night to the haunts of his prey. When he dies, it is with flames shooting from his eyes and claws unsheathed. But his step cannot be heard, for he comes on velvet paws. When the prey awakes, the tiger is upon him. The colony lives on in the republic; and our America is saving itself from its grave errors—the arrogance of the capital cities, the blind triumph of the scorned country people, the influx of foreign ideas and formulas, the wicked and unpolitic disdain in which the aboriginal race is held—through the superior virtue, backed by the necessary conviction, of the republic that struggles against the colony. The tiger lurks behind each tree, waiting at every turn. He will die with his claws unsheathed and flames shooting from his eyes.

But "these countries will be saved," as the Argentine Rivadavia announced, whose sin was to be gentlemanly in crude times; a silk scabbard does not become the *machete*, nor can the lance be discarded in a country won by the lance, for it becomes angry, and presents itself at the door of Iturbide's congress demanding that "the blond one be made emperor." These countries will be saved because a genius for moderation, found in Nature's imperturbable harmony, seems to prevail in the continent of light, where there emerges a new realistic man schooled for these realistic times in the critical philosophy, which in Europe has succeeded the literature of sect and opinion in which the previous generation was steeped.

We were a strange sight with the chest of an athlete, the hands of a coxcomb, and the brain of a child. We were a masquerade in English trousers, Parisian vest, North

American jacket, and Spanish hat. The Indian circled about us in silent wonder, and went to the mountains to baptize his children. The runaway Negro poured out the music of his heart on the night air, alone and unknown among the rivers and wild beasts. The men of the land, the creators, rose up in blind indignation against the scornful city, against their own child. We were all epaulets and tunics in countries that came into the world with hemp sandals on their feet and headbands for hats. The stroke of genius would have been to couple the headband and tunic with the charity of heart and daring of the founding father; to rescue the Indian; to make a place for the able Negro; to fit liberty to the body of those who rose up and triumphed in its name. We were left with the judge, the general, the scholar and the prebendary. As if caught in the tentacles of an octopus, the angelic young men lunged toward Heaven, only to fall back, crowned with clouds, in sterile glory. The natural people, driven by instinct, swept away the golden staffs of office in blind triumph. The European or Yankee book could not provide the answer to the Hispanic-American enigma. Hate was tried, and the countries wasted away, year by year. Exhausted by the senseless struggle between the book and the lance, of reason against dogma, of the city against the country, of the impossible rule by rival city cliques over the natural nation alternately tempestuous and inert, we begin almost without realizing it to try love. The nations stand up and salute each other. "What are we like?" they ask; and they begin to tell one another what they are like. When a problem arises in Cojimar, they do not send to Danzig for the answer. The frock coat is still French, but thought begins to be American. The youth of America roll up their sleeves and plunge their hands into the dough; it rises with the leavening of their sweat. They understand that there is too much imitation, and that creation holds the key to salvation. "Create" is the password of this generation. The wine is from plantain, and if it proves sour, it is our wine! It is understood that the forms of government must accommodate themselves to the natural elements of the country, that absolute ideas must take relative forms if they are to escape emasculation by the failure of the form, that liberty, if it is to be viable, must be sincere and complete, that the republic which does not open its arms to all, and move ahead with all, must die. The tiger within enters through the fissure, and the tiger from without. The general restrains his cavalry to a pace that suits his infantry, for if the infantry be left behind, the cavalry is surrounded by the enemy. Politics is strategy. Nations should live in continual self-criticism, because criticism is healthy; but always with one heart and one mind. Go down to the unfortunate and take them in your arms! Dissolve what is clotted in America with the fire of the heart! Make the natural blood of the nations course and throb through their veins! Erect, with the happy, sparkling eyes of workingmen, the new Americans salute one another from country to country. The natural statesman appears, schooled in the direct study of Nature. He reads to apply what he reads, not to copy. Economists study the problems at their origin. Orators begin to be lofty. Dramatists bring native characters to the stage. Academies consider practical subjects. Poetry shears off its romantic locks and hangs its red vest on the glorious tree.

Prose, lively and discriminating, is charged with ideas. Governors study Indian in republics of Indians.

America is escaping all its dangers. The octopus still sleeps on some republics; but others, in contrast, drain the ocean from their lands with a furious, sublime haste, as if to make up for lost centuries. Some, forgetting that Juárez rode in a mule-drawn coach, hitch their coach to the wind and entrust the reins to a soap-bubble; poisonous luxury, the enemy of liberty, corrupts the frivolous and opens the door to the outlander. In others, where independence is threatened, an epic spirit produces a heightened manliness. Still others spawn a rabble-in-arms in rapacious wars against their neighbors which may yet turn and devour them. But there is yet another danger which does not come from within, but from the difference in origins, methods and interests between the two halves of the continent. The hour is fast approaching when our America will be confronted by an enterprising and energetic nation seeking close relations, but with indifference and scorn for us and our ways. And since strong countries, self-made by the rifle and the law, love, and love only, strong countries; since the hour of recklessness and ambition, of which North America may be freed if that which is purest in her blood predominates, or on which she may be launched by her vengeful and sordid masses, her tradition of expansion or the ambition of some powerful leaders, is not so near at hand, even to the most timorous eye, that there is not time to show the self-possessed and unwavering pride that would confront and dissuade her; since her good name as a republic in the eyes of the world puts on the America of the North a brake which cannot be removed even by the puerile grievances, the pompous arrogance, or parricidal discords of our American nations, the pressing need for our America, is to show herself as she is, one in soul and purpose, swift conqueror of a suffocating tradition, stained only by the blood drawn from hands that struggle to clear away ruins, and the scars left us by our masters. The scorn of our formidable neighbor, who does not know us, is the greatest danger for our America; and it is imperative that our neighbor know us, and know us soon, so she shall not scorn us, for the day of the visit is at hand. Through ignorance, she might go so far as to lay hands on us. From respect, once she came to know us, she would remove her hands. One must have faith in the best in men and distrust the worst. If not, the worst prevails. Nations should have a pillory for whoever fans useless hates; and another for whoever does not tell them the truth in time.

There can be no racial hate, because there are no races. The rachitic thinkers and theorists juggle and warm over the library-shelf races, which the open-minded traveler and well-disposed observer seek in vain in Nature's justice, where the universal identity of man leaps forth from triumphant love and the turbulent lust for life. The soul emanates, equal and eternal, from bodies distinct in shape and color. Whoever foments and propagates antagonism and hate between races, sins against Humanity. But as nations take shape among other different nations, they acquire distinctive and vital characteristics of thought and habit, of expansion and conquest, of vanity and greed, which from the latent state of national preoccupation could be converted in a period of internal unrest, or precipitation of the accumulated character of the nation, into a serious threat to the neighboring countries, isolated and weak, which the strong country declares perishable and inferior. The thought is father to the deed. But it must not be supposed, from a parochial animus, that there is a fatal and ingrained evil in the blond nation of the continent, because it does not speak our tongue, nor see the world as we do, nor resemble us in its political faults, which are of a different order, nor favorably regard the excitable, dark-skinned people, nor look charitably, from its still uncertain eminence, on those less favored by History, who climb the road of republicanism by heroic stages. The self-evident facts of the problem should not be obscured for it can be resolved, to the benefit of peaceful centuries yet to come, by timely study and the tacit, immediate union of the continental soul. The hymn of oneness sounds already; the actual generation carries a purposeful America along the road enriched by their sublime fathers; from the Rio Grande to the straits of Magellan, the Great Semi, seated on the flank of the condor, sows the seed of the new America through the romantic nations of the continent and the sorrowful islands of the sea!

# DRAMA

# Iván Acosta

Iván Acosta was born in Santiago de Cuba in 1943 and came to the United States in 1961. He graduated from the New York University Film Institute. His involvement in theater includes the direction of plays at the Henry Street Playhouse and the New Federal Theater. He was awarded the ARIEL, O.C.L.A., and Thalia awards for his musical hit *Grito 71* in 1971. Acosta is the founder of the Centro Cultural Cubano de New York, where he has produced many plays. *El Súper* went from the stage into the film industry, winning awards.

## El Súper[1]

AURELIA:  Lower your voices, someone's at the door. It must be Philip.
ROBERTO:  At this hour?

---

Primary works by Iván Acosta: *El Súper* (Miami: Ediciones Universal, 1982); *Un cubiche en la luna: Tres obras teatrales* (Houston: Arte Público Press, 1989).

[1]The Superintendant

PREACHER:  Good evening. (*He enters without permission.*)

AURELIA:  What can we do for you?

PREACHER:  The eternal purpose of God now triumphs for the good of man ...

AURELIA:  Young man, please forgive me, but ...

PREACHER:  In the Bible it is written that Jesus resurrected Lazarus from the dead after four days.

AURELIA:  That's fine son, but ... I believe in Santa Bárbara ...

PREACHER:  Does it make sense to you that some people live on earth in perpetual hunger, as is the case with millions today?

PANCHO:  Yeah, we'll take care of that right away, bro' ...

AURELIA:  What? ... Okay, I don't think that ...

PREACHER:  So, what you mean is that the Bible story about Jesus providing food for thousands of people isn't—perhaps—important to you?

AURELIA:  Well, yes, but look, couldn't you come another day? Right now we're. . . .

PREACHER:  Christ is the only Savior. You have to save yourselves. It's better late than never. We all have to be born again ... (*He hands Ophelia a religious pamphlet.*)

OPHELIA:  Okay, but I'm Catholic, son.

PREACHER:  (*He goes to the living room and hands pamphlets to Roberto and Pancho.*) The super-powers spend more than 40 billion dollars on weapons, and to keep one soldier armed, uniformed and equipped. . . . I'm telling you, just one soldier ... (*He sits down.*)

ROBERTO:  (*Roberto stands up quickly.*) Okay, okay. Young man, I understand what you're sayin', but you've got to understand that we have visitors. We're busy.

PREACHER:  You should never be too busy to receive the word of God. For that reason I urge you, in the name of Christ, for everyone to speak with one voice, end the divisiveness, everyone come together in one mind, with a unified point of view ...

PANCHO:  Bro', that's what they call Communism. Get'm outta here already!

PREACHER:  That is the Bible, the word of God ...

OPHELIA:  But he won't leave!

PREACHER:  Does it make any sense that a simple turtle lives more than 150 years while the superior creation, man, despite modern medical science has to resign himself to a life expectancy half as long, or less?

ROBERTO:  All right. Young man, we're busy. I've already told you. (*He escorts him to the door.*) Do me the favor of hittin' the road. If you like, come another day, but for now, that's enough.

PREACHER:  Jehovah has declared his plans for the future in symbolic language. (*He continues talking as he is leaving.*) Read Genesis 3:15, read Galatians 3:18, read Ezekiel 38:23, and Joseph 9:11. The creator, God, Jehovah ... (*From outside.*) Save yourselves now. Your names will be praised on earth and in heaven when you settle your score with Satan, the demons and the wicked people on earth.

(*The words of the preacher continue to be heard backstage. Roberto begins to talk to Aurelia and an improvisation starts among the four people.*)

AURELIA: What was that all about?

ROBERTO: Remember, I've told you not to open the door without lookin' out the window first.

OPHELIA: That's why I don't open the door for anyone without lookin' first to see who it is.

PANCHO: They line up right here and grab whatever they can.

ROBERTO: It's just not right, and especially with the bunch of nuts runnin' around this city. What about that serial killer? That son of Sam? Right? That woman never learns. If I've told her once, I've told her a thousand times, but she just doesn't learn.

AURELIA: I thought it was Philip.

ROBERTO: The bottom line is that you have to be careful. (*They all talk at the same time about the same topic.*)

PANCHO: Hey Roberto, you know what? This reminds me of when we were down there durin' the invasion and there's this guy, like the one who just left. Well . . . (*Roberto interrupts him.*)

ROBERTO: That's enough, Pancho. Why don't we talk with the women some, okay? Ophelia, come 'ere. Aurelia, give it a rest in the kitchen. Come 'ere. (*Aurelia and Ophelia go to the living room.*)

PANCHO: Ophelia, bring me another beer, would ya'?

AURELIA: You wanna 'nother too, Roberto?

ROBERTO: (*He rubs his stomach.*) No, no more. I don't wanna mess up my diet.

OPHELIA: Speakin' of diets, look at you Aurelia. You're lookin' thinner, right? Or is it that dress?

AURELIA: Oh, come on, girl, trapped in that kitchen, who can resist stuffin' their face?

ROBERTO: Now Aurelia, she's the one who's careful about what she eats. She doesn't touch bread, or rice, or beans, and she won't eat meat fried in oil.

OPHELIA: Think about it. She's in her prime. Here, it's fashionable to be skinny. Even so, back home, the fatter you were, the healthier they thought you were. I remember when I was in high school and they'd call me "skinny cat." Here they'd h've said I had a great figure.

PANCHO: A figure like Mahatma Ghandi's! As far as I'm concerned, I'm not interested in any skinny cat, 'cause the way I like it is to have some meat before I get to the bones! (*He laughs loudly.*)

AURELIA: There're so many ads about diets that ya' just get sucked in. I mean, they use those young models, who are perfect: perfect teeth, perfect hair, those legs, those eyes. They're genuine little dolls. People see that on TV, and then everybody wants to look like 'em.

ROBERTO: That reminds me of when I was young . . . you know, those American movies, about cowboys and the war. Everybody was blond with blue eyes, there wasn't one Black.

PANCHO: Yeah, right. And they were six and seven feet tall. Not one of 'em was short. Think about what happened to Alan Ladd. That guy was 5' 4", and when his movie was comin' out, they made him taller by havin' him stand on an empty milk crate.

ROBERTO: Don't forget, they never lost a battle either.

PANCHO: Lose a battle? Are you crazy? To the Japanese, to the Germans, to the Koreans? Forget it. They were always the heroes and the enemy was always sent packin'. And the heroes never even got shot either. You better believe it. I mean come on, these are the same folks who invented Superman.

OPHELIA: That's right, and those Americans just eat it all up.

ROBERTO: (*Yawning.*) Right. And by eatin' so much, they get indigestion. (*The conversation shifts to a slower pace.*) How much longer do we have to shovel snow for these people, my friends?

PANCHO: Until you decide to move to the Exile capital.

AURELIA: Fine. I'll tell you Pancho that I prefer the snow and the boiler and all the rest compared to going to Miami. Geez! The whole Cuban thing and all that gossip! Here, at last nobody sticks their nose into other people's lives.

PANCHO: Yeah, well, what about when you have a little heart attack in the morning and there isn't one neighbor who even prepares ya' a cup of coffee or tea. Forget it. There's nothing can replace Cuba. (*Aurelia yawns, and without speaking, gestures to Roberto asking for the time, and he answers her in the same way. Ophelia also yawns.*) The rooster's cock-a-doodle-doo in the morning, a little cup of hot coffee, greetings from the neighbor passin' by, that sun that burns like the devil, the juice of the sugar cane. Oh, my dear Cuba, dear little Cuba! (*Singing badly.*) When I left Cuba, I left my life. La, la, la, la, la. Guantanamera, guajira, guantanameeera ... (*The lights have been dimming.*)

OPHELIA: Pancho, whadda ya' say we go?

PANCHO: Okay, you're the boss. Right? (*He laughs.*)

# Transcultural

What happens when you no longer worry about whether or not you belong in the United States or in your native homeland? When do you stop thinking that a return to your native country is a must if you wish to be considered a native of your nation? When are you as comfortable living in the United States as you are living anywhere else? Does this mean that you are less Mexican, Argentinean, Panamanian, or any other ethnicity you were before coming across or over the Rio Grande, the Atlantic or Pacific ocean? When does a writer reflect these changes, themes, or preoccupations in his or her writing? When are you allowed to embrace another culture as your own without losing the authenticity of your native heritage? When is it acceptable to acknowledge the acquisition of Anglo-American cultural habits, traditions, and language? When does one recognize that we live in a transcultural environment? What does this mean? How does it affect us? Transculturation is understood as a process in which a culture experiences changes as a result of its constant interaction with foreign cultures. US culture is transcultural in that people of all cultures in the world live in US territories, and although not all cultures are allowed to participate equally, they are present and in many ways reshape US culture. This is done through food, music, literature, daily interaction, and so on. Therefore, it is easy to see why Latino authors can maintain their native heritage while they participate in everyday life in the United States.

Transcultural literature features authors whose texts evidence the participation of several worlds in one space and offer examples of how these worlds compliment one another. The selections present views that encompass the search for identity to issues that pertain to a multiplicity of identities that permit Latinos to adapt to life in the United States. Authors in this category demonstrate that they are no longer worried about returning to their countries because with advances in technology, this can easily be accomplished by computer or telephone. As a matter of fact, being in two places is not a thing of the future or something out of the ordinary.

Authors in this category share the perspective that Latinos in the United States must create identities that will facilitate their accommodation, identities that also enable them to keep strong ties with their own countries although they live in an Anglo-American environment. The writers included reflect on their experiences in North America, often as minorities but also as survivors who are looking to overcome the special circumstances that surround them and inform who they are. Authors and characters represent immigrants in search of better opportunities who discover that life in the United States does provide economically for them and for their families back home, although this involves working at low-paying jobs that take a toll on their bodies and lives. Many authors notice a connection with the country left behind through the material objects that are purchased and sent back: a radio, a television, a VCR, a computer are items symbolically charged as examples of life away from the native land. They are symbols of transculturation in that through them images and ideas on US life and culture are transmitted.

Roberto Quesada's *Never Through Miami*, in a humorous tone, explains the ways in which a person can and should arrive to the United States and extols the influence of the images sent via television and the Hollywood film industry. Through his characters Quesada presents the situation of coming to a land to which one has been exposed only via Hollywood and television. Quesada, in a scene in which a mother and daughter discuss life in the United States, speaks of the influences of US television on Ecuadorian women, and signals, too, the influence of Latin American *telenovelas* on US television and culture. This is a fine example of the transculturation dialog that takes place between the United States and the rest of the world in that transculturation is not a one-way street. Ramón "Tianguis" Pérez's autobiography, *Diary of an Undocumented Worker*, also bridges two countries, the United States and Mexico. Pérez recounts his odyssey to and through North America as he tries to earn enough money to help him open a small wood shop in Macuiltianguis, Mexico.

Transculturation is a process that also has negative repercussions, as is presented by several poets such as Carolina Monsivais whose poem "Somewhere Between El Paso and Houston" demands justice for the hundreds of women who are abused physically and emotionally in both the United States and Mexico. Monsivais touches on issues of transnationalism as she discusses many instances whereby young Mexican women, working in US-owned and operated factories, are murdered and kidnapped and the atrocities go unpunished. Monsivais attests to the experience not only of living between two worlds but within many cultures. Her journey oscillates between Houston and El Paso, two major cities in Texas, each too preoccupied in its own development and too busy to care for the victims of its capitalistic expansion. In such places, women are often easy targets for abuse and crime, and, in many ways, are disposable.

Spoken word poetry by Latino artists also crosses the border between languages and cultures. Spoken word poetry is a type of verse that is intended to be performed; for that reason, rhythm and rhyme are respected in the works.

Brenda Cárdenas, in her poem "ñ", presents an ode to the unique sound that this letter produces in the Spanish vocabulary, a sound that is not present in English. Cárdenas provides a variety of examples in which this letter enriches the Spanish alphabet as well as the English. Her poem can also be read as a symbol of the richness of Mexican culture, tradition, and language, a wealth that complements American language and culture. Another salient issue is presented in Olga Angelina García's poetry is the role that Latinas have in US society, where they are not only sexy and exotic but also significant contributors to society. In "Lengualistic Algo: Speaking Tongues," she renders homage to bilingualism, to the ability to speak in code, in tongues, and in dialects. She states that this is a positive skill in Latinas and Latinos, who must find ways to negotiate their space in United States. She believes that one way to execute this task is through one's voice, which in the end is an indicator of one's tradition and cultural background.

Tradition as a source of strength and belonging is also a theme analyzed in "The Seven African Gods" by Frank Varela, a Nuyorican poet, who delves into the repercussions of the loss of traditions and customs for a community. The loss of something as significant as the praying to a religious symbol translates as the end of humanity because this also represents the loss of faith or belief in what is integral to the creation of a specific community. Also reinforcing the value of tradition, robertokarimi's "The Reinvention of the Zero" parts from the LA riots of early 1990s to speak of the value recognizing each person's ethnic background. This acknowledgment reinforces identities and culture in the United States. Both poets underline the transcultural environment in which they live, where they can acknowledge and value their heritage without repercussions.

The primary role of this category, then, is to provide texts that describe behaviors and actions by which the Latino authors experience life in the United States—a life that is not based on one culture but on a multiplicity of cultures that complement, compete, and dialog with each other and within each author. This section takes us a step further in recognizing that Latinos negotiate identities in the United States; away from their countries, they acquire methods that incorporate US culture, traditions, and language in their lives and in their families. In this fashion, we can began to understand how it is that Latino literature now enriches our culture, our schools—that it is as much a part of US culture as Coca-Cola and McDonald's.

# POETRY

## Carolina Monsiváis

Carolina Monsiváis is from El Paso, Texas. She worked as an outreach advocate at Sexual Trauma and Assault Services, Inc., in El Paso, and as a school educator for the Houston Area Women's Center. She received an Individual Artist Grant from the City of Houston/Harris County in 2002, which funded the publication of *Somewhere between Houston and El Paso*. Her poems speak of her activism on behalf of issues that afflict women of all races.

### Somewhere between Houston and El Paso

As always, I anticipate the sunset
that greets me with a different face
each time I make my way back home
to desert, I carry always right
below skin in sand swept pulses.
It drops red, behind mountains,
then seems to rise like lava over
ridges. I reach out from the car
window cup heat in hands to carry
back to my desk in the city of concrete
and weld thoughts shifting in mind.
I'd been walking heavy with rage
for weeks after meeting many girls
during presentations on getting out
of violent relationships, now
behind in Houston carrying the burden
of being disbelieved,
of being blamed or of being silent
over how their bodies have been
made into war zones.
They tell me life is as it is and a good
relationship means surviving with
minimal scarring.
Ahead, in Juarez awaits black crosses
painted over pink backgrounds
on telephone poles around the market,
for girls disappearing nightly on their way

*purposely making grammatical errors*

*emphasis on setting*

Primary work by Carolina Monsivais: *Somewhere between Houston and El Paso* (San Antonio: Wings Press, 2000).

home from maquiladoras.
One can no longer
pass through the market
without noticing
200 blazing headstones of pink.
I'm asked what can we do,
when there is nothing we can do?
All I can offer is the heat in my hands
to burn the wall between reality
of violence we have only ever known
and the uncharted landscape
of imagination where the tools
of a different life lay buried beneath
the soot blown over from this world.

# Sandra Cisneros

Sandra Cisneros was born in Chicago to a Mexican father and Chicana mother. She has garnered wide critical acclaim and popular success through her poetry and short story publications. Her writing addresses her childhood experiences, ethnic heritage, issues that pertain to poverty, cultural suppression, self-identity, and gender roles. She received a B.A. in English from Loyola University of Chicago in 1976 and attended the University of Iowa's Writers' Workshop, where she found her voice—a working-class, Mexican-American woman with an independent sexuality. She received many awards for her writing, among them the MacArthur Foundation Fellowship. She currently lives in San Antonio, where she continues to be an advocate for Latinas and Latinos.

## Tango for the Broom

I would like to be a poet if
I had my life to do over again.
I would like to dance with the broom,
or sweep the kitchen as I am

sweeping it today and imagine
my broom is a handsome
black-haired tango man whose

Primary works by Sandra Cisneros: *The House on Mango Street* (New York: Vintage Books, 1985); *My Wicked, Wicked Ways* (Bloomington: Third Woman Press, 1987); *Loose Woman: Poems* (New York: Vintage Books, 1995); *Woman Hollering Creek* (New York: Vintage Books, 1991); *Caramelo* (New York: Vintage Books, 2003).

black hair scented with Tres Flores[1]
oil is as shiny as his
black patent leather shoes.

Or, I would like to be a poet laundress
washing sheets and towels,
pulling them hot and twisted
from the dryer, wrapping

myself in the warmth of
clean towels, clean sheets,
folding my work into soft towers,
satisfied. So much done in a day!

Or, I would like to be a poet eating soup
today because my throat hurts. Putting
big spoonfuls of hot soup
into my big fat mouth.

---

[1]Three Flowers (a hair treatment used for styling)

# Alicia Gaspar de Alba

Alicia Gaspar de Alba was born in El Paso, Texas. She received her B.A. and her M.A. in English and Creative Writing from the University of Texas at El Paso and her Ph.D. in American Studies from the University of New Mexico. Her literary publications include a collection of poetry, *Beggar on the Córdoba Bridge* (1989); a collection of short stories, *The Mystery of Survival and Other Stories* (1993); a novel, *Sor Juana's Dream* (1999); and the collection of poetry *La Llorona on the Longfellow Bridge* (2003). She currently teaches at the University of California, Los Angeles.

## Huitlacoche Crepes

*(for Antonia and Arturo)*

### I.

Your friend tells you she is afraid

---

Primary works by Alicia Gaspar de Alba: *Chicano Art Inside/Outside the Master's House: Cultural Politics and the CARA Exhibition* (Austin: Univ. of TX Press, 1998); *La Llorona on the Longfellow Bridge: Poetry y otras movidas* (Houston: Arte Público Press, 2003); *The Mystery of Survival and Other Stories* (Tempe: Bilingual Press Editorial Bilingüe, 1993); *Sor Juana's Second Dream* (Albuquerque: Univ. of NM Press, 1999); *Three Times a Woman: Chicana Poetry* (Tempe: Bilingual Review Press, 1989); ed, *Velvet Barrios: Popular Culture of Chicana/o Sexualities* (New York: Palgrave Macmillan, 2003).

she has lost her voice
somewhere in the surcos[1]
of her hot Texas memories.

## II.

At the reception a woman shakes
your hand, tells you how magical
your story was and how Mexican
literature is so loved in this town
she calls "plain vanilla."
You wonder if she has ever tasted
the chocolate chips and mocha swirls
the strawberry juice marbled
like blood in the jasmine-scented earth
of San Antonio de Bexar.

## III.

The güera[2] journalist sits
at your table—thick plates of cabrito[3]
and huitlacoche[4] crepes, café de olla[5] —
and asks the Mexicans who got there
first what they think about bilingual
education, and doesn't immersion
make much more sense if the goal
is to become American citizens?

## IV.

México always reminds us
she is there—in the pall of smoke
that stretches over the border,
on the brown backs of travelers
bent low over beets or strawberries,
Virgin of Guadalupe tattooed to their
shoulder blades or dangling from the rear-
view mirror of their American dreams.

## V.

"What do you think about bilingual education?"

---

[1]Furrows
[2]Blond woman, US American
[3]Goat
[4]Corn smut, fungi
[5]Coffee brewed with cinnamon

The question hangs in the air, obscene
as the flash of exposed genitals. A sarape
of silence falls over our chocolate-
dipped strawberries.
Do the Mexicans get up and leave?
*Beam us up, Scottie!*
Do we throw the gourmet fungus
huitlacoche crepes
in her face, lecture her
about beans and corn and strawberries?
Do we take a sharp blade
to her native lengua,[6]
slice all the way down
to the agave heart of silence
where nothing but mezcal grows
and the tongue shrivels like the worm
at the bottom of a bottle labeled
Freedom of Speech?
In another year, every immigrant's
new social security number will be
187-209-227.

## VI.

Write about your feet, you tell your friend,
about the earth your toes have traveled,
the surcos
where you planted the seeds
of your working heart, where your mother
and father pulled the master's tongue
out by the roots, immersed it in
the hundred-and-twelve degree glare
of the south Texas sun while their Mexican
voices filled the fields with song.

------

[6]Tongue

# Tony Medina

Tony Medina was born in the Bronx and lives in Harlem. He makes the struggle for life in these places the subject of many of his poems. Rumba and salsa, the blues, jazz, hip-hop, and reggae supply the rhythm for his verse and permit his imagination to embrace the

Americas as a diverse world. His poetry forces today's poetry out of its academic confines into explosive spaces in which questions emerge to engage the workplace, where many people are harassed, demoralized, and oppressed daily. He exhorts readers to stop "being illiterate," to realize that those rap artists who are admired are, in fact, intellectuals in their field. They take the time to research music, beats, and language.

## The Illiterati

They write
but they don't read
They read
but they can't write

~they~

Hip on the scene
they are the afro sheen
cosmetic queens
wanting to be seen
in perpetual commercials
of posh bohemian cafés
or as a side order
in an underground entrée
of shrimps reading to shrimps
& allergic to each other's ears

*juxtaposed adjectives*

They fight
but they can't cite
the sources of their anger
instead they rely on
2nd hand info
& other poets' lines
Reactions & Impressions
is what they must have
not the quest for ideas
nor the investigation
of their soul
trapped in the barbed wire fence
of the filthy shit hole we stuck in
while they suckin
on somebody else's vapors

*not smart enough to philosophize*

Primary works by Tony Medina: *No Noose Is Good Noose* (New York/London: Harlem River Press, 1996); Ed. with Derrick I.M. Gilbert *Catch the Fire!!!: A Cross-Generational Anthology of Contemporary African-American Poetry* (New York: Riverhead Books, 1998); Ed. with S.E. Anderson *In Defense of Mumia* (New York: Writers and Readers Pub., 1996); *Love to Langston* (New York: Lee & Low Books, 2002); Ed. *Bum Rush the Page: A Def Poetry Jam* (New York: Three Rivers Press, 2001); *Committed to Breathing* (Chicago: Third World Press, 2003).

miming & rhyming
on time
relying on a line
they copped
& memorized
from the peers they
think they have
but shrimps are minor
keys that mimic major keys
like monkeys
chained to a
music box
for money

To them ideas are spooky
heavy unwanted
trash
what they read
is not ishmael reed
or books or
papers but
the backs of
iodine
bottles
where one
day their
poems
will
land

To them
history is
an oxymoron
that makes
them morons
& a mockery
of their fantasy
of thinking that
they're the
only one's
to use

*shift in lineation = anger* (handwritten annotation)

the words
fuck & shit
in the same
poem
& that the petty
bourgeoisie
owe 'em
respect
    & money

To them attitude
is where it's at
not longitude
not latitude
nor the clear & direct
vertical violence
visionary integrity
would entail
but the whine
& wail of
superficial
horizontal
back biting
jealousies
of who's gonna
read first
before they burst
or shit they drawers
they want applause
so bad
only to soon realize
they've been had
not by the state or system
or instigating agents or puppets
but by their own
ignorance & greed
& desire to bleed
the people of their
common sense & money
       (cents)
Has beens is what we have

speed
&
rhymes

because they've never been
serious about anything
but trying to be rich
                &
           famous
with antics upon antics
of wordless semantics
& what Beatty calls
"Verbal Mugging"

w/ all the tidily tease & tidily toes
of wanna be has been ho's
& all the other foes
working
against
progress
fo'
MONEY MONEY MONEY
        MONEY
Milk Duds & honey
candy coated
cotton candy fluff
to stuff in your head
& keep your memory
dead
to the violence
that they seek
from the ignorance
that they reek
& speak
& pipsqueak
off the curb
or from around
the corner
of their minds
tap dancing to
rhymes
that stay
silent

& = lazy

we won't remain silent

# Radames Ortiz

Radames Ortiz's poems have appeared in numerous publications, including *Exquisite Corpse, Pacific Review, Gulf Coast, Open City,* and *Borderlands.* He was awarded a 2003 Archie D. and Bertha Walker fellowship from the Fine Arts Work Center in Provincetown, Massachusetts. He currently resides in Houston, Texas.

## Night Cruising

We cruise past city lights, past
a new stadium on Clay & Walker.
Enter the darkest part of the city
where old warehouses are without
plumbing or electricity.
Where language is of no use &
words are rat droppings behind a sink.
Brutal. A waste.
That's how we cruise the streets.
Our chins high above sludge of night,
our eyes winking small skirts & firm breasts.
That's where it's at, our happiness,
drifting like love songs boasted
out of old jukeboxes in bars
where patrons shake their hips,
scoot their snakeskin boots,
tap their brims of hats. Elemental
like horses, snakes—shoes hanging
off phone wires. At 90 mph the wind
is a blessing, a bump on the road.
We curve turnpikes, wail thru tollways,
our mouths brilliant wounds
yellowing every shade of green.
On ribcage of train tracks
we are heroes outgrowing their confetti

Primary work by Radames Ortiz: *between angels monsters* (Houston: n.p., 2002).

while under a blanket of bright stars
we reinvent ourselves thru windshields
& gas pedals floored to the ground.

# Ruth Irupé Sanabria

Ruth Irupé Sanabria was born in Argentina and grew up in Washington, D.C. She is an activist and poet organizing a school for undocumented people in New Jersey.

## Las a-e-i-o-u's de los ums seeking tongues of migratin' letras que ain't no way hiding[1]

gyrating spanglish verses in the rundown where dominicans loved and I
watched in a city so black
they call it chocolate
is the root
word
behind this eloquence.
yo[2] elaborare on every detail para que usted[3]
tenga la oportunidad[4] to fully comprehend
the logistics of
mi latina[5]
oral stream.

**2.**

The fortune tellers in the den of thieves
predict the future:
the temperature is changing
due to a warm front sweeping in from the south
south of the equator,
all of miami and east of L.A.

---

Ed. Sam Hamill, *Poets Against the War* (New York: Thunder Mouth's Press, 2003).

[1]The aeious of the letters seeking tongues of migratin' that ain't no way hiding
[2]I
[3]So that you (formal)
[4]Have the opportunity
[5]My Latin

actually, the ravage of tropical storm
TwoTongue LenguaFresca[6]
has been taking its toll on these
southern areas
for a few centuries now
with the surfacing of a dark and mysterious dis ease.
The exotic natives of these lands were the first
to show symptoms of this
dis ease
that, according to doctors and some medicine men,
is acquired in the rare instance
that the YoNo SpeakNoInglesh Virus[7]
comes in contact with U.S. borders or shores.
Consequently,
these inhabitants were also the first
to show signs of immunity to this malady
as their tongues
*(the area most affected by this deter mental dis ease)*,
developed a thick coat of repellent
resistant to psychologically induced
OneTongue-Antibodies.
Though officials sought to quarantine
those unfortunates
afflicted with this debilitating
enfermedad, [8] excuse me, I mean dis ease
we now have a report
that a new strain of this grave condition
has been found spreading
through most metropolitan and urbanized areas
throughout the country
this new strain, like the previous bug,
is being attributed to the radical climatic
change
triggered by a warm front sweeping in from a new southern region,
the south Bronx.
However, amid the ensuing panic,
we must remember that this dis ease

---

[6]Fresh tongue
[7]I do not  speak English
[8]Illness

is completely preventable,
all that is required to protect you and your loved ones from catching this
dis ease
is to remain celibate from any form of unbiased cultural intercourse
in the case that such intercourse becomes inevitable,
don't think, simply be closed minded
lack of communication is crucial, remind your infected partner that
he/she should go home, be sure to specify that you mean Mexico,
or if he/she is black you might want to suggest Puerto Rico . . .
do not compromise your ignorance, remain firm
in forbidding the presence of any infected individual
amidst the company of you and your family,
help the community—support intolerance
donate votes to abolish bilingualism, i.e. the promiscuous abandon of
conformity.
Spread the word
against the dis ease at your work place by promoting
mandatory acculturation and random tongue searches,
be sure to report any suspicious
dialect behavior and seize all forms of deviant rhetoric.
Promote Safe Assimilation,
with your help we can stop the spread of this dis ease.
Remember the INS is on your side.
This has been Maria Rosa Garcia Lopez
reporting en vivo, I mean quise decir[9]
live from America

**3.**

i ain't denyin' nothing
i'm a contradiction
in it's self
an' this
is how I SPEAK so listen y escúchalo bien[10]
cuz you know how I be feelin'
'bout repitiéndome[11]
tú ve, es que[12]

---

[9]Live/I meant to say
[10]Listen well
[11]Repeating myself
[12]You see, it's that

this is what I have become
ha ha ha
I laugh at all the
pimp mack daddy hos hooker dope crack feign perverted greasy head
mexican big tit mami rosa maria holy jesus jose superfly coke dealing
rapist rican mammies maids peabrained
illiterates
projected on the screen
cuz we resemble,
you know what I mean?
She always look like me
and at times,
if they did a lot of anthropological research
they even master the sound of we

## 4.

In college I am
an English major
thus,
fully capable of expressing
clarity of thought
in the properness of textbook
fashion, *shit*,
I mean, furthermore, I can
assess your own thoughts, so do not think too loud  . . .  yes yesss
you grapple with
spics, us spanish folk whosho loves to talk like dat . . . ¡arriba arriba ándale
ándale! 13
but does it scare you
to know that
in the privacy
of our own homes
of our own minds
many sp, pardon me, latinos
you know the *good ones*
who bachelored
and mastered the white
eloquence
of *proper* English

---

13Up, up, hurry, hurry!

speak this urban and rural
broke up and to'up
southern and backward
norteño[14] and forward
speech?
and that you can't understand
or even pretend like you do?
how does it feel to be left out and out
of control?
It must feel like
time for some action
some good legal action and moral
enforcing time for some national
headbanging tongue lynching
and
none of it works
we
just
can't
seem
to get
the fucking picture.

## 5.

we speak
this tree of tongued jewels
from which origins seep forth
like a brook in a forest
we gurgle the isms of recurring nightmares and
like the earth we decompose
shackles into vital minerals

listen
you will hear
staggering languages
of crossed oceans
crutched by seashells held to ears
so natural our tongues be

---

[14]Northern

free of constraints
in a land where living
on earth has a fee and we are
a national nightmare realized
by the influx of aliens
encountering in-a-city realities
copulating lenguas entre labios[15] creating
spoken masterpieces with fluid affinity
displaced immigrant words
becoming spoken refugees
as blackboards give birth
to the ya tú sabes[16] what's up

## 6.

recuerdo yo[17]
mi primer paso[18]
un día[19]
a grip of years ago
en mi school
can't you see it
ooh ooh teacha look it
we took a problem and resolved it
entre los morenos[20]
y los dominicanos[21]
each was forced to choose
and I thought well coño[22] fuck it
being la tremenda[23] smartass que soy yo[24]
I'm a let the teacher know
that I speak the reflection of where i'm from
I mirror the voices from the drone

---

[15]Tongues between lips
[16]You already know
[17]I remember
[18]My first step
[19]One day
[20]Among black people
[21]And Dominicans
[22]Damn
[23]The tremendous
[24]That I am

now, she said I spoke broken
the language of the broke
the black and the foreign
so I asked her
but how bright could we be
to take two languages and make them three


## 7.

let me continue
que quisiera brindar[25]
la elocuencia[26]
de nuestra realidad[27]
es muy simple[28]
en su complejidad.[29]
I scream you scream
the grandiose immigrant dream
between heaven and earth
like limbo we steam
in praise of language,
sweet words from the soul,
furiously spoken
this tongue is
as rebellious as freedom
and we speak
in slave tongues
that gum
drop stick
to the air like
the pollution
of dust
the filmy darkness
that envelopes us
across the land
grammar book anarchy
is at hand.

---

[25]That I would like to offer
[26]The eloquence
[27]Of our reality
[28]Is very simple
[29]In its complexity

# SPOKEN WORD POETRY

## Brenda Cárdenas

Brenda Cárdenas was born and raised in Milwaukee, Wisconsin, and lives in Chicago. She enjoys spending time at a Chicago coffee shop in which all the borders cross: "news from around the hood mixes with news from other lands." She comes from a working-class family and is a granddaughter of mom-and-pop shopkeepers. Her performances range from recitals at universities—readings accompanied by new chamber music, for example—to installations that have included video and audio art with her spoken word. Cárdenas adapts folkloric traditions into her storytelling, and is often accompanied by the band Sonido Inkquieto. Cárdenas is an advocate of interlingualism, which is blending or mixing two languages in-line, within sentences, as they're used organically and naturally by people who speak both languages fluently.

## Intensidad[1] - Ñ

*from Spanish Sound Waves, a Series*

El campesino[2] rolls
his shoulder blades as he turns
from the furrows toward
the road's curve home,
Otro año, otro día, otra estación[3];
le ha añejado con su añojal.[4]

~ Ñ, the yawn in mañana ~[5]

La araña[6] weaves her web of music,
tuning its strings while she sings
de sus compañeras obrando[7]
en las cabañas, labrando[8]
en los campos de caña.[9]
She holds the high notes,
pulling filaments taut.
And when a fly's wing

---

Primary works by Brenda Cárdenas: *Book of Voices*, e-poets network online, <http://voices.e-poets.net/index.shtml>; *Between the Heart and the Land: Entre el corazón y la tierra: Latina Poets in the Midwest* (Chicago: MARCH/Abrazo Press, 2001).

[1]Intensity
[2]The farm worker
[3]Another year, another day, another season
[4]I have aged it with its years
[5]Morning
[6]The spider
[7]Of her comrades working
[8]In the cabins, working
[9]In the sugarcane fields

touches one fiber,
everything vibrates.

~ la añagaza del balance ~ [10]

A cat's arch and curled spine
stretches into the long afternoon.
Sueña con alimañas[11]
espiando de las montañas;[12]
sueña con carne,[13]
the wiry tension
of spring and pounce
on the small-boned
and the broken-winged.

~ the sneer of engaño ~ [14]

Deep heat of day rises
like a serpent from its cool tomb
entrañado[15] beneath the sand,
leaves its tilde trace, la señal,[16]
that loosens and fades,
one moment sliding
into centuries of terrain.

~ el diseño antiguo del futuro ~ [17]

Diamond-skinned Kukulcán,
guiñando desde el cielo,[18]
slides past clouds over the edge
of sun at the tip of Chichén
onto a shadow of stone,
the equinox of a plumed past.

~ the slow and brilliant tilt de los añosos ~

Coiled in mantillas pañosas,[19]
y la[20] rumble of streetnoise
the fire-eater waits for night

---

[10]The truce of balance
[11]Dreams with pests
[12]Spying from the mountains
[13]Dreams with flesh
[14]Treason
[15]Involved
[16]The signal
[17]The ancient design of the future
[18]Winking from the sky
[19]Dull mantillas
[20]And the

to define the sharp outlines
of sustenance—
su extrañeza y su ceño,[21]
sus llantos oscuros de daño[22] —
eyes squeezed tight
above the blackened rim
of his open mouth

~ Ñ, the grimace of resistance ~

~ La ñacanima y la luz ~[23]

---

[21]Its strangeness and its brow
[22]Its dark cries of harm
[23]The large poisonous snake and the light

# Olga Angelina García

Olga Angelina García is a Chicana poet who was born and raised in East Los Angeles, California. Her poetry masterfully employs code switching, demonstrating the politicized identity that many bilingual speakers adopt. She holds a BA from the University of California, Santa Barbara, in ethnic studies, and an MFA from the University of Texas, El Paso. She has performed at several places in Los Angeles and El Paso/Ciudad Juárez. Her poetry is featured in *Raza Spoken Here* and *When Skin Peels*.

## Lengualistic Algo[1]

Qué quieren conmigo los puristas,[2]
all tongue-tied
& sitting proper
behind fat stoic dictionaries?
I've already eaten the thin white skeletons
of foreign words
choked on the bones of Inglés[3] Only,
learned the art of speaking in codes
and code switching,
learned to spit palabras[4]

---

Primary works by Olga Angelina García: *When Skin Peels*, cd recording, Calaca Press, 2000; *Raza Spoken Here*, cd recording, Calaca Press, 1999; *no contaban con mi Lengua* (Toulouse: np, 2002).

[1]Something
[2]What do puritans want from me
[3]English
[4]Words

out of boca abierta[5]
like bullets
like fire
like fuego[6]
like poems
have already licked alive
the crevices of open-legged borders
bleeding the histories and languages
of my name
Have already been witness to silence
to white-haired first grade teacher
bringing finger to lips and saying,
Shhhhhh! Speak English.
You're in America now,
speak English.
Mi bisabuela fue Yaqui[7]
Mi abuela Mexicana[8]
Mi madre mestiza[9]
y yo?[10]
Your worst linguistic nightmare
hecho realidad[11]
Aquí se le hecha
de todo;[12] East Los attitude,
chile chipotle,[13] Chicana power fist.
Aquí el inglés se quita sus moños,[14]
wears khakis guangos[15]
and dances slow motion to oldies.
Aquí el inglés[16] trips over itself
Y el español[17] comes down
off its high Spanish horse,
cruises down Whittier Boulevard
in a cherry-red Impala lowrider,

---

[5]Mouth open
[6]Fire
[7]My great grandmother was Yaqui (Indian from Northern Mexico)
[8]My grandmother Mexican
[9]My mother mestiza
[10]And I?
[11]Made real
[12]Here everything is added
[13]Chipotle chile
[14]Here English gets off its high horse
[15]Lose
[16]Here English
[17]And Spanish

wátchala[18] it rides the bus,
eats chile spiced mangos
and elotes smothered in mayonesa,[19]
it learns to say pá instead of para,[20]
'cá instead of acá[21]
'llá instead of allá,[22]
travel pá cá y pá llá[23]
pá llá y pá cá
pá Caló. Órale![24]
Somos las chicas patas lenguas que se no rajan
cruzando fronteras sin papeles,[25]
illegal tongues jumping over barb-wire fences
and running como las cucarachas[26]
when you hit the light switch!
Córrele Cuquita! Córrele![27]
Aquí el lenguaje existe en el momento
que[28] Conejo hits up Pablo for a ride
con, Come on vato. Give me un aventón[29]
to la marqueta. Y Pablo lo manda a la fregada[30]
with a wave of a hand y con Chale dude![31]
Qué me vez? cara de taxi-cab?[32]
Aquí se usa lo que sirve,
el rascuache, el mestizaje,[33]
las left-overs y lo yet to be born,
Aquí cada palabra está viva. Respira.[34]
And all the Chicas Patas, las Wátchalas,
los éses y ésas of the world
stand up and shout:
Hey! And ain't I a word?

---

[18]Watch it / Look at it
[19]Corn on the cob with mayonnaise
[20]for
[21]here
[22]there
[23]here and there
[24]There you go
[25]We are the long-legged tongues that cross borders illegally
[26]like cockroaches
[27]Run Cuquita, run!
[28]Here, language exists the instant in which
[29]with, come on, dude, give me a ride
[30]to the store, and Pablo sends him to hell
[31]and with a, no way, dude!
[32]Who do think I am?
[33]Here we use what works/the down to earth, the mixture/
[34]Here every word is alive. It breathes.

Caigo[35] from hungry mouths
of thousands. Salgo como bala[36]
en los barrios de Califas,[37]
broto como lluvia en el desierto de Arizona,[38]
canto mi Tex-Mex junto a Flaco Jiménez[39]
And tell me, ain't I a word?
Los académicos me ignoran[40]
los puristas dicen que contamino,[41]
Webster y el Pequeño Larousse
no me conocen y Random House me escupe.[42]
No manchen![43]
Aquí mi raza no se detiene[44]
cada nueva palabra[45] remembers, relives, speaks
the many conquests of our bleeding tongues.
Our language, como cuerpo de serpiente,[46] moves
it shape-shifts
it sheds
en un instante muere[47]
y aún vuelve a nacer.[48]

---

[35]I fall
[36]I come out like a bullet
[37]in California neighborhoods
[38]I spring like rain in the Arizona desert
[39]I sing my Tex-Mex next to
[40]Academics ignore me
[41]purists say that I contaminate
[42]do not know me and Random House spits on me
[43]Don't bother me!
[44]My race does not stop here
[45]Each new word
[46]like a serpent's body
[47]dies in an instant
[48]and continues to be born.

# Leticia Hernández-Linares

Leticia Hernández-Linares was conceived in El Salvador, born in Hollywood, and now lives in San Francisco. She has worked as an educator and youth advocate for the past ten years, teaching writing and art classes to young people. Her writing appears in *Raza Spoken Here 2*. She has presented her work in California and El Salvador. The poem included here, "Cumbia de salvación," demonstrates the mixture of two cultures in the United States through the rhthym of music as well as to that of life, where one learns that all cultures can and should exist without the erasure of any one of them.

Primary works by Leticia Hernández-Linares: Raza Spoken Here 2, CD recording, San Diego: Calaca Press, 2001; *Razor Edges of My Tongue* (San Diego: Calaca Press, 2002).

# Cumbia de salvación[1]

*Cumbia sabrosa cumbia** 
*para ti yo bailo hasta amanecer*[2]

Legs
wrapped around each other
on the floor where wood and skin meet
caderas[3] to the right, caderas to the left
and what it is that en realidad *manda en mi país*[4]
no es[5]
*el ritmo sabrosón de*[6] *El Salvador*
it's el dólar, el peso, el colón,[7]
los pedacitos de hueso[8] that you find on the floor
keeping us in need of salvation
and that painful inflammation in my hips, my feet
isn't from dancing
but from scrubbing the greed from the corners of the room
from the plates we use to eat

watch
my body move through all kinds of beats
but first, I gotta go to el 99c and then to the carnicería[9]
shiny dishes new towels red juice of tripas bowels yummy
are you watching
as I take lessons in how to make deals that will keep me
sweeping
7 days a week
I save my pennies here, so that before I visit my peeps
I can stop by the neon lit duty free store
tommy hilfiger striped american feel
it's what everyone finds

*pa pa ra ra pa rap cu cu cumbia*
yes girl it's the remix
I used to think that meant the record skipped

---

*Words in italics are sung. Most are samples or twists of the song "Sabrosa Cumbia" by Marito Rivera y su Grupo Bravo.
[1]Song of salvation
[2]Cumbia delicious cumbia for you I dance until day break
[3]Hips
[4]Rules in my country
[5]Is not
[6]The tasteful rhythm of
[7]The dollar, the peso, the colón (currency)
[8]The bone pieces
[9]Meat market

now it reminds me of how my shoes
pass over the same places on the concrete
stains on the street left
from people tripping over how and what to acquire
sellers nod their heads, open their shoulders for people who
need want desire
plenty
of clients dancing right into their arms
deseos[10] de El Salvador trailing after them

*Es dinero el que manda en mi país[11]*
*Es el ritmo sabrosón de El Salvador*

para allá, para acá, y para qué[12]
ay, you don't need to buy
another useless thing
hey did you hear about fulanita[13]
heard she's out of work
and never goes dancing anymore

¿y eso?[14]

es que,[15]
she danced right into the store
and choked
on her debt

*Cumbia de mis amores[16]*

---

[10]Wishes
[11]Money rules in my country
[12]There, here, why
[13]Some girl
[14]And that?
[15]It's that
[16]Cumbia of my love

# Nancy Mercado

Nancy Mercado is the author of *It Concerns the Madnes*, a collection of poetry. She is also editor of *Long Shot*, a literary and arts publication. Her work has been anthologized in *ALOUD: Voices from the Nuyorican Poets Café* and *Identity Lessons: Contemporary Writing about Learning to Be American*, among others. In her dedication to the arts, she has served as curator for the Latina Writers Coffeehouse Series at the Brooklyn Public Library in 2000

Primary works by Nancy Mercado: *It Concerns the Madness* (New Jersey: Long Shot Productions, 2000); Ed. *Tripping over the Lunch Lady: And Other School Stories* (East Rutherford: Dial Books for Young Readers, 2004); in *BumRush the Page: A Def Poetry Jam* (New York: Three Rivers Press, 2001).

and the Word Power Literary Series at the New Jersey Performance Arts Center (NJPAC) in 1999. She earned an MA from New York University and is the founding director of the Lola Rodriguez de Tió Cultural Institute in New Jersey. For ten years, she developed and was artistic director of the Young Life Theatre Group, completing six plays with grants from the New Jersey State Council on the Arts. She has taught courses and conducted workshops in playwriting and poetry for Boricua College and Rise & Shine Productions—the Poetry Video Learning Project. Mercado is a professor at Boricua College in New York City.

# Jetties Were the Bridges I Crossed

*—for Salomon, Maria & Javier Mercado*

## I.

The Atlantic City Steeplechase Pier
Was the playground I ran in,
Scaled roller coasters as far as my eye could climb
Peered into deep mysterious seas
Sand mounds were the backyard
In which I dreamt,
Converted them to hills of snow
The ocean rolled up to meet

Jetties were the bridges I crossed
Dark-green and black
Majestic beyond their smoky veil of ocean mist

> *I was often afraid for my father*
> *Who braved them in winter*
> *Sitting at their very edge*
> *Fishing for hours and for years*
> *His solitary tiny figure far off—*

The Boardwalk
Was the unfinished hardwood floors of my home
Where I strolled for hours with Mother
Amid giant giraffes and
Clouds of cotton candy overhead

## II.

*(Massachusetts Avenue School, USA)*

In Massachusetts Avenue School
My hours were spent
In day dreams of Puerto Rico
Waves rolling up
To my second floor window

In Massachusetts Avenue School
As I gazed at the snowy sidewalk below,
Mr. Grant, my middle-aged white teacher
Bellowed into my ear
Smashing it to pieces

Fourth graders made easy targets
Little brown pegs hobbling
Around concrete school yards
Speaking Spanish to each other
I washed Mr. Grant's blackboards
Thinking this would buy my escape
But, I could not wash away myself
I could not wash away my family

## III.

*(En Mi Casa Toman El Pico)*[1]

The kitchen was the hub
From which all toil
And a splash of ignorance
Generated good memories
For the years to come

Spanish spilled over
Turkey preparations,
Chicharron[2] & plátano[3] stuffing
And adobo[4] spices
Brought the bird
Closer to the swine
Puerto Ricans preferred
On such occasions

My brother holed up in his room for hours
Played rock & roll
The lyrics danced inside my brain all night
Iron Butterfly
Jimi Hendrix
The Doors
Dance inside me
'Til this day.

---

[1]In my house they drink El Pico
[2]Pork rinds
[3]Banana
[4]Spice

# Marisela Norte

Marisela Norte is a Chicana who grew up in East Los Angeles in a working-class environment. Both of her parents migrated from Mexico. Her father was a film projectionist who enjoyed his work but was unable to find work in the United States. Norte's poetry, like her father's film passion, invites readers to join her in the bus whose window projects the daily images of her daily life in California. Her writing focuses on women of color—not only Latinas but all women, thus crossing racial and ethnic lines. Her poetry takes as subject urban communities in which women and Latinos are described in their daily activities as she watches them, leaving the reader with enough information to determine a possible future for each one.

## Peeping Tom-Tom Girl

I am a Peeping Tom girl
and from my seat on the downtown bus
I have been driven through,
been witness to
invaded by las vidas de ellas.[1]
I've made myself up to be the girl who sits in the back
with the black mask over her eyes,
the high school doll
too anxious to experiment.
La muchachita[2] stuffed into the pink lampshade dress
who listens as her parents argue through different neighborhoods.
She shuts her eyes and tries to memorize
the menus on the chalkboards outside.
And then there is this woman
the widow with the gladiolas who never misses a day of forgiveness,
who gladly lays her flowers down. This woman,
la viuda y la otra, esa.[3]
She just sits and sits and counts todos los días en inglés y en español.[4]
la mandaron al diablo con su bolsa del mandado
mujer de papel, corazón de cartón.[5]
She sleeps in doorways, Hefty-bag wardrobe,
broken tiara and too much rouge.
1, 2, 3, 4, 429, 13, 13, 0, 0, X, 2.
She is the countess, Nuestra Señora,

---

Primary work by Marisela Norte: *Norte/Word* (San Pedro: Alliamnce Recors, 1991).

[2]The little girl

[3]The widow and the other one, her

[4]The days in English and Spanish

[5]They sent her to hell with her shopping bag / paper woman, heart of carton

La Reina Perdida que cayó en Los.[6]
And then there is silent who taught a friend of mine
how to flick her cigarettes out of her car window and be so bad in the process.
Silent who spends a lot of time in the Welfare office now
filling out those pink and blue forms.
Can't find a baby sitter,
a good man, a job.
She smiles blowing the smoke out of her nose
and sending the butt of her Marlboro out of the office window,
and into the boulevard.
She rides those buses I do balancing boxes of Pampers marked half price
and pulling two kids, a pink one and a blue one behind her on a string
just pull my little string, and I'll do anything,
I'm your puppet.
Fifteen years ago Robert gave her that 45,
they used to ride the Kern bus home
and make out in the driveway until they thought
their lips would fall off, but they didn't.
Puppet, passion, Pampers
What were those words in the middle?
And then there's Rosemary who's still in junior college
and can't decide between a career in real estate or dancing.
She hangs out at the local hangouts fluttering her long lashes
and flashing her long legs at some men's eyes.
And sometimes older men buy her drinks and make vague promises:
"I'll take care of you,
i'll drive you straight home,
let me take care of that car payment,
I wanna take you out to dinner."
And almost always they are old enough to be her father or uncle
silver hair, lose tongue, quick-handed nit witted men,
dangling electro-plated lollipops in front of her eyes.
And Rosemary says, "Sure, why not?
I want someone to take care of me,
someone who'll make me his forever m'ija,[7]
pay my bills, take me dancing.
send me day-old roses, I don't care."
Her friend Rosary thinks she's crazy and doesn't mind telling her so.
They've been friends now for about ten years,
been through absent menstrual cycles, low-paying jobs,
conceited men they both thought they'd never be able to live without.
And everyone used to get them confused

---

[6]Our Lady / The Lost Queen who fell in L.A.
[7]My daughter, sweetheart

until Rosemary made the distinction in everyone's yearbook
in red ink right below her hollow smile, she scribbled:
Rosary beads,
Rosemary bleeds.
Bells ring,
it is my cue to start walking and I make all the cracks on the sidewalk.
Like a lost tourist I curse the crowds
and can't help wondering why so many of us are getting pregnant,
getting gray hair, or being lied to.
I see the girls, las chicks,
I follow them around, become them for the afternoon,
the light goes red as two doñas discuss lipstick,
"Fíjate que lo compré a medio precio,
¿no?
Sí, y es de Revlon."[8]
Downtown Los, when I'm alone
Dark-eyed men speak to me in languages I don't understand.
A standing destruction, the blank man in the Brookes Brother's suit,
he smells like leather-bounds books.
Our heads turn, it is a short ceremony:
We spend long summers back east raising baby alligators.
To him, I am a beautiful terrorist, an unsuccessful advance,
glancing, avenues, lights go on and off inside me.
Inside me it is all white heat sometimes
and the dark eyes are persistent, insisting,
I flirt back,
shrug my shoulders, I should be barefoot on some Italian coast,
Steamy, smoldering, a burning girl, red toenails, a devilish laugh,
my long hair, dark skin,
his soul tangled in mine
suddenly I am beautiful,
too beautiful for my own good.
But the dream dies fast as I am pushed away by an angry woman carrying too many
packages and an unwanted child in her swollen belly.
Suddenly, I am back, sick, weak,
I haven't written in days, guilt ridden.
Not half a woman, I want out of my own skin,
I can't stand the stupid image,
the pink sponge rollers, the imperfect body.
Never been to Europe, only half a million films
1, 2, 3, 4, 400, 13, 13, 0, X, 2, X, 2, U2.
May I take you out to dinner?
Cloth napkins

---

[8]Look, I bought it at half price / really? / yes, and it is a Revlon

ay Dios, ruega por nosotros
ruega por nos,
por Los.
Entonces le daremos fin a esta pesadilla
donde muchos solamente somos actores sin papeles.[9]

---

[9]Dear God, pray for us/ pray for us, for L.A. We will then end this nightmare / where many are only actors without papers

# Luis J. Rodríguez

Luis J. Rodríguez was born in El Paso, Texas, in 1954. He grew up in Watts and the East Los Angeles area. His first book of poems, *Poems across the Pavement,* won the Poetry Center Book Award. *The Concrete River* won a PEN West/Josephine Miles Award for Literary Excellence. His recent autobiographical account, *Always Running: La Vida Loca, Gang Days in L.A.* was awarded the Carl Sandburg Award of the Friends of the Chicago Public Library. He is currently working with peacemakers among gang members in Los Angeles and other parts of the United States. He also runs Tía Chucha Press, which publishes emerging socially conscious poets.

## My Name's Not Rodriguez

It is a sigh of climbing feet,
the lather of gold lust,
the slave masters' religion
with crippled hands gripping greed's tail.
My name's not Rodriguez.
It's an Indian mother's noiseless cry,
a warrior's saliva on arrow tip, a jaguar's claw,
a woman's enticing contours on volcanic rock.
My real name's the ash of memory from burned trees.
It's the three-year-old child wandering in the plain
and shot by U.S. Cavalry in the S and Creek massacre.
I'm Geronimo's yell into the canyons of the old ones.
I'm the Comanche scout; the Raramuri shaman
in a soiled bandanna running in the wretched rain.
I'm called Rodriguez and my tears leave rivers of salt.
I'm Rodriguez and my skin dries on the bones.
I'm Rodriguez and a diseased laughter enters the pores.

---

Primary works by Luis J. Rodriguez: *Always Running: La Vida Loca, Gang Days in L.A.* (Willimantic: Curbstone Press, 1993); *The Concrete River* (Willimantic: Curbstone Press, 1991); *East Side Stories: Gang Life in East L.A.* (New York: Power House Books, 1998); *Hearts and Hands: Creating Communities in Violent Times* (New York: Seven Stories Press, 2001); *The Republic of East L.A.: Stories* (New York: Rayo, 2002); *Trochemoche; Poems* (Willimantic: Curbstone Press, 1998).

I'm Rodriguez and my father's insanity
blocks every passageway,
scorching the walls of every dwelling.
My name's not Rodriguez; it's a fiber in the wind,
it's what oceans have immersed,
it's what's graceful and sublime over the top of peaks,
what grows red in desert sands.
It's the crawling life, the watery breaths between ledges.
It's taut drum and peyote dance.
It's the brew from fermented heartaches.
Don't call me Rodriguez unless you mean peon and sod carrier,
unless you mean slayer of truths and deep-sixer of hopes.
Unless you mean forget and then die.
My name's the black-hooded 98mm-wielding child in all our alleys.
I'm death row monk. The eight-year-old gum seller in city bars and taco shops.
I'm unlicensed, uninsured, unregulated, and unforgiven.
I'm free and therefore hungry.
Call me Rodriguez and bleed in shame.
Call me Rodriguez and forget your own name.
Call me Rodriguez and see if I whisper in your ear,
mouth stained with bitter wine.

# Frank Varela

Frank Varela is a Chicago spoken word artist. His poetry contains a lot of the magical realism from Latin American literature; it reflects the emergence of *borinqueños* in American life. Varela discovers magic in Chicago's neighborhoods, in a place that was never thought to have magic. He finds guiding spirits, family members, and Puerto Rican luminaries in the streets of Chicago, and memories of North Avenue, Humboldt Park, Roberto Clemente High School, Western Avenue all serve to demonstrate the presence of Puerto Ricans in the Midwest. This is also a celebration of Puerto Rico as well as a way to show how Puerto Ricans fit into U.S. American society.

## The Seven African Gods

Crazy Willie waited near the entrance of Humboldt Park,
motioned for me to hurry.
He ignored my outstretched hand
and fell into step beside me.

Primary works by Frank Varela: *Book of Voices*, e-poets network online, <http://voices.e-poets.net/index.shtml>; *Serpent Underfoot/Spanish and English* (Chicago: MARCH Abrazo Press, 1993); *Bitter Coffee* with Carlos Cumpian Ed. (Chicago: MARCH Abrazo Press, 2001).

"It all started with the Seven African Gods.
You see, bro', we stopped worshipping
the Seven African Gods."

I was perplexed.
"You're not making any sense,"
I said.

Crazy Willie winked, hummed *música de Machito*,[1]
but I noticed as we walked deeper into the park—
reality shifted: oaks lengthened into palm trees;
elms—strangler figs; the gray sky of winter—turquoise.

"*Tú sabes*,"[2] Crazy Willie said, "*cuando*[3] we stopped
worshipping the Seven African *Dioses*,[4]
they turned on us."

Numbed, it dawned on me.
"They got even."

"*Pues claro*,[5] damn right,
Puerto Ricans were banished
to Chicago."

[1]Machito's music
[2]You know
[3]When
[4]Gods
[5]But of course

# robertkarimi

robertkarimi is a bilingual-iranian-guatemalteco-hiphop-rockero-polisexual-chicken barbecue chef-performance poet from California, according to his biography on the Calaca Press website (www.calacapress.org). He is a member of the 1999 National Champion Silicon Valley Poetry Slam Team. He has worked with Guillermo Gómez Peña in the Brown Sheep Project. He has written two chapbooks: *get down with yr . . . muslim-catholic self to a funky disco beat* and *eat me, do me, be me*, published by y qué Press, which he funded. Karimi now teaches high school.

## The Reinvention of Zero

On the day, after the day, the media called the LA Riots,
we pushed together into LA downtown darkness
assembled, not freely, into an Asian-owned club called The Mayan.
Our heads pumped as the band played, you know,
the band you never heard of because Mexican radio only plays testosterone

Primary work by robertkarimi: *Raza Spoken Here 2*, cd recording, San Diego: Calaca Press, 2002.

and sugary sweet discos,
anything else litters the radio room floor
like our bodies did on the dance floor.
We, the circle of life.
We, the circle of death.
We, with our bodies like foreboding clouds rolling to the darkness
become tiny lightning storms in the middle of the floor and we sang!
Human cars engaged in demolition derby,
there's Marco, Filipino revolutionary who loved The Cure, Susy and the Smiths.
His community told him he could not love Resolve and Veracruz
or articulate the ails of his community.
Pues, he painted his car the colors of the Filipino flag
and put a Sex Pistols Sticker on top.
His sweat mixes and he slams into Beto,
the Lebanese-Mexican who slams harder into each person,
with each guitar lick, each drum kick.
His girlfriend left him because he did not understand that community politics does not
mean planting your seed in every Latino garden,
and he slams into Jaime, Ricky, Cera all collide into each other.
The bullet sweater grows larger in the middle of the pit, and slam.
Gloria pushes the circle faster, harder
guitaring through all the pendejos[1] who try to touch her tits
and she uses elbows slam style like at a roller derby y wáchala, wáchala,
no one dares bumping to her, except for Jorge X,
the militant macho man who just sits and watches,
sits and watches.
Wearing his oversize Ché t-shirt to show how down he is
even though he really listens to the New Kids on the Block, o algo así,[2]
and Cristina just pushes through.
She's been waiting all night like an atom.
She joins the molecular madness.
Her love for Tejano music kept her away,
scared of the violence, the commotion,
pero el potion de Budweiser took care of her trepidation and she kicks up her
feet zapateando como la gran diabla[3] and Mari screams "¡Pinche, putos!"[4]
And she slams into José who's just chillin'.
He doesn't want to get into the circle 'cuz he's not really Mexican,
his mom just gave him the name because she wanted a Mexican in the family.
He pushes the masses, and the masses push back,
he pushes the masses, and the masses push back,
he pushes the masses, and the masses push back,

---

[1]Dumb people
[2]Something like that
[3]Stamping with our feet like the great devil woman
[4]Damn, men

he pushes the masses, and the masses push back,
and push forward and push back and push forward
and todo,[5] todo pushing, todo forward, todo pushing, todo sangre,[6]
todo de alma, todo de corazón,[7] and all the dreams, desires, pain,
slammed, fused.
The Cure, Prince, Michael Jackson, Lord Krishna, Indian Mistakes,
slammed,
José José, Freddy Fender, Emilio, Stevie B., Rage,
slam,
Shakira, Smashing Pumpkins, Cypress Hill, Ozomatli, Nirvana,
slam,
All slam, together, mushed, in a dark LA club called The Mayan,
where everything revolves around the circle,
all collapses into zero.
Puro amor
puro cero
puro slam[8]
puro amor
puro amor
puro cero.
This night, I learned that the Maya never left this earth,
they are here,
they slam,
and I learned why people fear the mash pit,
and I learned why people fear mixed culture,
you can't package zeroes, putos.[9]

---

[5]Everything
[6]All blood
[7]All soul, all from our heart
[8]Pure heart, pure zero, true slam
[9]Losers

# PROSE

# Norma Cantú

Norma Cantú is an award-winning author and professor. She received her BS and MS from Texas A & I University in Laredo and Kingsville, respectively. She completed her Ph.D. in English at the University of Nebraska, Lincoln. Cantú has worked extensively with folklore, Chicana literature,

---

Primary works by Norma Cantú: *Canícula* (New Mexico: U of New Mexico Press, 1997); and *Canícula: Imágenes de una niñez fronteriza* (Boston: Houghton Mifflin, 2001).

and borderlands studies. She has taught at various universities in the United States and currently teaches at the University of Texas at San Antonio in the English Department.

## Tino

He did it at four. And again at nine. He stands to the side with his hand out as if pointing a gun or a rifle. Everyone else is crowded around me, the piñata in the shape of a birthday cake sways in the wind above our heads. Everyone's there: aunts, uncles, cousins, the neighbors, my madrina, everyone, even Mamagrande Lupita from Monterrey. I'm holding the stick decorated with red, blue, yellow tissue paper that we will use to break the piñata. And he's playing, even in the picture, at being a soldier. Only ten years later, 1968, he is a soldier, and it's not a game. And we are gathered again: tías, tíos, cousins, comadres, neighbors, everyone, even Mamagrande Lupita from Monterrey, and Papi's cousin Ricardo who's escorted the body home. We have all gathered around a flag-draped coffin. Tino's come home from Vietnam. My brother. The sound of the trumpet caresses our hearts and Mami's gentle sobbing sways in the cool wind of March.

## Piojos[1]

With joyous anticipation I arrive home to find Mamagrande and Tía Lydia visiting from Monterrey. I can't wait to tell Mami the news, so right after kissing the visitors hello, I blurt it out—tengo piojos.[2] I explain that at recess, the nurse who had come from the main office had lined us up for inspection and along with checking our eyes and our ears she had taken a popsickle stick and parted our hair, checking for lice. Just like Sanjuana and Chelito and Peewee, and most of my friends, I too wanted to be sent to the office to get the yellow slip that confirmed we had lice. And when the nurse nodded and pointed to the office, I felt I belonged. Just the same way that I would sometimes misspell a word during spelling bees so that I could go sit with my friends and not have to stay up and be teased later and called teacher's pet. With my announcement, I handed Mami the precious yellow slip with instructions for taking care of the problem, but the instructions were in English. So I translated, down to the gory details of what would happen if I didn't get this problem solved. Poor Mami, here she was trying to impress her mother-in-law and I come and ruin it. Mamagrande was scandalized, but had solutions. She told Mami what kind of soap to buy and proceeded to "espulgar"[3] right then and there. I soon realize the big event was no fun. I had to sit with my head on Mamagrande's lap that smelled of Monterrey, and she would pull and tug at my hair whenever she spotted a liendre or a louse crawling on my scalp. The whole weekend was spent taking care of my problem. By Monday, we all compared notes on what torture having piojos meant—the stinking shampoo, the rough soaps, the pink plastic comb with teeth so fine only the tiniest of lice could get away. Only Olegario teased and bragged that he liked having the critters running on his scalp, and how his hair was so black they could hide really well; but in a few days, he came back with his parents' solution to the problem, a shaved head. From then on he became Pelón, a name he kept through junior high and high school when he fought the dress code so he could wear his hair long. Next time the critters found a home in my hair, I didn't brag nor did I come home with the sense of anticipation I did that first time. I knew better. Sometimes, though, I'd pretend to feel the crawling, itching signs of lice so I could lay my head on Mami or Bueli's lap and feel their gentle fingers caress my hair lovingly and find nothing.

———

# Junot Díaz

Junot Díaz was born in Santo Domingo in 1969. He came to the United States, to New Jersey, when he was seven. Díaz grew up in Parlin, "There was an Army recruitment center on my block. In a predominantly black and Latino neighborhood, you had these Army guys riding around, trying to recruit you. My sense of the world at the time was once high school was finished, I could either get a job or join the army." He survived poverty, and his father's abandonment to attend Kean College and Rutgers University. He earned an MFA degree in creative writing from Cornell University. He received a Guggenheim Fellowship and the Lila Wallace Readers Digest Grant. His stories have been published in The *New Yorker* and he was chosen as one of the Top Twenty Writers under Forty in *The New Yorker* Summer Fiction Issue for 1999, "20 Writers for the 21st Century: The Future of American Fiction." Díaz teaches in the English Department at Syracuse University.

## Aguantando[1]

I lived without a father for the first nine years of my life. He was in the States, working, and the only way I knew him was through the photographs my moms kept in a plastic sandwich bag under her bed. Since our zinc roof leaked, almost everything we owned was water-stained: our clothes, Mami's Bible, her makeup, whatever food we had, Abuelo's tools, our cheap wooden furniture. It was only because of that plastic bag that any pictures of my father survived.

When I thought of Papi I thought of one shot specifically. Taken days before the U.S. invasion, 1965. I wasn't even alive then; Mami had been pregnant with my first never-born brother and Abuelo could still see well enough to hold a job. You know the sort of photograph I'm talking about. Scalloped edges, mostly brown in color. On the back my moms's cramped handwriting—the date, his name, even the street, one over from our house. He was dressed in his Guardia uniform, his tan cap at an angle on his shaved head, an unlit Constitución squeezed between his lips. His dark unsmiling eyes were my own.

I did not think of him often. He had left for Nueva York when I was four but since I couldn't remember a single moment with him I excused him from all nine years of my life. On the days I had to imagine him—not often, since Mami didn't much speak of him any more—he was the soldier in the photo. He was a cloud of cigar smoke, the traces of which could still be found on the

———

Primary work by Junot Díaz: *Drown* (New York: Riverhead Books, 1996).

[1]Hanging on

uniforms he'd left behind. He was pieces of my friends' fathers, of the domino players on the corner, pieces of Mami and Abuelo. I didn't know him at all. I didn't know that he'd abandoned us. That this waiting for him was all a sham.

We lived south of the Cementerio Nacional in a wood-frame house with three rooms. We were poor. The only way we could have been poorer was to have lived in the campo[2] or to have been Haitian immigrants, and Mami regularly offered these to us as brutal consolation.

At least you're not in the campo.[2] You'd eat rocks then.

We didn't eat rocks but we didn't eat meat or beans, either. Almost everything on our plates was boiled: boiled yuca,[3] boiled plátano,[4] boiled guineo,[5] maybe with a piece of cheese or a shred of bacalao.[6] On the best days the cheese and the platanos were fried. When me and Rafa caught our annual case of worms it was only by skimping on our dinners that Mami could afford to purchase the Verminox. I can't remember how many times I crouched over our latrine, my teeth clenched, watching long gray parasites slide out from between my legs.

At Mauricio Baez, our school, the kids didn't bother us too much, even though we couldn't afford the uniforms or proper mascotas.[7] The uniforms Mami could do nothing about but with the mascotas she improvised, sewing together sheets of loose paper she had collected from her friends. We each had one pencil and if we lost that pencil, like I did once, we had to stay home from school until Mami could borrow another one for us. Our profesor had us share school books with some of the other kids and these kids wouldn't look at us, tried to hold their breath when we were close to them.

Mami worked at Embajador Chocolate, putting in ten-, twelve-hour shifts for almost no money at all. She woke up every morning at seven and I got up with her because I could never sleep late, and while she drew the water out of our steel drum I brought the soap from the kitchen. There were always leaves and spiders in the water but Mami could draw a clean bucket better than anyone. She was a tiny woman and in the water closet she looked even smaller, her skin dark and her hair surprisingly straight and across her stomach and back the scars from the rocket attack she'd survived in 1965. None of the scars showed when she wore clothes, though if you embraced her you'd feel them hard under your wrist, against the soft part of your palm.

Abuelo[8] was supposed to watch us while Mami was at work but usually he was visiting with his friends or out with his trap. A few years back, when the rat problem in the barrio had gotten out of hand (Those malditos[9] were running off with kids, Abuelo told me), he had built himself a trap. A destroyer. He never charged anyone for using it, something Mami would have done; his only commission was that he be the one to arm the steel bar. I've seen this thing chop off fingers, he explained to the borrowers but in truth he just liked having something to do, a job of some kind. In our house alone Abuelo had killed a dozen rats and in one house on Tunti, forty of these motherfuckers were killed during a two-night massacre. He spent both nights with the Tunti peo-

---

[2]Country
[3]Yucca
[4]Plantains
[5]Banana
[6]Codfish
[7]Pets
[8]Grandfather
[9]Damn

*Rafa = brother*

ple, resetting the trap and burning the blood and when he came back he was grinning and tired, his white hair everywhere, and my mother had said, You look like you've been out getting ass.

*life's not bad*

Without Abuelo around, me and Rafa did anything we wanted. Mostly Rafa hung out with his friends and I played with our neighbor Wilfredo. Sometimes I climbed trees. There wasn't a tree in the barrio I couldn't climb and on some days I spent entire afternoons in our trees, watching the barrio in motion and when Abuelo was around (and awake) he talked to me about the good old days, when a man could still make a living from his finca,[10] when the United States wasn't something folks planned on.

*cool*

Mami came home after sunset, just when the day's worth of drinking was starting to turn some of the neighbors wild. Our barrio was not the safest of places and Mami usually asked one of her co-workers to accompany her home. These men were young, and some of them were unmarried. Mami let them walk her but she never invited them into the house. She barred the door with her arm while she said good-bye, just to show them that nobody was getting in. Mami might have been skinny, a bad thing on the Island, but she was smart and funny and that's hard to find anywhere. Men were drawn to her. From my perch I'd watched more than one of these Porfirio Rubirosas say, See you tomorrow, and then park his ass across the street just to see if she was playing hard to get. Mami never knew these men were there and after about fifteen minutes of staring expectantly at the front of our house even the loneliest of these fulanos[11] put their hats on and went home.

We could never get Mami to do anything after work, even cook dinner, if she didn't first sit awhile in her rocking chair. She didn't want to hear nothing about our problems, the scratches we'd put into our knees, who said what. She'd sit on the back patio with her eyes closed and let the bugs bite mountains onto her arms and legs. Sometimes I climbed the guanábana[12] tree and when she'd open her eyes and catch me smiling down on her, she'd close them again and I would drop twigs onto her until she laughed.

*things are shitty, but they're happy.*

## 2

When times were real flojo,[13] when the last colored bill flew out Mami's purse, she packed us off to our relatives. She'd use Wilfredo's father's phone and make the calls early in the morning. Lying next to Rafa, I'd listen to her soft unhurried requests and pray for the day that our relatives would tell her to vete pa'l carajo[14] but that never happened in Santo Domingo.

*Family cxn*

Usually Rafa stayed with our tíos in Ocoa and I went to tía Miranda's in Boca Chica. Sometimes we both went to Ocoa. Neither Boca Chica nor Ocoa were far but I never wanted to go and it normally took hours of cajoling before I agreed to climb on the autobus.[15]

How long? I asked Mami truculently.

Not long, she promised me, examining the scabs on the back of my shaved head. A week. Two at the most.

How many days is that?

Ten, twenty.

*math, not very smart*

[10]Farm
[11]Unknown men
[12]Soursop
[13]Lazy/slow
[14]Go to hell
[15]Bus

You'll be fine, Rafa told me, spitting into the gutter.

How do you know? You a brujo?[16]

Yeah, he said, smiling, that's me.

He didn't mind going anywhere; he was at that age when all he wanted was to be away from the family, meeting people he had not grown up with.

Everybody needs a vacation, Abuelo explained happily. Enjoy yourself. You'll be down by the water. And just think about all the food you'll eat.

I never wanted to be away from the family. Intuitively, I knew how easily distances could harden and become permanent. On the ride to Boca Chica I was always too depressed to notice the ocean, the young boys fishing and selling cocos[17] by the side of the road, the surf exploding into the air like a cloud of shredded silver.

Tía Miranda had a nice block house, with a shingled roof and a tiled floor that her cats had trouble negotiating. She had a set of matching furniture and a television and faucets that worked. All her neighbors were administrators and hombres de negocios[18] and you had to walk three blocks to find any sort of colmado.[19] It was *that* sort of neighborhood. The ocean was never far away and most of the time I was down by the beach playing with the local kids, turning black in the sun.

Tía wasn't really related to Mami; she was my madrina,[20] which was why she took me and my brother in every now and then. No money, though. She never loaned money to anyone, even to her drunkard of an ex-husband, and Mami must have known because she never asked. Tía was about fifty and rail-thin and couldn't put anything in her hair to make it forget itself; her perms never lasted more than a week before the enthusiasm of her kink returned. She had two kids of her own, Yennifer and Bienvenido, but she didn't dote on them the way she doted on me. Her lips were always on me and during meals she watched me like she was waiting for the poison to take effect.

I bet this isn't something you've eaten lately, she'd say.

I'd shake my head and Yennifer, who was eighteen and bleached her hair, would say, Leave him alone, Mamá.

Tía also had a penchant for uttering cryptic one-liners about my father, usually after she'd downed a couple of shots of Brugal.

*He took too much.*

*If only your mother could have noticed his true nature earlier.*

*He should see how he has left you.*

The weeks couldn't pass quickly enough. At night I went down by the water to be alone but that wasn't possible. Not with the tourists making apes out of themselves, and with the tígueres[21] waiting to rob them.

Las Tres Marías,[22] I pointed out to myself in the sky. They were the only stars I knew.

But then one day I'd walk into the house from swimming and Mami and Rafa would be in the living room, holding glasses of sweet lemon-milk.

---

[16]A witch
[17]Coconuts
[18]Businessmen
[19]Store
[20]Godmother
[21]Tigers
[22]The three Marías

You're back, I'd say, trying to hide the excitement in my voice. *only thing to stay sane*

I hope he behaved himself, Mami would be saying to Tía. Her hair would be cut, her nails painted; she'd have on the same red dress she wore on every one of her outings.

Rafa smiling, slapping me on the shoulder, darker than I'd last seen him. How ya doing, Yunior? You miss me or what?

I'd sit next to him and he'd put his arm around me and we'd listen to Tía telling Mami how well I behaved and all the different things I'd eaten.

## 3

The year Papi came for us, the year I was nine, we expected nothing. There were no signs to speak of. Dominican chocolate was not especially in demand that season and the Puerto Rican owners laid off the majority of the employees for a couple of months. Good for the owners, un desastre[23] for us. After that, Mami was around the house all the time. Unlike Rafa, who hid his shit well, I was always in trouble. From punching out Wilfredo to chasing somebody's chickens until they passed out from exhaustion. Mami wasn't a hitter; she preferred having me kneel on pebbles with my face against a wall. On the afternoon that the letter arrived, she caught me trying to stab our mango tree with Abuelo's machete. Back to the corner. Abuelo was supposed to make sure I served my ten minutes but he was too busy whittling to bother. He let me up after three minutes and I hid in the bedroom until he said, OK, in a voice that Mami could hear. Then I went to the smokehouse, rubbing my knees, and Mami looked up from peeling platanos. *Punishment*

You better learn, muchacho,[24] or you'll be kneeling the rest of your life.

I watched the rain that had been falling all day. No, I won't, I told her.

You talking back to me?

She whacked me on the nalgas[25] and I ran outside to look for Wilfredo. I found him under the eaves of his house, the wind throwing pieces of rain onto his dark-dark face. We shook hands elaborately. I called him Muhammad Ali and he called me Sinbad; these were our Northamerican names. We were both in shorts; a disintegrating pair of sandals clung to his toes. *us.*

What you got? I asked him.

Boats, he said, holding up the paper wedges his father had folded for us. This one's mine.

What does the winner get?

A gold trophy, about this big. *sounds like depression kid*

OK, cabrón,[26] I'm in. Don't let go before me.

OK, he said, stepping to the other side of the gutter. We had a clear run down to the street corner. No cars were parked on our side, except for a drowned Monarch and there was plenty of room between its tires and the curb for us to navigate through.

We completed five runs before I noticed that somebody had parked their battered motorcycle in front of my house.

Who's that? Wilfredo asked me, dropping his soggy boat into the water again.

I don't know, I said.

Go find out.

*they don't care that they're brown*

---

[23]A disaster
[24]Boy
[25]Butt
[26]Bastard, bugger

I was already on my way. The motorcycle driver came out before I could reach our front door. He mounted quickly and was gone in a could of exhaust.

Mami and Abuelo were on the back patio, conversating. Abuelo was angry and his cane-cutter's hands were clenched. I hadn't seen Abuelo bravo in a long time, not since his produce truck had been stolen by two of his old employees.   *survival of the fittest*

Go outside, Mami told me.

Who was that?

Did I tell you something?

Was that somebody we know?

Outside, Mami said, her voice a murder about to happen.

What's wrong? Wilfredo asked me when I rejoined him. His nose was starting to run.

I don't know, I said.

When Rafa showed himself an hour later, swaggering in from a game of pool, I'd already tried to speak to Mami and Abuelo like five times. The last time, Mami had landed a slap on my neck and Wilfredo told me that he could see the imprints of her fingers on my skin. I told it all to Rafa.

That doesn't sound good. He threw out his guttering cigarette. You wait here. He went around the back and I heard his voice and then Mami's. No yelling, no argument.

Come on, he said. She wants us to wait in our room.

Why?

That's what she said. You want me to tell her no?

Not while she's mad.

Exactly.

I slapped Wilfredo's hand and walked in the front door with Rafa. What's going on?

She got a letter from Papi.

Really? Is there money?

No.

What does it say?

How should I know?

He sat down on his side of the bed and produced a pack of cigarettes. I watched him go through the elaborate ritual of lighting up—the flip of the thin cigarrillo into his lips and then the spark, a single practiced snap of the thumb.

Where'd you get that lighter?

Mi novia[27] gave it to me.   *chuckle*

Tell her to give me one.

Here. He tossed it to me. You can have it if you shut up.

Yeah?

See. He reached to take it. You already lost it.

I shut my mouth and he settled back down on the bed.

Hey, Sinbad, Wilfredo said, his head appearing in our window. What's going on?

My father wrote us a letter!

Rafa rapped me on the side of my head. This is a *family* affair, Yunior. Don't blab it all over the place.

Wilfredo smiled. I ain't going to tell anybody.

---

[27]My girlfriend

*joking?*

Of course you're not, Rafa said. Because if you do I'll chop your fucking head off.

I tried to wait it out. Our room was nothing more than a section of the house that Abuelo had partitioned off with planks of wood. In one corner Mami kept an altar with candles and a cigar in a stone mortar and a glass of water and two toy soldiers we could not touch ever and above the bed hung our mosquito netting, poised to drop on us like a net. I lay back and listened to the rain brushing back and forth across our zinc roof.

Mami served dinner, watched as we ate it, and then ordered us back into our room. I'd never seen her so blank-faced, so stiff, and when I tried to hug her she pushed me away. Back to bed, she said. Back to listening to the rain. I must have fallen asleep because when I woke up Rafa was looking at me pensively and it was dark outside and nobody else in the house was awake.

I read the letter, he told me quietly. He was sitting cross-legged on the bed, his ribs laddering his chest in shadows. Papi says he's coming.

Really?

Don't believe it.

Why?

It ain't the first time he's made that promise, Yunior.    *nickname*

Oh, I said.

Outside Señora Tejada started singing to herself, badly.

Rafa?

Yeah?

I didn't know you could read.

I was nine and couldn't even write my own name.

Yeah, he said quietly. Something I picked up. Now go to bed.

## 4.

Rafa was right. It wasn't the first time. Two years after he left, Papi wrote her saying he was coming for us and like an innocent Mami believed him. After being alone for two years she was ready to believe anything. She showed everybody his letter and even spoke to him on the phone. He wasn't an easy man to reach but on this occasion she got through and he reassured her that yes, he was coming. His word was his bond. He even spoke to us, something that Rafa vaguely remembers, a lot of crap about how much he loved us and that we should take care of Mami.

She prepared a party, even lined up to have a goat there for the slaughtering. She bought me and Rafa new clothes and when he didn't show she sent everybody home, sold the goat back to its owner and then almost lost her mind. I remember the heaviness of that month, thicker than almost anything. When Abuelo tried to reach our father at the phone numbers he'd left none of the men who'd lived with him knew anything about where he had gone.

*Still loves father*

It didn't help matters that me and Rafa kept asking her when we were leaving for the States, when Papi was coming. I am told that I wanted to see his picture almost every day. It's hard for me to imagine myself this way, crazy about Papi. When she refused to show me the photos I threw myself about like I was on fire. And I screamed. Even as a boy my voice carried farther than a man's, turned heads on the street.

First Mami tried slapping me quiet but that did little. Then she locked me in my room where my brother told me to cool it but I shook my head and screamed louder. I was inconsolable. I learned to tear my clothes because this was the one thing I had whose destruction hurt my mother. She took all my shirts from my room, left me only with shorts which were hard to damage with bare fingers. I pulled a nail from our wall and punched a dozen holes in each pair, until Rafa cuffed me and said, Enough, you little puto.

Mami spent a lot of time out of the house, at work or down by the Malecón,[28] where she could watch the waves shred themselves against the rocks, where men offered cigarettes that she smoked quietly. I don't know how long this went on. Months, maybe three. Then, one morning in early spring, when the amapolas[29] were flushed with their flame leaves, I woke up and found Abuelo alone in the house.

She's gone, he said. So cry all you want, malcriado.

I learned later from Rafa that she was in Ocoa with our tíos.

Mami's time away was never discussed, then or now. When she returned to us, five weeks later, she was thinner and darker and her hands were heavy with calluses. She looked younger, like the girl who had arrived in Santo Domingo fifteen years before, burning to be married. Her friends came and sat and talked and when Papi's name was mentioned her eyes dimmed and when his name left, the darkness of her ojos[30] returned and she would laugh, a small personal thunder that cleared the air.

She didn't treat me badly on her return but we were no longer as close; she did not call me her Prieto[31] or bring me chocolates from her work. That seemed to suit her fine. And I was young enough to grow out of her rejection. I still had baseball and my brother. I still had trees to climb and lizards to tear apart.

## 5.

The week after the letter came I watched her from my trees. She ironed cheese sandwiches in paper bags for our lunch, boiled platanos for our dinner. Our dirty clothes were pounded clean in the concrete trough on the side of the outhouse. Every time she thought I was scrabbling too high in the branches she called me back to the ground. You ain't Spiderman, you know, she said, rapping the top of my head with her knuckles. On the afternoons that Wilfredo's father came over to play dominos and talk politics, she sat with him and Abuelo and laughed at their campo stories. She seemed more normal to me but I was careful not to provoke her. There was still something volcanic about the way she held herself.

On Saturday a late hurricane passed close to the Capital and the next day folks were talking about how high the waves were down by the Malecón. Some children had been lost, swept out to sea and Abuelo shook his head when he heard the news. You'd think the sea would be sick of us by now, he said.

That Sunday Mami gathered us on the back patio. We're taking a day off, she announced. A day for us as a family.

We don't need a day off, I said and Rafa hit me harder than normal.

Shut up, OK?

I tried to hit him back but Abuelo grabbed us both by the arm. Don't make me have to crack your heads open, he said.

---

[28]Dike, jetty

[29]Poppy

[30]Eyes

[31]Dark-skinned

She dressed and put her hair up and even paid for a concho instead of crowding us into an autobus. The driver actually wiped the seats down with a towel while we waited and I said to him, It don't look dirty, and he said, Believe me, muchacho, it is. Mami looked beautiful and many of the men she passed wanted to know where she was heading. We couldn't afford it but she paid for a movie anyway. *The Five Deadly Venoms.* Kung fu movies were the only ones the theaters played in those days. I sat between Mami and Abuelo. Rafa moved to the back, joining a group of boys who were smoking, and arguing with them about some baseball player on Licey.

After the show Mami bought us flavored ices and while we ate them we watched the salamanders crawling around on the sea rocks. The waves were tremendous and some parts of George Washington were flooded and cars were churning through the water slowly.

A man in a red guayabera stopped by us. He lit a cigarette and turned to my mother, his collar turned up by the wind. So where are you from?    *temptation*

Santiago, she answered.

Rafa snorted.

You must be visiting relatives then.

Yes, she said. My husband's family.

He nodded. He was dark-skinned, with light-colored spots about his neck and hands. His fingers trembled slightly as he worked the cigarette to his lips. I hoped he'd drop his cigarette, just so I could see what the ocean would do to it. We had to wait almost a full minute before he said buenos días[32] and walked away.

What a crazy, Abuelo said.

Rafa lifted up his fist. You should have given me the signal. I would have kung-fu-punched him in the head.

Your father came at me better than that, Mami said.

Abuelo stared down at the back of his hands, at the long white hairs that covered them. He looked embarrassed.

*doubt*    Your father asked me if I wanted a cigarette and then he gave me the whole pack to show me that he was a big man.

I held on to the rail. Here?

Oh no, she said. She turned around and looked out over the traffic. That part of the city isn't here anymore.

## 6.

Rafa used to think that he'd come in the night, like Jesus, that one morning we'd find him *rumors* at our breakfast table, unshaven and smiling. Too real to be believed. He'll be taller, Rafa predicted. Northamerican food makes people that way. He'd surprise Mami on her way back from work, pick her up in a German car. Say nothing to the man walking her home. She would not know what to say and neither would he. They'd drive down to the Malecón and he'd take her to see a movie, because that's how they met and that's how he'd want to start it again.

I would see him coming from my trees. A man with swinging hands and eyes like mine. He'd have gold on his fingers, cologne on his neck, a silk shirt, good leather shoes. The whole barrio would come out to greet him. He'd kiss Mami and Rafa and shake Abuelo's reluctant hand and then he'd see me behind everyone else. What's wrong with that one? he'd ask and

---

[32]Good morning    *self-conscious*

Mami would say, He doesn't know you. Squatting down so that his pale yellow dress socks showed, he'd trace the scars on my arms and on my head. <u>Yunior, he'd finally say, his stub-bled face in front of mine, his thumb tracing a circle on my cheek.</u>

he's alright

# Rigoberto González

Rigoberto González was born in Bakersfield, California, and raised in Michoacán, Mexico. He is the son and grandson of farmworkers. He received an MA from the University of California, Davis, and an MFA from Arizona State University. He was honored by the Academy of American Poets and has received three Pushcart Prize nominations. His book of poetry, *So Often the Pitcher Goes to the Water Until It Breaks*, received great reviews and was selected for the National Poetry Series. He lives in New York City. "La Quebrada" is an excerpt from the novel *Crossing Vines*.

## La Quebrada

The workers ate their lunches at the ends of the rows, beneath the vine canopies for shade, each group with its own colored ice chest. Still, a crowd gathered behind Merengue's truck to use the water tanks and to buy generic soft drinks for fifty cents a can. Aníbal had just squeezed in through the cluster of bodies to reach for his lunch when a violent tug forced him back.

"Check the weight on some of those boxes before the cargo truck hauls them off," Jesse demanded. "We've been getting complaints from the warehouse so make sure today's first shipment is perfect."

Jesse walked off with the static-ridden walkie-talkie bouncing against his hip. Flat-footed, he left behind a pair of parallel prints, like tire tracks.

Aníbal scowled, muttering under his breath but conscious about being heard by the pickers. The scaleboy earned a salary, the pickers worked for hourly wages and piecework; what was he complaining about?

"I'll have the piña colada, a piña colada, bartender!" El Caraballo Uno yelled out to the amusement of those around him. He pushed his way to the front.

"Mexicans go first, *puertorriqueño*,"[1] Ninja said through his cigarette. Pifas, also annoyed, muttered, "*Pinche puertito*."[2]

"There's plenty for everyone. Back away. Don't crowd," Naro said. He and Amanda took charge of the soda sales for Merengue.

"Small bills only, Sebastián, this isn't a bank," Amanda said.

"Is this diet? I hate diet," someone among the crowd complained. Aníbal only saw the hand raised up, waving the can of soda in the air. He missed the soda rush. It was the same chaos and excitement as with the paycheck rush on Fridays—everyone pushed and shoved,

---

Ed. Jaime Manrique with Jesse Dorris *Bésame mucho* (New York: Painted Leaf Press, 1999); *Crossing Vines: A Novel* (Norman: Univ. of Oklahoma Press, 2003); *So often the Pitcher Goes to Water Until It Breaks: Poems* (Champaign: Univ. of Illinois Press, 1999).

[1]Puerto Rican
[2]Damn little Puerto Rican

but politely made way for the person exiting the mob. Minutes later the dust at the scene of the soda sale settled. The volume on a transistor radio went up.

When he bent down to lift a box from a low stack near group 15 Aníbal smelled chipotle sauce. His mouth watered. The scale read twenty-two pounds. Aníbal pressed his thumb down the plate to complete the minimum twenty-three-pound weight requirement.

"No lunch?" Don Nico asked.

Aníbal smiled back at the old man and shook his head. "I'm on a hunger strike," he said.

"He's trying to keep his weight down," Doña Ramona volunteered, biting into a crisp corn tortilla while using her free hand to blow into a miniature battery-powered *brasero*.[3]

Doña Gertrudis removed her orange hard hat. The damp strands of hair stuck to her skin around the hairline. "Poor thing," she said, "working through the break. The union would never put up with this."

"Here we go," said Doña Ramona, tapping her finger against her temple. Around her neck hung a large stop-watch and a camera with its cap dangling from the lens. She broke a chip off the toasted tortilla to dip into her bowl of rice and sauce.

"Grape picking back in the seventies with Chávez," Doña Gertrudis began, staring out into space, "the union was so strong we could have had the gringo owners feed us with their own hands."

"Don't exaggerate, *comadre*,[4]" Doña Ramona said. "You sound like those women that come down from San Joaquín, telling us the grape pickers there get one-hour lunch breaks through the union. *¡Tonterías!*"[5]

"One-hour lunch breaks?" Don Nico laughed.

Tamayamá, sitting just behind Don Nico, let out a quick, "*¡Aijodesutamayamá!*"[6]

"We should be so lucky to get some decent hours working," Don Nico said.

"Well, we need the union," Doña Gertrudis said. "I heard talk about a strike down at Freeman's company. They'll show all of us how it's done."

"Strikes don't work anymore," said Don Nico. "Not like they used to."

"That's for sure," Doña Ramona said. "It's not the same nowadays, not down here in the Caliente Valley."

Aníbal walked farther down, the sun already pressing down hard on his back. He had been looking forward to getting out of the heat, at least for the short duration of the break since he spent the entire morning walking back and forth down the length of the block. As soon as one of Los Caraballos saw him coming, he elbowed the other.

"Well, well, look here, Demetrio," El Caraballo Uno said. "The scaleboy came to look at us. But I bet he likes me better than he likes you."

"That's because he thinks you have the bigger cock," El Caraballo Dos said. "But just wait until he gives me a chance."

Aníbal ignored them. Los Caraballos were loud and obnoxious. Mostly harmless but annoying just the same. From the corner of his eye he noticed Tinman observing from a distance. Tinman never ate. He only drank four of Merengue's cheap sodas, enough to let out a belch the entire crew could hear. During the break he read his book. His long hair brushing both sides of the open cover.

---

[3]Grill

[4]Close friend, godmother to one's child

[5]Nonsense!

[6]Son of . . . !

"The pretty boy's getting mad, Estanislaus," El Caraballo Dos said, making mock prissy gestures as he made his list. "Blowing up like the bullfrog. Glaring like the glass. He's going to break like the firecracker. Aim like the gun. He's—"

"He's scheming, Demetrio. Look at him. What's he thinking? What does he want and how bad does he want it?"

Aníbal checked the reading on the scale.

El Caraballo Uno kept goading in a whisper. "I bet that ass is real tight."

"It's this tight," El Caraballo Dos whispered, making a fist.

"Enough, already!" Aníbal said, hoping that an outburst would settle them down.

"Easy, easy," El Caraballo Uno said. "What do you think, Tinman? Should we let this pretty fish go?"

Tinman put his book down, pressed his hands together, and imitated a fishtail plunging back into an imaginary surface. Afterward he released his belch.

"Tinman says you're not that good a catch," El Caraballo Uno said between chuckles.

"But at least an appetizer," El Caraballo Dos chimed in, puckering his lips and throwing Aníbal a kiss. "A nice sweet mouthful." He grabbed for his crotch.

"And we can net ourselves Tiki-Tiki for a main course," El Caraballo Uno said. "Where is that *jotete?*[7] Behind him, Tinman stood up and swayed his hips, wrists limp.

"Does anyone here have salt?" Eva came up behind Aníbal. Both Caraballos quickly scrambled for the lunch bag.

"I've got your salt here, Evita," El Caraballo Uno said. "Take your grimy hands away!"

"I brought the salt, *pinche boricua*.[8] Let me see."

"I'll let you see it when I find it. Move!"

Aníbal seized the opportunity to sneak away, but was stopped by Doña Pepa with an offering of a piece of sandwich. "Take it," she said, bringing the slice of folded bread up to his face.

"No, thank you, Doña," Aníbal said with embarrassment.

"Take it, take it. You're going to thank me later."

Aníbal quickly stuffed the bread into his mouth. It soaked up the last traces of saliva, which nearly made him choke. He wasn't starving, but he wanted to please Doña Pepa, who reminded him of Nana back in Mexicali.

"If you get dizzy, suck on a lemon," Doña Pepa advised.

Doña Pepa sat on a box turned upside down. Grape boxes weren't made to withstand the weight of a human body, but Doña Pepa was petite, frail-looking, yet as strong as any other worker. Aníbal had seen her lift boxes of grapes that were twice the size as those her grandsons carried.

"Your grandsons?" Aníbal asked, to be polite.

"They're back there pissing," she answered. "*Cochinos*.[9] I told them not to wear those propaganda shirts. What's Merengue going to think? That we're troublemakers? That we want to strike?"

Doña Pepa was the crew's *abuela*.[10] Everyone knew she was beyond retirement age, but she came back to pick every year using her daughter's Social Security number. This year she brought with her two *pocho* grandsons who weren't very popular with the crew because they spoke broken Spanish.

---

[7] Gay man, derogatory term
[8] Damn Puerto Rican
[9] Pigs
[10] Grandmother

"Tell your packers the boxes are a little heavy," Aníbal said. Doña Pepa chewed her food slowly. Los Pepitos, her grandsons, pelted grapes at each other farther down the row.

"Scaleboy!" Amanda yelled. Aníbal turned to meet his reflection on her sunglasses. "We've finally got the identification stamp," she said. She handed him the metal numeral stamp and ink pad. "The shippers will stamp what's already been loaded; you need to stamp what hasn't. Start at the other end."

Aníbal looked to the end of the block. The bright umbrellas stood out, adjusted against the sun. As he walked, he considered that this would be over for him in a few weeks. It was the heat that was killing him, not Amanda or Jesse or Los Caraballos. The heat was beating them up as well.

When he reached the end of the block, he bent down to begin stamping each box above the label. The ink pad was dry so he spat on it. In the absence of workers, the sandy avenue between the blocks widened, framed by the neat stacks of boxes and the litter of damaged covers and torn cushions. Aníbal knelt down in front of a stack. The vibrations of the electricity cables hummed from the end of the block. With his body pressed low to the ground, he imagined himself camouflaged, his eyes following the stamp, roving like the anxious horned toad.

"It's actually a lizard," Carmelo would clarify. Carmelo was fanatic about desert wildlife, especially birds. Aníbal could only point out the roadrunner from the quail; Carmelo knew shrike from mockingbird.

"It's all in the black bar along the head, see it?"

Carmelo had stood behind him that time, his arm propped over Aníbal's shoulder and pointing into the spindly mesquite. Aníbal's vision had blurred with excitement. Bird or no bird, the instant Carmelo's muscle touched Aníbal their entire bodies connected.

Aníbal caught the glare of the sun on the metal stamp each time he turned his wrist. He was careful not to make contact with the metal, or else it blistered his skin.

What Aníbal liked best about life in the fields was the privacy. Despite the occasional trouble from Los Caraballos, no one really cared who he was when he wasn't a grape picker. There was no prying. In Mexicali, he could never lose himself among the network of neighborhoods that knew him, his parents, and his parents' parents. Once a well-to-do family settled on its property it engraved itself on a map. There was little chance of escaping mention in the gossipy society columns. The unwritten rule was that if a man had roots on the border he maintained them. Only poor migrant campesinos from southern Mexico actually crossed it; if they lived on the border they did so in *ejidos*,[11] the barren outskirts of the city, with no running water and no street names. They didn't live anywhere. But if a long-term border resident took that extra step into foreign soil then everyone would wonder: no money? no pride in Mexico? no place to hide?

Aníbal's parents were scandalized after he made his decision to become a field worker in the U.S. "A slave," quipped his father. They wanted him to stay and repair the damage he had done. For years he had worked as an assistant accountant for his father's construction business, saving up his money for Talina, the daughter of two lawyers. His mother anticipated the union, and the subsequent climb up the social ladder. And just when the engagement was about to be printed in the papers, Jorge came forward. Silly, romantic, and beautiful Jorge came forward, pleading with him to call off the engagement, to run away with him

---

[11]A town's common land

the way they fantasized after making love. Aníbal and Jorge. Forever. In an act of desperation, Jorge revealed everything to Talina, who revealed everything to his father.

"Who's Jorge?" his father had asked. And within minutes the room exploded into stutterings and incoherent explanations. Then the cover-up: *Talina had a change of heart; Talina's too young to marry, say parents; Young Pérez Ceballos needs to secure his future first.* Finally, the escape: the move out of his parents' household and into Nana's, the resignation from Industria Pérez, and the jump across the international border, without Jorge who had betrayed him. He was no longer Aníbal, but Scaleboy.

This afternoon Aníbal was going to tell Carmelo he was joining him on the grape route north, to Sonoma and San Joaquín. The understanding was clear, but left unspoken. Carmelo would keep his girl on that side of the border, and his male companion on this one. Last month Carmelo had Aníbal take pictures of him standing outside a house with a nicely kept lawn. Then more standing next to some stranger's Cadillac. The best ones Aníbal took were shot at the downtown shopping mall, where Carmelo asked the blonde from the ice-cream parlor to pose with him by the indoor fountain. Aníbal imagined the look of envy on the faces of those who saw the pictures across the border—a deception that probably compelled others to seek similar fortunes. Little did they suspect that it was the eye behind the camera that saw the truth, the whole truth, the necessarily hidden truth.

Aníbal kept one of those photographs with him at all times for comfort. Carmelo's smile was his. Only one side of his cheek perked up when he smiled, revealing the crooked canine. After his meal, Carmelo sat hunched on the hood of the car with a plastic case of dental floss. Aníbal followed the green string from the case to Carmelo's mouth to the ground. He studied the waves and loops of its design, attractive as chest hairs.

Down the block, one of the foreman honked the horn to signal the end of the break. Merengue yelled out "Merengue!" and Los Caraballos let loose a barrage of whistling. Bodies merged one last time at the path between the block, scrambling to steal one last drink of water before heading back into the sulfurous rows of vines. At his end, Aníbal felt like the solitary woodpecker that no one sees or hears but that everyone has been around because it pecks pecks pecks, leaving its mark behind. Peck peck peck. A distant knock so faint it remains unnoticed when it ceases, as if there had been no knock at all.

# Jaime Manrique

Jaime Manrique was born in Colombia. He is a novelist, poet, essayist, and translator. He has published extensively in English and Spanish. He has taught in the MFA programs at Columbia University, Mount Holyoke, and New York University. Among his publications are *My Night with Federico García Lorca, Colombian Gold, Latin Moon in Manhattan, Twilight at the Equator,* and *Eminent Maricones: Arenas, Lorca, Puig, and Me,* his autobiography.

Primary works by Jaime Manrique: *My Night with Federico García Lorca* (Wisconsin: Univ. of Wisconsin Press, 2003); *Columbian Gold* (New York: Painted Leaf Press, 1998; N. Potter, 1983); *Twilight at the Equator* (Madison: Univ. of Wisconsin Press, 2003), 1997; *Latin Moon in Manhattan* (Madison: Univ. Wisconsin Press, 2003); *Eminent Marrones: Arenas, Lorca, Puig, and Me* (Madison: Univ. of Wisconsin Press, 1999); Ed. with Jesse Dorris *Bésame Mucho* (New York: Painted Leaf Press, 1999).

## Señoritas in Love

Manolo was very excited, which, if you know Manolo, can be cause for alarm—he has the energy of a hurricane. We were going to N.Y.U. to hear Ramón Ariza give a talk. He was a famous Cuban author who had escaped from the island a couple of years ago and was now making his first public appearance in New York. Because Ramón was one of the few openly gay Latino. American writers, and because he had suffered persecution and incarceration for his beliefs, he was one of our heroes.

The weather had suddenly turned chilly, reminding us that we were in late November, that winter was around the corner Ramón Ariza was lecturing in a small auditorium in the Spanish Department. Though he was well known in Latin America, and two of his novels had been translated into English while he was still jailed on the island, he was not exactly a household name in New York. We were such ardent fans that we had left early so we could get front-row seats. Manolo had brought his camera and tape recorder to document the event, which he considered of historical importance.

By seven o'clock the auditorium was packed with an audience of mostly older, academic-looking women and a dozen men, though few seemed openly gay. Ramón arrived accompanied by the department chairman. Up until this point, I just knew the crush-inducing photo of him on the editions of his books published in Spanish. He was older now, in his mid-forties, but he was still handsome, though thin, borderline thin, so thin that it was hard to say if he had the virus. He had prominent cheekbones, sunken cheeks, and big, black intense eyes, and a mane of brown hair. Though he had a stocky, strong peasant build, there was something coquettish and queenie about his manner as he stood there while being introduced.

While Manolo took photos like any vulgar paparazzo, I found myself completely unable to take my eyes off Ramón. I loved his two novels about life in rural Cuba just before and right after the revolution. I also thought he was one of the greatest poets in the Spanish language. Even if he hadn't been jailed, tortured, his manuscripts destroyed, I would have been a big fan of his work. But of course the story of his incarcerations and his confrontations with Fidel added a whole other mystique to his persona. In Latin American artistic circles, which were traditionally left-wing and pro Castro, Ramón was considered a pariah. I, too, was divided in my admiration of Ramón—I considered myself a socialist and yet I couldn't forgive Fidel Castro for his treatment of homosexuals. As far as I was concerned, I was tired of putting the needs of the people above my own. Either I was considered one of the people—homosexuality and all—or I wanted no part of a system that wanted justice for all, except the homosexuals. Castro's track record spoke for itself, indicting him as someone who had perpetrated great crimes against gay people. So I often had found myself arguing with my Latino friends who were pro gay rights but also pro Fidel and who therefore dismissed and ridiculed Ramón.

Ramón was a magnetic speaker. As soon as he began to talk, he turned on some kind of inner light that made him shine like a true star. He was charming, deadly serious, irreverent, subversive as he talked about his life and the evolution of his work under communism. He had as many bad things to say about the Cuban communists on the island as about the Cuban exiles in Miami whom he called materialistic, racist, homophobic. I was astonished by his courage and his determination not to simplify his talk into black and white issues.

Ramón was telling us about how one of his novels had been confiscated by Fidel's police and all the existing manuscripts destroyed and how he had had to rewrite it from memory, when suddenly a male voice in the audience cried, "Liar! It's all lies!"

All the heads in the auditorium turned in the direction the voice had come from. Four younger men stood in the back, against the wall, looking defiantly at Ramón and at the rest of us. "You are a liar paid by the CIA," one of the men said. "Tell us how much they pay you to lie about the revolution."

Intense whispering was heard in the auditorium. "Faggot," one of the men called. "Faggot. You should all be dead."

"*¡Malparido hijo de puta!*"[1] Ramón screamed, losing all control, blanching, shaking. "If you were a man you wouldn't scream from up there. You'd say it to my face."

Like a stampede of hungry beasts, the men raced down the stairs in Ramó's direction. Pandemonium broke out in the auditorium. The ladies in the audience started screaming, Manolo began to snap pictures and before I knew it, the four men started beating Ramón, who fought all of them with incredible fury. Two of the men had pinned Ramón against the wall and were hitting him. Seeing this, I couldn't let the four goons beat one person so I decided to help Ramón and started throwing blows. When Manolo saw me enter the scuffle he joined in. Suddenly I realized some of the screaming ladies had entered the tussle and were hitting the attackers with their umbrellas and pocketbooks. One of the men ran out of the room, and as soon as they saw him flee, his companions followed him.

Ramón was on the floor bleeding, so I knelt to assist him. "Careful," he said. "Don't touch the blood. I have AIDS."

I froze. It was the first time our eyes met. He seemed surprised, hardly believing that a total stranger had come to his help. We were surrounded by a chorus of women. "Ramón, *¿estás bien? Ay, Dios mío.*[2] Somebody call an ambulance. *¡Ay, pobrecito!*"[3] was heard all at once.

Ramón had bunched a hand against his nose to stop the profuse bleeding.

"He has to go to the hospital," one of the ladies said.

"My car is parked right outside," another one offered.

Ramón placed a hand on my shoulder to help himself up. "Who are you?" he asked suddenly and I saw paranoia in his eyes. Perhaps he thought I was a Cuban agent. Later I would learn that he behaved in the States as if he were still in Cuba—he was suspicious of everyone and saw conspiracies everywhere. He had escaped the island but had brought the police state mentality with him.

"I'm a fan," I said. "I love your books. I'm a writer from Colombia. And this is my friend Manolo, another fan," I said, nodding in Manolo's direction.

Ramón winced and decided I was telling the truth. We helped him get up and into the elevator. When he was inside the car, it occurred to me that I should go with him. I told Manolo I'd call him later and, accompanied by the driver and another woman, we headed for Saint Vincent's Hospital in the Village. The women were academics who knew Ramón

---

[1]Ill-born son of a bitch!

[2]Are you okay? Oh, my God.

[3]Oh, poor

and had written papers about his work. I was the only stranger in the car. They talked among themselves with great animation without paying attention to me.

The waiting room was a madhouse, and when Ramón's turn came I helped him fill out the forms because he was still bleeding. It turned out he had no health insurance. One of the women with us, whose name was Sara, pulled out her American Express card, gave it to the attendant, and said, "Here's my card. You can charge everything to me."

Finally, a nurse came out pushing a wheelchair and whisked Ramón away. The women and I chatted for a while about Ramón, whom they worshipped, about themselves, the places where they taught, and about me. They were Cuban refugees who had been in the States for decades, though they still talked about Cuba as if they had left it yesterday. Both were in their fifties. Sara was plump, matronly, and very proper; Sonia was her junior, thin, full of nervous energy. Sara spoke slowly, measuring her words with precision. Sonia had a spitfire delivery. Sara was seductive in a motherly way; whereas Sonia was edgy, almost sharp. When they spoke about Castro and Cuba and how Ramón had been treated, I saw another side of them. I saw that they were strong, determined women and that they could be formidable adversaries.

Finally, I suggested that they should leave; that I would wait for Ramón and take him home. I convinced them that they could leave the situation in my hands. The women talked to the nurses, and when they were satisfied that Ramón's cuts were minor, that he would be discharged that night, we exchanged kisses and they left.

A couple of hours later a dazed Ramón appeared, accompanied by a nurse. I walked up to him. He looked surprised to see me there. "I told Sara and Sonia they could leave. That I would make sure you'd get home all right."

Instead of thanking me, he said, "Why are you doing this? You don't know me."

"I told you earlier, I'm a fan. That's why." I became apprehensive that I sounded like a groupie. I added, "I'm also a poet. I'm writing my first novel."

"Who's your favorite poet?" he asked aggressively. The way he put the question it sounded as though if I said the wrong name all communication between us would be over. The people pleaser in me wanted to guess who his favorite poet was. I did not want to alienate him, but I did not want to lie. Martí sounded like a safe bet, since all Cubans are nuts about Martí, but I did not care for his poetry, though I certainly liked "Guantanamera." "You mean, of all the poets in the world?" I asked, trying to gain time.

"Who comes to mind right now?" he asked, point-blank.

"Cernuda," I blurted. "Luis Cernuda."

"I love Cernuda too," he said and tried to smile. Ramón looked awful: his face swollen, his nose wrapped in a bulky, wet bandage. His shirt was liberally covered with dry blood. He had a black eye, so inflamed that it was shut. There was also blood splotched on his hair. He took a step in my direction and wobbled, as if he were dizzy. I offered him my arm.

When Ramón gave his address to the taxi driver, I felt déjà vu. The address he gave, 690 Eighth Avenue, was just next door to O'Donnell's Bar, which I had lived over for more than a decade. When I told him about this, Ramón said, "This is a good omen, don't you think?"

Was he flirting with me? I wondered. We were silent riding the taxi uptown. Ramón seemed morose, and he was drowsy from the sedatives and painkillers they had given him. The taxi stopped one door past my former abode. When I saw how weak he was, I offered to help him to his apartment. He accepted my offer without protesting. We climbed and climbed, all the way to the sixth floor. Several times we had to stop so that Ramón could catch his breath.

"Now that you're here," he said when we reached his door, "you must come in for a cup of coffee."

After we entered the apartment, which had half a dozen locks, Ramón secured it from the inside, sliding all kinds of chains and bolts across the door. For a moment, I was alarmed. Then I relaxed, as I realized this was just routine for him. Later, when I knew him better, I understood that he still felt as if any minute the Cuban Secret Police would break down the door of his apartment without any notice. We walked into the living room, which had a window looking in the direction of the Hudson. Because it was night, all I saw were the lighted silhouettes of some tall buildings.

Despite the fact that a couple of Ramón's books had been translated into English and into many foreign languages and that he had received some important cash awards, the apartment was shabby. A primitive oil landscape depicting the Cuban countryside hung in the living room. It was the only decoration. Ramón indicated that I sit in a sunken couch. He said he could offer me a Cuba Libre or a cup of coffee.

"Whatever you're having, it's fine," I said.

"Oh, you're so accommodating," he said coquettishly. "Coffee it will be. I'm going to write after you leave. I need a shot of caffeine to keep me awake. I feel so groggy from the damn sedatives."

I wanted to say, Forget about writing tonight. What you need is to rest. What was it in him that awoke my need to want to play Florence Nightingale? Was it that he had AIDS? Or was this part of my Al-Anon disease? I could hear Dallas screaming in my ear, "Keep the focus on yourself!"

Ramón served two mugs of strong black coffee and sat on the couch, at the opposite end. There was no light on in the living room but, because of the light on the buildings and billboards outside, no other illumination was needed. We sat there bathed in a muted neon glow that was a hodgepodge of colors, so that the place seemed unreal, like a stage. It looked like neither night nor day, as though time had ceased to exist at that moment and we were in a room in another galaxy where neither the sun nor the moon were the main sources of light.

It turned out that Ramón was also a client of Tim Colby's, and that he had moved into this apartment shortly before I moved away to Bank Street.

"I wonder if I ever cruised you," he said.

"Are you flirting with me?" I asked.

His face changed colors but he looked at me even more intently. "It's cultural, you know."

"I was hoping it would be more specific than that."

His face got even redder and mine got very warm. "Tell me the story of your life. I want to know everything," he said.

"My life's really boring." I wanted to talk about the people who had attacked him, but Ramón dismissed them as "Castroite scumbags" not worth talking about.

I was full of questions: I wanted to ask him about Cuba, about growing up in the countryside, about the early days of the revolution, about the persecution he had endured, jail, torture, and finally his escape. By comparison, my life had been dull and lackluster. Later, it occurred to me that, as a successful writer who traveled and spoke to audiences, he was probably sick and tired of having to repeat his story wherever he went. So much of it was public record, anyway. The truth is that I had never had many gay Latino friends. When Bobby Castro died of AIDS, he had left a large void in my life.

Right away, a spark was created between Ramón and me. Though we were strangers, I gabbed away about my childhood, my adolescence, about coming out as an adult in the States, about my writing. At every turn, he found some point of identification with my story. Like me, he had grown up with his mother's family. Like me, both his maternal grandparents were country people. We both had developed a love of books in early adolescence and had started to write when we were barely out of puberty. I had arrived in the States in my late teens. At that point, his experience and mine diverged. But everything that had to do with Latin America, with growing up in a culture of machismo, united us in a potent bond. We had been talking for a couple of hours when he asked, "What was the worst time for you when you were an adolescent?"

I didn't have to think about that one. "Sunday afternoons," I said.

"Exactly right," he said. "It was the same for me."

I talked about the terror of those sweltering afternoons in Barranquilla when the world seemed to come to a standstill. Many of the people in the city went to the soccer stadium and, if I didn't have a plan—for example, to go to the movies with Wilbrajan—the afternoon seemed endless and I felt a loneliness that was unbearably painful because I thought it would never end. As much as I hated school, where the boys tormented me for being an intellectual sissy, I preferred it to being at home when my mother and sister had gone out to visit friends and I sat by the window reading a novel. Next I talked about Tarzan, the only known homosexual in Barranquilla, an outcast who was supposed to prey on the boys. How I was both drawn to him and repelled by him. How I sat by my window reading and studied him when he went by the house, strutting like a peacock in his tight jeans and close-fitting T-shirts over his muscular torso. Here Ramón interjected that in Holguín, where he grew up, the only known homosexual was also an outcast, and that he dreaded he'd become one. I talked about discovering Oscar Wilde through the movie *The Trials of Oscar Wilde* and reading all his works. And the devastation I felt when I thought that, like Wilde, I would also be put in jail for my homosexuality. I talked about my first experiences with a neighbor, and about experimenting with animals, which was very common in Colombia, especially in the countryside. From reading his novels I knew that he, too, had done his share of that.

It was dawn when we stopped exchanging anecdotes. The lights on the buildings and billboards were out and the sky was a satiny ivory tent above Manhattan. I was so tired I was barely able to get up from the sofa. Ramón suggested that I stay and sleep on the couch. "I promise not to molest you," he teased me. There was no chance of that, I thought. Bandaged in bloody rags, he looked most unappealing. However, as we faced each other in front of his door, a momentary awkwardness ensued. We hugged, the way old friends do, but as we pulled away, our faces brushed and we kissed lightly on the lips. At that moment, it surprised me to find out that I was romantically attracted to him.

"Let's talk later today," he said. "Maybe we can catch a movie."

"Okay," I said, feeling myself blush.

When I stepped on the deserted sidewalk of Eighth Avenue at dawn, I felt light-headed, younger. Suddenly it hit me that another, entirely different life—risky but thrilling—had begun.

The ringing phone woke me up. *"Buenas tardes,"*[4] said Ramón's voice.

"What time is it?" I asked.

"It's noon, Sleeping Beauty."

Though we had just met, he was talking to me as an old intimate friend, and I liked the familiarity. I sat up on my bed and yawned.

"Should I call you back later?"

"No, it's nice to hear your voice. How are you feeling this morning?"

"My face is even more swollen than yesterday. But I'm not in pain." Ramón paused. "Hey, want to go see a movie later this evening?"

"Sure," I said. We had already established that we were both movie nuts and that we liked many of the same directors. "Do you have anything in mind?"

That night we met across from Lincoln Center to see Jean Vigo's *L'Atalante* which had recently been restored and which we hadn't seen before. There were few people in the audience and sitting so close to Ramón, being so aware of his breathing, once in awhile touching as we shifted positions on our chairs, heightened the trancelike mood created by Jean Vigo's masterpiece. Afterward, we walked out of the theatre discussing the film. It was a cold night, but we were both feeling so exhilarated and energized by the movie and our discussion that we walked down Broadway, to 43rd Street. Before I knew it, we arrived in front of the door to his building. It was like déjà vu: instant replay of the night before. It also felt as if a whole year of knowing each other (not a measly twenty-four hours) had gone by. It was like being with an old friend.

"Want to come up for a drink?" Ramón asked.

I hesitated; I didn't want Ramón to take over my life; I needed to get back to my old routine.

"I promise not to keep you up very late. Just a quick cup of coffee."

I didn't want to go home, yet I demurred. I wasn't sure whether he was just being polite. But I said yes because I didn't want the night to end. Inside his apartment, after we took off our jackets, we sat down in the same exact spots where we had sat the night before. Our eyes met. Ramón leaned over and took my hand. "Look," he said. "I like you. I am attracted to you, Santiago."

I squeezed his hand. With his red bruised face and bandages he looked quite monstrous. I closed my eyes so that I could see him the way he had appeared before the men attacked him in the auditorium.

"But I understand if you don't want to get involved with someone with AIDS."

With my eyes still closed, I put a finger to his lips. "Hush," I murmured. "I like you too," I added, to my own surprise. Until that moment I hadn't thought the potential was there for a romance. I opened my eyes. Now he looked handsome to me. "I don't care about the HIV."

"I don't just have HIV," he insisted. "I have full-blown AIDS. Last year I almost died of pneumonia. It's a miracle I've recovered this much. One thing I can tell you is that I never want to be that sick again. Once was enough. I know what's down the road so I don't want to lie to you."

I reached over, took his face gently in my hands, and kissed his lips. "I don't care," I said, not sure if I really meant it.

He took my face in his hands. "Then let's be lovers. I'm not into games and I don't have the time for a long courtship."

---

[4]Good afternoon

What can I say? I didn't want to reject Ramón because he was sick. I'd be a hypocrite if I didn't admit that I was terrified of what had happened. Was getting involved with a man with AIDS the ultimate Al-Anon caretaker dream? *Involvement* sounded like too light a word for the demands such a relationship would make.

All this was too much for me to deal with on my own. I called my free therapist—my Al-Anon sponsor. I was apprehensive about how Dallas might react. Would he approve of the affair? After all, how wise was it to get involved with a sick man? What kind of future was there in starting a relationship with someone who had no future? Ramón wasn't just positive—he was sick, the next time he got sick it might be fatal. We hadn't discussed the T-cell count or the various hospitalizations, etc., but I had already known enough sick people to realize that in Ramón's case the illness was quite advanced.

I voiced my hesitations to Dallas, whose advice was, "Santiago, it's not the length of a relationship that matters, but the quality of the time you have together." After I hung up, I thought about what he had said. I was thirty-five years old: I knew that the chances were slim that anyone of Ramón's exceptional qualities would ever appear again.

My fears hadn't been completely quelled by Dallas's words. I wanted to talk with at least one other person before I saw Ramón again—before we had sex. We had kissed passionately and I knew that kissing was all right, that the chances of getting HIV that way were almost nonexistent. I also knew that the best way to stay HIV-negative was not to share needles or have sex with an HIV-positive man. Lots of guys were having sex with positive men and were staying negative, but I couldn't just reject the idea of having sex with Ramón (whom I passionately desired) just because I wasn't quite sure about all the dos and don'ts.

I called Manolo but got his machine. Though I didn't feel comfortable discussing the nitty-gritty of sex with Laurette, I called her to get her take on the situation. Laurette heard me patiently, and then remarked, "When you're an old man, Santiago, you're not going to regret the affairs you had, but the ones you didn't have." More than anything else I would hear in the next few weeks, this made up my mind. I would not reject Ramón just because he carried the virus.

Right away I understood that I was getting involved in a three-some: that HIV was the third party in the equation—a noisy, insistent monster who would always come between us.

# Ramón "Tianguis" Pérez

Ramón "Tianguis" Pérez was born in San Pablo Macuiltianguis, Mexico, in a Zapotec village in the Sierra Juárez region of Oaxaca. His family ran a cabinetmaking shop. His experiences as a *mojado*, or undocumented worker, were chronicled in his first book, *Diary of an Undocumented Immigrant*, a first-hand testimonial of the process of immigration and labor contracting that Mexican workers experience in the United States at the hands of the US Immigration and Naturalization Service.

---

Primary works by Ramón "Tianguis" Pérez: *Diary of an Undocumented Immigrant* (Houston: Arte Público Press, 1991); *Diary of a Guerrilla* (Houston: Arte Público Press, 1999).

# "Crossing The Border" from *Diary of an Undocumented Worker*

My luggage is a small vinyl suitcase that holds one change of clothes. It's a bag for a person who has left home for a couple of days, but I don't know when I'll return to my village. Bigger than my bag is the mountain of goodbyes I'm carrying. My mother was so touched that she made the sign of the cross over me with a wax candle that is probably burning upon the altar of the church right now. My father, more used to goodbyes than mothers, told me, "Stay on your toes, boy," while he was giving me a hug. My brothers told me to send them postcards from the places I will find myself. Last night, my friends and I made the rounds, drinking.

It's about eleven o'clock in the morning and I'm walking the eight kilometers that separate my village from the highway that snakes over the peak of the mountain range. There's a dirt road that comes from it to my village, but there isn't always a passing truck on which to catch a ride. But this time, I'd rather walk the distance anyway.

The summer sun isn't extreme, but the exercise makes me sweat. Before leaving, I spent more than an hour beneath the showerhead and then changed into the clothes that my mother had ironed. It took more time for me to shower and change than it has for me to get bathed in sweat. But at least it made my mother happy to see me leave clean and in fresh clothes.

If my ancestors had known that the international highway was going to pass just eight kilometers from the village, maybe they would have decided to establish the village farther up, but I can't blame them. They probably had their own reasons for putting the village midway down the mountains, and I myself have learned that the closer land is to the peaks, the less fertile it is. Higher up, the cold is more intense and the peak is covered with snow. Beneath us, the heat is sultry, while in our village, the climate is mild. Now that I think about it, my ancestors were entirely right, and I'm sure that before digging the groundwork for the foundation of the village's first house, they set it precisely at the midpoint of the mountain.

Halfway between the village and the highway is a hill from which you can view the panorama of the village, and I rest there for a minute. In the middle of the thick forest of pines and oaks and other trees, a mild breeze comes up to me, fresh and comforting, but the rays of the sun don't let it become cold. There below, encircling the village, the cornfields have begun to dry, a sign that within two months people will bring in the harvest. The cornfields are a coffee-colored scene, and their sameness gives the impression of a giant blanket whose stitches sway with the wind. Below are the tin roofs of the village, shining beneath the sun, and in the middle, the church of thick, whitewashed walls with a dome on one side and a bell tower on the other. Next to the church I can see the top of the big ash tree that is probably as old as the village. The tree has been pruned to avoid accidents, they say, ever since the days when the electric lines came. From here, I can also see a white haze over the houses, smoke that comes from kitchen hearths. But by afternoon, gusts of wind will blow it far away.

Sure, I know, everybody loves his hometown and the region where he was born. But I've been in tropical climates where people have to resort to a fan to create a little breeze, and in those places, the greeting among people is, "How hot it is!" and the response is, "Yes, man, how hot!" I guess I'm lucky not to know how the Eskimos say good morning. Here, you don't need a fan and much less do you need a heater in the summertime.

Of course, not everything about my village is so temperate. It, too, has suffered inclemency. Several little creeks run around the village, and three of them run right through it, and right now the creeks are running too deep. The old people say that back in 1945 it rained day and night for forty days and people thought that the end of the world was coming. The rains were so plentiful that they deepened the course of the creeks, which before, had run almost level to the ground. The dirt kept mixing with the water until the land was cut with gullies that got deeper as the canals of the creeks grew wider. Those creeks grew and grew until it was impossible to cross them. The mudholes broke open and they, too, became like springs and they added their water to the swollen creeks. The waters carried trees, rocks and houses with them, everything that they found in their path. In the village, food grew scarce. The little that was in the stores didn't last long, and people began eating their chickens and the pigs that they were keeping to fatten. The roads became impassable. Cows drowned. The harvest was lost. One of my townsmen, worried because he had left his cattle tiedup outside of the village, tried to cross one of the creeks by floating on a log. But the water wasn't only running swiftly, it was also full of mud, branches and the trunks of trees. He was drowned before he got to the middle of the creek. The townspeople say that after the rains, or the flood, his family tried to find his body to bury it, but all they encountered was his hat, which was stuck in the branches of a bush. Those people who stayed afterwards are still in town, and they will stay even if another flood comes, because water can't dig as deep as the roots of our Zapotec village.

## Headed North

In another half hour of walking, I'll arrive at the highway where I'll catch a bus to take me to Oaxaca City. From there another bus will carry me to Mexico City, then yet another one will take me to Nuevo Laredo, on the border. My plan is to go to the United States as a *mojado*, or wetback.

It didn't take a lot of thinking for me to decide to make this trip. It was a matter of following the tradition of the village. One could even say that we're a village of wetbacks. A lot of people, nearly the majority, have gone, come back, and returned to the country to the north; almost all of them have held in their fingers the famous green bills that have jokingly been called "green cards"—immigrant cards—for generations. For several decades, Macuiltianguis—that's the name of my village—has been an emigrant village, and our people have spread out like the roots of a tree under the earth, looking for sustenance. My people have had to emigrate to survive. First, they went to Oaxaca City, then to Mexico City, and for the past thirty years up to the present, the compass has always pointed towards the United States.

My townsmen have been crossing the border since the forties, when the rumor of the Bracero[1] program reached our village, about ten years before the highway came through. The news of the Bracero program was brought to us by our itinerant merchants, men who went from town to town, buying the products of the region: corn, beans, coffee, *achiote[2]*, *mescal*, eggs, fabric dye, and fountain pen ink. The merchants carried these items on the backs of animals, or sometimes, on their own backs, until they reached the city of Oaxaca, about a three days walk from home. On their return trips, they brought manufactured prod-

---

[1]Farm worker
[2]Vegetable

ucts, like farm tools, cooking utensils, coarse cotton cloth, ready-made clothing and shoes, candies and so on. They sold their goods from house to house, town to town. One of them came with the news that there were possibilities of work in the United States as a *bracero*, and the news passed from mouth to mouth until everyone had heard it.

To see if the rumor was true, a merchant and two others went to the U.S. embassy in Mexico City. The only document the embassy required them to provide was a copy of their birth certificates, for which they came back to the village. On their return to Mexico City, they were contracted to work in California.

From the day of their departure, the whole town followed the fate of those adventurers with great interest. After a little while, the first letters to their families arrived. The closest kinsmen asked what news the letters contained, and from them the news spread to the rest of the villagers. Afterwards, checks with postal money orders arrived, and their families went to Oaxaca City to cash them. The mens' return home, some six months later, was a big event because when they came into town they were seen carrying large boxes of foreign goods, mainly clothing.

Their experience inspired others, but not all of them had the same good fortune. Some were contracted for only short periods, because each time there were more people waiting for the same opportunity at the contractors' offices. That's when some men smelled a good business; the men called *coyotes*, the forerunners of today's alien smugglers. They were men who, for a sum of money, intervened in the Mexican offices where contracts were given to make sure that their clients were included in the list of men chosen.

The contractual system came to an end with the Bracero program, in the mid-sixties, but ending the program didn't end Mexican desires to cross the border. People had learned that in the United States one could earn a wage much higher than the standard Mexican wage, even if to do it one had to suffer privations, like absence from one's family. So when the Bracero program ended, the *coyotes* kept working on their own. They looked for employers in the U.S. and supplied them with workers illegally.

I, too, joined the emigrant stream. For a year I worked in Mexico City as a nightwatchman in a parking garage. I earned the minimum wage and could barely pay living expenses. A lot of the time I had to resort to severe diets and other limitations, just to pay rent on the apartment where I lived, so that one day I wouldn't come home and find that the owner had put my belongings outside.

After that year, I quit as night watchman and came back home to work at my father's side in the little carpentry shop that supplies the village with simple items of furniture. During the years when I worked at carpentry, I noticed that going to the U.S. was a routine of village people. People went so often that it was like they were visiting a nearby city. I'd seen them leave and come home as changed people. The trips erased for a while the lines that the sun, the wind and the dust put in a peasant's skin. People came home with good haircuts, good clothes, and most of all, they brought dollars in their pockets. In the *cantinas*[3] they paid for beers without worrying much about the tab. When the alcohol rose to their heads, they'd begin saying words in English. It was natural for me to want to try my luck at earning dollars, and maybe earn enough to improve the machinery in our little carpentry shop.

During my infancy, I always heard people say "*Estadu*," because that's the way that "*Estado*," or state, is pronounced in Zapotec, our language. Later on, people simply said "*El*

---

[3]Bars

*Norte,*" "The North," when referring to the United States. Today when somebody says "I'm going to *Los,*" everybody understands that he's referring to Los Angeles, California, the most common destination of us villagers.

But I'm not going to Los Angeles, at least not now. This time, I want to try my luck in the state of Texas, specifically, in Houston, where a friend of mine has been living for several years. He's lent me money for the trip.

# The Runner

The waiting room at the bus station in Nuevo Laredo is spacious and well-lit. It is full of people walking in different directions with bags in their hands. Some are just coming in, some are leaving. Some are in line to buy tickets, and others are seated in the terminal, nervous or bored. A tattered beggar has laid some cardboard sheets on the floor of one corner and he's sitting there, chewing on a piece of hardened bread, his supper before retiring for the night. The waiting room clock marks nine p.m. My traveling companions seem content to have arrived, but I notice them yawning from tiredness; the trip took fourteen hours. Some of them try to comb their disheveled hair and others rub their red eyes. On seeing them, I decide that I probably have the same appearance.

Disoriented, I take a seat in the waiting room, hoping to shake off my own sleepiness. I know what I should do next. I should go out onto the street, take a taxi to a hotel, rest a while and then look for a *coyote*, or alien smuggler. Before setting out, I take my belongings and head towards the restroom, thinking that a stream of cold water across my face will help me wake up.

With the first steps I take towards the restroom, a dark-skinned guy comes up alongside me. He's short and thin and he's dressed in a t-shirt and jeans. He greets me familiarly, with a handshake. After looking him up and down, I'm sure that I've never seen him before. I give him a stern look, but he smiles broadly at me, anyway.

"Where are you coming from, my friend?" he says.

"From Mexico City," I answer.

"From Mexico City!" he exclaims. "Well, man, we're neighbors! I, too, am from Mexico City."

He reaches out and shakes my hand again.

I already know the type from memory. It's not the first time that a stranger has come up to me, saying almost the same things. I am waiting for him to tell me that he had suffered such and such instances of bad luck and that he had a relative in danger of dying and that he had to go to the relative's bedside and that, though it pained him to be without resources, he at least felt encouraged to have come upon a townsman who could give him a little money. But instead of saying that, the stranger keeps walking at my side.

"Where are you headed?" he asks.

I keep silent and without breaking my pace I give him an inquisitorial look, trying to figure out why in the devil's name he's trying to insert himself into my affairs. Still smiling and talking, he repeats his question, as if I hadn't heard him the first time.

"To Houston, I hope to arrive in Houston, with luck, and I'm going to have to find a *coyote,*" I tell him, because, given his insistence, I suspect that he might know something about the border-crossing business.

"Are you looking for a particular *coyote?* Has somebody recommended one?" he asks with growing interest.

"I don't know any and nobody has recommended one, and in just a minute, I've got to begin looking for one."

"Well, you're in luck, friend!" he exclaims, adopting the mien of a happy man, content to have brought good news. "You don't have to keep looking, because I"—he points to his chest with the index finger of his right hand—"work for the best and the heaviest *coyote* in Nuevo Laredo. . . . The heaviest," he repeats, emphasizing every syllable as if pronouncing the word really was a task of heavy labor.

After entering the restroom, I go up to the urinal, an earthen-colored, tiled wall with a narrow drainage canal at its foot. I start making water and my stranger friend does the same.

"A Mexican never pisses alone," he says, recalling an old saying.

"Right now we have forty *chivos*[4] ready to leave in the early morning, and they're going precisely to Houston, your same destination, my friend."

I'd later learn that they call us *chivos*, or goats, because of the odor we exude from lack of bathing facilities and clean clothing. I am surprised by the ease with which I've run into at least the assistant of a *coyote*, but I don't show much interest in knowing more about his work. After urinating, I go to a sink, open a faucet, and with cupped hands I wet my face a time or two. My friend follows me to the sink and plants himself nearby, without pausing in his praises of his *coyote* boss.

"How much is it going to cost me?" I ask, without raising my head from the sink.

"Four hundred and fifty dollars, plus four thousand pesos for the boat," he answers.

"Good, if that's all, paying will be no problem."

"Very good!," he exclaims with a triumphant gesture. "Well, my friend, in less than eighteen hours you'll be in Houston."

"That's even better," I say, holding back my happiness.

Then my unexpected friend takes a couple of steps and thinking, he says to me, "There's something missing. We've got to be sure that you'll pay that amount or that it will be paid for you."

"That's no problem. You will be paid when I get to Houston."

I'm carrying the money, but my distrust tells me that I shouldn't let the stranger know. The money is a loan of $650. I've got $100 in my billfold. The other $550, in bills of $50 each, is sewn into the lining of my jean jacket.

"Oh," he says, answering himself, "you've got a relative who is going to pay for you in Houston. It's incredible how everybody has relatives in the United States."

Without my asking, he has told me what my answer should be, should anyone else question me about money. I'll say that my friend will pay in Houston. Nobody will know that I'm carrying the money myself.

"It's not really a relative that I've got, it's a friend," I say, to get the story rolling.

"You should give us the phone number of your friend so that we can make sure that he really knows you and will pay for you."

"That's no problem," I tell him, just for the moment. The telephone number could be a problem because my friend has asked me to use his name only if it's urgent. He also asked

---

[4]Illegal aliens, people to smuggle

me not to carry his telephone number and address with me. I have complied with his requests. I memorized his name and address. The only problem I can foresee will be to find a way to tell him that if the *coyotes* call, he should promise to pay for me.

The friendly stranger doesn't stop trying to convince me that his boss is a powerful man. He says that his boss is invulnerable because he has paid off the police.

"On top of that," the stranger says, "he treats the *chivos* better than anyone else, because he gives them a house to stay in while they're waiting. The other *coyotes* put people out in the brush without jackets and a lot of times, without food. Not to mention the way he treats me," the guy adds. "He doesn't pinch pennies when we're out drinking."

I'm more interested in what he says about payment than in his endless homage to his boss.

"Do I have to pay for the boat every time it crosses the Rio Grande, or only to cross without incident?" I ask him, while I'm drying my face with the sleeve of my jacket.

"Oh, no!" he says, as if scolding himself for having forgotten an important detail. "If *La Migra*[5] catches you ten times, we'll put you across ten times for the same money. And what's more"—his face brightens as if with surprise—"my boss is right here in the station. Come on, I'll introduce you!"

We go walking towards the station's cafeteria, and the stranger who says he's my townsman points towards a group of three men seated at a table, each one in front of a can of beer.

"Do you see that dude who's wearing the cowboy hat? Well, that's Juan Serna, he's my boss," he tells me, with the pride and arrogance of someone who has introduced a Pancho Villa. "All you have to do is say that you're a client of Juan Serna, and the police will leave you alone, because— let me tell you—if you go outside to the street right now and you take a taxi at the next block, or if you catch a city bus, the Judicial Police will grab you—and forget it!—they'll let you go on the next corner, with empty pockets. They'll rip off your change, man. But if you tell them that you're with Juan Serna, they themselves will take you to the house where we keep the *chivos*."

"Wait for me here," he says when we've come within a prudent distance of the table where the three men are chatting. "I'm going to tell the boss that you're going to Houston."

He walks towards the table and speaks to the man named Juan Serna, then looks towards me. With a movement of his hand, he tells me to come nearer.

Juan Serna is dressed in an orange, nylon t-shirt with black lettering on its frontside that says, "Roberto Durán #1." He's dark-complexioned with somewhat fine facial features. His eyes seem very deep in their sockets. He's clean-shaven, with a wispy moustache. Beneath his eyes are the wrinkles of a man bordering on fifty. Several tattoos adorn both arms, most prominent among them is the head of Jesus, dripping blood from his crown of thorns. Juan Serna doesn't waste good humor like his assistant. He remains rigid, as if preoccupied with other affairs. He leans forward a little, supporting his body upon the table with his forearms, his hands clasped around a can of beer. He makes no gesture and gives no greeting when his assistant introduces us, only a rapid look, a look as indifferent as if he'd been handed the next can of beer. His two companions are seated in front of him, and they're saying something that I can't hear. My "townsman" stands, waiting expectantly at Juan Serna's side.

---

[5]The border patrol

"Where are you going?," Serna says to me in a northern accent and in a voice so dry that it sounds like he's formed his question not in his mouth, but in his throat.

"To Houston."

"Do you have someone to pay for you there?"

"My friend who lives in Houston."

"So should I take him?" my townsman says.

Juan Serna gives his consent by nodding at my townsman, but he nods without moving a single muscle of his face. I follow my townsman, with the impression that behind us Juan Serna is still nodding, like the branch of a tree that sways involuntarily after somebody has pulled on it.

Outside the bus station, the townsman leads me to a station wagon. He and I get into its back seat.

"We have to wait until the driver arrives," he says.

From the floor of the vehicle he picks up a six-pack and hands me a can.

"What's your name?," he asks.

"Martin," I say, just to give a name.

"My name is Juan, just like the boss," he says without my having asked him. "And I won't give you my last name because I don't know you, but I'll gladly tell you my nickname. You can call me Xochimilco, just like everybody here does."

While I sip on my beer, Xochimilco drinks one, then another, and a third, chatting all the while.

He says that he was a taco vendor in the Xochimilco district of Mexico City, and that was the reason for his nickname. The taco business had been a good one because his boss had lent him a car to go to places where people amassed, like soccer games. But things went bad when the boss had to sell his car. Xochimiloco says that he found himself first without work, and then without money. He found it necessary to ask a friend for a loan of five thousand pesos.

Xochimilco began to worry when his friend put twice the amount he'd asked for into his hands. He accepted only after making long declarations of gratitude. A month later, that same friend came to his house in a luxurious new car. "When from the doors to my house I saw him pull up," Xochimilco says, "I immediately thought about the loan he'd made me, and I was really relieved when he said that I should forget about it, because I still didn't have anything in my pockets."

His friend told him that if he was still in need, he'd help him get past his troubles, on the condition that he cooperate with the friend's plans. When Xochimilco asked in what way he could help, his friend laid a .38 calibre automatic pistol in his hands. Xochimilco didn't know what to say, but he looked with fascination upon the gun given to him.

"At first, it frightened me," Xochimilco tells me, "because I'd never shot a pistol, much less shot at a human being."

"Who said that you're going to kill anybody?" his friend said when Xochimilco expressed reservations. Xochimilco decided to trust his friend in the hopes that he, too, would someday have a car like his. His friend and another guy had planned a hold-up.

"Five hundred thousand pesos for only one simple hold-up!" Xochimilco bragged after a long swig of beer. "Your nerves make you tremble after the first job."

But Xochimilco's money troubles were finished. After the first job came others. The gang's biggest and last hit came after they had gotten to know the son of the owner of a slaughterhouse. The son was firmly resolved to rob his father, who he said was swimming in money but was so cheap that he wouldn't spend a cent, not even on himself. And the son, who knew his father's routine, conspired with Xochimilco and his friends. The four of them went into the father's office just as he was counting bills on his desk with the company safe open. When he realized that he was being robbed, the father reached for a pistol that he kept in his desk, but the bandits all opened fire, even the son. They made off with four million pesos; Xochimilco's cut came to half a million. Time passed and investigations began. When the son was arrested, Xochimilco decided to flee to *El Norte*.

"I had enough money to pay a *coyote*," Xochimilco says, with a slight and fleeting expression of nostalgia. After two attempts, he managed to reach Houston but he only stayed a month because one night, on leaving a beer joint drunk, the police stopped him and turned him over to agents of *La Migra*, the Immigration and Naturalization Service. A couple of days later, he was taken back to Nuevo Laredo. Now with only ten thousand pesos to his name, he could neither return to Mexico City nor cross the border again. He asked the man who is now his boss to give him a job.

"And here you have me," Xochimilco says. "I'm a runner. They call us that because we're always running behind guys that we suspect are headed to the United States."

I ask him how much he earns. He says that of the four thousand pesos that I'll pay for the boat, two thousand are for him. "I make that much for every *chivo* I take to Juan Serna's house."

"I imagine that you're not exactly poor," I tell him.

"Well, okay," he says, teasing, "I've made enough to have money, but I don't have it saved, because ... well, what good is money? Huh, my friend?" His eyes open into an interrogatory look as he leans closer to me. "To spend it! If not, what good is it?"

His job, he says, pays him different sums on different days, especially because he isn't the only runner.

"You can ask for 'Shell,' for the 'Mosquito,' or for the 'Dog.' Anybody can tell you about them, they're in the same business as me. Today I can pick up ten clients and tomorrow, none. That's the way this job is."

Xochimilco interrupts his explanations to point out a car that has parked in front of the terminal.

"That car without license plates belongs to the Judicial Police, and I can assure you that it won't be long before Juan Serna comes out to talk to them."

Just as he said, a minute later Juan Serna comes out of the terminal and walks directly up to the car without plates.

"Do you see it! Look at that!" Xochimilco exclaims. "What I tell you is no lie. That son-of-a-bitch is well-connected."

A few minutes later, a middle-aged man sits down in front of the steering wheel of the car where Xochimilco and I are waiting. Without saying a word, he starts the motor and we pull off.

"That idiot," Xochimilco says, pointing to the driver, "is the one they call 'Shell.' "

The car passes over paved streets, and for a few minutes, bumps down dirt streets full of chugholes. Meanwhile, I'm thinking that my circumstances are like those of a fugitive. To avoid being stopped by the police I have to keep company with thieves and maybe murderers, who, oddly enough, enjoy police protection. If the police stop me, I could argue that I'm a Mexican citizen, with a right to be in any part of the Republic, and I could point out that the police don't have the right to suppress my rights unless I'm committing a crime. To be a wetback, to go into the United States illegally, isn't a crime that's mentioned in our Constitution, but whether or not it is, it's not important. Here, he who's going to be a wetback, if he has money, will have trouble with the police, and if he doesn't have money, he'll have even more trouble. The idea that the police watch over the social order is an old tale that's true only in my village, where we name the policemen from among our own townsmen. If they find you drunk, they're likely to drag you home. If you deserve a punishment, the worst that can happen to you is a night in jail.

# Roberto Quesada

Roberto Quesada was born in Olanchito, Honduras, in 1962. He has lived in New York since 1989. His works include *The Big Banana, The Ships, The Human and the Goddess,* and *Never through Miami.* He founded and directed the literary magazine *Sobrevuelto.* His novels master the recreation of Honduran dialogs and situations that immigrants encounter in the United States.

## Miami International Airport

*silence = bad*

Control, control, control. Yes, that's the word that will save me. Words save; words are divine; they can rescue you. But sometimes they can do you in, too. Speak little, only what you must, or not at all. Silence is not as wise as people think; sometimes an opportune word trumps silence. I can't look nervous. This is the final test, the decisive one, the final door into the United States. That line is long. So many people! How many will get in? Will we get in? How many will be detained? How many deported? Being here is like *to be or not to be*. I have to practice my English mentally. The little bit that I know can save me. Once again, words can save me but this time in another language. Which language's words are more important? I have to concentrate on practicing while the line is moving; I must practice my pronunciation because if I say *two beer or not two beer*, they will probably deny me entry for being drunk. My documents are in order, my visa is valid, I look like the person in the photograph—yes, it's me, this is me. Nothing is fake, everything is legal. Legal, that is the word that saves. More than anything I am worried about this damned line. "Possession of this visa does not guarantee entry to the United States." What reason would they have for not letting me enter? Documents in order, a letter of invitation. I have no criminal record in my country or any other one. The most important thing is that I be apolitical and not apocalyptical.

Primary works by Roberto Quesada: *The Ships* (New York: Four Walls Eight Windows, 1992); *The Big Banana* (Houston: Arte Público Press, 1999); *Never through Miami* (Houston, Arte Público Press, 2002).

Helena will be overjoyed when I tell her I was in Miami. Her beloved Miami. What is it about Miami that makes so many fall in love with it? It must be pretty. It's a pity I'm only in the airport, but they say the best place for an artist is New York. I'll soon see New York. They say that the most difficult part is this: passing through customs. Everything is in order. I'm not bringing in any avocados or chickens or dogs or butter or cardboard boxes or anything that is not allowed. Will those two sculptures in my suitcase be a problem? No, they are mine; it's art. Art should get through without any problem because this is a developed country where they say art is respected. Yes, I think I meet all the requirements of those who enter with their heads held high. Here I go . . . It's my turn. Damn, I got that mean one with the scowl. Be quiet, mind, and stop thinking that here, they have technology that can read your mind and, *adiós*,[1] New York. Deported for saying "scowl" in your mind about an immigration officer.

"How long do you plan to stay in America?" the immigration officer asked without looking at him.

He hesitated before that annoyed face. How could that fat little woman with glasses and the snout of a Pekinese, who was studying the photo like an x-ray, have more power than he? The freckled little midget looked up and glared into his eyes, urging him for a response. He managed to say, "I'm sorry. No English."

She looked at the passport from back to front, page by page, as if looking for the *corpus delicti*, and then she translated her question.

"*¿Cuánto tiempo piensa quedar en América?*"[2]

He wanted to respond with the lyrics of a romantic Latin song, "My whole life I would spend with you," but that intimidating freckled face was there fulfilling its purpose of terrifying the new arrivals. He knew he had to say a number of months, and the maximum for his visa was six; there was no minimum. Saying six might be cause to deport him. How will you earn a living all that time? Saying less—two weeks, for example—could mean laying his own trap, for they would stamp his passport for two weeks and he would have to leave on that day or sink to the miserable status of an illegal, something he had never even considered.

"Six months."

"*¿Cuál ser la razón de su viaje?*"[3]

"To visit my family?" He said as quickly as possible so she wouldn't understand and wouldn't ask the next question: "What family do you have here?"    *disrespectful*

What could I say? I had no one here. I would have to say my great big family, all the Gonzálezes, Pérezes, Lópezes, Martinezes, Ruizes, Fernándezes . . . my great big Latin American family. Fortunately, the officer was more interested in concrete things than in what family I had here.

"*Mostrarme su boleta para regresar a su país.*"[4]

---

[1]Goodbye

[2]How long do you plan to stay in America?

[3]Why are you traveling?

[4]Show me your return ticket to your country

"I don't have a return ticket. My family will buy it for me when it's time for me to go back." She closed the passport like a door through which the stamp he needed would never enter. *"Nadie puede entrar a América sin su boleta de⁵round-trip."*

"Without what?"

*"Sin boleta para regresar a su país."*[6]

He had to help himself somehow, try to convince her or convince himself that dogs are man's best friends, and use his eyes to talk to that Pekinese-faced woman to get her to sympathize with him.

"I didn't buy one because I don't know the exact date I will return. I may stay less than I thought, or maybe I'll buy a car and leave by land."

The officer opened the passport. Elías felt that same feeling he felt when Helena had refused for so long to open her legs and then, without any warning, opened them like an invitation. But the two situations were very different. In Helena's case, he had the advantage of being owner and lord of the stamp, while the officer had left him without doors and without stamps, and worse yet, without keys. The officer examined the passport page by page, even more scrupulously than before. He felt the blow on his face of every door that was opened, the infinite passport, as long as a novel before the age of television.

*"¿Haber estado en América?"*[7] the officer asked in broken Spanish and her legs open.

"Yes, I have," he replied hurriedly, before the hinges announced another slam of the door.

*"¿Cuántas veces?"*[8]

"Three times."

She looked at the wide-open passport.

*"Aquí no dice."*[9]

"That passport is new."

*"Mostrarme su pasaporte anterior."*[10]

"I left my old passport in my country."

The officer placed her index finger between her legs and closed the door halfway. Elías was sweating, and he felt the stamp would never fit through such a tiny opening.

"It doesn't show here that you have been in America. Here it shows that it's your first time. We need your old passport. *¿En qué trabajar usted?"*[11]

*"Soy escultor,"*[12] he said almost proudly, under the illusion that the magic of art would also be useful for passing through customs.

She was pensive and appeared to be thinking over the word so it would come out perfectly.

---

[5]No one can enter to America without a return ticket . . .

[6]Without a return ticket to your country

[7]Have you ever been in America?

[8]How many times?

[9]It does not say anything here

[10]Show me your last passport

[11]What do you do?

[12]I am a sculptor

"*¿Escalator?*" she said in English. "Odd job, I don't know what an *escalator* is exactly."

Elías was losing hope; he could not let the door close, leaving him outside. He gestured and used body language.

"*Soy escultor*," and just as the agent was removing her finger from the middle of the passport, with just a sliver of light coming through the door, something brilliant came to him. "I am Leonardo da Vinci."

For the first time the passport-checking machine had a human reaction; she was surprised. "*¿Sentirse usted bien?*"[13]

Sweating as if untangling a spider web from his face, Elías said, "No, no, I'm not da Vinci . . . I have the same job."

Then, having understood, she took off the human mask and returned to her normal state.

"Oh, yes, I see, *comprende . . . escultor*.[14] Wait here," and she removed her finger from between her legs and closed the passport with a blow that hit Elías in the face. Dejected now and trying to invent some heroic reason to explain to his family, friends, and enemies why he was deported, he headed for the room the midget woman indicated to him, to wait, along with all the others, for the final judgment.

Just as he had found the peace that comes from resignation and was close to finding that empty space we all need to escape from reality and plunge into sleep's refuge, he heard his name in the distance, as if his soul were being called from Purgatory. His name resonated in his eardrums, weak, transparent, and elastic. It fell on his ears slowly, letter by letter, as if released from a dropper. E l í a s S a n d o v a l. It couldn't be him they were calling because the other Elías who had recently left his country was full of optimism and dreams of triumph. It was a name made of stainless steel. They brought him back from his refuge as if he were dreaming and passing through customs by way of another dimension, where documents were not needed. He woke up completely, and in a fraction of a second his mind was clear: the airport in Miami, the long wait, and now getting up from his seat to come face to face with another officer. Something told him it was worth giving it another try with the new officer because he saw a very different person from the small-faced Pekinese woman. This was a stylish, very good-looking man who carried himself in the manner of those who are proud of their features, their bodies and their inner selves do.

"How long do you plan to stay?" the officer asked in perfect Spanish.

Elías felt the relief that comes with being abroad and all of a sudden hearing someone speak your language.

"Six months."

"How much money do you have?"

---

[13]Do you feel fine?
[14]Do you understand . . . sculptor

"A thousand dollars."

"That's not much for six months."

"I have family in New York, a place to stay and meals. I won't have other expenses, and besides. . . . "

"Show me the thousand dollars."

Elías had not anticipated an interrogation of his finances, but, fortunately, he had a response handy that he felt was satisfactory.

"I spent some of it in the airport in my country in the duty-free shops. I bought gifts for my family in New York."

"How much money do you have, then?"

"Not quite five hundred."

"Show me what you have."

He felt the final door coming down on him like a tombstone. He decided to end the lying and his trip.

"The truth is, I'm a sculptor. One of my sculptures was bought in New York, and I'm going to be paid for it when I get there. Right now I only have eighty dollars."

The officer blew a little air out of his mouth, as if he was about to whistle, and he shook his head from side to side.

"With eighty dollars you can't last a single night in New York."

"I have family in. . . . "

"Go sit down. We'll talk when it's your turn."

"I think I missed my flight."

"I can only give you a visa for one day."

"I don't want one day. I'd rather be sent back to my country."

"Go sit down."

An hour went by, the longest hour of his life. Elías found himself in the tunnel that connects life with death. It was a tunnel with a life of its own; it could be longer than you could possibly imagine or so short that you could pass through it in less than a second. Whoever found himself in that tunnel did not fear either end but rather the tunnel itself. Desperation led to escape through the closer of the two exits. If you were closer to the death end, you would beg, because the doctor of death might feel sorry for you and administer euthanasia. But if you were near the other end, you would ask God not to take you yet, to give you a little more time to settle your affairs.

Elías was in the worst part of the tunnel—the middle. From there he sat up and shouted, "Are you going to send me back to my country or am I going to see my family? I missed one flight and I'm going to miss another. What have I done to be kept here like this? I'm not a murderer, I'm not a thief; I'm just an artist. I can't believe this is happening. You send whomever you want to my country. We've let you install more than twenty military bases. Three airports were built for you and your wars. We protect you from the Commies . . . and me, a harmless artist, can't enter your country. Where is that famous democracy?"

*anger, losing patience*

The officer interrupted his speech. "All right, calm down, we're seeing what we can do for you. Your case is sensitive," he said as he patted Elías a couple of times on the shoulder with an expression meant to comfort him. Then he signaled for him to follow, and they went into a cubicle. The officer sat down in front of a computer and offered him the seat across from him.

"Our country always gives preferential treatment to artists, but, of course, the artists I'm talking about are those who have already distinguished themselves in other countries, those who have respected résumés, those who stand above the rest. Can you imagine if that preferential treatment were given to all artists indiscriminately? The country isn't big enough for all the artists in the world who want to live here."

"Yes, I know. And I also know that others whose work is very good and important have been denied entry."

"Of course, it has to be that way. If you spotted an enemy of yours trying to enter your house, would you let him in?"

"No."

"Well, it's the same with countries, only your case isn't political. It's a matter of law: You can't enter the country without a return ticket."

Hoping that the officer would forget about the matter of the ticket, Elías asked naively, "You're Cuban, right?"

The officer, who was inspecting the passport, looked at him from over his eyeglasses. "Cuban-American."

"It was a tragedy what happened in Cuba."

The officer feigned surprise. "What tragedy? Was there a hurricane or an earthquake?"

"No, the political situation. What happened with the Russians . . . "

"I am apolitical."

"But this is about your country."

"It's not my country. I've never been there; I don't know it at all. I was born here. It may be my parents' country, but it's not mine."

"But your Spanish is so good."

"Naturally, my parents are educated people. I speak Castilian Spanish like they do."

"Your parents must have suffered a great deal to get out."

"Suffered? Not my parents. My grandparents maybe, especially my grandmother. She married my grandfather when she was very young, and ever since elementary school when she found out that Cuba was an island, she was unable to live in peace. It got worse as she got older. The idea of living in a place surrounded by water tormented her. That was why my grandfather, as soon as the economic situation permitted, had to leave the island, and Miami was the closest place. My grandmother liked Miami, but she would have liked any place that wasn't an island."

"I thought it was because of politics. . . . "

"Your passport doesn't show that you have been in this country before."

"But I have, believe me, three times."

"Where?"

"In New Orleans."

"Doing what?"

"Showing my work."

"It doesn't show that here."

"But it does in my old passport."

"It's too bad you didn't bring it . . . maybe then you would have been able to enter."

"This is unbelievable."

"What is unbelievable?"

"That you send thousands of soldiers to our country and have military bases and airports there, and an artist can't come into yours."

"It's not a question of politics, it's the law. Besides, you asked us to send the Marines."

"Who? I didn't."

"Your government."

"I am apolitical."

The officer looked at him as if giving him one last chance. "Show me the eighty dollars."

"It's sixty, actually."

The officer shook his head from side to side. "That's nothing."

"It's hard to get dollars in my country, but I'm going to be paid two thousand dollars for a sculpture in New York. Really."

"By whom?"

"My fellow countrymen in New York."

"What kind of sculpture?"

"A bust. A bust of Francisco Morazán."

"Who's that?"

"He's a Central American hero from the last century who fought for the unity of Central America, as a single nation that would be great and powerful."

"That's political."

"No, it's my job."

"But it's political. Politics are always involved."

"Not with me. Today I might do Morazán, but tomorrow if they ask me to do a bust of Hitler, I'd do that, too, as long as they pay me, of course."

"There's nothing wrong with being apolitical and doing what you have to, to earn a living, but you shouldn't be so cynical. This country fought against Hitler. Did you bring any sample of your work?"

"In my suitcases . . . Photos . . . "

Elías pulled a small album out of his carry-on bag. "This is the Morazán."

"Looks like mostly busts."

"That's what they want in my country. Everyone wants to have a bust of his own."

"It's not like that in New York."

"I also have another kind of. . . ."

"Yes, it's too bad you didn't bring your old passport," the officer said, unconvinced.

Elías sensed that the door was opening by the magic of an unexpected key, which could well have been the officer's affinity for artists or the simple desire to let him in.

"Look me up in the computer. I have to be there."

The officer looked as if he was about to enter his name but then changed his mind and took off his glasses. "I'll let you in. But don't come again without a return ticket."

"I missed my flight."

"Go to the airline office and they can resolve that."     he wins

"Thank you."

"How long do you want me to give you?"

Elías hesitated. "Six months."

The door was wide open, and the stamp was about to come smashing down. For Elías the moment was never-ending. He remembered Helena's legs and his triumphant entrance. The officer returned his passport.

"Good luck in New York."

"Thank you, thank you very much."

# DRAMA

## Josefina López

Josefina López was born in 1969 in San Luis Potosí, Mexico. She and her family moved to Los Angeles in 1974. They lived illegally in East Los Angeles for almost thirteen years until her family obtained amnesty. She graduated from the Los Angeles County School for the Arts and majored in theater. She wrote her Emmy-winning play, *Simply María, or The American Dream*, at seventeen. López states that her frustration about the lack of Latino voices in theater inspired her to write her first play. "I hope to give Latinas an opportunity to play characters that have dignity and courage, qualities that are representative of who we are." Her play *Real Women Have Curves* was produced as a film in 2002. *Unconquered Spirits, Confessions of Women from East L.A., Food for the Dead,* and *La Pinta*, are some of her other works.

Primary works by Josefina López: *Real Women Have Curves: A Comedy* (Woodstock: Dramatic Pub., 1996); *Food for the Dead: La Pinta: Two One-Act Plays* (Woodstock: Dramatic Pub., 1996); *Confessions of Women from East L.A.* (Woodstock: Dramatic Pub., 1997); in *Shattering the Myth: Plays by Hispanic Women* Ed. Linda Feyder (Houston: Arte Público Press, 1992).

# Simply María or The American Dream

## CHARACTERS

### Principals:

MARÍA: daughter of Carmen and Ricardo.
CARMEN: mother of María.
RICARDO: father of María.

JOSÉ: María's husband.
PRIEST

### In order of appearance:

GIRL 1
GIRL 2
GIRL 3
MOTHER: Carmen's mother.
WOMAN
NARRATOR
IMMIGRANT 1
IMMIGRANT 2
IMMIGRANT 3
IMMIGRANT 4
STATUE OF LIBERTY
MEXICAN MAN
MEXICAN WOMAN
POSTMAN
PERSON 1
VENDOR 1
VENDOR 2
BAG LADY
PROTESTER
MAN 1
DIRTY OLD MAN
CHOLO 2[1]
VALLEY GIRL 1
VALLEY GIRL 2
CHOLO 1

PERSON 2
PERSON 3
PERSON 4
ANGLO BUYER
MYTH
MARY
MARÍA 2
REFEREE
ANNOUNCER
FLOOR MANAGER
HUSBAND
WIFE
SALESMAN
HEAD NURSE
NURSE 2
NURSE 3
NURSE 4
BAILIFF
JUDGE
PROSECUTOR
JUROR 1
JUROR 2

*Note: Many of the above characters can be played by the same actor/actress.*

## PLACE

The play begins in an unspecified town in Mexico and moves to downtown Los Angeles.

## TIME

Over a period of years chronicling the growth of María from birth to her womanhood.

### Scene One

*There is a long thin movie screen on the top and across the stage that will be used to display slides of titles for a couple of seconds each. Lights rise.*

---

[1]Homeboy

MARÍA, *a young woman with a suitcase, enters. She goes to the center and remains still.* THREE GIRLS *enter and stand behind her.*

GIRL 3:   (*Loud introduction.*) Romeo and Juliet elope. Or, where's the wedding dress? (*Lights slowly fade. Then dim lights slowly rise.* RICARDO, *a tall, dark and handsome young Mexican man enters. He tries to hide in the darkness of the night. He whistles carefully, blending the sound with the noises of the night.*)

CARMEN:   (*From her balcony.*) Ricardo, ¿eres tú?[2]

RICARDO:   Yes! Ready?

CARMEN:   Sí. (*She climbs down from her balcony, then runs to* RICARDO, *kissing and consuming him in her embrace.*) Where's the horse?

RICARDO:   What horse?

CARMEN:   The one we are going to elope on.

RICARDO:   You didn't say to bring one. All we agreed on was that I would be here at midnight.

CARMEN:   I would have thought that you would have thought to ...

RICARDO:   Shhhh!!! ¡Mira![3] (*Points to* CARMEN's *room.*)

CARMEN:   ¡Mi madre![4] Let's go! And on what are we going?

RICARDO:   On this. (*Brings an old bike.*)

CARMEN:   ¡Qué![5] On that? No! How could ... Everyone knows that when you elope, you elope on a horse, not on a ... Ricardo, you promised!

MOTHER:   (*Discovering* CARMEN *gone.*) ¡Carmencita! Carmen! She's gone!

CARMEN:   Oh, no! Hurry! Let's go!

RICARDO:   (*Hops on the bike.*) Carmen, hurry! Get on!

CARMEN:   We won't fit!

MOTHER:   ¡M'ija![6] Where are you?

CARMEN:   We better fit! (*Jumps on, and they take off. She falls and then quickly hops back on.*) Ricardo, marry me! (*Crickets are heard, lights dim. Fade out.*)

   *Scene Two*

THREE WOMEN *enter a church with candles. A fourth, much older, enters with a lighted candle and lights the other candles. The* THREE WOMEN *then transform into statues of the saints in the church.* PRIEST *comes downstage, waiting for a wedding to begin.* CARMEN *enters, pregnant.*

PRIEST:   Will he be here soon?

CARMEN:   Soon. He promised.

---

[2]Is that you?
[3]Look!
[4]My mother!
[5]What!
[6]Daughter!

PRIEST:  I was supposed to start half an hour ago.

WOMAN:  (*Enters with a note.*) Is there anyone here named Carmen?

CARMEN:  Yes . . . Is it from Ricardo? (*Reading the note.*) "I haven't been able to get a divorce. It will be some time soon, believe me . . . Just wait. I'm working hard so that I can save money to buy a little house or a ranch for the three of us. If you wait, good things will come." (*To* PRIEST.) There won't be a wedding today. (*Exits crying with* PRIEST. *The statues become* WOMEN *and they all ad lib malicious gossip about the pregnant bride.* CARMEN *enters again, holding baby.* PRIEST *enters.* WOMEN *become statues again.*)

PRIEST:  Will he be here? (RICARDO *enters.*)

CARMEN:  He is here.

PRIEST:  Good. Now we can start.

CARMEN:  (*To* RICARDO.) I thought you wouldn't show up.

PRIEST:  (*Begins his speech, which is more or less mumbled and not heard except for:*) Do you, Carmen, accept Ricardo as your lawfully wedded husband?

CARMEN:  I do.

PRIEST:  Do you, Ricardo, accept Carmen as your lawfully wedded wife?

RICARDO:  I do.

PRIEST:  Under the Catholic Church, in the holy House of God, I pronounce you husband and wife. (*Takes baby from* CARMEN, *and sprinkles holy water on baby.*) Under the Catholic Church, in the holy House of God, this child shall be known as María. (*The* PRIEST *puts the baby on the center of the stage.* CARMEN, RICARDO *and* PRIEST *exit. On the screen the following title is displayed:* THE MAKING OF A MEXICAN GIRL.)

NARRATOR:  The making of a Mexican girl. (*The statues now transform into* THREE ANGELIC GIRLS *who begin to hum, then sing beautifully with only the word "María." They come center stage and deliver the following, facing the audience:*)

ALL:  María.

GIRL 1:  As a girl you are to be

GIRL 2:  Nice,

GIRL 3:  forgiving,

GIRL 1:  considerate,

GIRL 2:  obedient,

GIRL 3:  gentle,

GIRL 1:  hard-working,

GIRL 2:  gracious.

GIRL 3:  You are to like:

GIRL 1:  Dolls,

GIRL 2:  kitchens,

GIRL 3:  houses,

GIRL 1:  cleaning,

GIRL 2:  caring for children,

GIRL 3:  cooking,

GIRL 1: laundry,

GIRL 2: dishes.

GIRL 3: You are not to:

GIRL 1: Be independent,

GIRL 2: enjoy sex,

GIRL 3: but must endure it as your duty to your husband,

GIRL 1: and bear his children.

GIRL 2: Do not shame your society!

GIRL 3: Never,

GIRL 1: never,

GIRL 2: never,

ALL: Never!!!!

GIRL 1: Your goal is to reproduce.

GIRL 2: And your only purpose in life is to serve three men:

GIRL 3: Your father,

GIRL 1: your husband,

GIRL 2: and your son.

GIRL 3: Your father. (RICARDO *enters*.)

RICARDO: Carmen, I must go.

CARMEN: Ricardo, don't go. Not after all the time I've waited.

RICARDO: I don't want to leave you, but we need the money. There's no work here. I must go to el norte,[7] so I can find work and send for you.

CARMEN: I don't want to be alone.

RICARDO: You have María. I'm going so that we can have the things we don't have.

CARMEN: I would prefer to have you and not the things I don't have.

RICARDO: I want something else besides a life on this farm.

CARMEN: María will not see you.

RICARDO: She will. When I am on the other side, I will send for you. She will be very proud of me.

CARMEN: You promise?

RICARDO: I promise.

CARMEN: Well, then I will wait; we will wait.

RICARDO: I will write. (*Kisses* CARMEN *on the forehead*.)

CARMEN: Ricardo, remember that I love you. (RICARDO *leaves*.) Don't forget to write. (*Fade out*.)


### Scene Three

NARRATOR: Yes, write a lot; they will miss you. All who are in search of opportunity go to the same place: America. And America belongs to those who are willing to risk. (*A giant sail enters the stage brought on by* FOUR EUROPEAN IMMIGRANTS.)

---

[7]The North (United States)

IMMIGRANT 1:  All for a dream.

IMMIGRANT 2:  Ciao, mia Italia!

IMMIGRANT 3:  Auf Wiedersehen, mein Deutschland!

IMMIGRANT 4:  Au revoir, mon France!

IMMIGRANT 2:  Hello, America! (*In the background "America the Beautiful" plays, the music growing louder. The* STATUE OF LIBERTY *enters.*)

IMMIGRANT 3:  The Lady!

IMMIGRANT 4:  Up high in the sky, incapable of being brought down.

IMMIGRANT 2:  And like her . . .

IMMIGRANT 3:  . . . we carry . . .

IMMIGRANTS 2 & 4:  . . . a similar torch.

ALL:  A torch of hope.

STATUE OF LIBERTY:  Give me your tired, your poor, your huddled masses yearning to breathe free . . . (*At the bottom of the* STATUE OF LIBERTY *are* THREE MEXICAN PEOPLE [RICARDO *is one of them*] *trying to go across the stage as if it is the border. They run around hiding, sneaking, and crawling, trying not to get spotted by the border patrol.*)

RICARDO:  ¡Vénganse! ¡Por aquí![8]

MEXICAN MAN:  ¿Y ahora qué hacemos?[9]

MEXICAN WOMAN:  What do we do now?

MEXICAN MAN:  ¡Vámonos! ¡Por allá![10]

MEXICAN WOMAN:  ¡Nos nortearon![11]

RICARDO:  Let's go back. (*They go to hide behind the* EUROPEAN IMMIGRANTS. *The* STATUE OF LIBERTY *composes herself and continues.*)

STATUE OF LIBERTY:  I give you life, liberty and the pursuit of happiness for the price of your heritage, your roots, your history, your relatives, your language . . . Conform, adapt, bury your past, give up what is yours and I'll give you the opportunity to have what is mine.

MEXICAN MAN:  Pues bueno,[12] if we have to.

MEXICAN WOMAN:  Sounds good.

IMMIGRANT 4:  Look, fireworks!

RICARDO:  ¡Nos hicimos![13] (*"America the Beautiful" becomes overwhelming; lights flash, representing the fireworks. A few seconds later the same lights that adorn the celebration for* EUROPEAN IMMIGRANTS *become the lights from the helicopters hunting after the* MEXICAN PEOPLE. *Hound dogs are also heard barking, and the* MEXICAN PEOPLE *scatter and try to hide.*)

---

[8]Come! This way!

[9]And now what should we do?

[10]Come! That way! [7]The North (United States)

[11]They lost us!

[12]Good then

[13]We did it!

RICARDO:  ¡La migra!¹⁴
MEXICAN MAN:  The immigration!
MEXICAN WOMAN:  ¡Córranle!¹⁵ (*The* EUROPEAN IMMIGRANTS *and the* STATUE OF LIBERTY *all keep pointing at the* MEXICAN PEOPLE *so that they can be caught. The* MEXICAN PEOPLE *run offstage, and with the sail tilted down, they charge after them. Fade out.*)

### Scene Four

POSTMAN:  (*Throwing in paper airplane.*) Air mail for Carmen García.
CARMEN:  (CARMEN *enters and reads letter.*) "Mi querida Carmen,¹⁶ how are you? How is María? I've sent you some more money. This is the last letter I write to you because I am now sending for you. I fixed my papers with the help of a friend, and I got an apartment where we can live. Tell María I love her, and to you I send all my love . . . " María! . . . "Leave as soon as possible . . . " Leave as soon as possible . . . María, ¡ven acá! ¹⁷
MARÍA:  (MARÍA *enters.*) Yes, Mami.
CARMEN:  María get ready; we're going.
MARÍA:  Going where?
CARMEN:  To join your father in the city of the angels.
MARÍA:  Angels? (MARÍA *puts on her coat for the journey. Fade out.*)

### Scene Five

*On the screen the following title is displayed:* LOS ANGELITOS DEL NORTE.¹⁸ *The following is the making of a city. Actors will take on many roles. It will be organized chaos. Noises of police and firetruck sirens, along with other common city noises are heard. The lights rise on* VENDORS *selling on the streets, and all sorts of unusual and not so unusual* PEOPLE *found in downtown L.A. on Broadway.* CARMEN *and* MARÍA *are engulfed in the scene, appalled to see what they have come to.*

PERSON 1:  Broadway! Downtown L.A.!
VENDOR 1:  Cassettes, ¡cartuchos, dos dólares ¹⁹
VENDOR 2:  Anillos de oro sólido.²⁰ Solid gold. Not plated.

---

¹⁴The border patrol!
¹⁵Run!
¹⁶My dear Carmen
¹⁷Come here!
¹⁸The little angels of the north
¹⁹Eight-tracks two dollars!
²⁰One hundred percent gold rings

CARMEN:  Perdone, señora,[21] could you tell me . . .

BAG LADY:  Get out of my way!

PROTESTOR:  Homosexuality is wrong! No sex! No sex! ¡Se va a acabar el mundo![22] The world is coming to an end! (*Separates* CARMEN *from* MARÍA.)

CARMEN:  María! María, where are you?! (*Searches frantically*.)

MARÍA:  Mami! Mami! (*Cries for* CARMEN.)

WOMAN 1:  Buy this! ¿Sombras para verte como estrella de cine?[23]

WOMAN 2:  Hair brushes, all kinds, a dollar!

WOMAN 3:  You want to buy handbags?

WOMAN 4:  ¡Vámonos![24] Here comes the police. (*All the* VENDORS *on the street run away*.)

MAN 1:  Jesus loves you! (*Hands* CARMEN *a pamphlet*.) He died for our sins!

CARMEN:  ¿Qué?[25]

WOMAN 1:  That RTD bus is late again!

DIRTY OLD MAN:  Hey! Little girl! You want to get married? The world is coming to an end and you don't want to die without having experienced it.

CARMEN:  María! María! ¿Dónde estás, hija mía?[26]

CHOLO 2:  East L.A.!

TWO VALLEY GIRLS:  We love it!

CHOLO 1:  Hey, bato![27]

TWO VALLEY GIRLS:  Party and let party!

CHOLO 2:  ¡Oye, mi carnal![28]

PERSON 2:  ¡Viva la huelga![29] Boycott grapes!

PERSON 3:  Chicano[30] Power!

TWO VALLEY GIRLS:  We love it.

PERSON 3:  Chicano Power!

TWO VALLEY GIRLS:  We love it.

PERSON 4:  A little culture for the gringuitos.[31] ¡Tostadas, frijoles![32]

ANGLO BUYER:  How much? ¿Cuánto? ¿Salsa? ¿Cerveza?[33]

---

[21]Excuse me, ma'am

[22]The world is going to end!

[23]Eyeshadows to make you look like a movie star?

[24]Let's go!

[25]What?

[26]Where are you my daughter?

[27]Dude

[28]Hey bro!

[29]Hooray for the strike!

[30]Mexican American

[31]Little Anglos

[32]Chips, beans!

[33]How much? Salsa? Beer?

CARMEN:  María! (MARÍA *runs scared and bumps into* CARMEN. *They hug each other.* RICARDO, *dressed in a charro*[34] *outfit enters and gives some yells as if ready to sing a corrido.*[35] *All the chaos of the city stops, and all the city people recoil in fear.* RICARDO *becomes the hero rescuing* CARMEN *and* MARÍA *from their nightmare.*)

TWO VALLEY GIRLS:  We love it!

CARMEN:  ¡Ayyy! What a crazy city! It's so awful! People here are crazy! (*Almost about to cry, she embraces* RICARDO.) But Ricardo, I'm so happy to be here.

MARÍA:  (*Trying to get attention.*) An ugly man chased me!

RICARDO:  But you are all right?

MARÍA:  Sí. Now that you are here.

RICARDO:  Carmen, we are finally together like I promised.

CARMEN:  Ricardo, where's our home?

RICARDO:  Follow me. (*They leave the stage. Fade out. Props for next scene are set up quickly.*)


   *Scene Six*


NARRATOR:  They are going to the housing projects; Pico Aliso, Ramona Gardens, Estrada Courts. No one likes it there, but it's cheap. Es Barato.[36] (*On the screen the following title is displayed:* LITTLE HOUSE IN THE GHETTO.) Little house in the ghetto.

RICARDO:  Here we are.

CARMEN:  ¿Aquí?[37]

RICARDO:  Yes, I hope it's all right. It's only for now.

MARÍA:  (*Smiling.*) I like it! Look, Mami! There are swings and grass.

RICARDO:  There are a lot of kids in the neighborhood you can play with.

MARÍA:  Really, Papi? Would they want to play with me?

RICARDO:  Sure. (*Noticing* CARMEN's *displeasure.*) What's wrong? You don't like it?

CARMEN:  Oh. No, I'm just tired from the trip.

RICARDO:  How was the trip?

MARÍA:  (*Cutting in.*) It was great!

CARMEN:  Great? You threw up on me the whole way here.

MARÍA:  Except, I don't understand why the bus never got off the ground. Where are the angels? And where are the clouds? And the gate? And the music ... Like in the stories Mami used to tell me. I thought we were going to heaven. I thought you had been called to heaven because you are an angel. Are you an angel?

---

[34]Cowboy
[35]Ballad
[36]It's cheap
[37]Here?

RICARDO:  Yes, I'm your angel always.

MARÍA:  So if this isn't heaven and you're an angel, what are we doing here?

RICARDO:  María, I brought you to America so that you can have a better life. It wasn't easy for me. I was hiding in a truck with a lot of other people for hours. It was so hot and humid that people preferred to get caught by the migra than die of suffocation. But I was going to make it because I knew that I had a daughter to live for. I did it for you. In America, the education is great! You can take advantage of all the opportunities offered to you. You can work hard to be just as good as anybody. You can be anything you want to be! (*Pause.*) Carmen, let me show you the kitchen. (CARMEN *and* RICARDO *exit.*)

MARÍA:  America, I don't even know you yet and I already love you! You're too generous. Thank you. I'll work hard. I can be anything I want to be! (*Starts changing clothes to end up wearing a casual shirt and pants when she finishes the following:*) America, I'm ready to play the game. I'm gonna show those boys in this neighborhood how to really play football! (*She makes some football moves. Then she runs out.* CARMEN *enters.*)

CARMEN:  María, ¡ven aquí![38] (MARÍA *enters.*)

MARÍA:  Yes, Mami.

CARMEN:  La señora Martínez[39] told me you were playing football with the boys.

MARÍA:  Yes, Mami; I was.

CARMEN:  I don't want you playing football with the boys. It's not proper for a lady.

MARÍA:  But I'm good at sports. I'm better than some of the boys.

CARMEN:  It doesn't look right. ¿Qué van a decir?[40] (*In the background appear the* THREE GIRLS *who are only seen and heard by* MARÍA. *They whisper to her.*)

GIRL 1:  Never shame your society.

GIRL 2:  Never,

GIRL 3:  never,

GIRL 1:  never,

ALL:  NEVER!!!

MARÍA:  But my Papi said . . .

CARMEN:  You are not going to play with boys! (CARMEN *exits.*)

MARÍA:  I don't understand. Papi tells me to compete, Mami tells me it doesn't look right. I like to compete, too. (MARÍA *exits to her room.*)

RICARDO:  (*To* MARÍA.) María, ¡ven aquí! Who were you walking home with today?

MARÍA:  A friend.

RICARDO:  A boyfriend?

---

[38]Come here!

[39]Mrs. Martínez

[40]What are they going to say?

MARÍA: No, just a friend I have in my last class. He lives close by.

RICARDO: I don't want you walking home with or talking to boys. Study!

MARÍA: (*Dares to ask.*) Papi, why?

RICARDO: You're thirteen and you are very naïve about boys. The only thing on their minds is of no good for a proper girl. They tell girls that they are "special," sweet things, knowing that girls are stupid enough to believe it. They make pendejas[41] out of them. They get them pregnant, and shame their parents . . . Go to your room! (*The* THREE GIRLS *appear again and whisper to* MARÍA.)

GIRL 1: Never shame your society!

GIRL 2: Never,

GIRL 3: (*Does not continue, but slowly walks away from the two girls.*)

GIRL 1: Never,

GIRL 1 AND 2: Never!! (*Spotlight on* MARÍA. MARÍA *goes to the mirror,* GIRL 3 *appears in the mirror.* MARÍA *brushes her hair and so does* GIRL 3. *Then* GIRL 3 *begins to touch herself in intimate ways, discovering the changes through puberty, while* MARÍA *remains still, not daring to touch herself. Finally, when* MARÍA *does dare to touch herself,* CARMEN *comes into the room and discovers her. Lights quickly come back on.*)

CARMEN: María, what are you doing?

MARÍA: Nothing.

CARMEN: María, were you . . . (*Before* MARÍA *can answer.*) It is a sin to do that. Good girls don't do that. (GIRL 3 *goes behind* MARÍA.)

GIRL 3: (*Whispering.*) Why? Why? Why?

MARÍA: Why?

CARMEN: (*Somewhat shocked.*) Because it is dirty! Sex is dirty.

GIRL 3: Why is it dirty? What makes it dirty?

MARÍA: (*Suppresses and ignores* GIRL 3.) I'm sorry, I didn't know what I was doing.

CARMEN: María, I'm telling you for your own good. Women should be pure. Men don't marry women who are not unless they have to. Quieren vírgenes.[42] It's best that way, if you save yourself for your wedding night. Be submissive.

GIRL 3: Why? Why? Why?

MARÍA: Yes, but . . . Why?

CARMEN: That's the way it is. I know it's not fair, but women will always be different from men. Ni modo.[43]

MARÍA AND GIRL 3: I don't understand. Why must a woman be submissive? Why is sex dirty? (GIRL 1 *appears.*)

---

[41]Dumb (female and plural)

[42]They want virgins

[43]Too bad

GIRL 1:  María, stop questioning and just accept.

GIRL 3:  No, María! God gave you a brain to think and question. Use it!

GIRL 1:  But it is not up to us to decide what is right and what is wrong. Your parents know best, María. They love you and do things for you.

GIRL 3:  María, they are not always right . . .

RICARDO:  (*Interrupting the argument.*) María! Come and help your mother with dinner right now!

MARÍA:  All right! (*She goes to the table and chairs.*)

RICARDO:  What do you do in your room? You spend so much time in there.

MARÍA:  I was doing my homework.

RICARDO:  It takes you all that time? (RICARDO *has the mail and pulls out a letter from the pile.*)

MARÍA:  Yes, I want my work to be perfect so that I can win an award . . .

RICARDO:  All for an award? How about if I give you a trophy for washing the dishes when you are supposed to, and for doing the laundry right? (*He begins to read the letter.* MARÍA *searches through the pile. She finds a letter, reads it and becomes excited.*)

CARMEN:  (*To* RICARDO.) Who's the letter from?

RICARDO:  My cousin, Pedro.

CARMEN:  What are you going to tell him?

RICARDO:  The truth. I'm going to tell him his Martita did a pendejadita[44] and is due in three months. (*To* MARÍA.) What do I tell you?

CARMEN:  Ayy, ¡qué vergüenza![45]

RICARDO:  ¡Tanto estudio y para nada![46] It's such a waste to educate women. How is all that education helping her now. She's pregnant and on welfare . . . What's that smell? The tortillas are burning!

MARÍA:  Ayyy!!!! (MARÍA *runs to the kitchen.*)

CARMEN:  When you get married, what is your husband going to say?

MARÍA:  I'm sorry; I completely forgot.

CARMEN:  You can't cook, you can't clean . . .

MARÍA:  I try to do all the chores you ask.

CARMEN:  You can't do anything right. Not even the tortillas.

MARÍA:  I really try . . .

RICARDO:  No Mexican man is going to marry a woman who can't cook.

CARMEN:  You're almost eighteen! (*Looks to* RICARDO.) I married your father when I was eighteen and I already knew how to do everything.

---

[44]Stupid little thing

[45]Ay, how embarrassing!

[46]So much studying for nothing!

MARÍA:  Mamá, papá, there are other more important things . . . (*She holds the letter, but decides not to say anything.*) I just don't care for housework. (MARÍA *goes to her room. Spotlight on* MARÍA. *She looks at the letter and* GIRL 3 *appears. They look at the letter and* GIRL 3 *reads.*)

GIRL 3:  "Congratulations! You are eligible for a four-year scholarship . . . Please respond as soon as possible . . ." (MARÍA *jumps up in excitement. She then gets a typewriter and begins to type her response. The typewriter is not working. She goes outside to look for her father. Fade out.*)

*Scene Seven*

*RICARDO and MARÍA enter.*

MARÍA:  Papá . . . ¿Está ocupado?[47]

RICARDO:  I'm reading the paper.

MARÍA:  Do you think . . . well . . . maybe when you have finished reading you can fix this for me? Here is the manual. (*She shows it to him. He pretends to look, but cannot understand it.*)

RICARDO:  Go get my tool box. I'll do it my way. (RICARDO *begins to check the typewriter carefully.* MARÍA *looks attentively and also tries to think of a way to introduce the subject of college.* GIRL 1 *appears.*)

GIRL 1:  There is no one who can take the place of my father, who loves me but cannot show it any other way. If I wasn't scared, I would hold you. I love you. (RICARDO *finishes fixing the typewriter and hands it to* MARÍA.)

CARMEN:  ¡Ayy! ¡Qué huebona![48] Where is María?

RICARDO:  She's in her room typing. I fixed her typewriter.

CARMEN:  What is she typing?

RICARDO:  I don't know. Ask her.

CARMEN:  (*She goes to* MARÍA's *room.*) María, come help me fold the clothes.

MARÍA:  I'm busy!

CARMEN:  Busy? Busy! Can't it wait? I have things to do, too.

MARÍA:  All right. (*They start folding the clothes.* RICARDO *enters.*)

CARMEN:  María, your birthday is almost here. Do you want me to make you a beautiful dress for your birthday? Maybe you can wear it for your graduation? Oh, our neighbor, la señora Martínez, told me today her daughter Rosario is graduating from a good business school. She says she already has a good job as a secretary.

MARÍA:  Mamá, Papá, I don't want to be a secretary. (*Pause.*) I want to go to college.

---

[47]Are you busy?
[48]She is so lazy!

RICARDO:  What?

CARMEN:  It's too expensive.

MARÍA:  (*Quickly.*) I was awarded a big, four-year scholarship!

RICARDO:  ¿Qué? College? Scholarship?

CARMEN:  ¿Para qué?

MARÍA:  I want to be educated . . . (*Courageously.*) I want to be an actress.

RICARDO:  You want to go to college to study to be an actress? ¿Estás loca?[49]

CARMEN:  Ayyy, María, you are crazy! You don't know what you want.

RICARDO:  I didn't know you had to study to be a whore.

CARMEN:  What have we done to make you want to leave us? We've tried to be good . . .

MARÍA:  Nothing. It's not you. I want to be something.

RICARDO:  Why don't you just get married like most decent women and be a housewife?

CARMEN:  That's something.

RICARDO:  That's respectable.

MARÍA:  I don't understand what you are so afraid of . . .

RICARDO:  I don't want you to forget that you are a Mexican. There are so many people where I work who deny they are Mexican. When their life gets better they stop being Mexican! To deny one's country is to deny one's past, one's parents. How ungrateful!

MARÍA:  Papi, I won't. But you said that with an education I could be just as good as anybody. And that's why you brought me to America.

RICARDO:  No. Get married!

MARÍA:  I will. But I want a career as well. Women can now do both.

RICARDO:  Don't tell me about modern women. What kind of wife would that woman make if she's busy with her career and can't tend to her house, children and husband.

MARÍA:  And that's all a woman is for? To have children? Clean a house? Tend to her husband like a slave? And heat his tortillas?

RICARDO:  ¡Qué atrevida![50] Why do you make it seem as if it would be some sort of nightmare? (*Sarcastically.*) Women have always gotten married and they have survived.

MARÍA:  But surviving is not living.

CARMEN:  María, listen to your father.

MARÍA:  Papi, I listened to you. That's why! You encouraged me when I was young, but now you tell me I can't. Why?

RICARDO:  (*Trying to find an answer.*) Because . . . you are a woman.

MARÍA:  Papi, you're not being fair.

---

[49]Are you crazy?

[50]She is so daring!

RICARDO:  (*Trying to keep face and control.*) You ungrateful daughter! I don't want to see you. Get out of my face! (MARÍA *runs to her room, crying.*)

CARMEN:  Ricardo, why don't you even let her try, ¿por favor?[51] (*She goes to* MARÍA's *room.* RICARDO *stands, and then exits. Lights change to* MARÍA's *room.*) María, don't cry. Don't be angry at us either, and try to understand us. ¡M'ija! We are doing this for you. We don't want you to get hurt. You want too much; that's not realistic. You are a Mexican woman, and that's that. You can't change that. You are different from other women. Try to accept that. Women need to get married, they are no good without men.

MARÍA:  Mami, I consider myself intelligent and ambitious, and what is that worth if I am a woman? Nothing?

CARMEN:  You are worth a lot to me. I can't wait for the day when I will see you in a beautiful white wedding dress walking down the aisle with a church full of people. This is the most important event in a woman's life.

MARÍA:  Mother, we are in America. Don't you realize you expect me to live in two worlds? How is it done? Can't things be different?

CARMEN:  No sé.[52] That's the way your father is. Ni modo.

MARÍA:  Ni modo? Ni modo! Is that all you can say? Can't you do anything? (*Gives up on her and just explodes.*) ¡¡Ayy!! Get out! Get out! (CARMEN *leaves and* MARÍA *continues to pound on her pillow with rage.* MARÍA *slowly begins to fall asleep. Fade out.*)

###### Scene Eight

*On the screen the following title is displayed:* THE DREAM. GIRL 2, *who will now portray* MYTH, *appears. She wears a spring dress and looks virginal. She goes to* MARÍA.

MYTH:  (*Shaking* MARÍA *lightly.*) María, get up and come see.

MARÍA:  Who are you?

MYTH:  I'm Myth. María, come see what can be.

MARÍA:  What do you mean? What's going on?

MYTH:  María, you are dreaming the American Dream. You can be anything you want to be. Follow me. (*The sound of a horse is heard.*)

MARÍA:  Is that a horse I'm hearing?

MYTH:  See . . . (*A* PRINCE *appears and he and* MYTH *begin to dance to a sweet melody. Just as they are about to kiss, the fierce sound of a whip accompanied by loud and wild cries of the horse running off are heard.*)

PRINCE:  (*In a very wimpy voice.*) My horse! My horse! (*Runs off to catch his horse.*)

---

[51]Please?
[52]I do not know

MARÍA:  What happened?

MYTH:  I don't know. (*Another crack of the whip is heard, but now* GIRL 3, *who will portray* "MARY," *appears with the whip.*)

MARY:  Sorry to spoil the fairy tale, but Prince Charming was expected at the castle by Cinderella . . . Hello, María.

MARÍA:  And who are you?

MARY:  My name is Mary. It's my turn now, so get lost Myth! (*She snaps her finger and a large hook pulls* MYTH *offstage.*)

MYTH:  You're such a meanie!

MARY:  Control, that's the thing to have. So come along and follow me!

MARÍA:  Where are you taking me?

MARY:  To liberation! Self independence, economic independence, sexual independence. We are free! María, in America, you can be anything you want to be. A lawyer. A doctor. An astronaut. An actress!! The Mayor. Maybe even the President . . . of a company. You don't have to be obedient, submissive, gracious. You don't have to like dolls, dishes, cooking, children and laundry. Enjoy life! Enjoy liberation! Enjoy sex! Be free! (GIRL 1, *who will portray* "MARÍA 2," *appears brandishing a broom.*)

MARÍA 2:  You bad woman! You bitch!

MARY:  I'm not!

MARÍA 2:  You American demon. You are. You are. You just want to tempt her, then hurt her.

MARÍA:  (*Throwing* MARY *her whip.*) Mary, catch!

MARY:  Thanks! Now we will see! (MARÍA 2 *and* MARY *have a mock sword combat, until a man blows a whistle and becomes a referee for a wrestling match.*)

REFEREE:  (*Taking away the broom and the whip.*) All right, c'mon girls. I don't want weapons. Give them. (*The women push him away and charge at each other.* MARY *tries some dirty tricks.*) I told you I wanted this to be a clean fight. What were you using?

MARY:  Nothing! I'm so innocent.

REFEREE:  Now come over here and shake hands.

MARÍA 2:  (*Asking the audience.*) Should I? Should I? (*Gets* MARY's *hand and twists it. They wrestle wildly, with* MARY *winning, then* MARÍA 2. *The* REFEREE *finally steps in.*)

REFEREE:  Break! Break! (*He holds* MARY *and pulls her out.*)

MARY:  (*Barely able to speak.*) María, before you are a wife, before you are a mother, first you are a woman! I'll be back. (*She's dragged out.* MARÍA 2, *who won the fight, acknowledges the cheers of the crowd, then gestures for* MARÍA *to kneel and pray.* MARÍA 2 *puts a wedding veil on* MARÍA.)

MARÍA 2:  A woman's only purpose in life is to serve three men. Her father, her husband and her son. Her father. (RICARDO *appears. He picks up* MARÍA *and escorts her to the church. The bells and the wedding march are heard. The following title is displayed:* WHITE WEDDING. MARÍA *walks down the aisle; the groom enters.*)

MARÍA 2:  Her husband. (*The couple kneels and a wedding lasso is put around them.*)

PRIEST: (*Same as first* PRIEST.) Dearly beloved, we are gathered here, under the Catholic Church, in the holy House of God, to unite these two people in holy matrimony. Marriage is sacred. It is the unification of a man and a woman, their love and commitment, forever, and ever, and ever; no matter what! Well, then, let's begin . . . María, do you accept José Juan González García López as your lawfully wedded husband to love, cherish, serve, cook for, clean for, sacrifice for, have his children, keep his house, love him even if he beats you, commits adultery, gets drunk, rapes you lawfully, denies you your identity, money, love his family, serve his family, and in return ask for nothing?

MARÍA: (*Thinks about it and turns to her parents.*) I do.

PRIEST: Very good. Now, José. Do you accept María García González López as your lawfully wedded wife to support?

JOSÉ: I do.

PRIEST: Good. Well, if there is anyone present who is opposed to the union of these two people, speak now, or forever hold your truth. (RICARDO *stands up, takes out a gun and shows it to the audience.*) Do you have the ring? (JOSÉ *takes out a golden dog collar. The* PRIEST *gives it his blessings.*) Five, six, seven, eight. By the power vested in me, under the Catholic Church, in the holy House of God, I pronounce you husband and wife. (*The* THREE GIRLS *take away* MARÍA's *veil and bouquet. They place the dog collar around* MARÍA's *neck. Then they get the lasso and tie it around her to make the collar work like a leash. To* JOSÉ.) You may pet the bride. (*The lasso is given to* JOSÉ. *He pulls* MARÍA, *who gets on her hands and knees. They walk down the aisle like dog and master. The wedding march plays, people begin to leave. Fade out.*)

### Scene Nine

*A table and two chairs are placed in the center of the stage.* MARÍA, *pregnant, walks in uncomfortably. She turns on the television, then the ensemble creates the television setting, playing roles of T.V. producer, director, make-up people, technicians, as if the actual studio is there. Brief dialogue is improvised to establish on-set frenzy.*

ANNOUNCER: And here is another chapter of your afternoon soap opera, "HAPPILY EVER-AFTER." Our sultry Eliza Vásquez decides to leave Devero in search of freedom!

FLOOR MAN: Okay everyone, tape rolling, standby in ten seconds. Five, four, three, two . . . (*He cues.*)

ACTRESS: Devero, I'm leaving you.

ACTOR: Eliza, why?

ACTRESS:  I don't love you anymore. Actually, I never did.

ACTOR:  Eliza, but I love you.

ACTRESS:  I faked it, all of it. I did it because I had to. But now I must go and be free! (MARÍA *claps loudly in excitement for her.*)

FLOOR MANAGER:  Cut! (*To* MARÍA.) What are you doing here?

MARÍA:  This is my living room.

FLOOR MANAGER:  Oh, sure it is. Well go into the kitchen, make yourself a snack; we'll have the carpet cleaned in an hour. (*Pushes her aside.*) I know, I'm sorry . . . Standby. Five, four, three, two, one.

ACTRESS:  . . . But now I must go and be free!

ACTOR:  You can't do this to me!

ACTRESS:  Oh, yes I can!

ACTOR:  But I've given you everything!

ACTRESS:  Everything but an identity! Well, Devero, Devero, Devero, I've discovered I no longer need you. There are unfulfilled dreams I must pursue. I want adventure.

FLOOR MANAGER:  And . . . cut! That's a take. Roll commercial. Five seconds. Four, three, two, one. (*The soap opera ends.* MARÍA *claps approvingly. A commercial quickly begins, with the ensemble creating a similar on-set frenzy. In the commercial a man comes home with a bottle of Ajax as a gift for his wife.*)

HUSBAND:  Honey, I'm home! I brought you something. (*Hides the can treating it as if he had flowers.*)

WIFE:  Hi, darling! (*They give each other a peck on the mouth from a distance.*) How was work?

HUSBAND:  Fine . . . Ta-Dah! (*Presents the can.*)

WIFE:  You shouldn't have. Oh, thank you! I need all the cleaning power I can get!

HUSBAND:  I can smell you've been cleaning.

WIFE:  Yes! I've mopped the floors, done the dishes, the laundry; this house is spotless.

HUSBAND:  What a wife! (*They give each other another peck on the mouth from a distance.*) You're a good wife! (MARÍA *goes to turn off the television. The doorbell rings. She goes to answer the door. It's her husband who grunts at her and comes in, asks for his dinner and sits at the table.*)

JOSÉ:  María! María! I'm home. I'm hungry.

MARÍA:  José, how was work? Dinner is ready. I made your favorite dish. Do you want to eat now? (JOSÉ *doesn't answer.*) Well, I'll serve you then. (MARÍA *places a plate on the table.*) My mother came to visit today and she asked me what we are going to name the baby. She thought it would be nice to call her Esperanza. (JOSÉ *grunts.*) Of course it isn't going to be a girl. It's going to be a boy, and we'll name him after you. That would be nice, wouldn't it? (MARÍA *feels pains.*) Ayyy! How it hurts. I hope after the baby is born, I will be better. I've been getting so many pains, and I have a lot of stretchmarks ... I know you don't like me to ask for money, but I need the money to buy a dress that fits. I have nothing I can wear anymore.

JOSÉ: (*After a spoonful.*) My dinner is cold.

MARÍA:  Oh, is it cold? Well, I'll heat it up right now. It will only take a minute. (MARÍA *runs to the kitchen.* JOSÉ *leaves the table and stares at the bed. The following title is displayed:* THE SEX OBJECT.

JOSÉ:  María! ¡Mi amor![53] Come here, baby! ... Come on, m'ijita. I won't hurt you ... (*He continues to try to persuade her. Eventually he gets his way. There are sounds of lust and pain. Finally,* MARÍA *gives out a loud scream of pain.*)

JOSÉ:  What is it?

MARÍA:  The baby! (*Fade out.*)

### Scene Ten

*The lights rise after the scream.* MARÍA *spreads her legs wide open, covering herself with a white sheet.* THREE NURSES *run in. On the screen the following title is displayed:* THE REPRODUCING MACHINE OR BE FRUITFUL. *Dolls will be used as babies.*)

SALESMAN:  Here we have it. Direct from Mexico. The Reproducing Machine. You can have one by calling our toll-free number. Get your pencil.

HEAD NURSE:  Now, relax. Just breathe like this. (*Example.*) Ahhh!! All in good rhythm. Good! Don't worry, millions of women have children, especially Mexican women, they have millions. But you'll get used to it. After your fourth child, they'll just slide right on out.

MARÍA:  'Amá! Mamá!

HEAD NURSE:  There's nothing I can do. I went through it myself. Now, isn't the pain great? You're giving birth! Why, it's the most satisfying feeling a woman can feel. Okay, I think it's coming! Push, Push, Push. (*A baby pops up, flying into the air. It is caught by one of the nurses. She presents the baby to the* HEAD NURSE.)

HEAD NURSE:  Oh, it's a girl.

NURSE 2:  (*Presenting the baby to* JOSÉ.) Here's your baby daughter.

JOSÉ:  A daughter? How could you do this to me? Well, I'll have to call her Sacrifice. (MARÍA *screams again.*)

HEAD NURSE:  What is it?

MARÍA:  There's another one inside; I can feel it!

---

[53]My love!

HEAD NURSE:  Nahhh! Well, I'll check just in case. (*She peeps under the sheet.*) Well, I'll be! Yeah, there's another one. Push! Push! Push! (*Another baby pops into the air.* NURSE 3 *catches the baby.*)

NURSE 2:  (*Presenting it to* JOSÉ.) Here's another lovely daughter.

JOSÉ:  Another daughter? I'll have to call her Abnegation.

SALESMAN:  (*Appearing from nowhere.*) Here we have this amazing machine. The world renowned Reproducing Machine! (MARÍA *screams again.*)

HEAD NURSE:  What is it?

MARÍA:  There's another one!

SALESMAN:  Ahh, but if you were watching earlier, you saw the other amazing function. It can also be used as a sex object.

HEAD NURSE:  Push! Push! Push! (*Another baby pops up.*)

NURSE 4:  (*Catching baby.*) I got it.

SALESMAN:  Yes siree! You can be the boss. It's at your disposal. Hours of pleasure. And if it ever does go out of control, a kick and a few punches will·do the job and it will be back to normal.

NURSE 2:  Here's another one.

JOSÉ:  Another girl? Why are you doing this to me? I'll call her Obligation.

SALESMAN:  It's made in Mexico. It's cheap! It cooks! It cleans! (MARÍA *screams again.*)

HEAD NURSE:  Push! Push! Push! (THREE BABIES *pop up into the air. Some land in the audience. All the nurses are busy collecting them.*)

SALESMAN:  Its stretchmarks can stretch all the way from here to Tijuana. Not even a Japanese model can beat this one.

NURSE 2:  (*To* JOSÉ.) Guess what?

JOSÉ:  No, don't tell me; another girl?

NURSE 2:  Surprise!

JOSÉ:  (*Sees babies.*) Three girls! I'll call them Frustration, Regret and Disappointment.

SALESMAN:  It delivers up to twenty-one children. It feeds on beans, chile and lies.

HEAD NURSE:  Are there any more babies in that Mexican oven of yours?

MARÍA:  I don't think so.

HEAD NURSE:  See you in nine months for your next Mexican litter.

SALESMAN:  You can have your own reproducing machine! Call the number on your screen now! (*Fade out.*)


   *Scene Eleven*

   *Lights rise after a brief pause. On the stage is a table which serves as a crib for the six crying babies. On the screen the following title is displayed:* THE NIGHTMARE. MARÍA *tries to quiet the babies by holding each one at a time, then by the bunch.* CARMEN, RICARDO *and* JOSÉ *enter. They stand behind her like demons.*

JOSÉ:  Shut those babies up!

CARMEN:  You're a bad wife!

RICARDO:  This house is a mess!

CARMEN:  You can't cook, you can't clean!

JOSÉ:  Where's my dinner?

RICARDO:  The dishes?

JOSÉ:  My tortillas?

RICARDO:  You're a bad wife!

CARMEN:  I did it all my life!

JOSÉ:  Bad wife!

MARÍA:  No! I'm not! I'm a good wife! I try. I really do! (*MARÍA goes to get the laundry and begins to fold it quickly, but nicely and carefully. Suddenly, the clothes begin to take on a life of their own. There is a giant coat, and a pair of pants surrounding MARÍA. They start pushing her around, then her wedding dress appears and heads towards MARÍA's neck. They wrestle on the ground.*)

CARMEN:  Martyr! (*MARÍA manages to get away, and runs upstage. As she is running, a giant tortilla with the Aztec Calendar emblem falls on her, smashing her to the ground.*)

MARÍA:  Help!

RICARDO:  Martyr! (*MARÍA manages to get out from under the tortilla; as she escapes, she is attacked by a storm of plates.*)

MARÍA:  Help!

RICARDO, CARMEN AND JOSÉ:  Martyr!!! Martyr!!! Martyr!!!

MARÍA:  (*Becomes uncontrollably mad.*) Enough! Do you want your dishes cleaned? I've got the perfect solution for them. (*MARÍA gestures. Sounds of dishes being smashed are heard.*) Now you don't have to worry. I'll buy you a million paper plates! Ohhhh! And the tortillas. Mamá! I'm going to show you how they should be done. (*She gets a bag of tortillas and begins tossing them into the audience like frisbees.*) Are these good enough? I hope so! I tried to get the top side cooked first . . . or was it last? Anyway, who cares! Here are the tortillas! (*Attacks her mother with a couple of tortillas.*) I hate doing the dishes! I hate doing the laundry! I hate cooking and cleaning! And I hate all housework because it offends me as a woman! (*There is a piercing moment of silence.*) That's right. I am a woman  . . .  a real woman of flesh and blood. This is not the life I want to live; I want more! And from now on I am directing my own life! Action! (*Lights come fully on. TWO GIRLS grab and pull MARÍA harshly to take her to another place. The stage now becomes a courtroom. MARÍA is sat next to the JUDGE. The following title is displayed:* THE TRIAL. *The courtroom is filled with people who create a lot of commotion. The* JUDGE, *the* BAILIFF *and the* PROSECUTOR *enter.*)

BAILIFF:  Please rise, the honorable hang-judge presiding.

JUDGE:  (*Bangs his gavel until everyone quiets down.* JUDGE *will be done by same actor who does* PRIEST.) Quiet in my courtroom! I am warning you, anyone who causes any such commotion like this again will be thrown out! Is that understood! Let's begin!

BAILIFF:  We are here today to give trial to María who is being accused by her husband of rebellion toward her implied duties of marriage.

JUDGE:  How do you plead?

MARÍA:  Plead? Innocent! Guilty! I don't know!

JUDGE:  Are you making a joke out of my question?

MARÍA:  No . . . Sir.

JUDGE:  It sounds to me like you wish to challenge these laws.

MARÍA:  I don't understand why I am on trial. What real laws have I broken?

JUROR 1:  She knows what she's guilty of.

JUROR 2:  She knows what laws not to break!

MARÍA:  Who are they?

BAILIFF:  Your jury.

MARÍA:  But they are women, Mexican, traditional . . . They can't possibly be objective.

BAILIFF:  They are a good jury.

MARÍA:  This is unjust! I must speak up to this . . .

BAILIFF:  You have no voice.

MARÍA:  Where's my lawyer? I do get one, don't I? (*The courtroom fills with cruel laughter, which quickly stops.*)

JUDGE:  No, you defend yourself.

MARÍA:  How do I defend myself when I can't speak?

PROSECUTOR:  (*To* MARÍA.) You're dead meat, shrimp. (*To audience.*) This trial is meant to help preserve the institution of marriage. Ladies and gentlemen of the jury . . . in this case, ladies of the jury. A man's home is his castle. Where he has his foundation. It is the place where he comes home to his family, and he becomes the king of his castle. But this poor man comes home one evening and finds his children unattended, his house a mess, his dinner unprepared and his wife sitting back, watching soap operas!

MARÍA:  I object!

JUDGE:  You have no voice.

MARÍA:  You said I was to defend myself.

JUDGE:  Not now!

PROSECUTOR:  What we are going to try to do is prove the guilt of this woman . . .

MARÍA:  I object!

JUDGE:  Shut up!

MARÍA:  I won't!

JUDGE:  Mister Prosecutor, call your first witness!

PROSECUTOR:  I call Ricardo Garcia to the witness stand. (RICARDO *takes the stand.*) Tell us about your daughter.

RICARDO:  She was very obedient when she was young, but when she came to the United States she began to think of herself as "American" . . . She studied a lot, which is good, but she almost refused to do her chores because she thought herself above them.

PROSECUTOR:  Could you tell us what happened that evening your daughter rebelled?

RICARDO:  I'd rather not . . . That evening Maria was hysterical. She threw dishes, tortillas . . .

PROSECUTOR:  Thank you, that will be all. My next witness will be Carmen Garcia. (CARMEN *takes the stand.*) Tell us about your daughter.

CARMEN:  She's really a good girl. She's just too dramatic sometimes. She's such a dreamer, forgive her.

PROSECUTOR:  Could you tell us what you saw that evening?

CARMEN:  Well, she was a little upset, so she did a few things she didn't mean to do.

MARÍA:  No, Mama! I meant it!

JUROR 1:  She admits it!

JUROR 2:  She's guilty!

ALL:  Guilty!

CARMEN:  No, she's just unrealistic.

MARÍA:  I'm guilty then! *(The whole courtroom becomes chaotic. Everyone yells out "guilty." CARMEN becomes so sad she begins to cry.)*

MARÍA:  Mami, don't cry! *(The lights go on and off and everyone disappears. Fade out.)*


  *Scene Twelve*


MARÍA *begins to regain consciousness and wakes up from her dream. She is awakened by* CARMEN's *actual crying, which continues and grows.* MARÍA *gets up and listens to* CARMEN *and* RICARDO *arguing in the kitchen.*

RICARDO:  ¡Cállate![59] Don't yell or María will hear you.

CARMEN:  Then tell me, is it true what I am saying?

RICARDO:  You're crazy! It wasn't me.

CARMEN:  Con mis propios ojos[60] I saw you and la señora Martínez meet in the morning by the park. You have been taking her to work and who knows what! Tell me, is it

---

[59]Shut up!
[60]With my own eyes

true? If you don't, I'm going to yell as loud as I can and let this whole neighborhood know what's going on.

RICARDO:  Okay. It was me! ¿Estás contenta?[61]

CARMEN:  ¿Por qué?[62] Why do you do this to me? And with our neighbor? She lives right in front of us.

RICARDO:  Look, every man sooner or later does it.

CARMEN:  Do you think I don't know about all of your affairs before la señora Martínez? She is not your first! I never said anything before because I was afraid you would send us back to Mexico. But now I don't care! You break it with that bitch or . . . I'll kill her and you. ¡Ayyy! Ricardo, I've endured so much for you. I knew you were no angel when we ran off together, but I thought you would change. You would change, because you loved me. I love you, Ricardo! But I can no longer go on living like this or I'll be betraying myself and I'll be betraying María.

RICARDO:  Carmen, ¡ven aquí! Carmen, wait! (CARMEN *and* RICARDO *exit. The* THREE GIRLS *enter.* GIRL 3 *hands* MARÍA *a piece of paper and a pen.*)

MARÍA:  "Dear Mamá and Papá. Last night I heard everything. Now I know that your idea of life is not for me—so I am leaving. I want to create a world of my own. One that combines the best of me. I won't forget the values of my roots, but I want to get the best from this land of opportunities. I am going to college and I will struggle to do something with my life. You taught me everything I needed to know. Goodbye."

GIRL 1:  Los quiero mucho. Nunca los olvidaré.[63]

GIRL 2:  Mexico is in my blood . . .

GIRL 3:  And America is in my heart.

MARÍA:  "Adiós." (*Fade out.*)

---

[61]Are you happy?

[62]Why?

[63]I love you so much. I will never forget you

# ESSAY

# Gloria Anzaldúa

Gloria Anzaldúa was born on the ranch settlement Jesus Maria of the Valley of South Texas in 1942. When she was eleven her family moved to Hargill, Texas. She and her family experienced the hardships of migrant farm workers; nevertheless, with unusual

---

Primary works by Gloria Anzaldúa: *Borderlands/La Frontera: The New Mestiza* (San Francisco: Aunt Lute Press, 1987); *Haciendo Caras/Making Face, Making Soul: Creative and Critical Perspectives by Women of Color* (San Francisco: Aunt Lute Books, 1990); and, with Cherríe Moraga, *This Bridge Called My Back: Radical Writings by Women of Color* (Berkeley: Third Woman Press, 2002).

determination, she managed to become "not just only a woman, but the only person from the area who ever went to college." She attended Pan American University in Texas and received an MA from the University of Texas at Austin. *Borderlands/La frontera: The New Mestiza* (1987), a bilingual book combining several genres, is a sort of literary *mestizaje* (racial mixing); the structure presents Anzaldúa's ideas of combining historiography with poetry in a broad thematic range, from philosophy to poetry. Perhaps her most important goal is one she has worked toward from an early age: to overturn Chicano patriarchal family traditions. Feminism, lesbianism, an intense ethnic identity, and a highly personal emphasis (including the use of her own family writing) characterize her work.

*Where does she present her (claim/ thesis?*
*+ How does she write for a dual audience*

# How to Tame a Wild Tongue

"We're going to have to control your tongue," the dentist says, pulling out all the metal from my mouth. Silver bits plop and tinkle into the basin. My mouth is a motherlode.

The dentist is cleaning out my roots. I get a whiff of the stench when I gasp. "I can't cap that tooth yet, you're still draining," he says.

"We're going to have to do something about your tongue," I hear the anger rising in his voice. My tongue keeps pushing out the wads of cotton, pushing back the drills, the long thin needles. "I've never seen anything as strong or as stubborn," he says. And I think, how do you tame a wild tongue, train it to be quiet, how do you bridle and saddle it? How do you make it lie down?

> Who is to say that robbing a people of
> its language is less violent than war?
> —Ray Gwyn Smith   — *painter/artist*

I remember being caught speaking Spanish at recess—that was good for three licks on the knuckles with a sharp ruler. I remember being sent to the corner of the classroom for "talking back" to the Anglo teacher when all I was trying to do was tell her how to pronounce my name. "If you want to be American, speak 'American.' If you don't like it, go back to Mexico where you belong."

"I want you to speak English. *Pa' hallar buen trabajo tienes que saber hablar el inglés bien. Qué vale toda tu educación si todavía hablas inglés con un[1] 'accent,'*" my mother would say, mortified that I spoke English like a Mexican. At Pan American University, I, and all Chicano students were required to take two speech classes. Their purpose: to get rid of our accents.

---

[1] In order to find a good job, you have to know how to speak English well. Your education is a waste if you still speak English with an accent.

Attacks on one's form of expression with the intent to censor are a violation of the First Amendment. *El Anglo con cara de inocente nos arrancó la lengua.*[2] Wild tongues can't be tamed, they can only be cut out.

## OVERCOMING THE TRADITION OF SILENCE

> Ahogadas, escupimos el oscuro.
> Peleando con nuestra propia sombra
> el silencio nos sepulta.[3]

*En boca cerrada no entran moscas.* "Flies don't enter a closed mouth" is a saying I kept hearing when I was a child. *Ser habladora*[4] was to be a gossip and a liar, to talk too much. *Muchachitas bien criadas,*[5] well-bred girls don't answer back. *Es una falta de respeto*[6] to talk back to one's mother or father. I remember one of the sins I'd recite to the priest in the confession box the few times I went to confession: talking back to my mother, *hablar pa' 'trás, repelar.* Hocicona, repelona, chismosa,[7] having a big mouth, questioning, carrying tales are all signs of being *mal criada.*[8] In my culture they are all words that are derogatory if applied to women—I've never heard them applied to men.

The first time I heard two women, a Puerto Rican and a Cuban, say the word "*nosotras,*"[9] I was shocked. I had not known the word existed. Chicanas use *nosotros* whether we're male or female. We are robbed of our female being by the masculine plural. Language is a male discourse.

> And our tongues have become
> dry the wilderness has
> dried out our tongues and
> we have forgotten speech.
> —Irena Klepfisz — Lesbian Jew

Even our own people, other Spanish speakers *nos quieren poner candados en la boca.*[10] They would hold us back with their bag of *reglas de academia.*[11]

---

[2]The Anglo with an innocent face took away our language.

[3]Drowned, we spit the dark. / Fighting with our own shadow / the silence buries us.

[4]To be outspoken, or to speak too much

[5]Ladies raised correctly

[6]It's a lack of respect

[7]To talk back, answer back, big mouth, back talker, gossiper

[8]Ill-bred woman

[10]They want to put locks on our mouths.

[11]Academia's rules

## OYE COMO LADRA: EL LENGUAJE DE LA FRONTERA[12]

*Quien tiene boca se equivoca.*[13]
—Mexican saying

"*Pocho,*[14] cultural traitor, you're speaking the oppressor's language by speaking English, you're ruining the Spanish language," I have been accused by various Latinos and Latinas. Chicano Spanish is considered by the purist and by most Latinos deficient, a mutilation of Spanish.

But Chicano Spanish is a border tongue which developed naturally. Change, *evolución, enriquecimiento de palabras nuevas por invención o adopción*[15] have created variants of Chicano Spanish, *un nuevo lenguaje. Un lenguaje que corresponde a un modo de vivir.*[16] Chicano Spanish is not incorrect, it is a living language.

For a people who are neither Spanish nor live in a country in which Spanish is the first language; for a people who live in a country in which English is the reigning tongue but who are not Anglo; for a people who cannot entirely identify with either standard (formal, Castilian) Spanish nor standard English, what recourse is left to them but to create their own language? A language which they can connect their identity to, one capable of communicating the realities and values true to themselves—a language with terms that are neither *español ni inglés,*[17] but both. We speak a patois, a forked tongue, a variation of two languages.

Chicano Spanish sprang out of the Chicano's need to identify ourselves as a distinct people. We needed a language with which we could communicate with ourselves, a secret language. For some of us, language is a homeland closer than the Southwest—for many Chicanos today live in the Midwest and the East. And because we are a complex, heterogeneous people, we speak many languages. Some of the languages we speak are:

1. Standard English
2. Working class and slang English
3. Standard Spanish
4. Standard Mexican Spanish
5. North Mexican Spanish dialect

---

[12]Listen how border language barks
[13]Whoever has a mouth makes mistakes.
[14]Latino/a who does not speak Spanish correctly
[15]Evolution, enrichment of new words that are invented or adopted.
[16]A new language; a language that corresponds to a way of life
[17]Neither Spanish nor English

6. Chicano Spanish (Texas, New Mexico, Arizona and California have regional variations)
7. Tex-Mex
8. *Pachuco*[18] (called *caló*[19])

My "home" tongues are the languages I speak with my sister and brothers, with my friends. They are the last five listed, with 6 and 7 being closest to my heart. From school, the media and job situations, I've picked up standard and working class English. From Mamagrande Locha and from reading Spanish and Mexican literature, I've picked up Standard Spanish and Standard Mexican Spanish. From *los recién llegados*,[20] Mexican immigrants, and *braceros*,[21] I learned the North Mexican dialect. With Mexicans I'll try to speak either Standard Mexican Spanish or the North Mexican dialect. From my parents and Chicanos living in the valley, I picked up Chicano Texas Spanish, and I speak it with my mom, younger brother (who married a Mexican and who rarely mixes Spanish with English), aunts and older relatives.

With Chicanas from *Nuevo México* or *Arizona* I will speak Chicano Spanish a little, but often they don't understand what I'm saying. With most California Chicanas I speak entirely in English (unless I forget). When I first moved to San Francisco, I'd rattle off something in Spanish, unintentionally embarrassing them. Often it is only with another Chicana *tejana*[22] that I can talk freely.

Words distorted by English are known as anglicisms or *pochismos*.[23] The *pocho* is an anglicized Mexican or American of Mexican origin who speaks Spanish with an accent characteristic of North Americans and who distorts and reconstructs the language according to the influence of English. Tex-Mex, or Spanglish, comes most naturally to me. I may switch back and forth from English to Spanish in the same sentence or in the same word. With my sister and my brother Nune and with Chicano *tejano* contemporaries I speak in Tex-Mex.

From kids and people my own age I picked up *Pachuco, Pachuco* (the language of the zoot suiters) is a language of rebellion, both against Standard Spanish and Standard English. It is a secret language. Adults of the culture and outsiders cannot understand it. It is made up of slang words from both English and Spanish. *Ruca* means girl or woman, *vato* means guy or dude, *chale* means no, *simón* means yes, *churo* is sure, talk

---

[18]Mexican American who dressed in a zoot suit
[19]Spanish dialect used by pachucos
[20]Recently arrived
[21]Migrant workers
[22]Woman from Texas
[23]Words created by pochos

is *periquiar, pigionear* means petting, *que gacho* means how nerdy, *ponte águila* means watch out, death is called *la pelona*. Through lack of practice and not having others who can speak it, I've lost most of the *Pachuco* tongue.


## CHICANO SPANISH

Chicanos, after 250 years of Spanish/Anglo colonization, have developed significant differences in the Spanish we speak. We collapse two adjacent vowels into a single syllable and sometimes shift the stress in certain words such as *maíz/maiz, cohete/cuete.*[24] We leave out certain consonants when they appear between vowels: *lado/lao, mojado/mojao.*[25] Chicanos from South Texas pronounced *f* as *j* as in *jue (fue)*.[26] Chicanos use "archaisms," words that are no longer in the Spanish language, words that have been evolved out. We say *semos, truje, haiga, ansina*,[27] and *naiden*.[28] We retain the "archaic" *j*, as in *jalar*,[29] that derives from an earlier *h* (the French *halar* or the Germanic *halon* which was lost to standard Spanish in the 16th century), but which is still found in several regional dialects such as the one spoken in South Texas. (Due to geography, Chicanos from the Valley of South Texas were cut off linguistically from other Spanish speakers. We tend to use words that the Spaniards brought over from Medieval Spain. The majority of the Spanish colonizers in Mexico and the Southwest came from Extremadura—Hernán Cortés was one of them—and Andalucía. Andalucians pronounce *ll* like a *y*, and their *d*'s tend to be absorbed by adjacent vowels: *tirado* becomes *tirao*. They brought *el lenguaje popular, dialectos y regionalismos*.[30]

Chicanos and other Spanish speakers also shift *ll* to *y* and *z* to *s*. We leave out initial syllables, saying *tar* for *estar*,[31] *toy* for *estoy*,[32] *hora*[33] for *ahora*[34] (*cubanos*)[35] and *puertorriqueños*[36] also leave out initial letters of some words). We also leave out the final syllable such as *pa* for *para*.[37] The intervocalic *y*, the *ll* as in *tortilla, ella*,[38]

---

[25]Side, illegal alien
[26]Was
[27]We are, I brought, there is, like this
[28]Nobody
[29]Work
[30]Popular language, dialects, and regionalisms
[31]To be
[32]I am here
[33]Time
[34]Now
[35]Cubans
[36]Puerto Ricans
[37]To, through
[38]She

*botella*,[39] gets replaced by *tortía* or *tortiya, ea, botea*. We add an additional syllable at the beginning of certain words: *atocar* for *tocar*,[40] *agastar* for *gastar*.[41] Sometimes we'll say *lavaste las vacijas*,[42] other times *lavates* (substituting the *ates* verb endings for the *aste*).

We use anglicisms, words borrowed from English: *bola*[43] from ball, *carpeta*[44] from carpet, *máchina de lavar* (instead of *lavadora*)[47] from washing machine. Tex-Mex argot, created by adding a Spanish sound at the beginning or end of an English word such as *cookiar* for cook, *watchar* for watch, *parkiar* for park, and *rapiar* for rape, is the result of the pressures on Spanish speakers to adapt to English.

We don't use the word *vosotros/as*[46] or its accompanying verb form. We don't say *claro*[47] (to mean yes), *imagínate*,[48] or *me emociona*,[49] unless we picked up Spanish from Latinas, out of a book, or in a classroom. Other Spanish-speaking groups are going through the same, or similar, development in their Spanish.

## Linguistic Terrorism

> *Deslenguadas. Somos los del español deficiente.*[50] We are your linguistic nightmare, your linguistic aberration, your linguistic *mestizaje*,[51] the subject of your *burla*.[52] Because we speak with tongues of fire we are culturally crucified. Racially, culturally and linguistically *somos huérfanos*[53] —we speak an orphan tongue.

Chicanas who grew up speaking Chicano Spanish have internalized the belief that we speak poor Spanish. It is illegitimate, a bastard language. And because we internalize how our language has been used against us by the dominant culture, we use our language differences against each other.

Chicana feminists often skirt around each other with suspicion and hesitation. For the longest time I couldn't figure it out. Then it dawned on me. To be close to another

---

[39]Bottle
[40]To touch, go play
[41]Spend
[42]Did you wash the dishes
[43]Group
[44]Carpet
[45]Washing machine
[46]You (formal)
[47]Clear
[48]Imagine
[49]It excites me
[50]We are the ones with the deficient Spanish, we are tongueless
[51]Crossbreeding
[52]Joke
[53]We are orphans

Chicana is like looking into the mirror. We are afraid of what we'll see there. *Pena*.[54] Shame. Low estimation of self. In childhood we are told that our language is wrong. Repeated attacks on our native tongue diminish our sense of self. The attacks continue throughout our lives.

Chicanas feel uncomfortable talking in Spanish to Latinas, afraid of their censure. Their language was not outlawed in their countries. They had a whole lifetime of being immersed in their native tongue; generations, centuries in which Spanish was a first language, taught in school, heard on radio and TV, and read in the newspaper.

If a person, Chicana or Latina, has a low estimation of my native tongue, she also has a low estimation of me. Often with *mexicanas y latinas*[55] we'll speak English as a neutral language. Even among Chicanas we tend to speak English at parties or conferences. Yet, at the same time, we're afraid the other will think we're *agringadas*[56] because we don't speak Chicano Spanish. We oppress each other trying to out-Chicano each other, vying to be the "real" Chicanas, to speak like Chicanos. There is no one Chicano language just as there is no one Chicano experience. A monolingual Chicana whose first language is English or Spanish is just as much a Chicana as one who speaks several variants of Spanish. A Chicana from Michigan or Chicago or Detroit is just as much a Chicana as one from the Southwest. Chicano Spanish is as diverse linguistically as it is regionally.

By the end of this century, Spanish speakers will comprise the biggest minority group in the U.S., a country where students in high schools and colleges are encouraged to take French classes because French is considered more "cultured." But for a language to remain alive it must be used. By the end of this century English, and not Spanish, will be the mother tongue of most Chicanos and Latinos.

So, if you want to really hurt me, talk badly about my language. Ethnic identity is twin skin to linguistic identity—I am my language. Until I can take pride in my language, I cannot take pride in myself. Until I can accept as legitimate Chicano Texas Spanish, Tex-Mex and all the other languages I speak, I cannot accept the legitimacy of myself. Until I am free to write bilingually and to switch codes without having always to translate, while I still have to speak English or Spanish when I would rather speak Spanglish, and as long as I have to accommodate the English speakers rather than having them accommodate me, my tongue will be illegitimate.

I will no longer be made to feel ashamed of existing. I will have my voice: Indian, Spanish, white. I will have my serpent's tongue—my woman's voice, my sexual voice, my poet's voice. I will overcome the tradition of silence.

---

[54]Sadness

[55]Mexican and Latin women

[56]Americanized women

My fingers
move sly against your palm
Like women everywhere, we speak in code. . . .
—Melanie Kaye/Kantrowitz

## "Vistas," corridos, y comida: My Native Tongue

In the 1960s, I read my first Chicano novel. It was *City of Night* by John Rechy, a gay Texan, son of a Scottish father and a Mexican mother. For days I walked around in stunned amazement that a Chicano could write and could get published. When I read *I Am Joaquín* I was surprised to see a bilingual book by a Chicano in print. When I saw poetry written in Tex-Mex for the first time, a feeling of pure joy flashed through me. I felt like we really existed as a people. In 1971, when I started teaching High School English to Chicano students, I tried to supplement the required texts with works by Chicanos, only to be reprimanded and forbidden to do so by the principal. He claimed that I was supposed to teach "American" and English literature. At the risk of being fired, I swore my students to secrecy and slipped in Chicano short stories, poems, a play. In graduate school, while working toward a Ph.D., I had to "argue" with one advisor after the other, semester after semester, before I was allowed to make Chicano literature an area of focus.

Even before I read books by Chicanos or Mexicans, it was the Mexican movies I saw at the drive in—the Thursday night special of $1.00 a carload—that gave me a sense of belonging. "*Vámonos a las vistas*,"[57] my mother would call out and we'd all—grandmother, brothers, sister and cousins—squeeze into the car. We'd wolf down cheese and bologna white bread sandwiches while watching Pedro Infante in melodramatic tearjerkers like *Nosotros los pobres*,[58] the first "real" Mexican movie (that was not an imitation of European movies). I remember seeing *Cuando los hijos se van*[59] and surmising that all Mexican movies played up the love a mother has for her children and what ungrateful sons and daughters suffer when they are not devoted to their mothers. I remember the singing-type "westerns" of Jorge Negrete and Miguel Aceves Mejía. When watching Mexican movies, I felt a sense of homecoming as well as alienation. People who were to amount to something didn't go to Mexican movies, or *bailes*[60] or tune their radios to *bolero*,[61] *rancherita*,[62] and *corrido*[63] music.

---

[57]Let's go to the movies
[58]We, the poor
[59]When the children leave
[60]Dances
[61]Romantic music
[62]Mexican folkloric music
[63]Mexican ballad

The whole time I was growing up, there was *norteño*[64] music, sometimes called North Mexican border music, or Tex-Mex music, or Chícano music, or *cantina*[67] (bar) music. I grew up listening to *conjuntos*,[65] three- or four-piece bands made up of folk musicians playing guitar, *bajo sexto*,[66] drums and button accordion, which Chicanos had borrowed from the German immigrants who had come to Central Texas and Mexico to farm and build breweries. In the Rio Grande Valley, Steve Jordan and Little Joe Hernández were popular, and Flaco Jiménez was the accordion king. The rhythms of Tex-Mex music are those of the polka, also adapted from the Germans, who in turn had borrowed the polka from the Czechs and Bohemians.

I remember the hot, sultry evenings when *corridos*—songs of love and death on the Texas-Mexican borderlands—reverberated out of cheap amplifiers from the local *cantinas* and wafted in through my bedroom window.

*Corridos* first became widely used along the South Texas/Mexican border during the early conflict between Chicanos and Anglos. The *corridos* are usually about Mexican heroes who do valiant deeds against the Anglo oppressors. Pancho Villa's song, *"La cucaracha,"* is the most famous one. *Corridos* of John F. Kennedy and his death are still very popular in the Valley. Older Chicanos remember Lydia Mendoza, one of the great border *corrido* singers who was called *la Gloria de Tejas*.[67] Her *"El tango negro,"*[68] sung during the Great Depression, made her a singer of the people. The everpresent *corridos* narrated one hundred years of border history, bringing news of events as well as entertaining. These folk musicians and folk songs are our chief cultural mythmakers, and they made our hard lives seem bearable.

I grew up feeling ambivalent about our music. Country-western and rock-and-roll had more status. In the 50s and 60s, for the slightly educated and *agringado* Chicanos, there existed a sense of shame at being caught listening to our music. Yet I couldn't stop my feet from thumping to the music, could not stop humming the words, nor hide from myself the exhilaration I felt when I heard it.

There are more subtle ways that we internalize identification, especially in the forms of images and emotions. For me food and certain smells are tied to my identity, to my homeland. Woodsmoke curling up to an immense blue sky; woodsmoke perfuming my grandmother's clothes, her skin. The stench of cow manure and the yellow patches on the ground; the crack of a .22 rifle and the reek of cordite. Homemade white cheese sizzling in a pan, melting inside a folded *tortilla*. My sister Hilda's hot, spicy *menudo*,[69]

---

[64]Northern

[65]Musical groups

[66]Bass

[67]The glory of Texas

[68]The black tango

[69]Beef tripe stew that is eaten on the weekends

[70]Red chile

*chile colorado*[70] making it deep red, pieces of *panza*[71] and hominy floating on top. My brother Carito barbecuing *fajitas* in the backyard. Even now and 3,000 miles away, I can see my mother spicing the ground beef, pork and venison with *chile*. My mouth salivates at the thought of the hot steaming *tamales* I would be eating if I were home.

## SI LE PREGUNTAS A MI MAMÁ, "¿QUÉ ERES?"[72]

> Identity is the essential core of who
> we are as individuals, the conscious
> experience of the self inside.
>
> —Gershen Kaufman

*Nosotros los Chicanos*[73] straddle the borderlands. On one side of us, we are constantly exposed to the Spanish of the Mexicans, on the other side we hear the Anglos' incessant clamoring so that we forget our language. Among ourselves we don't say *nosotros los americanos, o nosotros los españoles, o nosotros los hispanos.*[74] We say *nosotros los mexicanos*[75] (by *mexicanos* we do not mean citizens of Mexico; we do not mean a national identity, but a racial one). We distinguish between *mexicanos del otro lado*[76] and *mexicanos de este lado.*[77] Deep in our hearts we believe that being Mexican has nothing to do with which country one lives in. Being Mexican is a state of soul—not one of mind, not one of citizenship. Neither eagle nor serpent, but both. And like the ocean, neither animal respects borders.

> *Dime con quién andas y te diré quién eres.*
> (Tell me who your friends are and I'll tell you who you are.)
>
> —Mexican saying

*Si le preguntas a mi mamá, "¿Qué eres?" te dirá, "Soy mexicana."*[78] My brothers and sister say the same. I sometimes will answer *"soy mexicana"* and at others will

---

[70]Red chile

[71]Stomach

[72]If you ask my mom, "What are you?"

[73]We, Chicanos

[74]We, Americans; or we, Spanish; or we, Hispanics

[75]We, Mexicans

[76]Mexicans from the other side

[77]Mexicans from this side

[78]If you ask my mom, "What are you?" She will tell you, "I am Mexican."

[79]Race

say *"soy Chicana" o "soy tejana."* But I identified as *"Raza"*[79] before I ever identified as *"mexicana"* or "Chicana."

As a culture, we call ourselves Spanish when referring to ourselves as a linguistic group and when copping out. It is then that we forget our predominant Indian genes. We are 70 to 80% Indian. We call ourselves Hispanic or Spanish-American or Latin American or Latin when linking ourselves to other Spanish-speaking peoples of the Western hemisphere and when copping out. We call ourselves Mexican-American to signify we are neither Mexican nor American, but more the noun "American" than the adjective "Mexican" (and when copping out).

Chicanos and other people of color suffer economically for not acculturating. This voluntary (yet forced) alienation makes for psychological conflict, a kind of dual identity—we don't identify with the Anglo-American cultural values and we don't totally identify with the Mexican cultural values. We are a synergy of two cultures with various degrees of Mexicanness or Angloness. I have so internalized the borderland conflict that sometimes I feel like one cancels out the other and we are zero, nothing, no one. *A veces no soy nada ni nadie. Pero hasta cuando no lo soy, lo soy.*[80]

When not copping out, when we know we are more than nothing, we call ourselves Mexican, referring to race and ancestry; *mestizo* when affirming both our Indian and Spanish (but we hardly ever own our Black ancestry); Chicano when referring to a politically aware people born and/or raised in the U.S.; *Raza* when referring to Chicanos; *tejanos* when we are Chicanos from Texas.

Chicanos did not know we were a people until 1965 when César Chávez and the farmworkers united and *I Am Joaquín* was published and *la Raza Unida* party was formed in Texas. With that recognition, we became a distinct people. Something momentous happened to the Chicano soul—we became aware of our reality and acquired a name and a language (Chicano Spanish) that reflected that reality. Now that we had a name, some of the fragmented pieces began to fall together—who we were, what we were, how we had evolved. We began to get glimpses of what we might eventually become.

Yet the struggle of identities continues, the struggle of borders is our reality still. One day the inner struggle will cease and a true integration take place. In the meantime, *tenemos que hacer la lucha. ¿Quién está protegiendo los ranchos de mi gente? ¿Quién está tratando de cerrar la fisura entre la india y el blanco en nuestra sangre? El Chicano, sí, el Chicano que anda como un ladrón en su propia casa.*[81]

---

[75]We, Mexicans

[76]Mexicans from the other side

[77]Mexicans from this side

[78]If you ask my mom, "What are you?" She will tell you, "I am Mexican."

[79]Race

[80]Sometimes I am not anything, nobody. But even when I am not, I am.

[81]We have to fight. Who is protecting my people's ranches? Who is trying to close the gap between the indigenous woman and the white man in our blood? The Chicano, yes, the Chicano who goes around as a thief in his own house.

*Los Chicanos*, how patient we seem, how very patient. There is the quiet of the Indian about us. We know how to survive. When other races have given up their tongue, we've kept ours. We know what it is to live under the hammer blow of the dominant *norteamericano*[82] culture. But more than we count the blows, we count the days the weeks the years the centuries the eons until the white laws and commerce and customs will rot in the deserts they've created, lie bleached. *Humildes*[83] yet proud, *quietos*[84] yet wild, *nosotros los mexicanos*-Chicanos will walk by the crumbling ashes as we go about our business. Stubborn, persevering, impenetrable as stone, yet possessing a malleability that renders us unbreakable, we, the *mestizas* and *mestizos*, will remain.

---

[82]North American
[83]Humble ones
[84]Calm

# Guillermo Gómez Peña

Guillermo Gómez Peña was born in Mexico City in 1955. An internationally renowned performance artist, he migrated to the United States in 1978. At that time, he identified with the political and cultural concerns of the Chicano movement. He is one of the few writers who has explored themes of colonialism, cultural otherness, (trans)border realities, and the implications of globalization. His performances are a combination of traditional rituals and shamanistic practices postmodern electronic media.

## Danger Zone: Cultural Relations between Chicanos and Mexicans at the End of the Century

In February of 1995, the first stage of a binational performance project called "Terreno Peligroso/Danger Zone" was completed. For an entire month—two weeks in Los Angeles and two in Mexico City—eleven experimental artists whose work challenges stereotypical and/or official notions of identity, nationality, language, sexuality, and the

---

Primary works by Guillermo Gómez Peña: *A Binational Performance Pilgramage* (Manchester: Cornerhouse, 1993); *Warrior for Gringostroika: Essays, Performance Texts, and Poetry* (St. Paul, Minn.: Graywolf Press, 1993), *The New World Border: Prophecies, Poems, and Loqueras for the End of the Century* (San Francisco: City Lights, 1996); *Dangerous Border Crossers: The Artist Talks Back* (London, New York: Routledge, 2000).

creative process worked together daily. Representing Mexico were Lorena Wolffer, Felipe Ehrenberg, Eugenia Vargas, César Martinez, and Elvira Santamaría; from California were Elia Arce, Rubén Martínez, Nao Bustamante, Luis Alfaro, Roberto Sifuentes, and myself. Chosen by the curators and producers, Josefina Ramirez and Lorena Wolffer, this group was as eclectic and diverse as our two cultures (Chicano and Mexican). The performances were presented at the University of California at Los Angeles (UCLA) and in the Ex-Teresa Arte Alternativo (Mexico City).

The performance work we did covered a wide spectrum, ranging from the most intimate ritual actions to the most confrontational activist performance; including tableaux vivants, avant-cabaret, spoken word poetry, apocalyptic rituals, and street "interventions." Our goals (at least those we consciously expressed) were: to create art together (border art is collaborative by nature); to open the Pandora's box of North/South relations and unleash the border demons; to destroy taboos; and to replace simplistic views of cultural otherness with more complex visions. The following text attempts to outline some of the problems that the artists confronted during this binational encounter.

## I.

At the close of 1993, many artists of Latin American origin who were living in the United States ingenuously believed that NAFTA, or the *"Tratado de Libre Comer-se"*[1] —despite its grave omissions in the areas of ecology, human and labor rights, culture, and education—would, at least indirectly, create the conditions for a rapprochement between Chicanos and Mexicans. But that idea completely backfired on us. Instead, ferocious nationalist movements began to arise in response to globalization of the economy and culture. Xenophobic proposals reminiscent of Nazi Germany—such as Operation Gatekeeper and California's chilling Proposition 187—were brandished to confront the increasing and inevitable Mexicanization of the United States. We watched, perplexed, as the sudden opening of markets occurred almost simultaneously with the militarization of the border and the construction of a huge metal wall to separate several border cities. Capital, hollow dreams, and assembly plants easily crossed from one side to the other, but human beings—along with critical art and ideas—were prohibited passage. It seemed that culturally, as well as economically, the *maquiladora*[2] model had been perfected: Mexicans would provide the raw material and do the arduous, badly paid work; Anglos would run the show; and Chicanos would be left out of the picture.

We are like tiny, insignificant spectators at a great end-of-the-century wrestling match: "The Invisible Octopus of Pseudo-internationalization vs. the Hydra of Neonationalism." Round One: The neoliberal formula of a continent unified by free trade,

---

[1]Treaty of free eating each other (a play on Free Trade Agreement [Tratado de Libre Comercio])
[2]Factory

tourism, and digital high-technology is confronted by indigenous, campesino, environmental, and human rights movements. *Coitus interruptus*. The Mexican peso plummets, foreign capital flees, and the Marlboro dreams of neoliberal elites vanish in a cloud of sulfurous smoke. *Cambio*.[3]

The crises are also becoming globalized. In the topography of the end-of-the-century crisis, Bosnia is strangely connected to Los Angeles (L.A.—Herzegovina), just as Chiapas is connected to the Basque country and to Northern Ireland. Mexicans in California confront a dilemma similar to that faced by Palestinians and black South Africans, and the young people of Mexico City (members of Generation MEX) manifest the same existential and psychological illnesses that plague New Yorkers or Berliners.

The paradoxes multiply *loca r*hythmically.[4] In the era of computers, faxes, virtual reality, World Beat, and "total television" (à la CNN), it has become increasingly difficult for us to communicate across the borders of culture and language. The smaller and more concentrated the world becomes, the more foreign and incomprehensible it seems to us. We are now exposed to many languages, but we lack the keys to translation. We have access to incredible amounts of information, but we don't have the codes to decipher it. The seductive virtual universe, with its unlimited options and multidirectional promises, confounds our ability to order information and to act in the world with ethical and political clarity.

If anything could be said to define "postmodernity," it is the steady increase in symptoms of border culture, the endless syncretisms with a complete lack of synchronicity, misencounters, and misunderstandings: "I am, as long as you (as the representative of racial, linguistic, or cultural otherness) no longer are"; "I cross, therefore you exist (or vice versa)"; "Fuck you, therefore I am"; and others that would be better left unsaid. Contemporary art—at its most critical, irreverent, and experimental—is an involuntary chronicle of the ontological and epistemological confusion that is affecting all of us equally.

Chicano rap, Mexican alternative rock, independent cinema, and performance art converge on these key points: the brave acceptance of our transborderized and denationalized condition; the *ars poetic* of vertigo; the metaphysics of fragmentation; and the total collapse of linear logic, dramatic time, and narrative aesthetics. (This book is hopefully an example of this.)

## II.

The myths that once grounded our identity have become bankrupt. Sixties-era pan-Latinamericanism, *la mexicanidad*[5] (unique, monumental, undying), and Chicanismo (with thorns and a capital C) have all been eclipsed by processes of cultural borderization and social fragmentation. Like it or not, we are now denationalized, de-mexicanized,

---

[3]Change
[4]Crazy
[5]Mexicanness

transchicanized, and pseudo-internationalized. And worse, in fear of falling into a new century we refuse to assume this new identity, roaming around instead in a Bermuda Triangle. We live in economic uncertainty, terrorized by the holocaust of AIDS, divided (better yet, trapped) by multiple borders, disconnected from ourselves and others by strange mass cultures and new technologies that appeal to our most mediocre desires for instant transformation and psychological expansion.

In this bizarre landscape, politics becomes pop culture, and technology turns into folklore. Mass culture, popular culture, and folklore are no longer distinguishable from one another: it seems that our only true community is television. Perhaps our only real nation is also television. Mexico is, and continues to be "one" by virtue of television; without television perhaps it would cease to be. Televisa is Mexico's macro-Ministry of Communications, Culture, and Binational Tourism, all in one. In the United States of the '90s, the most famous Mexicans are TV personalities such as Gloria Trevi, Paco Stanley, "Verónica," and Raúl Velasco. Sadly, the main connection that Mexican immigrants maintain with that marvelous, imaginary country called Mexico is via soap operas. If we are familiar with "El Sup" (Subcomandante Marcos) and Superbarrio, it's because they are skillful manipulators of the symbolic (and performative) politics of the media. In this context, we "untelevisable" performance artists are asking ourselves what role will be left for us to perform in the immediate future. Maybe our only options will be to make conceptual commercials for MTV and/or appear in artsy rock videos. For the moment, I'm having a hard time imagining more dignified alternatives.

## III.         -

North Americans (in the United States) used to define their identity in direct opposition to the "Soviet threat." With the end of the Cold War, the United States fell into an unprecedented identity crisis. Today its place in the world is uncertain and its (fictitious) enemies are multiplying left and right. On the eclectic list of recent anti-American "others" one finds fundamentalist Muslims, Japanese businessmen, Latin American drug lords, black rap musicians, and more recently, "illegal aliens" in both senses of the word: cultural martians invading "our" institutions, and seditious laborers who are "stealing jobs from *real* Americans."

This identity crisis translates into an immense nostalgia for an (imaginary) era in which people of color didn't exist, or at least when we were invisible and silent. The political expression of this nostalgia is chilling: "Let's take our country back." The far right, like Pete Wilson, Newt Gingrich, Jesse Helms, and Pat Buchanan, along with many Democrats, are in agreement on the following: This country must be saved from chaos and collapse into Third-Worldization; "illegal" immigrants must be deported; the poor should be put in jail (three strikes, you're out); welfare, affirmative action, and bilingual education programs must be dismantled; and the cultural funding infrastructure that has been infiltrated by "liberals with leftist tendencies" (the National Endowment for the Arts and the Humanities and the Corporation for Public Broadcasting) must be decimated. In the euphemistic Contract with America, ethnic "minorities," independent artists and intellectuals, the homeless, the elderly, children, and especially immigrants from the South, are all under close watch.

In Mexico, ever since the implementation of NAFTA the border no longer functions as the great barrier of contention against which official Mexican identity is defined. This has created its own large-scale identity crisis. Without the continuous harassment from Washington's Power Rangers, the *yupitecas*[6] and the *mariachis*[7] have had no other alternative than to go off to a cantina and drown themselves in the depths of lost love and *neo-Porfirista* nostalgia. The social explosion in Chiapas has complicated things further and has literally torn the country in two. *Salinista*[8] Mexico preferred to think of itself as *posmoderno*[9] and international, desiring at all costs to look outward and northward, but the unfolding internal political crisis has forced the country's gaze back inward to confront its racism against indigenous peoples and its abysmal contradictions.

Although the roots of our crises are of a very different nature, both Califas (California) and Tenochtitlán (Mexico City) are living through unprecedented identity crises. And, for the first time in the twentieth century there is a growing consciousness on both sides of the border that the crises and dangers that we're undergoing are similar. This mutual recognition could be the basis for new, more profound cultural relations between Chicanos and Mexicans: If we recognize that we're all equally screwed, perhaps at the same time we are equally capable of greater compassion and mutual understanding.

## IV.

At present, the only thing that unites those who left Mexico and those who stayed is our inability to understand and accept our inevitable differences. We detect the existence of these invisible borders, but we are unable to articulate them, much less cross them with tact. This phenomenon is clearly evident in the area of cultural relations between Mexico and the United States, most especially, between Mexicans and Chicanos. It's here where the contradictions abound, where the wound opens and bleeds, and the poisoned subtext of mutual (and largely fictional) resentments rises to the surface.

We, the post-Mexican and Chicano artists from "over there/the other side" look to the South with a certain ingenuousness, a distorting nostalgia and admiration, always dreaming of our possible return. Meanwhile, the Mexicans who remain south of the border look at us with a combination of desire and repudiation, fear and condescension. The mirrors are always breaking. While we on the California coast—where the West literally ends—look toward the Pacific, those in Mexico City look attentively toward Europe and New York. (The paradox here is that Europe and New York—in spiritual and artistic bankruptcy—are carefully watching both Chicanos and Mexicans, searching for novelty, inspiration, and exoticism to decorate the blank walls of their nihilist crisis.)

The missed encounters continue. In the United States, Latino artists work in the flammable context of the multicultural wars and identity politics. We define ourselves as a

---

[6]Play on the words yuppie and Aztecs

[7]Mexican traditional musicians

[8]Followers of former Mexican president Carlos Salinas de Gortari, who stole a lot of money from Mexico

[9]Postmodern

culture of resistance, and in our eagerness to "resist the dominant culture" we frequently lose all sense of a continental perspective, and end up assuming ethnocentric and separatist positions. Meanwhile, the Mexican artistic communities—with some exceptions—are undergoing a stage of nonreflective extroversion and the rejection of textually political or politicized art, which they associate with "minor" art and with official Mexican cultural discourse. Although they are the protagonists and witnesses of their country's most serious crisis in modern history (perhaps comparable to that of Eastern Europe), many Mexican experimental artists have chosen not to "textually" use *la crisis*[10] as subject matter in their work. Right now, they are more inclined to create a personal, intimate art of an existential or neoconceptual style.

When Mexican artists "go North," they do so with the intention of breaking into the commercial gallery circuit. They are prejudiced by the solemnity and virtual failure of official cultural exchange projects, and to them Chicano art appears didactic, reiterative, and poorly executed. Our themes—racism, immigration, the obsessive deconstruction of identities, and the subversion of media stereotypes of Mexicans—seem distant and irrelevant to their purely "Mexican" reality. They seem not to fully grasp the magnitude of their own crisis and refuse (not entirely without reason) to be seen as a "minority." Chicanos, hypersensitive to this fragile relationship, feel rejected by the Mexicans, and the gap between the two cultures grows wider.

The long and convoluted history of cultural exchange between Chicanos and Mexicans can be translated as a chronicle of missed encounters. For fifteen years Chicanos have tried, without success, to "return" through the great door and to reconcile themselves with Mexican relatives. With few exceptions, the reception to their art has been openly hostile or, at best, paternalistic. Despite the numerous and fashionable projects of binational interchange facilitated (or inspired) by NAFTA, Mexico's predominant vision of Chicano art is still antiquated. In 1995, most Mexicans still believe that all Chicano artists make barrio murals, write protest poetry, and erect neon altars to Frida Kahlo and the Virgin of Guadalupe; that they all speak like Edward Olmos in *American Me* and dance to Tex-Mex music; that they all drive low-riders. They ignore the actual diversity and complexity of our communities, and remain unaware of the influence of the Central American, Caribbean, and Asian communities that have moved into the Chicano neighborhoods. The influence of gay and lesbian communities of color, with their challenge to the excessive dose of testosterone from which Chicano culture has suffered for the last two decades, is also completely overlooked. The processes that have brought us to more fluid and interactive models of a Chicano/Latino multi-identity are still unheard of Mexico City, and two generations of young artists who have publicly questioned conventional, static notions of Chicanismo remain outside the realm of most Mexicans' consciousness.

---

[10]The crisis

## V.

In 1995, *la mexicanidad* and the Latino/Chicano experience are becoming completely superimposed. The 200,000 Mexicans who cross the border every month bring us fresh and constant reminders of our past (for Mexican Americans, the continual migratory flow functions as a sort of collective memory). And the opposite phenomenon also happens: the mythic North (which represents the future) also returns to the South, searching for its lost past. Many of the Mexicans who come to "the other side" become "chicanized" and return to Mexico—either on their own or by force of the immigration authorities. In the act of returning they contribute to the silent process of Chicanization which Mexico is currently undergoing.

This dual dynamic, as expressed in popular culture, functions as a sort of X-ray of the social psyche: the "northern" sounds of *quebradita*[11] (a fusion of north Mexican banda[12] and techno-pop) and rap can already be heard from Yucatán to Chihuahua; while the songs of Mexican bands such as Los Caifanes, La Lupita, Maldita Vecindad, and Los Tigres del Norte are being hummed from San Diego to New York. Selena, the "queen of Tex-Mex" (RIP), is venerated in both countries. The sounds of "tecno-banda" and quebradita (no one can deny that these are immigrant sounds) re-mexicanize Chicano music. The "cholos" and the "salvatruchos" (young Salvadorans in L.A.) are wearing Stetson hats and cowboy boots, while Aztec punk-rockers in Mexico City, Guadalajara, and Tijuana are expropriating Chicano iconography and fashion, and talking in Spanglish, ¿que no?

Mexican identity (or better said, the many Mexican identities) can no longer be explained without the experience of "the other side," and vice versa. As a socio-cultural phenomenon, Los Angeles simply cannot be understood without taking Mexico City—its southernmost neighborhood—into account. Between both cities runs the greatest migratory axis on the planet, and the conceptual freeway with the greatest number of accidents.

As transnationalized artists, our challenge is to recompose the fragmented chronicle of this strange end-of-the-century phenomenon. And so, the performance begins . . .

*(Translated by Clifton Ross)*

---

[11]A traditional Mexican dance
[12]Band

# Questions to Consider

## NATIVE

1. Have you ever had to defend your claim to the United States as a foreigner or as a citizen? What did you say? How would you say it? Would you use some of the tools employed by Tomás Rivera in "Zoo Island"? Do you agree with the character's approach in this story?

2. Alurista and Tato Laviera make a case for multiculturalism in the United States. Alurista, for example, uses the serape to speak of the beauty that a variety of colors and ethnicities create when they come together. What articles or items in your surroundings that may be used in the same manner? Do you think a multicultural and multilingual existence is possible? Why or why not? Explain your answer.

3. What recurring symbols or icons do you find in the selections in this section? What effect do they have on the stories? Why do you think they are used?

4. "Dallas" by Rosaura Sánchez and "Exile" by Benjamín Alire Sáenz touch on the discrimination minorities face in the United States at the hands of the police. How do you see issues of discrimination or racism expressed in some of the other works included? Do you think such discrimination still exists? Why or why not?

5. Language is an important aspect of Latino literature. Writers are sometimes forced to choose English over Spanish, or vice versa. What do you think are the implications of this choice? Does it make a difference? What happens when an author uses Spanglish (combination of English and Spanish) to express his or her ideas?

6. Orality is a component of culture and tradition in Latino literature because it is believed to represent the life that is never recorded in books. For that reason, music and the art of storytelling are treasured, among other oral expressions. "Dichos" by Patricia Preciado Martín incorporates orality. What do you learn from this story? Can you think of examples in your community that could fall under this category? Do they tell you about the life and culture that is not recorded in books? Do other authors that you have read in this book or somewhere else incorporate orality in their writing? Explain your answer.

7. Growing up in the United States as a person with a hyphen—Mexican-American or Cuban-American, for example—can be difficult because one is constantly trying to prove that one is U.S. American and that one has not forgotten the homeland. Luis Valdez, in his play *Los Vendidos*, discusses the value of being a sellout and its repercussions for the Latino community. Do you agree with his ideas? Is this common nowadays?

8. Coming-of-age narratives are common in Latino literature, as they explore the issues young people experience growing up in the United States. Richard Yáñez and Helena María Viramontes present fine examples of literature that address this theme. Do you think their experiences have something in common with your own? How are their experiences similar to or different from yours?

# EXILE AND IMMIGRATION

1. What is your opinion of the hyphenation of an ethnic identity, such as Mexican-American? Can one be both? Richard Blanco's "América" discusses the need to combine Cuban and American culture in his house in order to adjust to life in the United States. Do you see this as a loss of one culture to the other? Have you ever had to reassess your cultural traditions to accommodate specific situations? How did you feel?

2. What do you think an immigrant or exile to the United States would say if they arrived in the 1950s? What would they say now? Do exiles or immigrants experience culture shock nowadays?

3. Have you traveled to another country? Can you explain what you felt experimenting with another culture? How did you manage? Read the testimony that Alicia Alarcón titles "All I Thought About Was Disneyland" and describe your opinion of a country to which you have never been to but have heard about. What do you think you will see? What will people be like?

4. Exiles and immigrants come to the United States for many reasons—especially politics, as is the case of Alicia Partnoy and José María Heredia, and economics, as in Alicia Alarcón's piece. What do you think are the advantages and disadvantages of being an exile or immigrant to the United States? If you had to explain what life would be like for an exile or immigrant in the United States, what would you say?

5. When writers write as exiles or immigrants, they often allude to the fact that they are not citizens of the United States. For that reason, their works either admire the United States or criticize it. Why do you think writers resort to either of these options? Are other options possible?

6. The writings of authors like Víctor Montejo and Tomás Borge describe the violent life in their homelands. What themes does this writing reflects? Why do you think these authors focus on the violence? What impact does it have you as a reader? What does this writing do for the writers themselves? What is the writers' message?

7. Compare and contrast the language used in José María Heredia's poem "Hymn of Exile" and Gustavo Pérez Firmat's "Bilingual Blues." What are your reactions to these poems? What are the authors trying to express? Do they achieve their goals?

8. The characters depicted in Exile and Immigration works represent either elite or working-class men and women. Compare and contrast characters from "Hymn of Exile" and "Toward Patzún" or "Testimony: Death of a Guatemalan Village." Are the differences major? Why or why not? Does this affect your observations?

# TRANSCULTURAL

1. In "Lengualistic Algo: Speaking in Tongues" we see that language is important in keeping one's culture alive as is the case of Spanish. Josefina López complicates this by questioning the values and traditions that are kept in the domestic space of Latino families. How can one maintain Latino culture in the United States? What can people do to preserve traditions and customs? Why or why not? How does the approach of each writer to this theme differ? Do external or internal factors affect their views?

2. How are the United States and other countries that have signed free trade treaties affected by the agreement? What do you think are the benefits to everyone involved? Guillermo Gómez Peña questions the value of such treaties and their benefits to Latin American countries. What are your own observations? Who do you think benefits? Who do you think plans the treaties?

3. Carolina Monsiváis and Josefina López use women and their roles in Latino environments to demonstrate the abuse that is often perpetrated on them, sometimes unknowingly. What messages does each author present?

Each author presents problems; what are some of the solutions they offer? Do you think the solutions are viable? Why or why not?

4. Memory is important in helping writers craft the works we read. When you read Norma Cantú's selections, think of the most vivid images she presents. Why does she share these memories? Why is it important for the reader to know that a memory is shared? What memories about your childhood would you share? Why?

5. Roberto Quesada and Ramón "Tianguis" Pérez speak of their experiences in coming to the United States. Quesada, on one hand, focuses on Miami International Airport, while Tianguis reports on the illegal crossing of the Rio Grande. Compare and contrast these observations. What do the characters have in common?

6. Jaime Manrique, in "Señoritas in Love," discusses several themes, what is the main message of this story? The phrase "you're not going to regret the affairs you had, but the ones you didn't have" can be applied to many things in our lives. How can this can be applied to your life?

7. Growing up in the United States affords young people interesting perspectives on multiculturalism. Both Luis Rodriguez and Brenda Cárdenas discuss the importance of Spanish in their lives. Do you have another heritage that enriches who you are? What are some of the spaces this characteristic opens for you? When did you become aware of it?

8. Writers who no longer worry about writing about their homeland as a way to keep their heritage alive, or are no longer preoccupied with their place in the United States, begin to explore many other themes. What themes affect your view of Latinos? Did you know that Latinos were writing of such themes?

# Chronology

**1492**    On 3 August, Christopher Columbus sails from Spain in his three ships: the *Pinta*, the *Niña*, and the *Santa María*. On 12 October, the Spaniards reach an island called El Salvador in the Bahamas, and later that same month, on the 27th, they reach the northeastern shore of Cuba. The crew is convinced that they have reached Cipango or Cathay in Asia.

**1508**    Juan Ponce de León sails from Puerto Rico and, a year later, is appointed governor of Puerto Rico.

**1513**    Juan Ponce de León lands in Florida. At that time, it is estimated, 100,000 Native Americans live there.

**1519**    Hernán Cortés arrives in the coast of Veracruz, Mexico. A year later, the Aztecs force the Spaniards out of Veracruz. This is referred to as *La noche triste* (The Sad Night). Moctezuma is stoned to death.

**1521**    Cortés leads his compatriots into Tenochtitlán, and they build Mexico City.

**1536**    Álvar Núñez Cabeza de Vaca returns to Mexico and begins to explore and colonize what is to become the American Southwest. While he is in Mexico City, there are rumors that Cabeza de Vaca has discovered cities laden with gold and silver.

**1573**    The Franciscan order arrives in Florida to establish missions.

**1598**    Juan de Oñate, a Portuguese, began to colonize New Mexico.

**1610**    Santa Fe, New Mexico, is founded.

**1680**    Popé, a Pueblo Indian, leads a rebellion that forces the Spaniards out of northern New Mexico into El Paso, where they found Ysleta.

**1690**    In May, the first Texas Spanish settlement, San Francisco de los Tejas, is founded near the Neches River.

**1716**    Spain reoccupies Texas when Spaniards discover a possibility that the French may try to take over the land. This allows them the opportunity to convert natives to Catholicism. San Antonio is founded in 1718.

**1769**    Fray Junípero de Serra establishes the first mission in Alta California in what became San Diego. He eventually founded ten missions, traveling 10,000 miles and converting 6,800 natives.

**1770–1790** Approximately 50,000 African slaves are brought to Cuba to work in the production of sugar.

**1776**   As a result of their alliance with France, Spain obtains lands all the way to Florida from Mexico/Central America. Anglo-Americans declare their independence from England.

**1781**   The thirteen former British colonies become the United States. The newly independent people of New Spain become the Republic of Mexico.

**1803**   Napoleon Bonaparte sells the Louisiana Territory to the United States in his quest for money and dominance.

**1810**   In Mexico, Father Miguel Hidalgo y Costilla leads a revolt against Spain, forcing their withdrawal on 16 September. Mexico's independence is gained in 1821.

**1819**   Florida is purchased by the United States for $5 million under the Onís Treaty.

**1823**   Erasmo Seguín persuades the US Congress to pass a colonization act allowing more Anglo settlers to migrate to Texas. By 1830, Texas has 18,000 Anglo inhabitants and their African slaves, who total more than 2,000.

**1836**   The Anglo settlers declare the Republic of Texas independent of Mexico. That same year, the Texas constitution stipulates that all residents of Texas at the time of the rebellion will acquire all rights of citizens of the new republic, but if they are disloyal, these rights are forfeited. Numerically superior Anglos forced Mexicans off their property, and many Mexicans cross the border to Mexico.

**1840**   To meet the wage-labor demands, 125,000 Chinese are brought to Cuba between 1840 and 1870 to work as cane cutters, build railroads in rural areas, and serve as domestics in the cities. The influx of Spaniards increases; the Spaniards concentrate in retail trades and operate small stores called *bodegas*.

**1845**   Texas is officially annexed to the United States.

**1846**   The Treaty of Guadalupe Hidalgo ends the Mexican-American War; half of Mexico, including Texas, California, most of Arizona and New Mexico, and parts of Colorado, Utah, and Nevada were ceded. Mexican nationals are given one year to choose their nationality. Approximately 75,000 Hispanic people choose to remain and become citizens by conquest.

**1848**   The gold rush lures Anglo settlers to California, which became a state in 1850.

**1853**   General Santa Anna, through the Gadsden Treaty, sells the land from Yuma, Arizona, along the Gila River to the Mesilla Valley (New Mexico) to the United States.

**1855**   The Supreme Court rules that the Treaty of Guadalupe Hidalgo does not apply to Texas.

**1862**   The Homestead Act is passed in Congress. This allows squatters in the West to settle and claim vacant lands, often those owned by Mexicans.

**1868**   The Fourteenth Amendment to the US Constitution is adopted, declaring that people of Hispanic origin born in the United States are US citizens. On 17 September, a decree in Puerto Rico frees all children born of slaves after this date, and in 1870, all slaves who are state property are freed. On 23 September, El Grito de Lares, the shout for Puerto Rican independence, takes place. In October, Cuba, under the leadership of Carlos Manuel de Céspedes, declares independence.

**1880**      Mexican immigration to the United States is stimulated by the advent of the railroad.

**1892**      The Partido Revolucionario Cubano is created to organize the Cuban and Puerto Rican independence movement. Three years later, José Martí and his Cuban Revolutionary Party open the final battle for independence.

**1897**      Spain grants Cuba and Puerto Rico autonomy and home rule.

**1898**      In April, the US declares war against Spain. On December, Spain signs the Treaty of Paris, transferring Cuba, Puerto Rico, and the Philippines to the United States.

**1900**      The Foraker Act establishes a civilian government in Puerto Rico under US dominance. Puerto Ricans are allowed to elect their own House of Representatives but are not allowed to vote.

**1959**      The Cuban Revolution overthrows Batista, and Fidel Castro takes power in Cuba. The majority of Cubans migrate to the United States between 1959 and 1962. (More than one million Cubans have entered the country since 1959.)

**1960**      A third phase of labor migration begins. Puerto Rican and Mexican patterns of migration are modified, and other countries begin to migrate to the United States. In 1964, the Bracero program ends.

**1961**      Aspira (Aspire) is founded to promote education of Hispanic youth, serving Puerto Ricans wherever they live in large numbers. Anti-Communist Cuban exiles attempt a foray into Cuba known as the Bay of Pigs invasion. This strengthens Castro and embitters Cuban exiles in the United States.

**1962**      The United Farm Workers Organizing Committee is led by César Chávez, and in 1965, it organizes its first successful Delano grape strike and first national boycott. The union comes to be known as the United Farmworkers of America.

**1964**      The United States passes the Civil Rights Act of 1964, which establishes affirmative action programs and the Equal Employment Opportunity Commission (EEOC).

**1965**      A border industrialization program, the *maquiladora*, is initiated. Mexico hopes to raise the standard of living in the border region, while the United States hopes to avoid the possible negative political and economic consequences of leaving hundreds of Mexican workers stranded when the Bracero Program ended. Fidel Castro announces that Cubans can leave the island nation if they have relatives living in the United States. He stipulates that Cubans already in Florida have to come and get their relatives.

**Late 1960s–** Young Mexican Americans throughout the country seek a new identity while struggling for the
**early 1970s** same civil rights objectives as previous generations. Their struggle becomes known as the Chicano movement.

**1968**      Chicano student organizations, such as the Brown Berets and La Raza Unida party in Texas, are formed to obtain control of community governments where Chicanos are the majority. Such organizations spring up throughout the United States.

**1969**      After the establishment of the Central American Common Place Market in the 1960s leads to economic growth and improved conditions in the region, the border war between Honduras and El Salvador brings its collapse and a rapid decline in economic conditions in Central America.

**1970s–early** The rise in politically motivated violence in Central America spurs a massive increase in
**1980s** undocumented immigration to the United States.

**1970** The amendments constituting the landmark Voting Rights Act of 1970 include a provision designed to guard against inventive new barriers to political participation.

**1972** Ramona Acosta Bañuelos becomes the first Hispanic treasurer of the United States.

**1973** The right of the Puerto Rican people to decide their own future as a nation is approved by the United Nations. In 1978, the United Nations recognizes Puerto Rico as a colony of the United States.

**1974** Congress passes the Equal Educational Opportunity Act to create equality in public schools by making bilingual education available to Hispanic youths. Students must also be given the programs to learn English.

**1978–1988** The proportion of Hispanic female participation in the workforce more than doubles, from 1.7 million to 3.6 million.

**1979** Political upheaval and civil wars in Nicaragua, El Salvador, and Guatemala contribute to large migrations of refugees to the United States.

**1980** A flotilla converges at Cuba's Mariel Harbor to pick up refugees. By year's end, more than 125,000 "Marielitos" migrate to the United States.

**1986** Congress enacts the Immigration Reform and Control Act (IRCA) granting legal status to applicants who held illegal status before 1 January 1982.

**1990** Latinos become the second-fastest growing segment of the US population. Spanish is named the official language of Puerto Rico.

**1991** Despite the US Congress's refusal to consider the statehood of Puerto Rico, a referendum is held on the island. It clearly shows that the population is in favor of statehood.

**1991** In March, a jury exonerates Los Angeles police of the brutal beating of African American Rodney King, which was captured on videotape. This leads to riots when African Americans and Latinos protest the verdict.

**1992** In February, the Farabundo Martí National Liberation Front (FMLN) ends its guerrilla movement by signing a peace treaty with the government of El Salvador. In exchange, the government agrees to sweeping changes in the military, including the retirement of more than one hundred officers. El Salvador was a key battleground for the Cold War during the 1980s, with the United States pouring more than $6 billion in economic and military aid to defeat the FMLN. In October, President George Bush signs the Cuban Democracy Act, also known as the Torricelli Bill, which bans trade with Cuba by US subsidiary companies in third countries and prohibits ships docking in US ports if they have visited Cuba.

**1993** President Bill Clinton appoints twenty-five Hispanics to positions that need confirmation by the Senate, including Nicolás Kanellos to the National Council for the Humanities.

**1994** The North American Free Trade Agreement (NAFTA) takes effect, eliminating all tariffs between trading partners Canada, Mexico, and the United States within fifteen years. This is an effort to integrate the economies of the three countries and possibly create a common market that will include the entire hemisphere. The agreement is opposed by US labor unions, which fear the continuing loss of jobs to Mexico. In Mexico, revolutionary outbreaks by Mayan peasant farmers in Chiapas are timed to coincide with the beginning of NAFTA. The Zapatista National Liberation Army (EZLN) takes over the important southern city of San Cristobal de las Casas, among others, which leads to bloody confrontations with and repression by the Mexican army until a ceasefire is accepted by both sides on 12 January.

**8 November 1994** Californians pass Propositon 187 with 59 percent of the vote. The initiative bans undocumented immigrants from receiving public education and public benefits such welfare and subsidized health care, except in emergency situations, and it requires teachers, doctors, and other city, county, and state officials to report suspected and apparent illegal aliens to the California attorney general and the Immigration and Naturalization Service (INS).

**2010** Latinos will make up 13 percent of the US population.

# Film List

## A

*A La Brava: Prison and Beyond*
*Abandoned: The Betrayal of America's Immigrants*
*Accordion Dreams*
*Adelante Mujeres!*
*Affirmative Action: The History of an Idea*
*Affirmative Action under Fire: When Is It Reverse Discrimination?*
*After the Earthquake*
*Algún Día (Some Day)*
*América de los Indios*
*American Me*
*An American Story with Richard Rodriguez . . . And the Earth Did Not Swallow Him*
*Animaquiladora: The Animation Sweatshop*
*Año Nuevo (New Year)*
*Arrow*
*The Art of Resistance*
*The Assumption of Lupe Velez*

## B

*The Ballad of Gregorio Cortez*
Ballad of an Unsung Hero
*La Bamba*
*The Battle of Glorieta Pass*
*Beca de Gilas: Rebeca's Story*
*Before Night Falls*
*Biculturalism and Acculturation Among Latinos*
*Bilingual Education*
*Birthwrite: Growing Up Hispanic*
*Black and White in Exile*
*La Boda (The wedding)*
*Bombing L.A.*
*Border Brujo*

*Border Economics*
*Borderline Cases: Environmental Matters at the United States–Mexico Border*
*Born in East L.A.*
*The Boxer*
*Bread and Roses*
*Break of Dawn: A True Story*
*The Bronze Screen*

## C

*Cafe con Leche (Coffee with Milk)*
*Califas: Chicano Art in California*
*California Since the Sixties: Revolutions and Counterrevolutions: Challenge of Multiracial Democracy, 2/6/99*
*Calle 54*
*Campus Culture Wars: Five Stories About PC*
*Captain from Castile*
*Carmelita Tropicana: Your Kunst Is Your Waffen*
*Carnalitos (Little Kin)*
*Challenging Hispanic Stereotypes: Arturo Madrid*
*Chasing Papi*
*Chicana*
*Chicano: The History of the Mexican American Civil Rights Movement Episode 1: Quest for a Homeland; Episode 2: The Struggle in the Field; Episode 3: Taking Back the Schools; Episode 4: Fighting for Political Power*
*Chicano Park*
*Children of Violence*
*Chulas Fronteras (Beautiful Barders)*
*Cisco Kid*
[Cisneros, Sandra] *Sandra Cisneros*
*La Ciudad (The City)*

Class Divided
The Closing Door: An Investigation of Immigration
    Policy
Colors
Color Schemes: America's Washload in 4 Cycles
Como Agua Para Chocolate (Like Water for Chocolate)
El Corazón Sangrante (The Bleeding Heart)
Corpus: A Home Movie for Selena
El Corrido de Cecilia Rios
Corridos!
The Couple in the Cage: A Guatinaui Odyssey
Crazy/Beautiful
El Crimen del Padre Amaro (The Crime of Father
    Amaro)
Crossing Borders: A Cuban Returns
Crossover Dreams
Cultural Bias in Education
Culture Clash's Bowl of Beings
The Culture of Poverty

## D

The Dancer Upstairs
De Colores: Lesbian and Gay Latinos: Stories of
    Strength, Family and Love (Lesbianas y gays
    Latinos: historias de fuerza, familia y amor)
Death on a Friendly Border
Del Mero Corazon (Straight from the Heart: Love
    Songs from the Southwest)
Desperado
The Devil Never Sleeps (El Diablo Nunca Duerme)
The Difference between Us
Distant Water
Dreams Ensnared: The Dominican Migration to New
    York
Duel in the Sun

## E

Empire
The English-Speaking Amendment
The Eye of the Storm

## F

Factory Farms
La Familia

Fear and Learning at Hoover Elementary
The Fight in the Fields: César Chávez and the
    Farmworkers' Struggle
Flyin' Cut Sleeves
The Forgotten Americans
Free Speech and Racism on Campus: Nightline:
    June 12, 1989
Frida
Frida
Frida Kahlo
From Here, From This Side: De Acá de Este Lado
From Sleepy Lagoon to Zoot Suit: The Irreverent Path
    of Alice McGrath
From the Other Side (De l'autre cote)
Frontierland
Frontline: Racism 101

## G

Gabriela
Gary Soto (May 3, 1995)
Gay Desperado
Getting to Heaven (Ganarse el cielo)
Go Back to Mexico!
Golden Cage: A Story of California's Farmworkers
Graffiti Verite: Read the Writing on the Wall
GV2: Graffiti Verite 2
GV3: Graffiti Verite 3 (The Final Episode)

## H

Hablas Inglés? (Do You Speak English?)
Hangin' with the Homeboys
Hate Crime
Hijos del silencio (Sons of Silence)
Hispanics in the Media
Home is Struggle
Homeboys
Homelessness Among Hispanics
The House We Live In

## I

I Am Joaquin (Yo Soy Joaquin)
I Like It Like That
Illegal Aliens Entering the U.S.: September 8, 1986
    (Nightline)

*Viva La Causa!*
*Viva Villa!*
*Viva Zapata!*
*Voces del Campo (Voices of the Fields)*

## W

*A Walk in the Clouds*
*Warrior of Light*
*Wars and Images*
*Watsonville on Strike*
*The Wedding Planner*
*West Side Story*
*When You Think of Mexico: Commercial Images of Mexicans in the Mass Media*
*Woman on Top*

*Women on the Verge of a Nervous Breakdown*
*The Wrath of Grapes*

## Y

*Y Este Encuentro Quiere Ser Canción (And This Meeting Wants to Be a Song)*
*Y tu mamá también (And your mother, too)*
*Yo Soy*
*Yo Soy Chicano (I Am Chicano)*
*Yo Soy Hechicero (I Am a Sorcerer)*
*Yo Soy Joaquin (I Am Joaquin)*

## Z

*Zoot Suit*
*Zoot Suit Riots*

# Author Websites and Other Resources

## Marjorie Agosín
http://www.chelseaforum.com/speakers/Agosin.htm
http://www.wellesley.edu/PublicAffairs/Profile/af/
    magosin.html

## Claribel Alegría
http://www.onlinepoetryclassroom.org/poets/
    poets.cfm?prmID=280

## Miguel Algarín
http://www.greatertalent.com/bios/algarin.shtml
http://www.pbs.org/shattering/algarin.html

## Alurista
http://cemaweb.library.ucsb.edu/alurista.html

## Julia Alvarez
http://www.middlebury.edu/~english/facpub/Alv-
    autobio.html
http://www.lasmujeres.com
http://voices.cla.umn.edu/authors/ JuliaAlvarez.html
http://www.alvarezjulia.com/
http://www.emory.edu/ENGLISH/Bahri/Alvarez.html

## Gloria Anzaldúa
http://www.princeton.edu/~howarth/557/border/html

## Jimmy Santiago Baca
http://www.jimmysantiagobaca.com

## Richard Blanco
http://www.smith.edu/poetrycenter/bios.php?name=rblanco

## Tomás Borge
http://www.hartford-hwp.com/archives/47/028.html

## Rafael Campo
http://www.poets.org/LIT/poet/rcampfst.htm

## Lorna Dee Cervantes
http://members.aol.com/tonytweb/loranlinks.html
http://www.poets.org/LIT/poet/ldcerfst.htm
http://www.pbs.org/wnet/foolingwithwords/
    main_cervantes.html
http://voices.cla.umn.edu/authors/LornaDeeCervantes.
    html

## Veronica Chambers
http://www.veronicachambers.com/

## Sandra Cisneros
http://bedfordbooks.com/litlinks/fiction/cisneros.htm
http://falcon.jmu.edu/~ramseyil/cisneros.htm
http://voices.cla.umn.edu/authors/SandraCisneros.html
http://www.lasmujeres.com/sandracisneros/

## Judith Ortiz Cofer
http://parallel.park.uga.edu/~jcofer/home.html
http://www.college.hmco.com/english/heath/syllabuild/
    iguide/cofer.html

## Lucha Corpi
http://www.accd.edu/sac/english/portales/corpi.htm
http://voices.cla.umn.edu/newsite/authors/
    CORPIlucha.htm

## Pablo Antonio Cuadra

http://www.filosofia.org/ave/001/a034.htm
http://www.literatura.us/cuadra/
http://www.dariana.com/Panorama/PAC_poemas.htm

## Junot Diaz

http://latnn.com/grafico/interview/articles/junot2.htm
http://www.thei.aust.com/sydney/biographies/diaz.html

## Alicia Gaspar de Alba

http://www.sscnet.ucla.edu/chavez/gaspar.html

## Olga Angelina García Echeverría

http://www.calacapress.com/olgagarcia.html

## Isaac Goldemberg

http://www.geocities.com/hibrido_literario/goldemberg.html

## Guillermo Gómez Peña

http://www.rhizome.org/member.rhiz?user_id=74
http://amsterdam.nettime.org/Lists-Archives/
    nettime-l-9805/msg00083.html
http://www.pochanostra.com/

## Ray González

http://www.poetry.org/issues/issue3/text/cnotes/rg.html
http://metroactive.com/papers/cruz/03.21.01/
    gonzalez-0112.html
http://www.poets.org/poets/poets.cfm?prmID=250

## Martín Espada

http://www.poets.org/poets/poets.cfm?prmID=250
http://www.english/uiuc.edu/maps/poets/a_f/
    espada/espada.htm
http:poetryflash.org/archive.espada.html
http://www.progressive.org/mpespada798.htm

## Víctor Hernández Cruz

http://www.poets.org/poets/poets.cfm?prmID=698

## Leticia Hernández Linares

www.yofoolio.com

http://www.pacificnews.org/jinn/stories/6.31/
    010315-spanglish.html

## Angela de Hoyos

http://voices.cla.umn.edu/newsite/authors/
    DEHOYOSangela.htm

## Tato Laviera

http://college.hmco.com/english/lauter/heath/4e/studen
    ts/author_pages/contemporary/laviera_ta.html
http://www.georgetown.edu/faculty/bassr/heath/
    syllabuild/iguide/laviera.html

## Josefina López

http://www.josefinalopez.com/

## José Martí

http://www.fiu.edu/~fcf/jmarti.html
http://members.aol.com/josemarticuba/index1.html

## Jaime Manrique

http://www.worldofpoetry.org/rs_manrique.htm

## Tony Medina

http://authors.aalbc.com/tony.htm
http://aalbc.com/authors/jazz.htm
http://www.horizonmag.com/2/tony-medina.asp

## Nancy Mercado

http://www.longshot.org/books/mercado/
    mercado1.htm
http://www.angelfire.com/ny/conexion/
    mercado_nancy.html

## Víctor Montejo

http://www.curbstone.org/authdetail.cfm?AuthID=51
http://www.curbstone.org/ainterview.cfm?AuthID=51

## Pat Mora

http://www.patmora.com/index.htm
http://college.hmco.com/english/heath/syllabuild/iguide/
    mora.html

## Cherríe Moraga

http://voices.cla.umn.edu/authors/CherrieMoraga.html
http://mchip00.nyu.edu/lit-med/lit-med-db/
    webdocs/webdescrips/moraga1268-des-.html
http://www.uic.edu/depts/quic/history/
    cherrie_moraga.html
http://www.queertheory.com/histories/m/
    moraga_cherrie.htm

## Rosario Morales and Aurora Levins Morales

http://www.georgetown.edu/faculty/bassr/heath/
    syllabuild/iguide/morales.html
http://college.hmco.com/english/lauter/heath/4e/students/
    author_pages/contemporary/morales_au.html

## Marisela Norte

http://www.salon.com/audio/2000/10/05/norte/

## Radames Ortiz

http://www.sundress.net/sometimescity/v3/1/
    rortiz.html
http://www.poetscanvas.org/feature_23.htm

## Américo Paredes

http://www.utexas.edu/admin/opa/paredes_folder/
    paredes4.html
http://www.galegroup.com/free_resources/chh/bio/
    paredes_a.htm

## Alicia Partnoy

http://lilt.ilstu.edu/smexpos/alicia_partnoy.htm
http://liberalarts.lmu.edu/mll/dr__alicia_partnoy.htm
http://www.literatura.org/Partnoy/Partnoy.html

## Miguel Piñero

http://www.ccc.commnet.edu/latinoguide/secondary/
    Mpinero.htm

## Roberto Quesada

http://www.hondurasliteraria.org/autores/novelistas/
    quesada.htm

## Alberto Ríos

http://www.poets.org/poets/poets.cfm?=51
http://www.public.asu.edu/~aarios/index.html

## robertkarimi

http://www.calacapress.com/robertkarimi.html

## Luis Rodriguez

http://www.luisjrodriguez.com/

## Nelly Rosario

http://www/bet.com/articles/1,,c4gb2774-3436,00.html
http://www.calabashfestival.org/pages/artists/
    artists_page/rosario_n.html
http://www.findarticles.com/cf_dls/m1295/
    7_66/90307161/p1/article.jhtml

## Benjamín Alire Sáenz

http://ccc.commnet.edu/latinoguide/secondary/
    saenz.htm

## Ruth Sanabria Irupé

http://mywebpages.comcast.net/richarddery/paw/poets.htm

## Michele Serros

http://www.muchamichele.com/
http://www.npr.org/programs/theride/mserros/

## Virgil Suárez

http://www.virgilsuarez.com/
http://arts.endow.gov/explore/Writers/suarez.html
http://english.fsu.edu/faculty/vsuarez.htm

## Piri Thomas

http://www.cheverote.com/piri.html

## Luis Valdez

www.elteatrocampesino.com
http://arts.endow.gov/learn/NCA/Valdez.html
http://www.galegroup.com/free_resources/chh/bio/
    valdez_l.htm

### Frank Varela

http://voices.e-poets.net/VarelaF/
http://www.vceducation.org/Events/Spring2002/
    020531varela.html

### Victor Villaseñor

www.victorvillasenor.com

### Tino Villanueva

http://www.accd.edu/sac/english/portales/villanue.htm
http://www.library.swt.edu/swwc/archives/writers/
    villanueva.html

### Helena María Viramontes

http://mchip00.nyu.edu/lit-med/lit-med-
    db/webdocs/webdescrips/viramontes753-des-.html
http://mchip00.nyu.edu/lit-med/lit-med-
    db/webdocs/webdescrips/viramontes1422-des-.html
http://voices.cla.umn.edu/authors/
    HelenaMariaViramontes.html
http://endeavor.med.nyu.edu/lit-med/lit-med-
    db/webdocs/webdescrips/viramontes753-des-.html
http://www.bedfordstmartins.com/litlinks/fiction/
    viramontes.htm

### General information on Latino/Latina publications

http://www.accd.edu/sac/english/bailey/mexamlit.htm
http://aalbc.com/writers/thirdworldpress.htm

http://www.artepublicopress.com
http://www.auntlute.com
http://www.bedfordstmartins.com/litlinks
http://www.calacapress.com
http://www.ccc.commnet.edu/latinoguide/
    authors.htm
http://cemaweb.library.ucsb.edu/cema_index.html
http://www.chicanas.com/
http://www.cincopuntos.com/
http://www.curbstone.org/
http://endeavor.med.nyu.edu/lit-med/
    lit-med-db/authors.html
http://www.escritoresdominicanos.com/
    gajitos.html
http://www.Hispanic.com
http://www.Hispanic Online
http://www.Hispanic Vista
http://home.uchicago.edu/~weorchar/authors.html
http://www.lif.org/
http://www.latinoweb.com/
http://www.loc.gov/rr/hispanic/
http://www.nclr.org/
http://www.quepasa.com/
http://www.sdlatinofilm.com/
http://www.southendpress.org/
http://www.sparcmurals.org/
http://voices.cla.umn.edu/newsite/index.htm
http://voices.e-poets.net/

# Credits

Miguel Algarín. "Taos Pueblo Indians: 700 Strong According to Bobby's Last Census" 1980.

Alurista. "el sarape de mi personalidad" (poem), From *Floricanto en Aztlán,* Reprinted with the Permission of The University of California Press, 1971.

Jimmy Santiago Baca. "Martín III." From *Decade II: A Twentieth Anniversary Anthology* ed. Julián Olivares and Vigil Piñón, Reprinted with the Permission of Arte Público Press, 1993.

Rafael Campo. "Belonging." From *The Other Man Was Me*, Reprinted with the Permission of Arte Público Press, 1993.

Lorna Dee Cervantes. "Refugee Ship." From *A Decade of Hispanic Literature*, Reprinted with the Permission of Arte Público Press, 1982.

Lucha Corpi. "Marina Madre." From *Palabras de mediodía/Noonwords*, Reprinted with the permission of Arte Público Press, 2001.

Sanda María Esteves. "Affirmations #3, Take Off Your Mask." From *Bluestown Mockingbird Mambo*, Reprinted with the permission of Arte Público Press, 1990.

Ray Gonzalez, "These Days" from *The Heat of Arrival*. Copyright © 1996 by Ray Gonzalez. Reprinted with the permission of BOA Editions, Ltd.

Víctor Hernández Cruz "loisaida" From *R Rhythm, Content, and Flavor.* Reprinted with the permission of the author.

Carolina Hospital. "Hyphenated Man." From *The Child of Exile*, Reprinted with the permission of Arte Público Press, 2004.

Angela de Hoyos. "Lessons on Semantics." From *Woman, Woman*, Reprinted with the permission of Arte Público Press, 1985.

Tato Laviera. "AmeRíkan." From *AmeRíkan*, Reprinted with the permission of Arte Público Press, 2000

Pat Mora. "Legal Alien." From *Chants*, Reprinted with the permission of Arte Público Press, 1984.

Rosario Morales and Aurora Levins Morales. "Ending Poem." From *Getting Home Alive* by Aurora Levins Morales and Rosario Morales.

Richard Blanco. "América" from *City of a Hundred Fires*, by Richard Blanco, © 1998. Reprinted by permission of the University of Pittsburgh Press.

Tomás Borge. "Nicaragua" by Tomás Borge Martínez, translated by Russell Bartley, Kent Johnson, and Sylvia Yoneda from *Have You Seen a Red Curtain in My Weary Chamber?* By Tomás Borge Martínez (Curbstone Press, 1989). Distributed by Consortium.

Pablo Antonio Cuadra. "The Campesinos Go Down the Roads," From *The Birth of the Sun* Unicorn Press, 1988.

Martín Espada. "Federico's Ghost" from *Rebellion is the Circle of a Lover's Hands* by Martín Espada. (Curbstone Press, 1990) Reprinted with permission of Curbstone Press. Distributed by Consortium.

Martín Espada. "Revolutionary Spanish Lesson" 1990, Reprinted with the permission of Arte Público Press.

Isaac Goldemberg, "Self-Portrait" 2001, Reprinted with permission of author.

Víctor Montejo. "The Dog" by Víctor Montejo, translated by Victor Parea from *Sculpted Stones* by Víctor Montejo (Curbstone Press, 1995) Reprinted with the permission of Curbstone Press. Distributed by Consortium.

José María Heredia. "Hymn of Exile." Trans. Arte Público Press. Reprinted with the permission of Arte Público Press, 2000.

Gustavo Pérez Firmat. *"Bilingual Blues."* From *Bilingual Blues*, copyright © 1987, Bilingual Review/Press.

Salomón de la Selva. *"A Song for Wall Street."* From *Tropical Town and Other Poems*, Reprinted with the permission of Arte Público Press, 1999.

Alicia Alarcón. *"All I Thought about Was Disneyland."* From *The Border Patrol Ate My Dust*, Reprinted with the permission of Arte Público Press, 2005.

Julia Alvarez. "Snow." From *How the García Girls Lost Their Accents*. Copyright © 1991 by Julia Alvarez. Published by Plume, an imprint of Penguin Group USA, and originally in hardcover by Algonquin Books of Chapel Hill. Reprinted by permission of Susan Bergholz Literary Services, New York. All rights reserved.

Arturo Arias. *"Toward Patzún."* by Arturo Arias, translated by Leland H. Chambers from *Contemporary Short Stories from Central America* ed. by Enrique Jaramillo Levi and Leland H. Chambers, copyright © 1994. By permission of the University of Texas Press.

Aurora Levins Morales. *"Immigrants,"* From *Getting Home Alive* by Aurora Levins Morales and Rosario Morales, copyright © 1986, Firebrand Books, Ann Arbor, Michigan.

Víctor Montejo. Excerpt from *Testimony: Death of a Guatemalan Village* by Víctor Montejo (Curbstone Press, 1987), translated by Victor Parea. Reprinted with the permission of Curbstone Press. Distributed by Consortium.

Alicia Partnoy. Excerpt from *The Little School* by Alicia Partnoy, pages 25-28, Published by Midnight Editions 1986, 1998.

Virgil Suárez. "Spared Angola" From *Spared Angola*, Reprinted with the permission of Arte Público Press, 1997.

Claribel Alegría, "The Politics of Exile," 1989. Reprinted with permission of the author.

# Index

323